Leisure in Your Life:
New Perspectives

Leisure in Your Life:
New Perspectives

by Geoffrey Godbey

Venture Publishing, Inc.
State College, Pennsylvania

Venture Publishing, Inc.
1999 Cato Avenue
State College, PA 16801
Phone: 814-234-4561
Fax: 814-234-1645
http://www.venturepublish.com

Production Manager: Richard Yocum
Manuscript Editing: Michele L. Barbin, Richard Yocum
Artwork by Bruce Storm
Cover by Echelon Design

Library of Congress Catalogue Card Number: 2007940631
ISBN-10: 1-892132-75-3
ISBN-13: 978-1-892132-75-8

for Galen

Contents

1 Leisure, Recreation, Play, and Flow   1

2 Leisure: Past and Present   29

6 Spending Money for Leisure:
The Best Things in Life Are Free (or Fee)   151

12 Leisure and Healthy Lives 317

13 Healthy Leisure—Celebrating Life 351

14 Leisure Service Organizations 387

15 The Future of Leisure 417

Acknowledgments

The author wishes to acknowledge Michele L. Barbin, Production Editor for Venture Publishing, for her central role in shaping and amending this edition of *Leisure in Your Life*. She has contributed to content and style as well as issues of language.

About the Author

Dr. Geoffrey Godbey is Professor Emeritus in the Department of Recreation, Park and Tourism Management at The Pennsylvania State University. He is also the President of Next Consulting, a company concerned with repositioning leisure and tourism services for the near future. The author of ten books and over 100 articles concerning leisure, work, time use, aging, recreation and parks, tourism, health and the future, he is past President of the Academy of Leisure Sciences and the Society of Park and Recreation Educators.

Godbey has testified before committees of the United States Senate and the President's Commission on Americans outdoors. A frequent public speaker to diverse groups, he has given invited presentations in twenty-four countries. Interviews and summaries of Godbey's writings have appeared in a number of mass media outlets including *U.S. News and World Reports, Newsweek, Time, Reader's Digest, The Economist, The Today Show, Good Morning America, CBS Morning Show, The New York Times, Psychology Today, The Wall Street Journal, USA Today, The Washington Post, Modern Maturity, The Chronicle of Higher Education, The Utne Reader, NBC Evening News, CNN News, ABC Evening News* and many others.

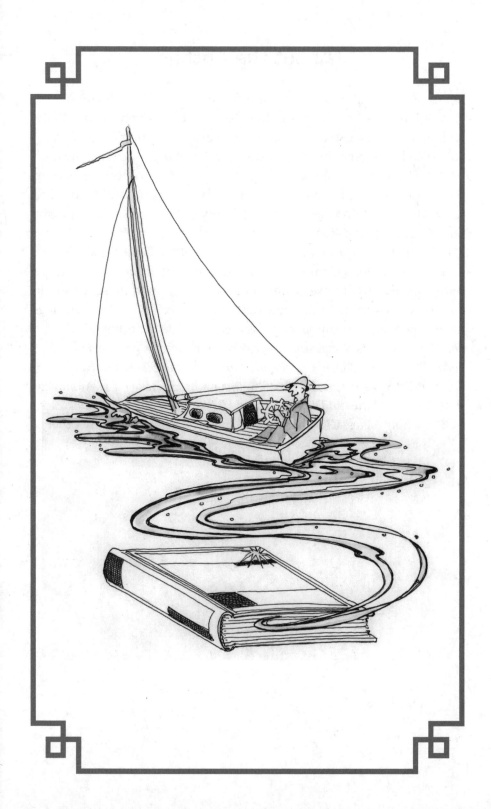

Leisure, Recreation, Play, and Flow

This book is about leisure in your life, what it means, and what it could mean. It is also about how leisure affects the lives of others. This new edition includes "voices" in each chapter—brief conversational statements from people that illustrate the ideas being discussed.

What you do during nonworking hours may determine your happiness, your contribution to the world, and even the meaning of your life as much as what you do in your occupational or obligated time.

To have leisure is one of the earliest dreams of human beings—to be free from an endless round of labor; free to pursue what one wants; free to spend time in voluntary, pleasurable ways; free to find and accept one's place in the world; free of the tyranny of nature and of other human beings; free to exist in a state of grace. Living life on your own terms, being free to do what you choose, is a central ideal of Western society and, quite probably, of you as an individual.

Leisure is not neatly confined to any one part of our lives or to any one place or organization. You may find leisure when you are alone, at school, church, clubs, shopping centers, in automobiles, tents, caves, bars, in front of a TV or computer monitor, behind home plate, in the formations of drifting clouds, and in many other circumstances. Consequently, when studying leisure, many different parts of the human condition must be examined. To understand leisure you must also try to clarify values about what role it can and should play in your life.

Despite these challenges, in a society where you may spend almost twenty solid years in leisure activity, it is essential to reach some understanding about leisure and the related concepts of recreation, play, and flow in order to shape both your life and your society more intelligently. Various questions must be considered:

- What do these terms mean?
- What roles have they played in other societies?
- Is a life of leisure desirable—or possible?
- What do people do for leisure?
- Are some leisure activities better than others?
- How does leisure behavior relate to our work, education, economy, religious beliefs, and so forth?

This book assumes that our examination must begin with the life of you, the reader, and then expand to consider society. This approach requires more of *you* because you will be asked to think about your own values and behavior. You might also gain some understanding about how you spend your time and speculate about what kind of work-leisure arrangements you would find pleasing. You will be asked to examine your own leisure life and then to compare your behavior and values to those of others. You will also be asked to increase your understanding of how leisure is used and the consequences of such use in society.

To do this, it will not be assumed that you should be led to certain beliefs or ways of behaving but instead that you should examine alternatives and understand more clearly your current position in regard to leisure. While the author admits to some biases (I love poetry, travel, playing conga drums and squash, gardening, reading, and playing with kids), at the end of this book, you should be a little closer to understanding your own leisure ideals rather than adopting mine. You should also know a little more regarding the role leisure does and can play in our society.

What Is Leisure?

The idea of *leisure* is complicated and diverse. The different perspectives reflect historical differences in the organization of societies as well as differences in concepts of both freedom and pleasure. The diverse concepts which have continued to shape our thinking about "leisure" have their origins in ancient Athens, the industrialization process begun in Britain, struggles between those in different social classes, the emergence of commercial enterprises which promoted specific forms of nonwork activity, and urban social reformers. More recently, the concept of "leisure" has been shaped by a huge range of communication technologies, from the cell phone, to the iPod, to plasma TV.

The term *leisure* has many shades of meaning and, in fact, has some meanings which are almost entirely distinct from each other. If you stopped people on the street and asked them to define leisure, what would they say?

Leisure has been conceptualized in four basic contexts: time, activities, state of existence, and state of mind.

Leisure Defined as Time

When we think of leisure in terms of time, it usually refers to some portion of our lives in which we have comparatively greater freedom to do what we want. Aristotle called this available time.[1] Such time may be thought of as something negative; Veblen took this perspective at the turn of the twentieth century when he bemoaned the emergence of a new leisure class which consumed time unproductively, merely displaying their wealth.[2] Another

> *"Leisure?" I don't know, I guess just free time—doing what I want. Having fun. Well, maybe you're never really completely free. I mean, a lot of the time I'm really rushed. There's so many things I have to do—or want to do. Sometimes leisure is just sitting and looking out the window—kind of doing nothing. Sometimes it's just hanging out with my boyfriend. Sometimes, an activity is leisure and sometimes not. I like to walk the dog sometimes; other times it's just because he needs to go out. Aerobic dance is fun sometimes and a pain other times. Leisure... It's pretty complicated—but I know it when I have it.*

way of conceptualizing leisure as time is "the time surplus remaining after the practical necessities of life have been attended to."[3]

Defining leisure as "free time" raises a number of issues. What is free time? Is it time which the individual doesn't sell for economic gain? Some of us freely and voluntarily choose to do certain things for which we are paid money. It is often difficult to draw the line between obligated and free time. Is going to church, synagogue, or mosque obligated? For some cultures it may be, but not for others. Is eating obligated in all instances, and is sleeping? In a society where only a small fraction of the population goes hungry, it is not always easy to define what must be done unless we define it in terms of what we believe we must do.

And, in a complex society such as ours, no time is free of the constraints of convention or social mores. We still have certain social rules to follow.

For some in our society, it is particularly difficult to determine what is free time and what is not. What is free time for the retired person, the student, the homemaker, the unemployed, the bedridden, the artist, the professor, or the homeless person? If we assume that "free time" is primarily time when we aren't involved in an activity for which we receive money, then the definition has no meaning to many in our society who do not do such work. Furthermore, we are compelled to do many things that don't involve money. We may sometimes feel compelled to attend a wedding, wash the car, exercise to lose weight, or do a number of other things for reasons other than economic ones. Many different factors may keep our time from being free; not only economic factors but also social, psychological, spiritual, and political ones. An individual may have time not related to economic survival, but may also not be politically free to travel or indulge in self-expression. One may also be prevented from having time due to spiritual emptiness or psychological injury suffered during work. Thus, the things which place limits on our free time differ for us as individuals and as members of different groups.

When leisure is defined as "free time," Kaplan identified several different kinds of free time which have emerged in our society, including

- the permanent, voluntary leisure of the rich;
- temporary, involuntary leisure of the unemployed;
- regularly allocated, voluntary leisure of the employed;
- permanent incapacity of the disabled; and
- the voluntary retirement of the aged.[4]

As you can see, these kinds of "free time" have very different consequences for those who have them. A holiday differs in meaning from retirement in fundamental ways.

Leisure Defined as Activity

Leisure has also been defined as certain types of activities. The ancient Greek word for leisure, *schole*, means "serious activity without the pressure of necessity."[5] The English word *school* is derived from the Greek word for leisure.[6] This term does not imply a strict distinction from work, nor is it synonymous with the term *recreation*, because the Greeks had another term meaning "playful amusement to pass the time." This conception of leisure as activity has been broadened to include

> ...a number of occupations in which the individual may indulge of his own free will—either to rest, to amuse himself, to add to his knowledge or improve his skills disinterestedly or to increase his voluntary participation in the life of the community after discharging his professional, family, and social duties.[7]

When leisure is defined as activities or occupations, it quickly becomes apparent that while no activity can be said to always serve as leisure for the participant, many activities are typically undertaken in the role of leisure. Playing softball, for instance, is typically undertaken more or less voluntarily during nonwork time and is pleasurable for the participant. There are exceptions. A few people play softball to earn money. Some may feel that they have to play the game to protect their jobs or to win the friendship of those who are important to them. For most people, however, playing softball is leisure activity.

Leisure Defined as a State of Existence or Mind

If leisure is defined as a state of existence it is, as Aristotle said, the "absence of the necessity of being occupied."[8] This state has also been thought of as "a mood of contemplation."[9] Thus, leisure is often used as an adjective to mean unhurried, tranquil, or without regard to time. Leisure defined as a state of existence may also be tied to religious celebration. Pieper believed that leisure was a sense of celebration which characterized the lives of some people who accepted the world and their place in the world with joy.[10] Leisure is therefore a state of grace bestowed upon those capable of spiritual celebration. You cannot obtain it just because you want to. It is a gift.

Leisure is also defined as a state of mind. Many psychologists have written about leisure in terms of *perceived freedom* or *internal locus of control*. That is, the important thing in defining an experience as leisure is that individuals believe that they are free or that they are controlling events rather than being controlled *by* events. According to psychologist John Neulinger

Leisure has one and only one essential criterion, and that is the condition of perceived freedom. Any activity carried out freely, without constraint or compulsion, may be considered to be leisure. "To leisure" implies being engaged in an activity as a free agent and of one's own choice.[11]

Problems with Conventional Ideas about Leisure

Each of these previous concepts contains some problems in terms of defining "leisure." Go back and examine each concept critically. After that, I'll propose my own definition of leisure, and you can judge it for yourself.

It was June and my parents were away. I was sitting on the back deck, maybe from around 7 p.m. or so. I was planning to go out that night; see what's happening downtown. So I sat there—and I sat there—and I kind of just let go and looked at the sky.

The longer I watched, the more wrapped up in it I became. It was like I had never seen the sky before from my own back deck. Clouds were moving very slowly—like dreaming elephants bound for home. The sun was red, turning slowly to purple, then gray, then black—stars began to appear.

What was I thinking about? Nothing. Just letting the world go by. After quite a while, in the dark, I realized I could hear the crickets. I spent the night alone that evening but I wasn't lonely at all.

Leisure as Free Time

"Free time" is often thought of as "leisure" itself or as a necessary but insufficient condition for "leisure" to take place. In either case, there are some difficulties in likening "free time" to "leisure."

First, "freedom" is not an absolute concept. It is an idea which may be applied to almost any part of life: politically "free," economically "free," morally "free," socially "free," physically "free," ecologically "free." These realms of freedom change constantly for many of us in terms of the extent to which they exist. At times they are thought of as necessary preludes to "leisure," yet "leisure" may emerge from situations that are unfree. A criminal forced to do community service by a judge may ultimately experience "leisure" in that service. An adolescent forced by his parents to take trumpet lessons may, nevertheless, eventually experience "leisure" when playing. A woman may feel obligated to go to the playground with her child or to the symphony with her fellow workers but still find "leisure" there. The prelude to vacations, for many of us, is sitting several hours in a space so small that we can't even extend our legs, yet we may experience "leisure" upon arrival. In many domains of freedom, our preludes to "leisure" often are not free. There may be a higher probability of experiencing "leisure" when the preludes to leisure are comparatively free, but "leisure" may also occur when they are not.

Although "leisure" is thought of as spending time "freely," those experiencing "leisure" often appear to be drawn further and further in a compulsive fashion through the leisure experience. They are drawn *through* the experience, and later, *to* the experience as are lovers. Later still, they are drawn toward the whole of existence. Those who experience leisure start by loving what has a name and continue until they love what has no name. Our love of a namable experience (e.g., gardening, sunbathing, playing golf, walking in the woods) proceeds until that focused love provides the inner resources to love what has no name. The pleasurable compulsion to love what has no name, does, itself, have a name—faith. If our love of a particular namable experience becomes only a desire to have an infinite number of other particular experiences, it may mean only that we have arrived at a different condition— wanderlust.

Wanderlust—the desire to do and see everything; to travel constantly; to experience, perpetually, the unknown—is not the same as leisure. Leisure occurs when the individual is intuitively drawn to certain activities or experiences, not toward all experience. These certain, specific activities have symbolic

Maybe it's a stage of life or something. When you're a teenager, you're always afraid of missing out on something. You always want out of the house—always want to go somewhere. Some people stay that way.

Michelle has all these travel websites that she shows me and she always wants to go to the next place—she never goes anywhere a second time. She's kind of like— "What's next, what's next, what's next." It's like those boxes of candy where every piece is different. I like peanut butter meltaways. You can give me a whole box and I'm happy to skip the other kinds.

My boyfriend Dave and I went fishing above Montreal last summer. We loved it. In July, we're going back.

value in affirming the meaningfulness, and hence, pleasurableness of existence. Wanderlust is looking—leisure is finding.

Must one live a life in which one is relatively "free" from the external compulsive forces of one's culture and physical environment to experience "leisure?" While such a concept is a hazy one, perhaps it may be said that slaves do not experience leisure. Those who are political slaves, slaves to externally compelled activity or physical survival, slaves to drugs, or slaves to the ravages of weather or physical misfortune are not likely to find leisure. The slave does not have leisure because either externally imposed compulsions prevent the development of internal compulsions or because the internally developed compulsions are not based upon love. Prisoners, for example, have little room for the development of behaviors in which they can grow to love (although it occasionally happens). The addict of cocaine or alcohol is internally compelled but has ceased to love the compulsion or to find a basis in the behavior for faith. As we will soon see, however, a slave might have "recreation" or might even "play."

Leisure as State of Mind

"Leisure" thought of as a state of mind is not the old Athenian notion, which was centered around state of being. Our state of being is more complex than our state of mind, since it has to do with our existence in the world and not just our existence in our mind. To assume that state of mind alone produces leisure reduces the concept to one of *solipsism*, the belief that nothing exists or is real but the self. If this were true, there would be no basis for the love of an individual experience to be transformed into the nameless love—faith. If nothing is real but the self, one can love only the self. One could not joyfully surrender oneself to experience. Psychologists who reduce "leisure" to the notion of perceived freedom ignore the consequences when one's perceived reality is at variance from an objective reality. For instance, a college student under the influence of drugs recently jumped from a high building, thinking he could fly. He was not at leisure; he was killing himself.

This is not to imply that one's state of mind is irrelevant in "leisure" experience; it is an important component. In leisure, one gets lost in an activity, joyfully surrenders or gives oneself to the experience, and in this process, the mind narrows its focus without effort and constricts awareness of self. From this constriction (loving the namable experience) comes an expansion (loving what has no name). Thus, state of mind is relevant, but two different states of mind are implied: first, a state of constricted attention to a joyfully compelling experience and, second, a state of wonder (contemplation and celebration) in which we realize that we are part of something larger, that "self" is an artificial boundary. There is also a tendency for social psychologists to think of leisure or the leisure state as emanating from an internal "locus of control." Control, however, does not describe leisure as well as "giving," "surrendering," or "letting go" do. Internal control may make it much more likely that leisure will happen, but leisure starts to occur when one begins to trust a specific activity enough to let go, act instinctively, on the assumption that the activity is superior to others.

In today's changing world, some individuals report that they feel rushed all the time. If one is always rushed, is leisure possible or even a relevant idea? Can one give oneself fully to an activity if they are always thinking, "What's next?" Perhaps not.

Leisure as a State of Being

A third idea that needs rethinking is leisure as a "state of being." Leisure as a state of being seems to have emanated from the ancient Athenian notion in which the political system granted a privileged minority of males the absence of the necessity of being occupied (although the

I started singing in the church choir by accident. The choir director asked me after church if I would like to join them one day and I said, "I don't know."

I love to sing, I was always singing, even when I was just walking down the street. Sometimes people would look at me funny because singing in public makes you look like you're a mental case. The next week I asked the choir director a few questions and then said "O.K."

The first rehearsals, even with all these people I didn't know, were great. I knew I had done the right thing. My first church service in the choir went well, and I wasn't too nervous. Then I was given a few solos.

Sometimes, when you sing with a choir, your own voice becomes part of something larger and you aren't sure if it is you, or us, or them, or everyone, or everything singing. When that happens—it's magic. The wonderful, surprisingly loud, collective sound—now that is celebrating. It doesn't matter so much what is being celebrated because the act of doing it is just so great. I'm pretty much Christian, and I love the psalm which says "make a joyful noise unto the Lord..." This is something I will continue to do.

society imposed some requirements on them in terms of government participation). Ideally, this "absence of necessity" applied to all realms of one's being and was specifically thought to include the spiritual dimension as well as the political and economic. An absence of necessity, however, seems to be a precondition of leisure rather than a description of what leisure is. When people experience leisure, they don't experience an absence of the necessity of being occupied. Instead, they feel a pleasurable compulsion, necessity, or desire to be occupied. One is drawn to an experience which has a magnetic attraction. This desire or compulsion is located internally, but it is, nonetheless, compulsion. We are exercising our human will when we give ourselves to what compels us because it has meaning and that meaning or importance is intuitive. Entering leisure experience and understanding its benefits is not rational or calculating. It is instinctive and intuitive.

Certainly we enter some new experiences by rationally weighing potential liabilities and benefits. But, as we develop the capacity for that experience to serve as "leisure," there is greater and greater trust in the experience, or willingness to give oneself over to it, and a diminishing interest in what external ends that activity will serve as a means to. Leisure, then, is not the "absence"—it is a presence—a compelling presence to which we can surrender our will. This surrender can be made because the experience is intuitively meaningful and provides pleasure that transcends the specific to embrace the universal.

The absence of the necessity of being occupied, of course, is absolute only for those who are dead, insane, or unconscious. In creating who we are as humans, we act because of the necessity of self-definition. Life presents the necessity of choice, the necessity of acting. These necessities are "occupying," and one may be "occupied" out of necessity by contemplation, for instance, as well as by the search to secure food or shelter. Leisure, then, does not involve the *absence* of the necessity of being occupied, but rather the necessity of being willfully and meaningfully occupied. Leisure is a response to that situation. As previously mentioned, leisure is an internally located compulsion. This compulsion, however, is not understood in terms of pleasure seeking but rather as the establishment of meaning through specific acts. The negation of absurdity through the joyful exercise of the human will, based upon faith, by which the individual intuitively understands that he or she has

It was going to be great. Both of us work 24-7 and our jobs have a lot of stress. It was going to be great to get away at a hotel with a big pool and good food. Just lie around and unwind. Lie in the sun and all. Well, she loved it—she can actually do nothing and be happy doing nothing. Me? I was nuts in about half an hour. Fortunately, I had stashed my laptop, and after she dozed off on the chaise lounge, I went back up to our room, plugged in, and started working.

become a part of something bigger—this understanding is pleasurable in the most fundamental sense.

Leisure has to do not so much with "freedom" as with the personal invention of meaning through one's actions. The opposite of leisure is not so much "work" as it is meaningless activity (although work, for some, is almost without meaning).

Leisure as Activities

Leisure may also be thought of as a cluster of activities, which may be specified by name or which are "voluntary" and "pleasurable." Defining "leisure" as a cluster of activities which can be identified in advance has the opposite problem from defining leisure only as a "state of mind." While the "state of mind" definition ignores the external world, defining "leisure" only as a specified cluster of activities ignores the internal world. Activities may be meaningful, pleasurable, or compelling to different individuals or only in certain situations, cultures, lifestyles, life stages, tastes, and so forth. Almost all individual activities have the capacity to serve as a basis for "leisure," although perhaps some have a higher potential than others. Leisure is not an activity but a process which involves some specific act.

While a wide range of activities may serve as part of the leisure experience, this is not to imply that the specific activity or activities are readily "substitutable" for the individual who experiences leisure through a specific activity. As the activity begins to serve as "leisure," it is no longer subject to rational comparison with alternative activities. This, of course, is the reason that economists have rarely understood anything about leisure behavior. They have assumed that it is based upon rational calculation when, in fact, it is based more on intuition and love.

Here's a list of the favorite leisure activities of Americans. I can't believe fishing was higher than computer activities! Also, where's sex? ➡

Table 1.1 Favorite Leisure-Time Activities by Percent, 1995–2004 [12]

Q: "What are your two or three most favorite leisure-time activities?"									
	1995	1997	1998	1999	2000	2001	2002	2003	2004
Reading	28	28	30	27	31	28	26	24	35
TV watching	25	19	21	22	23	20	15	17	21
Spending time with family/kids	12	12	13	12	14	12	11	17	20
Going to movies	8	7	8	8	6	7	6	7	10
Fishing	10	12	11	13	9	12	8	9	8
Computer activities	2	3	3	7	6	7	4	5	7
Gardening	9	11	14	15	13	10	8	6	6
Renting movies	5	5	3	4	5	4	3	3	6
Walking	8	8	7	9	8	6	4	4	6
Exercise (aerobics, weights)	2	4	3	3	6	5	4	6	6
Listening to music	5	3	4	4	4	4	4	4	6
Entertaining	7	3	5	3	2	1	2	3	5
Hunting	4	4	4	6	3	3	3	4	5
Playing team sports	9	9	9	8	5	5	7	6	5
Shopping	3	3	3	4	3	4	2	4	5
Traveling	4	5	4	4	5	4	4	4	4
Sleeping	2	3	1	2	2	2	3	2	4
Socializing with friends/neighbors	*	*	2	5	6	4	5	7	4
Sewing/crocheting	7	4	8	4	3	3	3	3	4
Golf	6	8	6	6	5	6	5	3	4
Church/church activities	3	4	2	3	4	3	2	5	4
Relaxing	*	*	1	3	3	3	3	3	3
Playing music	3	2	2	3	3	2	1	3	3
Housework	*	*	*	*	*	*	*	2	3
Crafts (unspecified)	*	*	*	3	4	4	2	4	3
Watching sporting events	*	*	2	5	4	2	2	5	3
Bicycling	4	3	3	3	2	3	3	2	3
Playing cards	*	*	*	*	*	*	1	2	2
Hiking	3	3	2	2	1	*	3	3	2
Cooking	2	2	2	2	2	1	2	3	2
Eating out/dining out	2	2	2	2	1	1	2	5	2
Woodworking	1	*	1	2	1	1	2	1	2
Swimming	7	6	7	6	5	8	5	2	2
Camping	4	3	3	4	4	3	2	1	2
Skiing	1	*	*	1	1	1	1	2	2
Working on cars	2	1	2	2	2	1	1	1	2
Writing	*	*	*	*	*	1	1	1	2
Boating	2	2	3	3	3	3	3	1	2
Motorcycling	*	*	1	1	1	1	1	1	1
Animals/pets/dogs	*	*	2	2	1	1	1	1	1
Bowling	4	3	2	2	2	1	1	1	1
Painting	2	1	1	2	1	1	2	1	1
Running	2	1	1	2	1	1	2	1	1
Dancing	1	*	2	1	1	1	1	2	1
Horseback riding	2	2	1	1	1	1	1	3	1
Tennis	2	1	2	1	1	1	1	1	1
Theater	1	1	1	1	1	1	1	1	1

* Less than 0.5%; Base: All Adults; spontaneous, unaided responses. Other activities mentioned by one percent include billiards/pool, beach, volunteer work, driving and outdoor activities.

Dylan Thomas mentioned a shepherd who, when asked why he made—from within fairy rings—ritual observances to the moon to protect his flocks, replied: "I'd be a damn fool if I didn't." [13] So it is with leisure.

Does "Leisure" Apply to Everyone?

Some aspects of the concept of leisure may not apply to everyone. If we think about the previous definitions of leisure from the standpoint of to whom they apply, for instance, it becomes apparent we have been talking about a concept that historically applies primarily to males. If leisure is defined in terms of time, it is frequently thought of in opposition to "work," and work frequently means paid employment. If leisure is what happens after work, how does the concept apply to women or men who are not in the labor force? Do mothers and homemakers have leisure in this sense? Also, how does the term apply to women who work for pay outside the home but have a "second shift" of work when they return home, consisting of housework, shopping, and childcare? As we will see in Chapter 2, the Industrial Revolution pulled men from rural life into industrial work far more frequently than women. "Leisure" became thought of as the time after this industrial work was completed, but such a definition did not correspond to the reality of women's lives.

If we define leisure in terms of activities, there is again a tendency to ignore women's lives. If we say that camping is a leisure activity, we could be thinking from only the male's perspective. Suppose the female has to do all the packing for the camping trip, prepare the children, plan the meals, cook the meals at the campsite, watch the children, wash up after each meal, get the children into their sleeping bags each night, and get up with them if they are afraid in the middle of the night. Camping may simply be a round of labor for the female—housekeeping under inferior conditions.

While leisure defined as a state of mind or being has the potential to apply to both men and women, in the ancient Athenian sense leisure was clearly for men. Aristotle advised men to avoid taking a wife or lose hope of obtaining leisure. Women's second-class status, their inability, with few exceptions, to travel out into the world, and their lack of political power made the Greek ideal of leisure unobtainable for women.

Thus, leisure has been a concept that historically has applied mainly to men and, in some cases, only to men in the labor force. As Rosemary Deem pointed out, "almost all the work on the history of leisure has connected itself with how men have spent their leisure time and what connections there have been between that and their main form of work or employment."[14] Consequently, we know much more about what leisure has meant in male terms than in female terms. It should be noted, of course, that women's roles have changed remarkably during the last few decades. Today's young women live in a different world from their mothers—and they are redefining leisure.

We may similarly question whether "leisure" applies to those who have experienced, and often still experience, institutionalized prejudice, such as African Americans, gays and lesbians, Mormons, and others. Can those in hospitals be said to have leisure? In a materialistic society such as ours, can the poor or the unemployed be thought to have leisure? While such issues are a matter of interpretation, it may quickly become apparent that those who are more privileged or fortunate are likely to find it easier to experience leisure in many senses of the term.

Proposing a Definition of Leisure

Given the previous information and definitions, leisure needs redefinition for our world and our time. I propose the following:

> Leisure is living in relative freedom from the external compulsive forces of one's culture and physical environment so as to be able to act from internally compelling love in ways that are personally pleasing, intuitively worthwhile, and provide a basis for faith.

This definition is a departure from commonly used ones since there is no reference to time or one's state of mind.[15] "Relative" freedom recognizes that freedom has to be and should be limited. This relative "freedom from" provides an opportunity to act—"freedom to." The motivation to act is "internally compelling love." This idea includes internal motivation but goes beyond it.

For an activity to be "intuitively worthwhile" may mean that the first several times we do it, it is not leisure. If we grow to love it, however, there is no longer any need to justify the experience—we begin to have faith in it.

This definition is also, hopefully, one that applies to both men and women. While men and women may sometimes differ in the extent to which they are free from the "external compulsive forces of one's culture…" there is no reason that this difference has to exist.

> Whose definition is that? It seems kind of weird. What religion is he?

Recreation

While words like "recreation," "leisure," and "play" are sometimes used interchangeably, the term *recreation* is often used in a more specific and limited sense. Recreation has traditionally been defined as activity done in opposition to work which refreshes and restores the individual. Margaret Mead has said that recreation represents a

> whole attitude of conditional joy in which the delights of both work and play are tied together in a tight sequence. Neither one may be considered by itself, but man must work, then weary and take some recreation so he may work again. [16]

Recreation, in other words, is dependent upon work for its meaning and function. Work comes first, then recreation, and then more work. Perhaps even a slave could have recreation. Historically, many slaves were given periods of time after work in which they could engage in a limited range of activities, such as games, sports, singing or dancing, to recover from work. If we think of leisure as "free time," then it may be said that recreation is

> any activity pursued during leisure, either individual or collective, that is free and pleasurable, having its own immediate appeal, not impelled by a delayed reward beyond itself. [17]

In popular usage, recreation may be thought of as activity which isn't serious—that is, "fun and games." Recreation may also refer to sports and related athletic activities. We often expect to find only sports and games at "recreation centers."

Sometimes definitions of recreation are limited to leisure time activities that are "morally sound, mentally and physically uplifting, respectful of the rights of others, voluntarily motivated, and [which] provide a sense

Sometimes you just need some R&R. Just blow off some steam. I play in a softball league—have for six or seven years. We don't take it too seriously, and we all clown around a bit and give each other a hard time. Then, after the game, we drink beer and swap a few lies. It's a chance to recharge and forget about work. Maybe that's why I lay in front of the TV sometimes, hardly even paying attention. Oh, also, I do woodworking. I've got a bunch of equipment in the basement: a wood lathe, jointer, table saw. A bunch of things like that. When I'm working with wood, I'm focused on the challenge and precision and forget about the outside world. I'm proud of what I make and I go back to work the next day refreshed—unless I stay up half the night working on a cabinet.

of pleasure and achievement."[18] If recreation is limited to morally sound activities, we are faced with the question of who decides what is morally sound: society. Sometimes through religion, we may reach a consensus regarding the moral soundness of some activities, but we may not be able to reach an agreement on many other activities. Another way of looking at this question would be to say that recreation activity has great potential for good or for harm, but the definition should not be limited to those instances in which goodness is achieved.

Recreation in our own society is often thought of as a given set of activities which are somehow inherently recreational. Such activities may be designated in the following categories: amusements; arts and crafts; dance, drama, games and sports; hobbies; music; outdoor recreation; reading, writing, and speaking; social recreation; spectating, special events, and voluntary service.[19] While we may commonly think of recreation in these terms, nearly any activity has the potential to be recreation. That is, it may be undertaken voluntarily, during leisure time, and provide pleasure. Some people earn their livings as carpenters while others undertake similar activity for recreation. Some ride bicycles to get to work; others ride as recreation. Thus, in an absolute sense, we can't limit our definition to a list of specific activities.

Gray and Greben have suggested that recreation, rather than being a set of activities, is:

an emotional condition within an individual human being that flows from a feeling of well-being and self-satisfaction.

It is characterized by feelings of mastery, achievement, exhilaration, acceptance, success, personal worth and pleasure. It reinforces a positive self-image. Recreation is a response to aesthetic experience, achievement of personal goals or positive feedback from others. It is independent of activity, leisure or personal acceptance.[20]

This definition stresses the response to activity rather than the activity itself. In fact, we don't always experience feelings of well-being from participation in activities commonly thought of as recreational. According to this definition, we might play volleyball during our leisure but still not be able to define it as recreation if we are playing poorly and are unhappy about it. Also, since the definition states that the emotional condition of recreation is independent of leisure, we might experience recreation as a job for which we are being paid. This is a major difference from most previous definitions.

As you can see, a number of disagreements exist among various definitions of recreation. These are concerned with whether or not recreation is a means to an end (such as achievement) or an end in itself, whether or not it should be limited to "moral" activity, whether or not it must refresh the individual for work, and whether or not it is determined primarily by the nature of the activity, the attitude of the respondent toward the activity, or the respondent's psychological state during the activity.

Play

What is "play?" If you thought "leisure" and "recreation" were complex ideas, perhaps you aren't ready to play around with "play." It is, at first consideration, an easy task to define "play." We know it when we see it. Dogs play, children play, we play—video games, the guitar, or roles on a stage. We may also, occasionally, play in ways very similar to dogs or children. Actually, "play," like "fun," is an easier concept to recognize in everyday life than it is to put into words.

The Dutch historian Johan Huizinga who wrote what is probably the most important book yet about play, *Homo ludens: A Study of the Play Element in Culture*, defined the six characteristics of *play* as follows:

- voluntary behavior

- a stepping outside of "ordinary life"
- secluded and limited in time and space
- not serious, but absorbs the player intensely
- bounded by rules
- promotes formation of social groups which surround themselves with secrecy.[21]

Think about these characteristics a minute. While we may think of play as being a time when there are no rules, Huizinga tells us that all play has rules. These rules are sometimes in existence before the play begins (e.g., checkers, football, tag) or they are made up as the play goes along (e.g., children's imaginary play, such as playing dolls or soldiers or just "playing" around with a Frisbee). If kids are playing make-believe, play won't begin until there is agreement concerning which child is which character and what action is taking place. When there is a disagreement over rules, the play will stop until players resolve the dispute. When at play, children know they are playing even though they are deeply absorbed in what they are doing. Play is irrational, done for its own sake, and cannot be understood in purely rational, scientific terms (even though scholars keep trying). We play because we want to and because it is fun.

Are you a playful person? Before answering, based on what we have learned so far, consider the following. Play may be divided into various forms of play. One way of doing so, developed by Caillois,[22] assumes that play has four forms: One form of play, which we all did in some way as children, is the pursuit of vertigo in which one tries to

> My dog Earl and I play a lot. I take this old chewed up tennis ball out back and Earl goes crazy. He knows the game is on. I hide the ball behind my back, fake throwing it, and Earl takes off. Then he sees I still have the ball, so I wing it a long way—in the other direction. Earl takes off again—like a rocket. Then he brings the ball and puts it on the ground just far enough away that he can get to it just before I can. I act like I don't see it—and then lunge for it. Earl beats me to it and then takes off. Next time he puts it closer. We have our rules. If I fake too much, Earl thinks I am breaking the rules. If he doesn't put the tennis ball close enough so that I have a chance to grab it before him, he is breaking the rules. So I guess dogs know how to play—so do I. I think it's wired into us.

momentarily destroy the stability of perception, escaping reality for the moment. Children roll down hills or turn in circles until they become dizzy and fall down. Some college students play drinking games, ride roller coasters and otherwise inflict a "voluptuous panic" on what was a lucid mind.

Play may also be games of chance; that is, games in which there is an outcome over which the player has no control or a decision takes place which is independent of the player. "Playing" slot machines would be an example, as would bingo, matching coins, or lotteries.

In some play, the player mimics, imitates, or makes-believe that he or she is something other than himself or herself. He or she forgets, disguises or temporarily sheds his or her personality to pretend to be another.[23] Thus, one may act in a "play," do impersonations or imitations of another person, animal or thing, or disguise themselves on Halloween or a costume party. Perhaps more people have "played" at being Elvis Presley than any other human—Thank-you-very-much.

Finally, we may most commonly think of play as a contest, in which there is sustained attention, appropriate training, the application of some level of skill, and the desire to win.[24] Such competition is carried out within the framework of rules, which players voluntarily accept.

So play may be, essentially, competition, mimicking, games of chance, or pursuit of vertigo. In some cases, there may be play forms which show elements of more than one of these play forms. If you were playing poker with friends, you might be engaged in competition in which you used skill—when should you draw a card trying to get a straight flush? There are also, however, elements of chance—if you get dealt four kings in seven card stud with no wild cards, you will probably win. Finally, there might be mimicry—you bluff other players by appearing to be a person with a winning hand although your hole cards don't even add up to two pairs.

Similarly, while riding a roller coaster which produces a sense of vertigo, you may start a contest to see who can hold their hands up in the air the longest as the coaster goes down the first big drop.

Even though play may not be done for any purpose outside itself, many social scientists believe that play serves as a way in which the child takes on the culture he or she is born into. It is also sometimes considered to be a way for the child to resolve conflicts without serious consequences. Researchers suggest that through play a child may "test out" his or her curiosities without experiencing repercussions in the event of failure.

Play can also be defined in social psychological terms. According to such definitions, people have a need to process information or knowledge. Berlyne believed a relation existed between information flow and various elements of uncertainty such that when a person is faced with a stimulus where he or she is unable to predict the outcome of an event, a conflict is created which motivates the processing of information to reduce uncertainty.[25] Theoretically, every individual has an optimal information-seeking level for such stimuli. As Ellis stated, play may be defined as "behavior that is motivated by the need to elevate the level of arousal towards the optimal."[26]

Some researchers have sought to explain play in terms of a need to show the ability to control or produce effects upon the environment. An example might be putting together a puzzle even though there is no reward for it or tossing a wadded ball of paper into a trash can from a long distance. Such behavior is a form of mastering the environment, even though it is not done for an external reward.

The previous two theories are closely related since producing an effect in the environment may be thought of as a kind of arousal-seeking or information processing. Ellis summed this up as follows:

> The formulations of play as caused by arousal-seeking and learning and the cognitive dynamics of development can be integrated in this way. The arousal-seeking model explains the mechanism driving the individual into engagement with the environment in ways surplus to the need of immediate survival. The consequences of such behavior come, via learning, to condition the content of the behavior so motivated. The accumulative effect of such learning interacts with the arousal-seeking motive to produce an upward spiral in the complexity of the interactions. Similarities in that developmental path have led to the separation of the continuous process of growth into developmental stages where growing individuals are seen to move through similar phases at approximately the same time.[27]

What does all this mean? It means that people need stimulation. If you put them in a tank of water heated to the same temperature as their body in a room which is dark and devoid of sound, their need for stimulation will be so great that they will usually start to hallucinate. We begin to play out of a need for stimulation. If you are walking down the street with nothing much absorbing your attention, you may start to notice cracks in the sidewalk and make up a game in which you have to avoid stepping on them. In effect, you have started to explore your environment as a way of seeking stimulation. What happens to the individual because of this play shapes future play so that, combined with continuing desire for arousal, the play becomes more complex. The development of more and more complex levels of play happens in most children at approximately the same age.

Berlyne thought that play could involve two different kinds of exploration: first, specific exploration which was aimed at finding a single answer to a problem or challenge; and second, diverse exploration aimed at finding in the environment elements that can produce excitement or distraction.[28] The complexity of the play thing or situation determines how much it will be explored. According to Bishop and Jeanrenaud, "an object or situation that has many things to see, hear, touch, smell, taste or manipulate, especially in unusual ways, is more complex than one with fewer of these features and is more likely to encourage exploration."[29]

A theme park, therefore, is more likely to encourage exploration than a dormitory room. A rubber ball is more likely to encourage exploration than a block of wood, since the ball can be manipulated in more ways than the block of wood.

After exploration, there may be assimilation in which there is a repetition of behaviors, often with subtle transformations in the play or in the play situation so the individual acquires proficiency. Finally, there may be creativity, "…the production of novel responses which have an appropriate impact in a given context."[30] Conversely, assimilation may lead to the environment or play object losing its novelty. When this happens, the situation

> My physical education teacher never lets us explore anything. When we had the classes on basketball, she told us—here's how to dribble, here's how to shoot, here's how to guard. We never got to try out our own ideas. So, I guess, we never got to play—only work. She knows a lot more about basketball than I do—but she doesn't know anything about me.

may return to what Huizinga referred to as "ordinary life,"[31] thus causing the player to either withdraw from the situation or object formerly used as play or to begin behaving toward the object or situation as toward ordinary life.

Flow

To our other concepts, we must add "flow." As defined by psychologist Mihalyi Csikszentmihalyi, flow is a kind of optimal experience which can take place as either "work" or "leisure."[32] Like some concepts of leisure or play, flow is activity which is an end in itself. It is self-contained (autotelic). Csikszentmihalyi describes the flow experience as follows:

> ... a sense that one's skills are adequate to cope with the challenges at hand in a goal-directed, rule-bound action system that provides clear cues as to how well one is performing. Concentration is so intense that there is no attention left over to think about anything irrelevant, or to worry about problems. Self-consciousness disappears, and the sense of time becomes distorted. An activity that produces such experiences is so gratifying that people are willing to do it for its own sake, with little concern for what they will get out of it, even when it is difficult, or dangerous.[33]

In flow experiences, there is a challenge which is in line with the skills of the individual involved. If the challenge is much greater than the skills of the individual, anxiety is produced. If the challenge is much less than the individual's skills, boredom is produced. Thus, if the Chicago Bulls played a basketball game with a team made up of your classmates, your class would probably experience anxiety while the players on the Bulls became bored. When children confront such situations, they balance the skill and challenge by trading players to form new teams—"you get Harry and Joan, and we get Michael Jordan"—or they handicap one team.

While flow experiences may happen by circumstance, they are usually structured. The normal state of the human mind, Csikszentmihalyi and other psychologists suggest, is entropy—a kind of mental chaos. This condition is neither pleasurable or useful. The human mind has a need for complexity which requires an ability to restructure consciousness, limit self-consciousness, and exercise skill if meaningful

It was the best Ramon and I had ever danced. It was a tango contest and we had really practiced hard—lots of hours in the studio—lots of critiquing from our dance instructor. The night of the contest we were both nervous, but for some reason, when it was our turn and the music started—we just let go. It sounds weird to say but it was like the rhythm and Ramon and the melody and I were all the same thing. I forgot about everything and just moved from instinct. Way past anxiety, past wanting to win. I just let go—I knew what to do. It was great: almost like I was in charge but blacked out at the same time. When the music stopped—it surprised me. Yes, we won the contest but the main thing was that wonderful feeling of certainty.

activity is to be attained. The normal condition of the mind, in other words, is a kind of unfocused chaos which must be controlled. Perhaps this is part of what the ancient Athenians meant when they referred to a life of leisure requiring great discipline.

In work or in leisure, flow can occur only when an individual is capable of concentration and has developed skill. When the ability to concentrate is fragmented, either by a lack of rules (anomie) or by a social system which makes people act in ways which go against their goals (alienation), flow experience is unlikely to occur.

Within family contexts, flow experiences for children are more likely to occur when there is clarity of what parents expect and give their children feedback about it, a centering of interest by the parents on what the child is presently doing, the opportunity for the child to make choices, the developing of commitment by the child in which they have enough trust to put aside their defenses and become unselfconsciously involved in what interests them, and finally—challenge—the parents providing increasingly complex opportunities for action to their children.[34] To do these things requires not only time and effort on the part of the parents but also a combination of both trust of the child and a willingness to exert discipline.

Many leisure (and work) experiences have little potential for flow. Those that don't require much skill, such as watching TV, provide neither the challenge nor the opportunity to use skill. As we will see later, there is evidence that such activities are not very satisfying. Thus, based upon the flow concept, judgments can be made about what is good leisure and what is not. Flow activity is basically the making of meaning, and doing so requires giving oneself in a focused way, whether climbing a mountain, performing surgery, or playing the trumpet.

Summary

Leisure, recreation, play, and flow are important ideas in our lives. Like most important ideas, they mean something slightly different to each individual. Also, each of these terms gets interpreted differently by each succeeding generation.

Historically, leisure has always implied an ideal. That is, without being able to imagine some specific things that were worth doing when you were free to do them, "leisure" would have no meaning. As you read this book, you will learn more about the leisure ideals of others and will explore those of your own. The following chapters will help expand your consciousness about leisure, clarify your values, and provide you with lots of information. After reading them, you will be better able to define leisure in your own life.

> I guess it's the biggest challenge you get in life. Your parents want you to succeed—which sometimes only means take care of yourself financially. Everybody worries about being healthy—sometimes obsessively. O.K. but financially independent and healthy for what? After you solve the problems of survival—what's next? Have fun? Do good? Become famous? Get comfortable? Explore? Leisure is very important—but it isn't easy!

Study Questions

1. Describe some situations in which you experience leisure. What makes it leisure?

2. Do you still play? Why or why not?

3. Are certain activities always recreation? Why or why not?

4. Do you have any "flow" experiences in your "work" or "free time?" If so, briefly describe them.

5. What functions does leisure serve in your life?

6. What do leisure, recreation, play, and flow have in common?

Exercise 1.1

Select two people with whom you come in contact in your everyday life and interview them concerning what leisure means to them and what role it has in their lives. Preface your interview by telling them about the course you are taking and a little bit about different concepts of leisure.

Design some questions for this very informal interview to try to determine what they think leisure means, the role(s) of leisure in their lives, what they do and would like to do during leisure, and the importance or lack of importance they associate with it.

You don't need a large number of questions. Probe further after they answer to see if they have more to say. Give them opportunity to clarify their answers or elaborate.

Write a brief summary of their answers and bring it to class to compare with the results of other interviews.

Endnotes

1   De Grazia, S. (1961). *Of time, work, and leisure* (p. 19). New York, NY: The Twentieth Century Fund.

2   Veblen, T. (1899). *The theory of the leisure class* (p. 40). New York, NY: B.W. Heubsch.

3   May, H. and Petgen, D. (1960). *Leisure and its uses* (p. 3). New York, NY: A.S. Barnes.

4   Kaplan, M. (1960). *Leisure in America* (p. 21). New York, NY: John Wiley & Sons.

5   Goodman, P. (1965). Leisure: Purposeful or purposeless. In P. Madow (Ed.), *Recreation in America* (p. 31). New York, NY: H.W. Wilson Company.

6   Larrabee, E. and Meyersohn, R. (1958). *Mass leisure* (p. 2). Glencoe, IL: The Free Press.

7   Dumazedier, J. (1960). Current problems of the sociology of leisure. *International Social Science Journal, 21*, 526.

8   De Grazia (1961)

9   Mead, M. (1958). The patterns of leisure in contemporary American culture. In E. Larrabee and R. Meyersohn (Eds.), *Mass leisure* (p. 11–12). Glencoe, IL: The Free Press.

10   Pieper, J. (1952). *Leisure: The basis of culture* (p. 40). New York, NY: New American Library.

11 Neulinger, J. (1974). *The psychology of leisure: Research approaches to the study of leisure.* Springfield, IL: Charles Thomas Publishers.

12 Harris Interactive. (2004, December 8). Table 1: Favorite Leisure-Time Activities (Spontaneous, Unaided Responses). *The Harris Poll #97.* Retrieved 2 October 3, 2007, from http://www.harrisinteractive.com/harris_poll/printerfriend/index.asp?PID=526

13 Thomas, D. (1939). Collected poems (p. 14). New York, NY: New Directions Books.

14 Deem, R. (1988). Feminism and leisure studies: Opening up new directions. In E. Wimbush and M. Talbot (Eds.), *Relative freedoms — Women and leisure* (p. 5). Milton Keynes, UK: Open University Press.

15 Goodale, T. and Godbey, G. (1989). *The evolution of leisure: Historical and philosophical perspectives.* State College, PA: Venture Publishing, Inc.

16 Mead (1958)

17 Fairchild, H. (1944). *Dictionary of sociology* (pp. 251–252). New York, NY: Philosophical Library.

18 Doell, C. and Fitzgerald, G. (1954). *A brief history of parks and recreation in the United States* (p. 127). Chicago, IL: The Athletic Institute.

19 Hovis, W. and Wagner, F. (1972). *Leisure information retrieval system city-wide recreation project* (pp. 17–18). Seattle, WA: Leisure Services, Inc.

20 Gray, D. and Greben, S. (1974). Future perspectives. *Parks and Recreation, 9*(6), 49.

21 Huizinga, J. (1950). *Homo ludens: A study of the play element in culture.* Boston, MA: Beacon Press.

22 Caillois, R. (1958). *Man, play and games.* Glencoe, IL: The Free Press.

23 ibid.

24 ibid.

25 Berlyne, D. (1968). Laughter, humor, and play. In G. Lindsay and E. Aronson (Eds.), *Handbook of social psychology* (pp. 131–168). New York, NY: Addison Wesley.

26 Ellis, M. (1973). *Why people play.* Englewood Cliffs, NJ: Prentice-Hall.

27 ibid.

28 Berlyne (1968)

29 Bishop, D. and Jeanrenaud, C. (1982). Creative growth through play and its implications for recreation practice. In T. Goodale and P. Witt (Eds.), *Recreation and leisure: Issues in an era of change* (pp. 85–86). State College, PA: Venture Publishing, Inc.

30 ibid.

31 Huizinga (1950)

32 Csikszentmihalyi, M. (1990). *Flow: The psychology of optimal experience.* New York, NY: Harper and Row.

33 ibid.

34 ibid.

Leisure:
Past and Present

It is often said that people today have more leisure than they used to. However, there is also talk about the fast pace of life and a longing for simpler times. This chapter will examine some ways leisure has changed, both in quantity and quality, from the past to the present. Do we have more leisure than previously?

> Does this generation have a lot of leisure? Hell, yes. Sure, they run all over the place like chickens with their heads cut off but, look— things were different in my day. My Mom had four kids and no modern appliances to help clean. She had a push sweeper and a broom. Ironed all our clothes so they looked neat. On Halloween, we had handmade costumes. I was a pirate, with an eye patch and a skull and crossbones on my hat. Didn't see much of my father. He worked at a factory—left the house early, came home late and very tired, and wanted to be alone for quite awhile. My friends started work early in life and many died within a year or two of retiring. We didn't have the money or the time to do what we wanted. We also didn't have permission. My Dad would have kicked my butt if I behaved like many kids do today. We had chores. We walked two miles to school and didn't go shopping for pleasure because we didn't have money. Yes, people have a lot of leisure today, but they don't get it. Maybe they expect too much. Maybe they don't know any better.

Arguments for Increasing Leisure

Perhaps, in our own society, we could point to the following arguments as to why leisure is increasing.

1. *The increased production of material goods through the application of technology.* This increased productivity, often two to three percent per year during the last half-century, has meant that workers have the potential for more leisure if the material standard of living is kept the same.

2. *The creation of laborsaving devices for household maintenance and other essential duties.* Laborsaving devices for maintaining households and other living spaces have meant that if the level of maintenance required stays the same and it takes less time to achieve that level, more time is available for leisure. Sometimes, however, the result of this has been an increase in the desired level of maintenance.

3. *The decline of the influence of social institutions, such as the church and the family, in establishing predetermined roles for individuals in all aspects of life.* This has, in effect, produced more individual discretion in the selection of activities. Changes in religious beliefs concerning man's relationship to the macrocosm and the decline of the influence of secular religion in the twentieth century have allowed humans to exercise their will to a greater extent than before because fewer usable guidelines for behavior based upon religious doctrine exist.

4. *Differences in attitudes toward pleasure.* It appears that contemporary society has become a pleasure-seeking one. The Puritans' distrust of pleasure and the Christian belief in original sin are losing prominence, thereby reducing many individuals' need to justify their lives through work or suffering.

5. *Substantial increases in the education level of individuals.* Valuing certain leisure activities is usually a product of exposure. For instance, individuals may not value reading novels until they have been exposed to several and have been taught about them. The increased education of the average citizen has caused an expansion of interest in various activities, which has brought about greater interest in pursuing leisure and a greater diversity of interests during leisure.

6. *Lack of physical fatigue associated with many forms of employment.* In many previous societies, work was physically exhausting. Because of this, recreation or leisure was synonymous with

resting or relaxing, but little else. The exhausting demands of work prevented life away from work from realizing its potential. Today many forms of work involve a minimum of physical energy and therefore leave the individual in a position to enjoy a variety of leisure activities that require intensive energy.

7. *An increase in discretionary income.* While some leisure activities cost the participant nothing in terms of money, most today have some cost associated with them. Because of this, the rise in personal disposable income during the last three decades has resulted in a generally proportionate rise in leisure spending and thus in the potential to participate in many activities. Certainly, however, this rise has at least temporarily stopped for many, particularly the young, which limits leisure options.

8. *Humanization of the workplace.* Compared to a century ago, many jobs are performed under more pleasant surroundings and more humane conditions. Part of this change reflects progress made by unions in obtaining rights for employees. Part, also, reflects the fact that the nature of many jobs has changed. Machines now do many of the dirty, dangerous tasks which humans previously did.

9. *Greater potential for choice among women and minorities.* Tremendous progress has been made during the last few decades to broaden leisure opportunities of women and minorities. This is not to imply that severe problems of opportunity no longer exist, only to acknowledge that things have changed. Only a few decades ago, many public recreation facilities were segregated, and women's participation in leisure activities outside the home was severely restricted.

10. *Earlier retirement and later entry into the labor force.* There is little doubt that people are retiring from paid work earlier in relation to their life expectancy than they did previously. Substantial portions of retirees live from one to three decades after retirement, often in good health and with considerable economic resources. At the same time, many young people enter the labor force later in life after completing college or other post-high school training. In combination, these trends mean the total percentage of our life devoted to work has declined considerably.

11. *Deferred marriage and smaller families.* Today in the United States, females and males marry at an average age of almost 25 and 27 respectively. A female will bear 2.0 children on average. Since single people have more free time than married people, as do parents of smaller rather than larger families, the trend toward deferred marriage and smaller families has increased free time dramatically.

Arguments against Increasing Leisure

Unfortunately, these same societal conditions that have created the increased potential for recreation and leisure have also created a number of other factors that have either negated this potential or altered the meaning of leisure in our society.

> Leisure? Get serious. I always feel rushed. Always! There are so many things to do. Life is complicated. I've got e-mails piling up. I just started this job as a technical writer for a big company, and they immediately gave me a quota of papers I have to complete by the end of this month. One of my credit cards was stolen; I have to cancel it and go through my online account. My wife works in retail and that's long hours. We want children, but I don't know when we would have time for them. We live in the "burbs" and have to drive everywhere— We even drive our bicycles to the bike path. I feel like I should be working out more, but I don't. Laura says she wants to go back to college for an MBA and that means I would need to do more clean up and meals. I guess I can if I have to. Leisure? Yeah, right.

Among the factors harming our potential for leisure are the following:

1. *Increased societal complexity and change.* Coping with the increased complexity and accelerated rate of change within our society has blunted our leisure potential in a number of ways. Decisions have become more complicated and time-consuming in a society where planning and regulation by the government are increasingly necessary and where citizens expect a greater

role in that process. The average individual is being forced to absorb more and more information, often of a complex technical nature, at an increasingly accelerated rate. Some scientists believe that much of the pathological behavior evidenced in most industrialized societies is due to "brain overloading"— a condition brought about by the constant mental strain resulting from the increased tempo of everyday life and the political, technical, and moral changes to which humans must adapt.

2. *Limitless materialism.* Many people in our society today have an inability to satiate their material desires. The acceleration of consumption has found no limits, even though we have no societal justification for it. The acquisition, maintenance, and use of the vast number of material goods which we increasingly want takes time and increases the amount of work we are compelled to undertake in order to sustain our lifestyle.

3. *The carry-over of "work values" into leisure.* Many of the goals, methods, and styles of our work institutions increasingly spill over into our leisure institutions. In much of our "leisure" activity, no less than in our "work" activity, we place a high value on advance planning and goal setting, competition, incremental improvement through the mastery of special knowledge and technique, the efficient utilization of time, and winning. What has emerged is a situation where one worries about doing the activity sufficiently well, regardless of whether it is work or leisure. This serious approach has led to the decline of many forms of pleasure.

4. *Higher percentage of the population in the labor force.* Today, the percentage of people who work outside the home for pay is at an all-time high. Not only are the majority of adult women working for pay outside the home but also more teenagers are as well.

Since 1973 there has been little change in productivity in the United States. Output has increased greatly not because of the improved efficiency of capital or labor, but because of increased amounts of capital and labor. "The rising number of families with two wage earners barely maintained household incomes, and only at the expense of parental childcare and involvement in schools, housekeeping, volunteer work and other services."[1] More immigrants have also joined the labor force, which is a means of expanding U.S. output. Thus, U.S. productivity has not continued on the infinitely upward cycle that many envision.

5. *Increased environmental limitations.* While pollution is as old as humans are, today's rapidly deteriorating condition of our environment limits many forms of leisure expression. The depletion of the ozone layer makes many forms of outdoor recreation more dangerous. Fishing or swimming may be limited due to water pollution. Air pollution may hinder running or make a picnic less pleasant. Both the quality and availability of many forms of leisure expression are greatly harmed by our unwillingness or inability to live in harmony with the environment.

6. *The continual speeding up of life.* There is considerable evidence that the pace of life is getting faster and faster. Computers, cellular phones and other technological changes have helped speed up life, as has the open-ended consumerism that characterizes our society. Things cost money—money costs time.

7. *An increased sense of what is necessary.* "Leisure," in many senses, depends on the feeling of an individual that there is nothing they have to do. For many individuals in modern nations, regardless of how much time they have free from work, housework or other obligations, the sense of what is necessary increases. One should work out everyday, take vitamins, read labels on cans, look good, feel good, learn to use every new computer software program which comes along, and have "quality time" with those they care about. This increased sense of the necessary may mean that there is little sense of leisure in our society, regardless of how many hours of time free from work we have.

8. *The threat of terrorism.* In recent years, the United States has begun to experience acts of terrorism, as have many other countries. The threat of terrorist acts may make some forms of leisure more difficult, such as tourist travel on commercial

airlines, and it may make some other leisure activities less tranquil and serene if one is afraid of bombings, kidnapping, or other terrorist acts.

In summary, while our potential for leisure has increased, we are nowhere near becoming the leisure society about which so much has been written.

Leisure: Past and Present

Leisure has differed historically in different societies, both in quantity and quality. The forces that shaped leisure—food supply, religious beliefs, political systems, rates of human reproduction, wars, weather, rate and type of learning, playfulness, amount of industrialism, and other factors—are so varied that it is difficult to make meaningful generalizations. Although the following section is certainly not comprehensive, it will illustrate some of the major differences in leisure for different societies and different ages.

> *I'm in the airport and people are eating food while sitting by boarding gates. They are also talking on cellphones. Some are also reading. I go into the restroom. There are people talking on cellphones in the toilets. There are people brushing their teeth. There are people text messaging. I walk back out. There are people shopping, drinking while talking on the phone, and ordering from a menu and talking to the bartender while trying to keep an eye on their carry-on bags. Only one person in the whole airport seems to be doing nothing—and he looks depressed. Oh, and most of these people are on vacation!*

Let's start with three broad statements. First, it is not always correct to say that societies continue to have more and more leisure. Rather, it is more correct to say that the quantity and quality of leisure have varied greatly within different periods of history and within different societies. Second, as societies become more urbanized and industrialized, work and leisure become more highly separated than previously. As they move toward a knowledge economy, this separation decreases. Work reaches out into the part of life that was previously reserved for leisure and leisure takes place during time that was once part of work. Third, what is satisfying and worthwhile during leisure varies greatly from culture to culture and reflects the values and conditions of that culture.

Leisure in Nonindustrial Cultures

While societies before industrialization were just as diverse as those after industrialization, if we examine such cultures, we may begin to wonder whether technology really has given us more or better leisure. Although it is certainly true that many preindustrial cultures were characterized by long hours of toil, some were not. Although it may be said that "...human social life is a response to the practical problems of earthly existence,"[2] the degree to which practical problems of staying alive shape our social lives may vary from culture to culture and from person to person. Additionally, the line between labor and leisure is not so distinct. Primitive people tend to approach a great many of their daily activities as if they were play. Anthropologists who have studied the daily routines of agrarian and hunter-gatherer societies report a pattern of work and leisure that is much more integrated than that of a modern industrial society. Thus, in their study of Maori culture, anthropologists Stumpf and Cozens reported that every aspect of Maori economic life was characterized by an element of recreation: "Whether engaging in fishing, bird-snaring, cultivation of the fields, or building a house or canoe, the occasion was marked by activities which we could definitely classify as recreational."[3] These activities—singing, loud talking, laughing—are also features of the cooperative work parties that are found in many parts of Africa.

Not only are there elements of recreation in the economic activities of some preindustrial cultures but, in some, the amount of time available for leisure appears to have been as great or greater than our own. Anthropologists Allen and Orna Johnson studied the Machiguenga Indians of Peru for 18 months and found this to be the case. These Indians survive by growing food in gardens, hunting, fishing, and collecting wild foods. "They are self-sufficient; almost everything they consume is produced by their own labors using materials that are found close at hand."[4] When the Johnsons divided the time of the Machiguenga into production time (work), consumption time (using consumer goods for pleasure, eating), and free time (idleness, rest, sleep, chatting), and then compared these time expenditures to those in current French society, they discovered that French men and women (both working and housewives) spent more time in production activities than the Machiguenga. The French also spent from three to five times more hours in the consumption of goods than the Indians. The Machiguenga's free time, however, was found to surpass that of the French by more than four hours a day. The Johnsons argued that while technological progress has provided us with more goods, it has not resulted in more free time for most people living in industrial society. They also pointed out that the pace of life for the Peruvian Indians was leisurely; daily activities never seemed hurried or desperate. Instead, "each task was allotted its full measure of time, and free time is not felt to be boring or lost but is accepted as being entirely natural."[5] (We will discuss this speedup in the pace of life shortly.)

These findings agree with those of Sahlins[6] who found that many hunter-gatherer societies, such as the Australian aborigines and the Kung San of South Africa, require only three or four hours of work per day to provide the material requirements for their simple way of life. Thus, as Sahlins pointed out, there are two ways to reach affluence—our own way, which is to produce more, or what Sahlins called the Buddhist way, which is to be satisfied with less.

It is difficult for us to appreciate the advantages of hunter-gatherer societies. There is a great tendency for us to think of such societies as being composed of ignorant savages. Nevertheless, "hunters and gatherers are not fools and, as recent studies show, their unique economy gives them all the time they need to build culture."[7] Lewin makes this point dramatically by reporting that the bushmen known as the Kung San work, on average, two and one-half days a week for an average of six hours a day yet their diet exceeds recommended allowances set by the U.S. Food and Drug Administration. However, there is great variation in such cultures; some may have appeared to have led tranquil lives because their limited food supply didn't provide enough energy to be more active.

We can conclude that the existence of large amounts of free time doesn't necessarily lead to what we think of as higher forms of civilization. It was once believed that by producing large food surpluses people would automatically experiment with various activities thought to characterize "higher" civilizations, such as art, mathematics, and written language. This, however, has frequently not been so.

In terms of amount of leisure, the Roman passion for free time reached its climax in the fourth century, when there were 175 holidays per year. Whatever the work schedules of slaves and women, leisure for the ruling class, for administrators and professionals, would never again be so abundant. In France and England, from the late Middle Ages to about 1800, the trend in manual occupations was toward longer hours. By the mid-nineteenth century, the workweek of factory workers in these countries and in America reached 70 hours or more. Farm workers were exceptions to this trend; estimates suggest that they worked very long hours during the whole period, with some reduction only in the twentieth century.

Games played an important role in most ancient cultures. Such games may be divided into categories that still make sense today. They include games that were competitive, involve training, sustained attention, and the desire to win. Such games were a kind of rivalry in which the winner was better in terms of speed, endurance, strength, memory, skill, ingenuity, or other qualities.[8] An example would be the southeastern Native American game of chunkey, a hoop and pole game:

> A hoop, variously made of wood, bark, cornhusk, pottery, or stone, was rolled across a level playing field. In some versions of the game, the rolling hoop was simply a target for arrows or darts shot or thrown by individual players, or more rarely by competing teams. A more common version, however, involved two players, one hurling the hoop and each subsequently sliding a pole after this moving target. The object was not to impale the hoop, but to have the poles come to rest as near to the fallen hoop as possible, an endeavor requiring great timing and dexterity.[9]

Other games were based on chance—gambling—in which a decision independent of the player, an outcome over which a player had no control, or in which winning itself was the result of fate rather than skill over an opponent.

A third kind of game involved mimicking—a person makes believe he or she is someone or something else and may also try to make others believe it. One "forgets, disguises or temporarily sheds his identity in order to temporarily become another."[10]

The pursuit of vertigo is the final kind of play—the kind of sensation which one may experience on amusement park rides today—or by smoking marijuana. In such "play," one's stable perception is temporarily altered and a kind of pleasurable panic is induced. Beer drinking games, for instance, are thousands of years old.

Games, in all the previous forms, had serious functions in ancient cultures. Such games might prepare children for adult roles, such as hunting, survival skills, domestic life and childrearing, or for social interaction and stratifying society. Games also helped ancient peoples deal with conflict, establish justice, and define relations with outside societies. Eskimo drumming contests, for instance, are a kind of insult contest in which two opposing parties with grievances against each other tried to outdo each other in insults. Those who listened determined the winner.

Such games could also be ways of determining the will of God(s), confirming or explaining the origins of the universe, or a part of religious practice or sacred beliefs.[11] Games were often behavior that could be considered sacred.

Industrialization

The decline of leisure from the end of the Middle Ages to the height of the Industrial Revolution is not, however, to be measured only by the increase in work hours. In preindustrial society, work was incorporated into everyday life, and leisure time was not separate. Work was carried on in the fields within sight of home or within the home itself, accompanied by friendly conversations and the business of village life. It was only when work came to be done in a particular place; at a special, separate time; and under certain conditions that leisure came to be demanded as a right. More precisely, "time-off work" was demanded, since there was no way that the intimate, preindustrial relationship between leisure and life could be restored in the factory towns of the nineteenth century.

Industrialization and organization during the Industrial Revolution brought about a greater separation between work and leisure and reduced the amount of leisure enjoyed by the ordinary citizen, at least in its initial stages. Thus, work came to be scheduled first, to suit those who owned the means of production. Leisure became leftover time.

In the early stages of industrialization, leisure became associated with a class of people, as it has at many other times throughout history. Not all countries industrialize in the same way, of course. Some countries, such as Japan, retained many elements of traditional culture even as the factory system was developed.

The Leisure Class

In ancient Athens, native-born male citizens were in some sense a privileged, leisure class. Their control of a system of slaves and the very limited rights of women empowered their lives of leisure. In the United States, the first leisure class that evolved did so on southern plantations; plantation owners had none of the prohibitions against pleasure that the Puritans to the north imposed and had slaves to do the work. It was in the second half of the nineteenth century that "society most flagrantly bent its pleasures to display."[12] Those who became rich after the Civil War—owners of steel plants, copper mines, textile mills, and cattle ranches—"sought to establish social leadership through their extravagance in entertainments and amusements."[13] Capitalism and the processes of urbanization and industrialization had brought about increasing divisions within society. One such division was "the Leisure Class."

In 1899, Thorstein Veblen launched an attack on the extravagance of the newly wealthy industrial capitalists. In *The Theory of the Leisure Class,* he argued that all consumption of goods, as well as leisure behavior, was shaped by the desire to impress others and to distinguish oneself from ordinary people. History, Veblen argued, showed a process by which man, through workmanship, at long last created the material surplus needed for economic security. This surplus, however, permitted a new group of self-centered motives to come into being, and some people "found their pleasure in invidious distinctions at the expense of others."[14] The primitive balance of production and consumption gave way to a world where too much productivity, in countries like Germany and Japan, put a military surplus in the hands of ambitious dictators, while in countries like England and America, too much consumption involved all classes in a meaningless chase to display material goods in an emulative manner.

Leisure, as Veblen described it, was the nonproductive consumption of time, undertaken because of a sense that productive work wasn't worthwhile and also to show that one could afford to be idle. Leisure was thought to be closely related to exploitation, and the achievements of a life of leisure had much in common with the spoils of war or the trophies of economic exploitation. Material goods were such trophies. But, since leisure did not generally result in material goods, those in the leisure class also had to provide evidence of nonproductive, immaterial, consumption of time:

Such immaterial evidences of past leisure are quasi-scholarly or quasi-artistic accomplishments and a knowledge of processes and incidents which do not conduce directly to the furtherance of human life. So, for instance, in our time there is knowledge of the dead languages and the occult sciences; of correct spelling; of syntax and prosody; of various forms of domestic music and other household art; of the latest properties of dress, furniture, and equipage; of games, sports, and fancy-bred animals such as dogs and racehorses. In all of these branches of knowledge the initial motive from which their acquisition proceeded at the onset, and through which they first came into vogue, may have been something quite different from the wish to show that one's time had not been spent in industrial employment; but unless these accomplishments had approved themselves as serviceable evidence of an unproductive expenditure of time, they would not have survived and held their place as conventional accomplishments of the leisure class.[15]

The use of leisure by the class of society who had it, obviously, didn't result in self-perfection or the improvement of culture or aid to the community. Instead, it resulted simply in unproductive uses of time in order to achieve status.

The roots of the leisure class, Veblen argued, could be traced to the ancient traditions of predatory cultures in which productive effort was considered unworthy of the able-bodied male. Thus, a leisure class existed before industrialism. It

> I am forced to agree with the proposition that working people really don't know what to do with free time. They lack all refinement that the proper use of leisure requires. They have no skills for leisure, and their baser instincts mean they will simply get drunk, have sex or play their awful music if given more time off the job. I honestly don't think they can be changed. Certainly it is worth attempting to provide a few amenities like public parks but, by and large, leisure must be reserved for people of a higher class. What the working class needs are brief periods of structured recreation, to refresh them for work. They can be dangerous if their free time is not controlled. We have been prepared for more graceful and refined living. That may sound elitist but then leisure is an elite idea. The differences between us and them is greater than the difference between them and other animals.

was the transition to a "pecuniary" culture, however, which brought the leisure class into full bloom. The captain of industry and the tribal chief, therefore, shared some things in common.

This portrait of the emerging leisure class, while containing some truth, was exaggerated. As sociologist David Riesman pointed out, there came to be lots of variation among those within the leisure class. Many, particularly women, were in the vanguard of modern movements in the arts and politics. Many became deeply involved in charity, and not always just to "show off." Some among the leisure class also recognized criticisms of their lifestyle and changed as a result.[16]

The Working Class

Not only did industrial capitalism bring about a small "leisure class" that had both time and money, it also brought about a class of workers who often had to be forced to work and, eventually, enticed into a model of open-ended consumption which they would come to accept and desire.

Those who lived the rural peasant life were often unwilling factory workers. Workers who formed the Luddite movement, for instance, tried to destroy the machines that were introduced into the work place "...until shot, hanged, and deported into submission."[17] According to De Grazia, the Luddites were mistaken in their attacks because what really changed and ruled their lives in a revolutionary manner was the clock. "The clock, to repeat, is an automatic machine whose product is regular auditory or visual signals. Who lives by it becomes an automaton, a creature of regularity."[18] Certainly the English villagers did not want this industrial life, but gradually, they were forced into it, driven off the land and into the factories. Prior to this

> ...The life they knew was unpunctual and chatty. A shoe-maker got up in the morning when he liked and began work when he liked. If anything of interest happened, out he went from his stool to take a look for himself. If he spent too much time at the alehouse drinking and gossiping one day, he made up for it by working until midnight the next. Like the Lapons or the Trobriand Islanders, he worked in enthusiastic spurts and spent long periods without toil; which, among nonindustrial communities, is a way of working more common than is generally supposed.[19]

Both the leisure class and the working class were, in many ways, historically new phenomena. The first generations of each group were put at almost opposite ends of the scale—one had plenty of money and plenty of free time but little experience in how to use either; the other had long hours of enforced, standardized, unfulfilling work, but little of the communal leisure they had previously experienced, and little in the way of personal resources to let them adjust to the small blocks of empty time they had. Both groups had great problems in responding to their situations. The working class, in many respects, had been enslaved not only by its dependence upon those who owned the means of production but also by a world that had sprung up only to accommodate the process of production.

She thinks she's better than I am just because she lives in that big house and has fancy clothes and all. She's not. The things she does in her free time are mainly showing off. Maybe she can play a song on the piano or say a few words in French, but I'll bet she can't sew like I can. She doesn't know anything about children—or how to make a good pie. I'll bet I'm a better dancer than her—when I get the time to do it—it's just that everything she does is fancier. I've got the imagination for free time—even if I don't get much of it. She and her old man just have a lot of money—nothing more.

Gambling, Drinking and Violence: Common Leisure Pursuits

In both Europe and North America, gambling and drinking either accompanied or were the source of most leisure activity of adult males and some females. Additionally, many leisure activities involved extreme violence to each other or toward animals. Historians, according to Cross,[20] identified a tremendous growth in wagering during the late-seventeenth century. While gambling was common to some extent in almost all cultures, the growth of racing and blood sports, from boxing to cockfights, in both Europe and North America, increased gambling greatly.

The practice of card playing for money and gaming spread to all sectors of society, involving women as well as men. One explanation for the rise of gambling was the rise of commercial enterprise and the spirit of capitalism, which took a positive attitude toward risk taking:

In America, according to historian John Findlay,

From the seventeenth century through the twentieth, both gambling and moving west thrived on high expectations, risk taking, opportunism, and movement: and both activities helped to shape a distinctive culture. Like bettors, pioneers have repeatedly grasped the chance to get something for nothing—to claim free land, to pick up nuggets of gold, to speculate on western real estate.[21]

While modern academic accounts of gambling usually center around gambling as an addiction, a pathological compulsion or as a masochistic desire to punish the guilty self, there has been little academic attention to pleasurable aspects of such risk-taking behavior. Much of the gambling that became popular in Britain during industrialization and later in North America certainly had a pleasurable element. It was a means of displaying wealth and bravery. It also provided, as Goffman[22] observed, an opportunity for euphoria, a flooding in of the experience of spontaneous yet all-encompassing action. It both channeled the excitement of competition and risk taking into relatively harmless endeavors and also frequently expressed the value of individuality and the dream of gain.[23]

In Britain, the government's attempts at controlling gambling were usually restricted to controlling gambling among the poor, while in North America greater church pressure led to numerous attempts to ban gambling. The Virginia Company sought to outlaw gambling in order to improve work discipline. There was also religious disdain for leaving things to chance, a characteristic of much gambling, as well as for the drinking and rowdiness that often accompanied it. Puritans in New England outlawed playing cards and horse racing. While casino gambling didn't prosper in North America as it did in Britain, generally attempts at banning gambling simply failed because people wanted to do it. Additionally, there was the matter of hypocrisy—both the church and state sponsored some forms of gambling, such as lotteries, from colonial times.

The popularity of gambling was such that some sports, such as boxing, horse racing, many forms of card playing, dog fighting, cockfighting, bear or bullbaiting and other forms of leisure expression, existed primarily to allow for betting. In all such forms of activity, considerable attention was eventually given to establishing rules that reduced cheating, which was common. Attempts were made to regulate boxing, establish written rules for card games, and license the operation of gambling casinos. Cheating, nevertheless, remained a significant part of the gambling scene.

The consumption of alcohol was no less popular. Not only were wine, beer, and spirits popular because they were an ageless means of conserving fruit and grain in an era before refrigeration but also because of different attitudes toward drinking. "It 'strengthened' the laborer and got him through a 10- or 12-hour day."[24] Drink played a central role in the taking of meals and in social conversation as well. Even in Puritan New England, there was much evidence of drinking on the Sabbath. Indeed, the notion of total abstinence was a nineteenth century phenomenon. "While Puritans and other reformers struggled against its excess, few opposed drink on principle."[25] Consumption of alcohol was thought of as much as a food as an intoxicant. "Drink was perhaps even more central to the meal and conversation than it is today."[26]

While attitudes toward the consumption of alcohol were different in North America than Europe, drinking was nonetheless common. Alehouses and retail dram shops could be found in every town in the colonies. Rum and other forms of drink were often an integral part of the pay of workers. On the frontier, special occasions such as barn raisings, weddings and corn huskings led to communal drinking of homemade whiskey. Taverns sprang up around waterfronts, and drinking was an integral part of the life of a seaman.

Finally, much of the leisure of working-class males involved violence. Blood sports such as bull-baiting and cock-scailing involved, respectively, setting fierce dogs on a bull tethered by a short rope and throwing a heavy stick at a rooster to see who could kill it. Boxing essentially had no rules. Opponents hit each other when they were down, used head butts and hit below the belt.[27] Football was an extremely violent combination of soccer and

> When you get right down to it, football fans are generally a bunch of losers. Mostly they only like their team when it wins. They get trashed at a moment's notice. They gamble on all these football pools. If their team wins a championship, they go bonkers and set cars on fire and such. They don't seem to care that most players end up crippled or that half of them are criminals. It's like there's a big hole in their lives and football is what they use to stuff the hole with.

rugby. While there is a tendency to romanticize the peasant culture that was transformed into the working class, the leisure of many was brutal.

The Reform of Leisure

Industrialism, as we have seen, produced changes that made former leisure habits impossible for the peasants who had become the working class. New work patterns, the emergence of capitalism and the urban environment, which was largely an unplanned phenomenon accompanying the factory system, made former ways of life and leisure obsolete. The factory system was a catastrophe for peasant culture. Likewise, peasant culture was a catastrophe for the factory system. Peasants often preferred idleness, drink, working when the mood struck them and the pleasures of the body over the pleasures of the mind. All these situations led to a series of attempts to reform the leisure of the peasants, who had now become the "working class." Those who were employers as well as upwardly mobile employees believed that changing the leisure habits of the working class was of fundamental importance in determining the success of industrialism. Many, including Victorian novelist Charles Dickens, also recognized that leisure time was the only arena for the "re-creation" of the physical and psychological capacity to work.[28] By the 1830s, reformers understood that new work patterns had deprived members of society of the means of expressing their religious, family and self-definitional values.

At the same time, these reformers held that leisure was perhaps the best place to inculcate the personal values essential for a growing commercial economy: self-control, familism, and "respectability."[29] As an English reformer Joseph Kay described the situation, the poor

> live precisely like brutes, to gratify... the appetites of their uncultivated bodies, and then die, to go they have never thought, cared, or wondered whither... They eat, drink, breed, work and die; and... the richer and more intelligent classes are obliged to guard them with police.[30]

At the heart of much reform of leisure in the early nineteenth century was fear of the urban working poor. Crime increased significantly in the early 1800s. Gang wars, prostitution, pickpockets, even the possibility of insurrection made the cities unsafe.

Certainly urbanization was to blame for much of the crime and pathological behavior that accompanied the transformation of peasants into the urban working class. As American historian Paul Boyer observed

> The bawdy servant girl was transformed into the painted prostitute soliciting on the street. The village tavern became the beer cellar in the slum; the neighborly wager on the horse race or a cockfight, the organized gambling of the city. The unruly child and the discontented farm youth quarreling with his father became the multiplied thousands of street Arabs and young urban newcomers who seemed to have broken free of all familial control.[31]

Much of the effort in the rational recreation and other reform movements was to counter such situations, both from altruistic motivations as well as self-interest. Evangelists on both sides of the Atlantic sought to "Christianize" leisure through developments such as Sunday School; the Sabbatarian Movement, which sought to ban many forms of leisure expression on Sunday; and the temperance movement, which sought to ban all use of alcohol. In Britain, the Temperance Movement was not very strong politically but in North America, a combination of clergy and business leaders gained enough political power to restrict alcohol use in 13 states and territories by the 1850s.[32] Temperance groups were often dominated by women, who saw the saloon culture of men as a threat to both family and community life. The various Teetotaler and Temperance Movements often resulted in fierce disputes, pitting neighbor against neighbor.

There were also movements against prostitution, sometimes called Social Purity Movements, also often led by women. Such groups, in the early eighteenth century, picketed brothels and published the names of patrons. Vigilante mobs occasionally hanged persistent brothel owners.

As British historian Hugh Cunningham argued, however, the various reform movements wanted not just to suppress various leisure behaviors, they also wanted to transform leisure behavior, replacing play which was public, inconclusive and improvised with play that was more highly ordered and planned. In doing so, the intent was to make the working class more "respectable, more predictable, less dangerous to others, and more amenable to industrial working conditions."[33]

Certainly there was also a genuine concern for broadening the intellectual horizons, improving family life and the general health and
welfare of those less fortunate.

The means of achieving these ends were as diverse as the promotion of reading, choral societies, structured sport experiences, adult
education, and a variety of other nonwork experiences. The nature of
many of these efforts were, themselves, offshoots of the techniques of
industrial work. Modern sport, for instance, was born during the nineteenth century during the transformation of work to the industrial system. In Britain, sports such as track and field, swimming, rowing, and
soccer became regulated contests with techniques drawn from industrial
production and from the unfolding world of capitalistic market relationships. The casual nature of many sports largely disappeared as they
became a noneconomic form of competition paralleling capitalism's
win-lose mentality.

While the transformation of work did cause the transformation of
leisure, such change was not systematic or complete. Many traditions of
preindustrial life remained intact; others were restructured—but some
were lost forever.

For the working class, the meaning and significance of leisure
slowly evolved. Gradually, there took place "...a critical change from
the nineteenth century vision of man fulfilling himself through the free
employment of his own natural gifts that leisure would release. In the
new approach, the emphasis was markedly upon a materialistic set of
goals."[34] The transition from preindustrial to industrial society brought
with it a speeding up of the pace of life. This occurred partly because
of the demands made upon factory workers by their employers, upon
whom they were almost completely dependent. It also took place
because technology enabled a worker to produce more in a given period
and, thus, his time increased in value. As his time increased in value,
it became more scarce, like most economically valuable commodities.
The increased scarcity of time also came about because the individual
in an industrial society had more options available in terms of what
could be done. For instance, opportunities for travel increased. Also,
minds were awakened to the potential of leisure as formal and informal
education increased. Interest was stimulated in many activities of which
individuals had previously been unaware or unappreciative.

The Increasing Role of Government in Controlling Leisure

The process of industrialization, in almost every country in which it takes place, has brought about an increased role of government in recreation and leisure in two ways: the provision of recreation and leisure facilities, programs and other services, and the increased regulation of leisure behavior.

In regard to the regulation of leisure activities, government had almost always, within Judeo-Christian cultures, sought to ban certain forms of leisure behavior. What changed under industrialization was the increased extent to which government sought to control such activity and the increased means at its disposal to do so. Clarke and Critcher discussed the increased role of police in regulating leisure activity owing to laws passed in the second quarter of the nineteenth century which established organized police forces at the municipal and county level. One of the tasks of such police forces was to clear the streets of nuisances to facilitate travel and commerce. "One of the biggest nuisances was popular culture."[35] Street trading, children's games and simply hanging around were now activities that were no longer appropriate for the streets. Police were also increasingly evident at almost any public occasion, including holidays, fairs, and wakes. They were also evident inside pubs and music halls.

Licensing was also a way in which the state maintained control over numerous forms of leisure activity. Licensing policies increasingly sought to control and regulate pubs, music halls, and the sale of alcohol. These were increasingly regulated and the operation of commercial recreation "rationalized." Negotiations between proprietors of music halls and local authorities resulted in music halls becoming much tamer and more orderly:

> Gone were drink, food and most of the prostitutes. Tables and chairs had been replaced by fixed rows of seats; and semiprofessional and amateur performers had been supplanted by full-time professionals tightly controlled by contract, including guarantees that they would not include in their acts any material "offensive" to political figures and institutions.[36]

The pub, also, was increasingly controlled and lost many of its social functions.

Here's how it works in my state—at least I think. You can have private beer distributors but only the state can sell wine and spirits, unless it's a state winery and they can sell their own wine on site. Six-pack shops can sell beer but no more than two six packs to a customer. A restaurant can sell alcohol if it has a license but half of its revenues must be from food. If you build a few hotel rooms onto the restaurant, you can get a different kind of license easier. So what I want to know is why is it so easy to buy cigarettes?

In all these changes, leisure was shaped, increasingly, to express the same values which industrialism had brought about rather than to provide an opposition to such values. While the working class often resisted such changes, generally they were only partially successful in keeping some part of leisure free from the emerging ideals of efficiency, rationality, and productivity.

The Basis of Increasing Free Time

Although free time became more controlled, it also increased in America for several reasons, including the rise in productivity of the labor force, the efforts of labor unions and a policy of support for shorter hours of work from the federal government. While owners of the means of production have historically been against any reduction of working hours on the assumption that such reductions would reduce profits, labor unions were successful in gradually promoting shorter hours. Such unions justified increases in free time as necessary for greater family involvement and community life. Most unions wanted work to be incrementally reduced toward zero hours as far as possible. While there were differences in the portion of increased wages and increased free time they desired from increases in productivity, more free time was a rallying cry of unions all the way up to the Second World War.

Although some progress was made in reducing hours to ten or eleven hours per day in the late nineteenth century, such limits were often restricted to women and children or to factory work. The more wealthy nations such as Britain and the United States reduced the work-day to nine or ten hours by the 1890s, but the international movement for an eight-hour day was frustrated from its inception in the 1880s until after World War I. The opportunity for retirement reached the United States only in the 1930s and vacations, while a right in Europe,

Sure, I joined the union. I'm glad I did. It's not just wanting better wages, but that's a big part of it. Management is making a fortune from this factory, and we're the ones who make it happen. I'm trying to support a family and it ain't easy. My wife even started working part-time and I don't like that—makes me feel like I can't provide. The union is also fighting for more time off—an eight-hour day. Imagine that. More time for my family. More time to work in the garden. Maybe even join the Elks Club. I'm a union man all the way. Eight hours for work, eight hours for sleep and eight hours for whatever we want to do!

remained a privilege granted at the discretion of the employer in the United States.

The U.S. government was supportive of decreases in the workweek until the Great Depression in 1929. More free time was viewed as a social good, a sign of progress. This changed during the Great Depression when mass unemployment created a link between free time and unemployment. As historian Ben Hunnicut pointed out, government policy changed as a result of the Depression. Emphasis was placed upon "full employment" rather than reduced hours of work. The Fair Labor Standards Act, which governs the official hours of work on many Americans, has not decreased from 40 hours since then. Basically, since the Depression, hours of work for full-time employees have changed very little, although national time diary research suggests an increase in free time of almost one hour per day between 1965 and 1985.[37]

In summary, the Industrial Revolution began a vast process of transformation. Gradually, through unionization, less brutal management and vast increases in production, the worker would find reduced hours and, in many cases, improved working conditions. Also gradually, the worker would begin to accept and then desire the consumption of material goods that was necessary for industrialism to flourish. As Riesman noted, "The working class has fallen heir to conspicuous consumption, which the leisure class is giving up."[38] Had the working class not begun to consume in an almost open-ended manner, the world would have unfolded quite differently.

This same process, with some cultural modifications, is going on in many different countries of the world today. In China, Peru, or Japan, some version of this process is unfolding.

> Government brags about "full employment" sometimes, and I think we forget what that means. Is it good to have a society in which everyone works full time? I don't think so. Suppose every person in the United States over the age of 14 worked every day of the year for eight or nine hours? Full employment! A culture of failure, but full employment. Many things, maybe most things worth doing, aren't things you get paid for—Did that ever occur to you?

The Changing Nature of Leisure

The transition from preindustrial to industrial society resulted in systematic changes in leisure's characteristics. This transition was one from societies that were rural and simple in their social organization to those which are socially complex and urban. In rural, conservative societies, there is a tendency for leisure activities to center around family and church groups while in more complex, urban cultures there is a tendency for leisure to be centered around individual interests and for the family to be less dominant in the use of leisure.

Industrialism also began to produce more material goods for the common people, and the desire to acquire goods became incorporated into a materialistic style of life. The acquisition, use, and maintenance of a progressively greater number of material goods further contributed to the speedup in the pace of life.

Postindustrial Society

Today, our society is past the stage of industrialization. Most workers are involved in the production of services rather than in the production of material goods. As Daniel Bell observed, our postindustrial society is characterized not by an absence of scarcity, although certain traditional forms of material scarcities such as food and shelter have been eliminated for the majority, but by new forms of scarcity.[39] Such costs or scarcities include the cost of information, the cost of coordination, and the cost of time.

Learning is mandatory in our society, and the rate at which we are bombarded with information increases daily. Every new social or political movement speaks of the need to "educate the people." The new consumer activist movement, for instance, is based upon providing more and more accurate information to the consumer so as to ensure a logical choice on his or her part. This movement's success, however, is

I don't know. It seems like leisure has disappeared. We live in a society where you can never have enough money, you can never be thin enough, you can never read enough about what foods are good for you. There don't seem to be any limits on things. My neighbor has traveled to twenty countries but wants to go to others. My friends are buying McMansions, which have five or six bathrooms for two people. I get 50 e-mails a day, not counting SPAM, and I can't even reply to all of them. Everyone says they are a "professional," but what that really seems to mean is that their job is open-ended in terms of what they try to accomplish and the bar on productivity is being raised all the time. I think to really have leisure there have to be some limits, and I don't see many limits in this culture. If you want to have it all, you can't have leisure.

dependent upon individuals internalizing huge amounts of information, processing it in a logical way, and then making calculated decisions (not unlike a computer). To buy a tennis racket intelligently, therefore, one would need to have reliable data concerning comparative price; durability; flexibility of head, throat, and shaft; weight and weight distribution; head shape; size of sweet spot; racket head torque; vibration; stringing pattern; grip size; grip composition; string type; string tension; etc., etc. Such an approach ensures that the individual pays for the racket not only with money but also with time, energy, and added complexity to his or her life. In many ways, the consumer movement is an apology for materialism that doesn't usually question the need for products but just gives the potential buyer instructions on how best to purchase them.

The increasing amount of communication in society may have literally "saturated" us, changing our concepts of self in the process. As a mass culture is replaced with a more diverse, individualized culture in which the amount of sensory input we get grows and grows, we think about ourselves differently. The Romantic and Modern notions of self are largely being replaced with "postmodern" ones. Psychologist Kenneth Gergen explains what has happened as follows:

Cultural life in the twentieth century has been dominated by two major vocabularies of the self. Largely from the nineteenth century, we have inherited a Romantic view of the self, one that attributes to each person characteristics of personal depth: passion, soul, creativity, and moral fiber. This vocabulary is essential to the formation of deeply committed relationships, dedicated friendships and life purposes. But since the rise of the Modernist worldview beginning in the early twentieth century, the Romantic vocabulary has been threatened. For Modernists, the chief characteristics of the self reside not in the domain of depth, but rather in our ability to reason—in our beliefs, opinions and conscious intentions. In the Modernist idiom, normal persons are predictable, honest and sincere. Modernists believe in educational systems, a stable family life, moral training and rational choice of marriage partners.

...both the Romantic and Modern beliefs about the self are falling into disuse, and the social arrangements that they support are eroding. This is largely a result of the forces of social saturation. Emerging technologies saturate us with the voices of mankind—both harmonious and alien. As we absorb their varied rhymes and reasons, they become part of us and we of them. Social saturation furnishes us with a multiplicity of incoherent and unrelated languages of the self. For every-thing we "know to be true" about ourselves, other voices within respond with doubts and even derision. The fragmen-tation of self-conceptions corresponds to a multiplicity of incoherent and disconnected relationships. These relation-ships pull us in myriad directions, inviting us to play such a variety of roles that the very concept of an "authentic self" with knowable characteristics recedes from view. The fully saturated self becomes no self at all.[40]

In the postmodern era, according to Gergen, the very concept of personal essence is thrown into doubt. People exist in a state of con-struction and reconstruction, placing the absolute answers provided by science, moral authority, and the law into question. The saturated self constantly changes and does so based upon an ever-widening array of relationships and communication.

Part of this saturated self comes from new costs of coordination. As society becomes more complex, as we become more interdependent, and as our ability to harm each other increases, planning and regulating our society becomes more important and more difficult. Additionally, the necessity of interacting with increasing numbers of people and a greater number of social situations is necessary and, to facilitate that, more travel is needed. Such coordination is not the prerogative of an elite but is necessary for everyone so that our own cars, chemicals, and radioactive wastes do not kill us.

Finally, of course, is the factor of time, the ultimate scarcity for those who wish to consume and experience at an historically unprecedented rate. How shall we view this ironic situation? What an extraordinary luxury to have, as a problem, a perceived scarcity of time not tied to economic production. The desire to experience all things pleasurable, to be needed and involved in as many sets of human experiences as possible is, in many respects, the ultimate greed—the greed of a small frog who tries to swallow the sun. Two things must be said about this greed for experience. First, it springs directly from the mentality and processes of economic capitalism, where competition for goods and the production process are divorced from need. It is natural that this progression has taken place. *Capitalism* may be defined as

> ...an economic system based upon the accumulation and investment of capital by private individuals who then become the owners of the means of production and distribution of goods and services. Capitalism is also characterized by economic motivation through private profit, competition, the determination of prices and wages primarily through supply and demand, an extensive system of credit, freedom of contract and a free labor market.[41]

In similar terms, the accumulation and investment of time by individuals in diverse pleasurable activity has taken place as a means of self-actualization. It has become a competition, with time the scarce resource, to find out who we are—literally, to recreate ourselves, experientially.

Capitalism also sowed the seeds of our open-ended desire for new experience by saturating us with unneeded material objects. As the ability of our economic system to create needs for new material products begins to find limits, the creation of needs is transferred to another realm—leisure experiences. People are sold the experiences of gambling, traveling through Europe, viewing other people's sexual activities, going down a wild river on a rubber raft, learning tennis from a Zen Buddhist perspective, changing personal relationships through a multitude of therapies, making wine, and any others they will buy. What

> When I lived in one room, I wanted an apartment, when I had an apartment, I wanted a detached house, when I bought the house, I wanted a bigger one—within about six months. When I got the bigger house, I wanted a second home—for vacations. When I got the second home, I had a heart attack. I was just as happy in the room—or at least the apartment.

is produced is wanderlust, not for other places but for other lives.

Postindustrial society also has brought about increased communication between those in different countries and more travel between countries. This has led to many countries developing a culture which is increasingly pluralistic; that is, shaped by many ethnic and minority groups who have a common culture and maintain their identity, rather than assimilate completely and become the same as their neighbors in values and behavior. The United States historically has represented a model of cultural pluralism; this has been due not only to its historic ties with Europe and Africa but also to immigration policies that continue to encourage the immigration of new groups. Canada has also experienced a more pluralistic culture during the last few decades, as immigrants from Europe, Asia, the Caribbean Islands, and the United States have transformed the country from one which was dominated by the English, French and, to a lesser extent, indigenous Canadians into a multicultural nation.

The effects of cultural pluralism upon the leisure behavior of a postindustrial society are illustrated in Table 2.1, which shows the characteristics of a mass culture that is moving toward having even more things in common, primarily due to the emergence of the mass media. *Mass culture* may be defined as

> elements of culture that develop in large, heterogeneous societies as a result of common exposure to and experience of the mass media…. The emergence of mass culture is a part of the process of the development of common unifying cultural values and attitudes in the new and vast population of modern national social units.[42]

Cultural pluralism emphasizes the role of leisure as anything the individual chooses to do for pleasure. The limits of such behavior are defined only by laws, with activity representing an expression of personal inter-

Table 2.1 Leisure in Singular and Plural Culture Societies

	Plural-Culture Society	Single-Culture Society
Concept	• Leisure is anything the individual chooses to do that he or she finds pleasurable • Leisure is unlimited, an end in itself	• Leisure is a set of identifiable experiences that the individual is taught to enjoy • Leisure is limited, a means to an end
Variation in behavior	• Wide range of acceptable behavior	• Narrow range of acceptable behavior
Standards to judge behaviors	• Laws set limits • No universally accepted mores by which to judge leisure behavior	• Mores and folkways set limits of behavior • Universal standards for leisure based on perceived cultural necessity
Role	• Individual and subcultural identity linked to leisure behavior	• Tribal, local, or national identity linked to leisure behavior
Role problems	• Difficult to judge leisure ethically • Disputes over leisure values, lack of meaning	• Lack of experimentation or alternatives • Persecution of that which is foreign • Easy to use leisure as a means of social control
Government's role	• Identification of recreation needs difficult • May provide only selected kinds of services or serve certain subcultures or groups disproportionately	• Identification of recreation needs easy • May provide services which act as a common denominator
Commercial organization's role	• Commercial sector has diverse opportunities • Easier to create needs and cater to individual's or subculture's tastes	• Commercial sector has limited opportunities • More difficult to create needs or cater to individual's or subculture's tastes

est, or "life style," rather than one's culture. Fads and created leisure needs may cause more innovation, a speeding up of the consumption of leisure experience with a corresponding questioning of what is worth doing. One resolution to this uncertainty is to do nothing, but a more common reaction is to try to do everything.

Just as capitalism is not essentially about industry but about the ownership of capital and the search to accumulate profit, so the working class is not essentially defined by manual work but by its exclusion from the ownership of capital and the need to sell its labor to survive.[43]

Thus, the question of ownership of the means of production continues to be a critical one, whether what is produced is televisions on an assembly line or insurance on your automobile. The movement to an economy in which most people are involved in providing services rather than material products does not necessarily change power relations between those who own the means of production and those they employ. Conversely, these power relations may be changed by worker investment in the company or other means regardless of whether the company "makes" televisions or life insurance. Postindustrial society, in summary, denotes a change in what is produced for economic profit but not necessarily in the power relationships in the production process.

In the emerging postindustrial society, the "leisure class" has almost disappeared. As economist John Kenneth Galbraith observed, while nearly all societies at nearly all times have had a leisure class—a class of persons exempt from toil. "In modern times and especially in the United States, the leisure class, at least in any identifiable phenomenon, has disappeared. To be idle is no longer considered rewarding or even entirely respectable."[44] In North America, as elsewhere, postindustrial society and democratization have led to the decline of a leisure class that is replaced by a larger class for whom work is no longer very painful. Today's privileged get good jobs rather than exemption from work.

In summary, leisure and its use have increasingly been shaped by organizations, and the goals of such organizations help determine the meaning and use of free time in modern society.

> When I was young I always wanted freedom—I mean I always wanted to be free. Do what I wanted. Go in the direction my interests were taking me. Now that I'm older, I don't think freedom or leisure are worth a damn unless you have discipline.
>
> Without self-discipline, freedom and leisure are bad ideas. Leisure is a situation where you get freedom from being controlled by other people or circumstances, but then you have to control and limit yourself. That's how I think it works. What do you think?

Study Questions

1. After reviewing arguments for and against increasing leisure, state whether you are convinced or unconvinced that the amount of leisure is increasing and why.

2. Identify the major characteristics of leisure in nonindustrial culture.

3. Compare and contrast the meaning and use of leisure among the "working class" and the "leisure class" which emerged during industrialization.

4. What new societal costs were associated with industrialization? How did these costs reshape the quality of our leisure?

5. Do you believe leisure would be more satisfying in a single culture society or a plural culture society? Why?

Endnotes

1   Paepke, C. (1993). *The evolution of progress — The end of economic growth and the beginning of human transformation.* New York, NY: Random House.

2   Harris, M. (1979). *Cultural materialism: The struggle for a science of culture* (p. ix). New York, NY: Random House.

3   Stumpf, F. and Cozens, F. (1947). Some aspects of the role of games, sports, and recreational activities in the culture of modern primitive people. *Research Quarterly, 18,* 104–108.

4   Johnson, A. and Johnson, O. (1978). In search of the affluent society. *Human Nature, 1*(9), 50–59.

5   ibid.

6   Sahlins, M. (1972). *Stone age economics* (p. 72). New York, NY: Aldine Atherton.

7   Lewin, R. (1980). An introduction of affluence. In J. Cherfas and R. Lewin (Eds.), *Not work alone: A crosscultural view of activities superfluous to survival* (pp. 14, 16). Beverly Hills, CA: Sage Publications.

8   Caillois, R. (1958). *Man, play and games.* Glencoe, IL : The Free Press.

9   DeBoer, W. (1993). Like a rolling stone: The chunkey game and political organization in eastern North America. *Southwestern Archaeology, 12*(2), 83–90.

10   Caillois (1958)

11   Orr, K. (1998). *Classification of games. A crosscultural perspective.* Honors project. The Pennsylvania State University, University Park, PA. Unpublished manuscript.

12   Dulles, F. (1965). *A history of recreation: America learns to play* (2nd ed.). New York, NY: Appleton-Century-Crofts.

13 ibid.

14 Veblen, T. (1899). *The theory of the leisure class.* New York, NY: Macmillan.

15 ibid.

16 Riesman, D. (1953). *Thorstein Veblen: A critical interpretation.* New York, NY: Charles Scribners Sons.

17 De Grazia, S. (1962). *Of time, work, and leisure.* New York, NY: Twentieth Century Fund.

18 ibid.

19 ibid.

20 Cross, G. (1990). *A social history of leisure since 1600.* State College, PA: Venture Publishing, Inc.

21 Findlay, J. (1986). *People of chance: Gambling in American society from Jamestown to Las Vegas.* New York, NY: Simon and Schuster.

22 Goffman, E. (1961). *Encounters.* London, UK: Penguin.

23 Cross (1990)

24 ibid.

25 ibid.

26 ibid.

27 Bailey, P. (1978). *Leisure and class in Victorian England.* Toronto, ON: University of Toronto Press.

28 Dickens, C. (1964). *Hard times.* New York, NY: Bantam.

29 Cross (1990)

30 Cunningham, H. (1980). *Leisure and the industrial revolution.* London, UK: Croom Helm.

31 Boyer, P. (1978). *Urban masses and moral order in America: 1820–1920.* Cambridge, MA: Yale University Press.

32 Cross (1990)

33 Cunningham, H. (1980)

34 Glasser, R. (1970). *Leisure—Penalty or prize.* London, UK: Macmillan and Company.

35 Clarke, J. and Critcher, C. (1985). *The devil makes work: Leisure in capitalistic Britain* (p. 190). Champaign, IL: University of Illinois Press.

36 ibid.

37 Robinson, J. (1991). Free time: Where it goes. *American Demographics, 13*(9), 47–48.

38 Riesman (1953)

39 Bell, D. (1973). The end of scarcity. *Saturday Review of the Society, 49,* 49–52.

40 Gergen, K. (1991). *The saturated self—Dilemmas of identity in contemporary life* (pp. 6–7). New York, NY: Basic Books.

41 Theodorson, G. and Theodorson, A. (1969). *Modern dictionary of sociology* (p. 245). New York, NY: Thomas Crowell.

42 Johnson and Johnson (1978)

43 Clarke and Critcher (1985)

44 Galbraith, J. (1958). *The affluent society.* Boston, MA: Houghton-Mifflin.

What We Do with Our Time: The Rhythm of Daily Life

Many songs and poems are written about time—where it goes, how sometimes in a magic moment one is able to step outside of it. There are also songs and poems about the lack of time to do what one wants. You may listen to such songs and agree with their sentiments. If so, I'll make you a deal you can't refuse. Here's the deal:

For the next 24 hours, beginning tomorrow morning when you wake up, you can do whatever you want. I'll see to it that any responsibilities you have are taken care of. Also, I will give you enough money to get you through the day. You will have no responsibility to anyone unless you choose it and no penalties later, since I will take care of your responsibilities. Will you accept my offer of doing what you want for one day?

For those of you who took the first offer, allow me to raise the ante. I'll make you the same deal and put enough money in the bank to support you in the manner to which you are presently accustomed. You can do what you want and I will see to it that any obligations you have, such as taking tests or working a part-time job, are taken care of. You can do your own thing for a week. Whatever you want. Is it a deal?

If you are still with me, let's make the offer for a month. All the same rules apply. Do whatever you wish. How about it?

By now many of you have decided not to accept my offer, but if it still sounds good to you, how about an offer of one year, beginning tomorrow, of doing exactly what you want? I will deposit enough money in the bank each month to support you to the tune of, oh, let's say $40,000 a year. You don't have to do anything for the money. O.K.?

If you are still playing "let's make a deal," you are ready for the ultimate question. Beginning tomorrow, for the rest of your life, you will have financial independence and can do whatever you like, where and with whom you please. Eat and sleep when you want and choose your own lifestyle. No strings attached. Do you accept?

At the end of this chapter, you will be asked to respond formally to these questions. A number of thoughts may have occurred to you when you were considering my offer. You may have thought that, since it is possible to do whatever you choose, you could continue to do just what you are presently doing. But, it would not be necessary since you would be financially independent and, if you desired, socially independent. You may have found it very easy to envision what you would do with one free day, but a year may be more difficult to imagine. How about a lifetime? You may not know how you would use, spend, or pass your time.

What, anyway, is "time?" Time is one of the most complex ideas in our language—and one of the most important. Different concepts of time condition the individual to behave in a certain way. Such differing concepts also affect his or her understanding of others. Concepts of time are directly linked to how different cultures view the world and to their stage of cultural development. The 2.6 billion Hindus in the world, for example, while they have a wide variety of beliefs and practices, tend to share a belief in inborn duty or virtue (dharma), a belief in a cosmic law of credits and debits for good and evil acts (karma), a belief in the transmigration of souls and their eventual release from time (moksha), and a belief in the ultimate ground of reality (brahama). The Vedas, sacred hymns, describe the world as

> one in which creation and destruction pursue their relentless labor simultaneously, hand to hand. As a defense against such a world, they advocate the insignificance of time's passage. Time, while real enough for daily chores, is judged unimportant in the economy of the universe.[1]

The Chinese have historically had a preference for organic naturalism in which time and nature are of conceived as aspects of dynamic, living systems which are to be qualitatively explored. Both the Hindu judgment of time as unimportant and the Chinese preference for thinking of time in natural, qualitative terms are systematically changed when a culture begins to modernize.

Nonmodern concepts of time, to some extent, thought of time as cyclic—consisting of daily, monthly, and seasonal rhythms of the natural world. The rising and setting of the sun, the fluctuations of tides, the moon's stages, and seasonal change were the measures of time around which tribal life was based. This view of time was cyclical; spring will come again. Time could not be "lost" under such a concept because it would come again.

The transformation of concepts of time from cyclic (a circle) to linear (a straight line) is wrapped up in changes in religious belief. Both Jews and Christians came to believe that history was not just a series of events but a progression from a well-defined beginning to an appointed goal or end. Ancient Hebrews preferred to believe in linear progress—progress toward the Promised Land. For Christians, the linear progression of history from the fall of Adam and Eve in the Garden of Eden to the birth, death, and resurrection of Christ and, from there to the last judgment became the foundation of Christian faith. As an expert in the study of time, J. T. Fraser pointed out

> With the meteoric advance of science and technology—made possible by the linear view of time and history—the relationship between God-the-timer and Man-the-timed has changed. In our epoch, carrying out the promise of salvation history became a responsibility of the created and not the Creator.[2]

Viewing time as a line (linear) with a beginning and an end made it a finite commodity. It made us begin to think of time as scarce, and that judgment is what, in many ways, characterizes the modern world and distinguishes it from the nonmodern.

The mechanical measurement of time, which has been measured by clocks since the thirteenth century, helped reinforce the linear concept of time. It allowed more accurate measurements of time to be made and shared among people. This was necessary as people began to earn their living in ways other than hunting and gathering, farming, or individual production of goods. Mechanical measurement of time paved the way for industrialization and splitting the day into segments of work and leisure.

Today the computer is the new time-allocating device. Computer programs predetermine how the future will unfold and control the sequence, duration, tempo, and coordination of activities. The computer, as Rifkin[3] observed, differs from a clock as a teller of time. While clocks are set in terms of sequence, duration, and rhythm, a computer can manipulate these by changing the program. Time is no longer a single fixed reference point that exists external to events. It is no longer bound in any way to the rhythms of the natural world. Computer time is a mathematical abstraction which separates us from the natural world.

If the computer increasingly defines and controls time in whatever capacity it is used, it may reshape our inner sense of time. All of us experience time in psychological terms, making qualitative judgments about it. For instance, if you enjoy reading this book, forty-five minutes spent reading it seem to pass more quickly than if you do not enjoy reading it. Psychological time or inner time is our perception or inner sense of the passage of events. In this sense, time can only be judged in terms of personal meaning.

Time may now be thought of as a relative concept rather than an absolute one, not only because of the computer's ability to "program" time in any way we wish but also because of changes in theoretical physics. Einstein's special theory of relativity assumes that space and time are relative and related concepts rather than constant, absolute and separate. While the speed of light is a constant throughout the universe, our perceptions of time are shaped by how fast we are moving. Nothing is at absolute rest. If we moved away at the speed of light from a clock tower which said 12 o'clock and continued to view the clock, it would always say 12 o'clock since the light that carried the image of the clock would be traveling at the same speed we were. Even looking at a wristwatch produces a little lag, since light must carry the image to our eyes and then our brain. Thus, there is no universal "present." People experience events differently depending on where they are on the planet and how fast they and what they observe are traveling.[4]

> What is time? Well, I guess it's what sort of organizes the world. You get so much time to live, so much time to do your work, so much time to sleep. It really isn't the same thing as money because you can make money, but you only get so much time. Some people think they go to heaven after they die, so they live forever. They have all the time of eternity. I don't believe that. When you're dead—you're dead. So you only have so much time. When you realize that, it makes you run around—you don't want to waste your time. The clock is ticking.

Measuring Time Use

It is very difficult to determine how people actually spend their time. First, people's psychological or inner sense of time is often at variance with the mechanical measurement of time. Thus, we may believe we spent eight hours at work, but if someone observed us at work and used a stopwatch to time our behaviors, our imagined eight hours might be much less, or more. To more objectively measure our use of time, the time budget or time diary has been used by researchers.

A time budget is a structured diary in which people record at certain regular intervals what they do during their waking hours. Usually the day is recorded in periods of one hour or less. In determining which of the recorded activities are really leisure pursuits, some researchers have excluded such nonleisure activities as "sleep, paid work, care of household and children, care of self, transportation, and other items which the record indicates are primarily instrumental or incidental to the other activities rather than ends in themselves."[5] Leisure includes all other activities. However, many human activities are not easily distinguishable as leisure or nonleisure pursuits. Therefore, some time budgets have sought to specify some middle category to include semi-leisurely activities.

One major advantage of the time budget is that it allows different categorizations of leisure and nonleisure activity to be made while using the same data. The time budget, however, presents many problems for the researcher. Many people, for instance, are not willing to participate in such a study. Additionally, time budgets are dependent upon the memory of the individual involved. People are likely to remember some leisure activities longer than they remember others, especially those that were most enjoyable, and to underestimate the amount of time spent in activities that they consider to be of "low status." Illegal activities and those considered immoral are likely to be omitted as well. Another problem is the actual recording of the activities. Right now, for instance, you might say that you are reading a book, doing homework, or learning about leisure. You might also have the television on and be eating an apple while you are reading. How would you describe this situation? Some studies have attempted to make the respondents record both primary and secondary activities undertaken simultaneously in order to solve this problem. Time budget data are often unable to represent more than a few days in the lives of the respondents, and people's activity patterns are different for different days of the week, months of the year, and so forth. In spite of these problems, time budget studies have contributed much to our knowledge about people's activity patterns.

> We had to keep a time diary in class for a week. It was a real pain in the butt. Still, it was worth it. I'm amazed at how I really do spend my time. My life is different from what I thought. Like, I couldn't believe it...

Increasing Free Time Across the Life Span

Peter Drucker and others argue that where business has succeeded in the noncommunist world, it has succeeded so well that people can consider satisfying noneconomic needs. "[H]alf of the expansion in wealth-producing capacity was used to create leisure time by cutting the hours worked while steadily increasing pay."[6] Drucker further notes that

> An additional third of the increased wealth-producing capacity has gone into healthcare, where expenditures have gone from less than 1 percent of gross national product to 8–11 percent (depending on the country) in fifty years. There has been almost equal growth—from 2 percent of GNP to 10–11 percent—in the expenditure on formal schooling; and with more and more schooling taking place outside the formal school system, especially in and by employing institutions, the portion of GNP that now goes to education is much higher than the 10 percent officially reported. Leisure, healthcare and schooling require goods; they are not spiritual. Very little of the new leisure is used for intellectual pursuits. The free hours are more likely to be spent in front of the television set watching "Dallas" or sports. Still, neither leisure nor healthcare nor education were ever considered economic satisfactions. They represent values quite different from those of the business society. They bespeak a society in which economic satisfactions are a means rather than a good in themselves, and in which business therefore is a tool rather than a way of life.[7]

This same phenomenon appears to be taking place in most other modern nations.[8] Figure 3.1 shows that the United States falls somewhere in the middle when compared to modern nations with regard to hours worked per year.

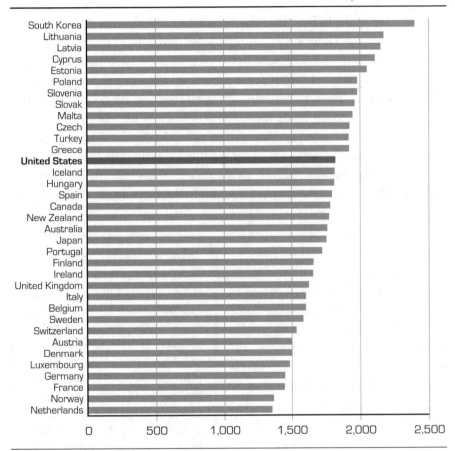

Figure 3.1 Annual Hours Worked, 2005[10]

Additionally, work is taking a smaller and smaller fraction of the hours of one's life. An analysis of British citizens, for instance, found that

> Although the average career length has remained around 40 years, the total life hours worked shrank from 124,000 hours in 1856 to 69,000 in 1983. The fraction of disposable lifetime hours spent working declined from 50 percent to 20 percent.[11]

Even if we have not achieved a society of leisure, we have gained free time—not only on a daily basis but as a percentage of our total lives. Free time is increasing in a wide range of countries, and the increases of free time are positively related to increased gross domestic product, in line with Drucker's thinking.

The big gains in free time during the last few decades have primarily had to do with later entry into the labor force, later marriage, fewer children, and earlier retirement in relation to life expectancy. In particular, it is in retirement where we have stored the big gains in free time. The life expectancy for an American who reaches age 65 is about 80 years for men and 84 years for women. On average, about twelve of these years will be healthy. Since, until recently, Americans have been retiring earlier, on average in their late fifties or early sixties, this means that most Americans are living an average of fifteen years in relatively good health after they cease participation in the labor force. This is where the huge gains in leisure have taken place during the last few decades.

Our current society hoards huge amounts of free time to be spent only in the last fifteen to twenty years of life. The Prussian bureaucrat who is reputed to have established 65 as the age of retirement payment is said to have done so completely arbitrarily. He probably never imagined that the institution of retirement that he helped establish would today consume almost one-fifth of a person's life. In the United States, the average age at which individuals retired in 1910 was 74 years old. In 2002, however, the average retirement age was 62. The age at which workers receive social security, however, is increasing. At this writing, if you were born in 1960 or later, you will need to be 67 to receive full Social

> Part of trying to understand how much free time people have is the issue of what people expect or want. When there are fewer opportunities, people don't rush so much. So some rushing is simply dashing after opportunities that your ancestors didn't have. My Dad didn't usually have access to a car when he was growing up, so going to the movie in a small town in Kentucky twelve miles away from the farm was out of the question—so he stayed home. Once in a while he would hitchhike, but if he didn't get a ride home from Danville after the movie, he would sometimes fall asleep by the side of the road. His mother didn't like him to do it. Going to a movie could take eight hours.

Security benefits. It is highly likely that this minimum age will continue to be raised.

An Average Day in the USA

How does daily life unfold in the United States? In terms of time spent, if we examine all those ages 15 and over, there are many surprises. A major study of time use—The American Time Use Survey[12] found that, on an "average day" in 2006, persons in the United States, ages 15 and over

- slept about 8.6 hours,
- spent 5.1 hours doing leisure and sports activities,
- worked 3.8 hours, and
- spent 1.8 hours doing household activities.
- The remaining 4.7 hours were spent in a variety of other activities, including eating and drinking, attending school, and shopping.
- Only 45 percent of all persons ages 15 and older reported working during an average day because some were not employed and others were employed but did not work on their diary day.

By comparison, persons employed full-time who worked during an average weekday spent

- 9.3 hours working,
- 7.6 hours sleeping,
- 3.0 hours doing leisure and sports activities,
- 0.9 hours doing household activities, and
- 3.2 hours spent on other activities, such as eating, drinking, and shopping.

Working by Employed Persons

- Many more people worked on weekdays than on weekend days. About 84 percent of employed persons worked on an average weekday, compared with 35 percent on an average weekend day.

- Employed persons worked an average of 7.6 hours on the days they worked. They also worked more hours on weekdays than on weekend days—8.0 versus 5.4 hours.

- On the days they worked, employed men worked about one hour more than employed women. The difference partly reflects women's greater likelihood of working part-time. However, even among full-time workers (those usually working 35 hours or more per week), men worked slightly longer than women— 8.4 versus 7.7 hours.

- Employed women living with a child under age 6 spent about one half-hour less per day working than employed women living in households with no children. On the other hand, employed men living with a child under age 6 worked about two hours more than those living in households with no children.

Household Activities

- On an average day in 2006, 84 percent of women and 65 percent of men spent some time doing household activities, such as housework, cooking, lawn care, or financial and other household management.

- Women who reported doing household activities during the diary day spent 2.7 hours on such activities while men spent 2.1 hours.

- On an average day, 20 percent of men reported doing housework—such as cleaning or doing laundry—compared with 52 percent of women. Thirty-seven percent of men did food preparation or cleanup versus 65 percent of women.

Care of Children by Adults in Households with Children

- In households with the youngest child age 6 or under, time spent providing primary childcare averaged 2.3 hours for women and 1.1 hours for men. Physical care, playing with children, and travel related to childcare accounted for most of the time spent in primary childcare activities.

- For adults living with children age 6 or under, women provided an average of 1.2 hours of physical care—such as bathing, dressing, or feeding a child—per day to household children, while men provided less than one-half of this amount—0.4 hour (less than 30 minutes).

Leisure Activities

- On an average day in 2006, nearly everyone ages 15 and over (>96%) reported some sort of leisure or sports activity, such as watching TV, socializing, or exercising. Among this group of participants, men spent more time doing leisure activities (5.7 hours) than women (4.9 hours).

- Men were more likely than women to participate in sports on any given day (20% vs. 15%). Men also spent more time in sports activities than women on the days they participated (2.0 hours vs. 1.2 hours respectively).

- Among individuals ages 25 and older, those with less than a high school diploma spent 1.7 more hours per day engaged in leisure and sports activities than those who had earned a bachelor's degree or higher.

- Married women spent 4.4 hours per day participating in leisure and sports activities. On average, this amounted to less leisure time than married men (0.8 hour less), unmarried women (0.7 hour less), and unmarried men (1.5 hours less).

The portion of our lives devoted to both paid work and housework is decreasing and it appears that such declines are predicted by rising economic standards of living within a country. Gershuny, after a meta-analysis of time use in fifteen countries drew this conclusion and added: "...there is no basis, theoretical or empirical, for thinking that we are 'running out of time.'" [13] While this is likely true, both the pace of life and its complexity seem to be increasing.

Measuring Time Spent at Work

There are many ways to attempt to measure the amount of time we spend at work. The most frequently cited statistic pertaining to work is workweek length. This measurement is made by the Bureau of Labor Statistics in our federal government and attempts to measure how long people who are "full-time workers covered by the provisions of the Fair Labor Standards Act" spend at work. This measure, although frequently cited, can be very misleading if taken at face value. Workers are simply asked how many hours they work and respond to the question in ten seconds or less. There is evidence that people tend to overestimate how long they work.[14] Additionally, it appears that about one quarter of the time that people are "at work" they are actually engaged in nonwork activity.

Many other kinds of information are also used in analyses of work time, including percentage of individuals in the labor force, percentage of those holding two or more jobs (moonlighting), the age of entry and retirement from the labor force in relation to life expectancy, the rate of unemployment, the number of vacations and holidays, and time spent traveling to and from one's job (commuting).

Segments of time such as vacations, commuting time, and job-related homework are typically not included in the measurement of an average workweek. Some studies, however, have shown that when the length of the workweek shortens, many workers take a second job.

Time use expert John Robinson has found that people have a tendency to overestimate how many hours they work when asked such questions. The same phenomenon happens in other countries as well.[15] Thus, what is clear is that people in the labor force think they are working longer hours, but time diary studies show that, on average, they are working less. The public, however, clearly believes that the amount of time they have for leisure is declining.

How We Spend Our Time

Now that we have examined some methods to tell us how we as individuals spend our time and have discussed the measurement of leisure as time, let's look at how our society spends its time.

The Amount of Free Time over One's Lifetime Continues to Increase

Americans average 35 to 40 hours of free time per week. This represents an increase of more than an hour per week compared to 1965. As may be seen in Figure 3.2 and Table 3.1, the activities that may typically be thought of as leisure activity, hobbies/play and other free time, account for just about as much time as television viewing. Time spent in uses

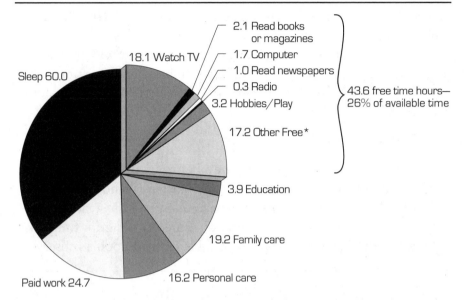

* Includes organizational activities (e.g., religious, civic, clubs), entertaining away from home (e.g., sporting events, movies, parties, bars), conversation, writing, thinking, and relaxing.

Figure 3.2 Hours Spent per Week on Free Time and non-Free Time Activities 1993–1996 (ages 18 and older)[16]

Table 3.1 Trends in Social Capital and Other Free Time Activities (in hours per week for those ages 18–64)[17]

	1965	1975	1985	1995	1995 minus 1965
Social Capital					
Socializing	8.2	7.1	6.7	7.3	– 0.9
Religion	0.9	0.9	0.9	0.9	0.0
Other organizations	1.3	1.5	1.2	0.9	– 0.4
Recreation					
Communication	3.6	3.4	4.4	4.6	+1.0
Sports/exercise	1.0	1.6	2.2	3.0	+2.0
Hobbies	2.2	2.8	2.8	2.7	+0.5
Sports/cultural events	1.2	0.6	0.9	1.3	+0.1
Adult education	1.8	2.3	2.2	2.4	+0.6
Total	20.2	20.2	21.3	23.1	+2.9

of leisure such as socializing and participation in formal organizations (which may be described as "social capital") has declined by 1.3 hours per week during this period, but time spent in a variety of other forms of recreation has increased. The biggest gain has been in sport/exercise, which increased an average of two hours per week.

The average amount of free time changes with age, with individuals in the middle period of life—25 to 54, having the least free time—37.2 hours per week. Thus, there is more free time early in life and later in life. Figure 3.3 shows the distribution of free time use by age.

The Time Famine

In spite of a greater portion of our life's hours spent at leisure, many residents of modern nations feel they are "starving"—not starving for lack of food as so many people have historically—but instead the ultimate scarcity of the postmodern world—time. Starving for time does not result in death; it results, as ancient Athenian philosophers observed,

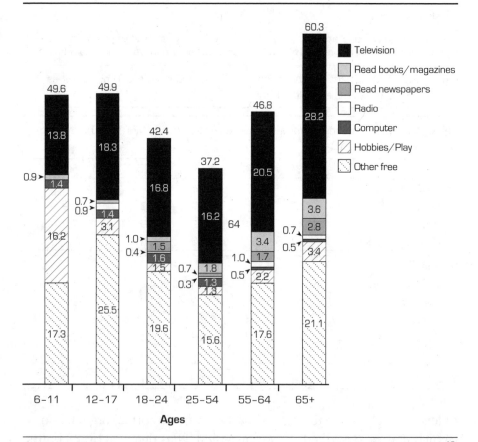

Figure 3.3 Free Time Use by Age (in hours per week per person ages 18 and older)[18]

in never having begun to live. Those who suffer the time famine seem to live lives of privilege when measured against the life and death dilemmas of less "developed" countries. In many ways, however, the consequences of starving for time are devastating. One never lives in the moment. There is always the next thing to do. The luxury of letting things happen—trusting the world to unfold as it should—is never present. Many wellness experts believe stress has become the biggest killer in our society. We have little tranquility but tons of tranquilizers.

One can never do enough in our time famine culture. Things can never happen fast enough. Organizations can never be efficient enough. The frantic state of mind produced by such a style of life makes us permanently anxious and perpetually stressed. It is only the dispossessed and the unfortunate who escape the time crunch. As Richard, a homeless man, told me: "I don't think there's any such thing as time." It is not by accident that those who are confined to hospitals are called "patients." Our society, however, does not widely admire patience. We favor short-term profits, brief conversations, sound bites, and microwave ovens. Even the life cycle of the cattle we raise for food is shorter than in other countries, since, in spite of a national surplus of milk, they are fed growth hormones. The "bottom line" mentality is evident in our personal relationships, our businesses, and even in our celebrations. Birthday parties are often celebrated only symbolically by a single candle in a cake served by restaurant wait staff—strangers who sing "Happy Birthday," then quickly return to their duties.

Thus, a paradox exists in our society: we have simultaneously gained free time while becoming more rushed. Our interior world and exterior worlds are out of sync. While increased free time was supposed to slow down the pace of life and make us more tranquil and leisurely, for many, the opposite appears to be happening. Even as free time increases, we feel more rushed, as though life is passing us by. What has changed is not the quantity of our free time so much as the qualities it possesses. True leisure is an idea that is not only forgotten in our society, it is no longer even understood. The real problem, the reason our mind's beliefs no longer reflect what is really happening in our daily lives, is that we have developed a dysfunctional attitude toward time for reasons previously discussed.

What this paradox also means, however, is that our society has progressed in spite of our perceptions of time. Those in modern nations have more time freed to do as they wish. The "leisure potential" has increased. The dream of more time freed from the necessity of labor is being realized but has not been recognized. The attitude of always having to do more represents a kind of cultural lag in which we continue to assume the need to rush, consume, and stay perpetually busy. Much of this need is a result of dysfunctional attitudes toward time rather than any temporal reality.

Slowing Down

Part of the desire to slow down the fast pace of life relates to reducing stress. It has been documented that stress levels are related to feelings of control. "We seem to have a deep-rooted need for control. If you are in a stressful situation and have the illusion you can control it, *even if you can't,* your stress reaction will be reduced."[19] This sense of control even affects our immune system. Optimistic beliefs that we are capable and competent to make changes are indeed critical to our health.[20] One may speculate as to whether the considerable time devoted to television viewing and the "dumbing down" of some aspects of North American culture may be a response to high stress levels. To the extent that high levels of complexity or sensitivity produce higher levels of stress, many in the public may have taken steps to minimize personal stress by reducing them. Other ways of anesthetizing oneself against stress seem increasingly prevalent in society, from hot tubs to marijuana to aerobic dance.

It is too early to tell whether the slightly greater decline in stress levels among women signals a move toward more equality in gender experiences of time and life pressures, but it is clear that men and women do continue to differ in their stress responses to the role demands of employment and marriage. Women's responses are notably more sensitive to both factors, particularly in relation to the "failed" situation of a marriage that results in divorce or separation. The reduced stress levels of men in this situation are not surprising, since after a divorce children reside with the mother in about 85 percent of the cases. Additionally, divorced males remarry considerably more often and more quickly than divorced women, and married males exhibit lower stress levels than never-married men.

Age and education, however, are more important predictors of stress than gender or role factors. Stress takes a dramatic downturn in later years, particularly after age 45—and that seems independent of the decline in career or family pressures or whether such individuals experience an "empty nest." Thus, an aged society may be a less stressful one.

Even greater differences are found by the factor of education. That may seem somewhat surprising, given that greater education is associated with higher income, job security, greater social activity and other features of the "good life." It is also at odds with the studies of objective stress that show that disruptive and stressful life events, like a relative's death or job loss, happen more to people with less education.

It may be that people with higher levels of education have a higher "sense of the necessary;" that is, more personal acts they feel are not optional but rather required of them. Such feelings may be exacerbated by increasing awareness of information concerning a wide range of topics from personal health to financial trends. Expectations as to what constitutes success, good looks, a good marriage or even a good vacation may have increased to the point that more stress is inevitable when such higher expectations cannot be met. As Zimbardo[21] has shown, individuals think about time differently. While those with a future orientation are able to achieve success as measured by a variety of tasks involving group and individual problem solving, such an orientation may lead to higher definitions of what should be done and how quickly it can be accomplished. More planning leads to setting more goals and, perhaps, the belief that one has failed if they are not accomplished. It may be argued, then, that much of such stress is self-imposed. During the last few years, Americans, overall, may be imposing less stress on themselves.

Differences in Time Use Between Weekdays and the Weekend Are Declining

One of the reasons it doesn't appear that free time is increasing is because the majority of those hours come during weekdays, not the weekend, and they come in small chunks of an hour here and there. Such smaller portions don't provide for the psychological release from work that people seem to prefer. While most of us have a cycle of activity that changes with the day of the week, overall, the difference between weekdays and weekends continues to decrease. In terms of free time, Sunday is the day when Americans typically have the most free time while on Thursday they have the least. More people are working for pay on weekends and catching up on household chores but still average five or more hours of free time on every weekday.

Flexible working hours are a central reason for the declining gap in free time on weekdays and weekends. In May 2004, over 27 million full-time wage and salary workers had flexible work schedules that allowed them to vary the time they began or ended work.[22] The proportion of workers with flexible schedules was 27.5 percent, down from 28.6 percent in May 2001, yet nearly double the proportion in 1991.

While U.S. survey respondents say they want their leisure to occur in large chunks of time, the 24-hour economy in which one may do almost anything at almost any time seems to have resulted in small periods of free time interspersed with other activity across the seven-day week.

With Regard to Leisure Activities, the Movement Toward the Democratization of Leisure Has Temporarily Ended

At the end of World War II, Americans entered an era of economic abundance and developed a mass culture which served to democratize the use of leisure. While poverty, racism, and other social problems continued to limit the use of leisure, free time and its use became democratized. That is, more people had more opportunity to do what they wished during their leisure, and the differences in leisure use between the elites and the rest of society became increasingly small. As many as seven out of ten Americans were in the middle class, meaning economic resources were more widely available. The Civil Rights Movement began to open up access to public recreation and park facilities to African-Americans and others who had previously lived in a segregated world. Similarly, social movements of women, people with disabilities, gays and lesbians, the elderly and others helped bring about increasing opportunity for recreation and leisure expression. The emergence of a mass society, with mass education, more standardized housing developments, network television and other mass media produced a culture in which leisure opportunity was greatly expanded.

Today, the democratization of leisure appears to have ended, at least temporarily. The gap in access to leisure resources has increased. One reason for this is the huge widening of the gap between rich and poor which has taken place. Also, massive government debt means that many recreation, park, and cultural experiences available to the public have been scaled back, eliminated, or paid for through fees and charges to participants.

The gap in education and economic resources between young and old has meant that many in the Thirteenth Generation (born between 1961 and 1980) are much poorer in relation to older people than previously. Younger people are less likely to be homeowners than previously, less likely to have health insurance, and less likely to save the money they earn.

Increases in one-parent families and declining educational achievement have sometimes meant that younger people are not socialized into as wide a variety of leisure experiences as previously. While a higher proportion of African-Americans are in the middle class compared to a few decades ago, many others are even poorer in relation to the rest of society than previously, living in dangerous neighborhoods with few public recreation resources.

Television Viewing Now Accounts for Almost Half of Our Free Time Use

Almost all the gains in free time since 1965 have been used for more television viewing. Of the 43.6 hours of free time that Americans ages six and older spend, more than half of it is with the media—TV alone accounts for an average of 18.1 hours per week. This figure doesn't include secondary viewing, which would add another five hours per week! Other media receive only a small share of our free time: 3.1 hours are spent reading, 1.7 hours are spent using computers and the Internet, and 0.3 hours are spent listening to the radio or recordings as a primary activity (although another 1.5 hours is spent with radio/recordings as a secondary activity).

As the scholar of architecture James Kunstler observed

> The American house has been TV-centered for three generations. It is the focus of family life, and the life of the house correspondingly turns inward, away from whatever occurs beyond its four walls. (TV rooms are called 'family rooms' in builders' lingo. A friend who is an architect explained to me: 'People don't want to admit that what the family does together is watch TV.') At the same time, the television is the family's chief connection with the outside world. The physical

envelope of the house itself no longer connects their lives to the outside in any active way; rather, it seals them off from it. The outside world has become an abstraction filtered through television, just as the weather is an abstraction filtered through air conditioning.[23]

Thus, television has become the pivotal use of free time, and most of its content is based around both escapism and consumption. The cultural historian Lasch describes how:

The appearance in history of an escapist conception of "leisure" coincides with the organization of leisure as an extension of commodity production. The same forces that have organized the factory and the office have organized leisure as well, reducing it to an appendage of industry.[24]

Leisure, then, is organized by large corporations rather than the people in local communities. Any thoughts of reordering leisure in society will have to start by considering television.

As television viewing has grown, it has dramatically restructured our use of time. With the advent of television, people have spent less time with activities which appear to be equivalent in terms of function, such as radio, movies and reading as well as nonmedia activities such as socializing, hobbies and conversation. Also, there has been a decrease in "non free-time" activities such as sleeping, housework and paid work. As a result of television, people are spending more time at home, indoors and with their

Everybody says TV is a bad thing, but almost everybody watches TV— a lot of TV.

If you say TV is bad for you, are movies bad for you? Is the Web bad for you? I mean, you are watching a screen in all these cases. It seems to me, it's what you watch—and why. I've learned a lot from TV—about issues like global warming. I've also been able to figure out from watching TV that the oil industry is trying to make us think global warming isn't a critical issue to our survival when it is. Oh, also, I think quite a bit of the comedy writing on TV is first rate. I still watch reruns of *Everybody Loves Raymond* and *Seinfield*. They have great story lines, well-developed characters, and very clever humor. So I'm not a snob about TV—even though most of it is crap.

families. Shaw, for instance, found that watching television dominated "family recreation."[25]

Since television viewing is our most time-consuming use of leisure, changes in television technology will reshape our use of leisure. The technology associated with television is undergoing a fundamental change—one which will decentralize the medium so that the television viewer has almost limitless choice of what is viewed. This possibility has come about due to changes in technology which allows all audio and video communication to be translated into digital information, the ability to store digitized information so it can travel through existing phone and cable lines, improvements in fiberoptic wiring so that there is a virtually limitless transmission pipeline, and new switching techniques which make it possible to bring all this to homes without rewiring them.

Television will be used in a variety of ways: movies can be ordered directly and entertainment shows replayed at your convenience; shopping by television will be done by viewing actual merchandise in stores; conferences can be held where people meet face-to-face with no travel; books and magazines can be displayed or printed; Christmas or other greeting "cards" sent; video games played with people in other homes; video telephoning; news reports come direct from wire services; hotel and airline tickets booked; and special events viewed on a pay-per-view basis. Students may shop for a college via television; elementary schools could make the school play available to parents who missed it; or the Sears catalog could be re-created. Even the morning newspaper may be on television. Interactive television technology will also mean that advertising can be customized to target markets. Auto showrooms could provide "infomercials" about their latest cars. According to former Vice President Al Gore, these changes will make television the most lucrative marketplace of the twenty-first century.

These changes will mean many other changes for businesses. The huge video rental market, a $12 billion industry, may largely disappear. The $70 billion catalogue shopping industry will also be directly affected. While network TV is not likely to disappear, their offerings may be more limited and their influence on our culture much less pronounced. Affiliate television stations may be in jeopardy.

Such changes will also have huge consequences for our culture. Multiplying TV listings and the viewers' ability to select from a vast menu of programs will likely mean a further breakup of the mass culture which arose at the end of World War II. The shared immediacy of network TV will be less and less evident. What we see, hear and know about the world will be more individualized. Television researcher George Gilder[26] argued that such changes will free us from programs regulated by a handful of bureaucrats and broadcasting professionals who must always appeal to the lowest common denominator. Narrowcast channels can broadcast specialized programming about a huge variety of subjects. Universities can reshape the way they operate so that many can take advantage of "distance education"—learning at home while perhaps working part- or full-time. In effect, we will be "voting" with our remote controls.

These changes will also produce many problems. There is the danger that people will spend most of their home life in front of a screen and most of their work life in front of another screen—a terrible constriction of life which would rob both work and leisure of much of its meaning. People could become less intellectually curious or simply lazier. Free TV could also be threatened. Since many people get their news from free TV (over-the-air antenna), this could lead to a less informed public.

Whether people will watch more or less TV after these changes is subject to debate. One line of reasoning is that people will actually watch it less. Turning on the set to see what's on may become essentially meaningless since what is on is up to you. Many people watch TV based upon program schedules which they base their home lives around. When these schedules disappear, the immediacy and routine nature of the experience will be fundamentally altered. People may start to suffer from information overload in one more area of their life and react by leaving the set off for longer periods of time.

Computers Are Taking More of Our Time But Have Not Revolutionized Our Leisure

While computers have become a part of everyday life for millions of Americans, today's online users are not at all typical of the American public. They are highly educated, upper income, and business focused. They are, however, becoming more diverse with each passing year. The online audience increasingly includes women and people with lower incomes, and "most users view the Net as a tool to save time and money."[27]

While there has been a tendency to think that the use of computers would lessen the time spent "reading," the opposite is generally true. Those who spend more time with computers also spend more time reading books and magazines. Actually, most time spent with computers is "reading."

The Internet and other information technologies represent a significant departure from previous communication technologies by combining features of both interpersonal communication and mass communication. According to the "functional equivalence" argument that has been applied to the diffusion of earlier communication technologies, one should expect decreases in both types of communication activities as Internet use increases. An effective and comprehensive method for testing which activities are most affected by the Internet is through 24-hour time-diary studies in which all daily activity is recorded.

When the time diaries of Internet users and nonusers in a 1998–99 national sample are compared, few differences in either interpersonal or mass communication of Internet users are found, or decreases in other free-time activities. As with the case of television, certain personal care and other non–free-time activities are most different. This raises questions about whether the Internet acts more to enhance communication behaviors rather than to displace behavior—which was the case for television as predicted by the functional equivalence hypothesis. It should be added that several studies find that people who use the Internet do not become more socially isolated than those who don't.[28]

A major study in 2002 by the Stanford Institute for the Quantitative Study of Society found that people who use the Internet do so for many purposes that can be considered leisure activity. As Figure 3.4 (p. 86) shows, 90 percent of users send and receive e-mail, 77 percent search for general information, 69 percent surf the web, with others using the web for reading, hobbies, entertainment and games, and chat rooms. The Internet, then, has become a source of leisure activity for millions.

From Specialists to Generalists

Perhaps the most important change in time use is that people in modern nations are in the process of moving from being "specialists" in regard to time use, for example, taking care of children and a household, working at a given occupation or pursuing a single form of leisure expression, to becoming generalists.

In the core theme of sociology—modernization—specialization is assumed to play a key role. The sociologist Linton assumed that a society's culture could be divided into three elements: *universals*—those habits, ideas and conditioned emotional responses which are shared by everyone; *specialties*—elements of culture shared by certain socially recognized categories of individuals but not the whole population; and *alternatives*—traits which are shared by certain individuals but not common to all members of any one of the socially recognized categories of society.[29]

In the ideal male-provider household, housekeeping is the specialty of women and earning the family's income is the specialty of men.[30] This "ideal" male provider household is changing. In the past few decades, in most modern societies, the percentage of people who are undertaking both paid work and housework is increasing.

Watching TV is a customary pattern of all people while pastimes, such as going to the theater, is an example of an alternative activity. The

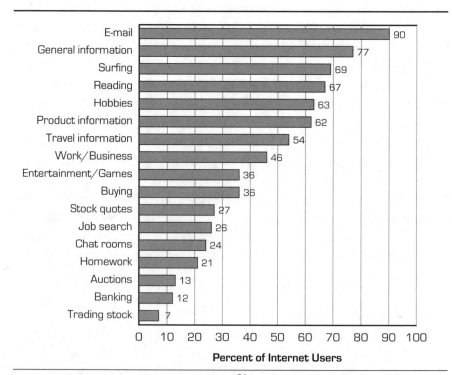

Figure 3.4 What users do on the Internet[31]

percentage of people who are doing alternative activities, such as going to the theater, are increasing as well:

> As a consequence of these trends towards greater universality of daily activities, growing numbers of people are involved in growing numbers of activities. With respect to both tasks and leisure, the degree of specialization is being reduced. Task combination and the combination of cultural with leisure activities are on the rise. In their respective domains, both combinations imply a time squeeze... Dispersion of the available leisure time over a greater number of pastimes means that the involvement per pastime is cut down. At the level of specific leisure pursuits, this implies that one more often is a passerby rather than a participant.[32]

Thus, people may have both more free time and feel more rushed. In the period of industrialization, people became specialists. "Professionalism" was built upon such specialization. The medical profession emerged in Britain, for instance, out of a period in which being a doctor was more a calling; something worth doing but not something that you could earn a living from. Women, at least middle-class women, often specialized in domestic life and childcare. They could bake, sew, decorate, and undertake the extraordinarily demanding task of caring for children.

Specialization in the use of time is disappearing. Today, many people are taking on more roles than they knew existed. Males are learning something about cooking, laundering and repairing their clothing, taking care of children and pets, and community life. Women are learning about mutual funds, careers, competitive sport, international politics, shooting firearms, and plumbing.

How those in modern nations use time, in summary, is changing—as is the way such individuals feel about time. The irony of modern life is that free time is increasing, but for many people it feels like there is never enough time.

Changes in Favorite Free Time Activity

When Americans are asked about their favorite free time activities in 2007, spending time with family and children, reading, socializing with friends and neighbors, and exercising had the biggest rise in popularity since 1995. Spending time on computer-related activities also increased.

The biggest declines in popularity were in swimming, watching television, playing team sports, gardening, sewing/crocheting, and bowling. The favorite leisure activities of Americans are listed below. Notice that, even though there is much discussion of the decline of reading and the end of literacy, reading remains the favorite free time activity.

Favorite activities of 2007[33] ranked in order of preference:

1. Reading: 35 percent
2. TV watching: 21 percent
3. Spending time with family/children: 20 percent
4. Going to the movies: 10 percent
5. Fishing: 8 percent
6. Computer activities: 7 percent

6 percent: Gardening, renting movies, walking, exercise (aerobics and weights), and listening to music

5 percent: Entertaining, hunting, playing team sports, and shopping

4 percent: Traveling, sleeping, socializing with friends/neighbors, sewing/crocheting, golf, going to church, and church-related activities

3 percent: Playing music, housework, crafts (unspecified), watching sporting events, and bicycling

2 percent: Playing cards, hiking, cooking, eating out/dining out, woodworking, swimming, camping, skiing, working on cars, writing, and boating

> My favorite free time activity is mostly based on who I'm doing it with. I don't like NFL football, but I watch it with Tommy and it's fun. He gets so excited and just passes that excitement along to me. Now he goes to women's lacrosse with me and says he likes it—even though he would never go by himself. So maybe, for lots of people, it's not about what you do but who you do it with.

1 percent: Motorcycling, animals/pets/dogs, bowling, painting, running, dancing, horseback riding, tennis, and theater

Many Asian Countries Have Increasing Amounts of Free Time

Many Asian countries are showing rapid change in the amount of free time available, particularly within urban areas. In China, for instance, a two-day weekend is becoming standard in urban areas. Also, the Chinese now have three holiday periods throughout the year with the potential for each to last for one week. In Korea, the *Korea Herald* newspaper reported in 2001:

> The announcement by the government that a five-day work-week will be introduced next year should be welcomed. Such a transition is overdue for the nation, which is the only member of the Organization for Economic Cooperation and Development that is holding on to the six-day workweek. The working hours would be reduced from the 44 hours a week to 40 in the near future to help "improve the quality of life and creativity of workers." The problem is whether or not Korea will be able to prepare itself in one year to meet the drastic changes that the shorter workweek will bring about in business, education, culture, tourism and others.[34]

In Taiwan, where the five-day workweek has become almost standard, two "Golden Week" holiday periods were recently introduced by the national government. Unlike the People's Republic of China, these holiday periods can potentially be individually selected by workers to fit their schedule. This may have the benefit of avoiding the problems the People's Republic of China has during their standardized golden weeks when hundreds of millions of people try to take leisure trips at the same time.

Japan also has an official 40-hour workweek and three holiday periods of about one week each.[35] The New Year holiday in late December to the beginning of January, is the most important holiday in which many Bonenkai (forget the year) parties are held in restaurants, followed by New Year's parties. A "Golden Week" celebrated from the end of April to the beginning of May is a time when many Japanese take tourism trips in Japan or to other countries. Finally, the Bon festival, celebrated around August 15th, is a period in which many people travel to be with their family and hold extensive family reunions.

India has a six-day workweek (although often with lots of breaks from the job) but now, in one week a month, either half or all of Saturday is taken off. Perhaps other Asian nations will follow the trend toward shorter working weeks as their economic standard of living increases.

Study Questions

1. Define and discuss some different ways of conceptualizing time. Do you operate under more than one of these concepts in your personal life? Why or why not?

2. In terms of the entire life span, is it accurate to say that people today are likely to spend a smaller portion of their life at work than they did in 1900?

3. What methods could you use to determine how your classmates spent their time over a one-week period?

4. Compared to other uses of leisure time, are time expenditures for sport and outdoor recreation major time expenditures?

5. Discuss changes in the time-use patterns of men and women.

Exercise 3.1

Beginning tomorrow, I will make you financially independent for as long as you like. It will be possible to do whatever you want, and with all duties taken care of so there will be no penalties when and if you return to your present life. Financial obligations will be met by money being deposited in a bank account for you that will average $40,000 a year.

1. Will you accept my life of leisure offer?

❑ Not at all   ❑ For one month

❑ For one day   ❑ For one year

❑ For one week   ❑ For the rest of your life

2. What opportunities and problems are there in such an offer?

3. If the offer were accepted, what would you do? Why?

4. If this offer were going to be accepted for the rest of your life, would any special educational preparation be needed? Why?

5. Would you be happier leading the life of leisure offered to you? Why?

6. Do you think most people would accept this offer for the rest of their lives? Why?

Exercise 3.2

It should be obvious to you by now that to many in our society time is a scarce resource. Probably, as a result of thinking about time and a few time-oriented exercises we will do, you may become a little more time-conscious. Sorry. The object here is not to bring about a change in the way you use your time but merely to create a little more awareness of how you "pass" or "use" your time.

Speaking of time-related exercises, let's take a look at how you spend your time.

Time Diary

The purpose of this exercise is to gain a better understanding of your usage of time and, in particular, your leisure time use. Additionally, the exercise will provide a basis for comparison of your leisure time usage with other students.

To complete the assignment, refer to the Time Diary Sheet and the Time Diary Activity Summary. For each of these days, your primary activities should be recorded in your own words as precisely as possible. For example:

Activity	Where	With Whom	Time Began	Time Ended
Woke up, showered (and shaved)	Home		7:45	8:15
Ate breakfast	Home	Wife and two daughters	8:15	8:45
Drove to work	Rec Hall		8:45	9:00
Attended meeting	Rec Hall	Professors	9:00	10:30

This record should be kept for all your waking hours (unless you believe that reporting some activity would be an invasion of your privacy). Do not report any illegal activities. Fill out your Time Diary just before going to bed.

After recording your activities for each of the days in question, fill out the Time Diary Activity Summary by recording the total minutes spent for each day in each of the categories of leisure activity. If your Time Diary has listed "played basketball 4:30–5:00," for instance, you would enter that 30 minutes in line 14 under active sports (participating). Complete the Time Diaries and the Summary, staple them together with the Time Diary Summary on top, and submit them.

Time Diary Activity Summary

Primary Activity	Total Minutes						
	Sun	Mon	Tue	Wed	Thu	Fri	Sat
1. Leisure travel							
2. Religion							
3. Organizations (voluntary)							
4. Radio							
5. Television (home)							
6. Television (away)							
7. Read paper							
8. Read magazine							
9. Read book							
10. Movies							
11. Social (home)							
12. Social (away)							
13. Telephone conversation							
14. Active sports (participating)							
15. Outdoors							
16. Entertainment (e.g., spectator at football, ice capades)							
17. Cultural events							
18. Resting							
19. Other leisure							
Totals							

How much leisure time did you spend with people other than students? (in minutes)

Sunday	min.	Wednesday	min.	Saturday	min.
Monday	min.	Thursday	min.		
Tuesday	min.	Friday	min.	**Total**	min.

How much leisure time did you spend away from campus or university facilities? (in minutes)

Sunday	min.	Wednesday	min.	Saturday	min.
Monday	min.	Thursday	min.		
Tuesday	min.	Friday	min.	**Total**	min.

Endnotes

1 Fraser, J. (1987). *Time: The familiar stranger.* Redmond, WA: Tempus.

2 ibid.

3 Rifkin, J. (1987). *Time wars: The primary conflict in human history.* New York, NY: Henry Holt and Company.

4 Shlain, L. (1991). *Art and physics—Parallel visions in space, time and light.* New York, NY: W. Morrow & Company.

5 Szalai, A. (1972). *The use of time: Daily activities of urban and suburban populations in twelve countries.* The Hague, Netherlands: Mouton and Company, pp. 132, 135.

6 Drucker, P. (1989). *The new realities* (p. 177). New York, NY: Harper Business.

7 ibid., p. 177–8.

8 Ausubel, J. and Grubler, A. (1994). Working less and living longer: Long-term trends in working time and time budgets. *Working Paper 94–99.* Laxenburg, Austria: International Institute for Applied Systems Analysis.

9 Maddison, A. (1991). *Dynamic forces in capitalistic development: A long-run comparative view.* Oxford, UK: Oxford University Press.

10 Gylfason, T. (2007). Why Europe works less, and grows taller. *Challenge, 50*(1), 21–39.

11 Ausubel, J. and Grubler, A. (1994)

12 U.S. Department of Labor, Bureau of Labor Statistics. (2007). *American time use survey summary: 2006 results* (USDL 07-0930). Washington, DC: Author. Retrieved September 25, 2007, from http://www.bls.gov/news.release/pdf/atus.pdf

13 Gershuny, J. (2002). Social leisure and home IT: A panel time-diary approach. *IT and Society, 1*(1), 58.

14 Robinson, J. and Godbey, G. (1999). *Time for life: The surprising ways Americans use their time* (Rev. ed.). University Park, PA: Penn State Press.

15 Robinson, J. (1993, June 10). Personal conversation.

16 Robinson, J. (1998, April). *Americans' use of free time*. Washington, DC: Discovery Communications, Inc.

17 Robinson and Godbey (1999)

18 Robinson (1998)

19 Ornstein, R. and Sobel, D. (1987). *The healing brain—Breakthrough discoveries about how the brain keeps us healthy* (p. 157). New York, NY: Simon and Schuster.

20 ibid.

21 Zimbardo, P. (1985). Time in perspective. *Psychology Today, 19*(3), 20–27.

22 U.S. Department of Labor, Bureau of Labor Statistics. (2005). *Workers on flexible and shift schedules in 2004 summary* (USDL 05-1198). Retrieved September 25, 2007, from http://www.bls.gov/news.release/flex.nr0.htm

23 Kunstler, J. (1993). *The geography of Nowhere—The rise and fall of America's man-made landscape* (p. 167). New York, NY: Simon and Schuster.

24 Lasch, C. (1979). *The culture of narcissism* (p. 217). New York, NY: Warner Books.

25 Shaw, S. M. (1999). Gender and leisure. In E. L. Jackson and T. L. Burton (Eds.), *Leisure studies: Prospects for the twenty-first century*. State College, PA: Venture Publishing, Inc.

26 Gilder, G. (1993). Life after television. Cited by Elmer-Dewitt, P. (April 12), Take a trip into the future on the electronic superhighway. *Time, 141*(15). 50–59.

27 Forrester Research. (1998). *Helping media companies build profitable new franchises—Media and technology strategies* (p. 2). Cambridge, MA: Forrester Research. Retrieved from http://www.forrester.com

28 Gershuny (2002)

29 Linton, R. (1937). *The study of man: An introduction*. New York, NY: Appleton.

30 van den Broek, A. (August, 1998). *From specialists to generalists? Despecialization in Daily Life in the Netherlands, 1975–1995*. Montreal, PQ: International Sociological Association World Conference.

31 Stanford Institute for the Quantitative Study of Society. (2002). What users do on the Internet. Retrieved October 15, 2007, from http://news-service.stanford.edu/news/2000/february16/igraph3-216.html

32 van den Broek (1998, p. 21)

33 Haris Poll cited in *Surprise! No. 1 Leisure Activity Is...* (2007). Retrieved September 25, 2007, from http://webcenters.netscape.compuserve.com/whatsnew/package.jsp?name=fte/leisureactivity/leisureactivity&floc=wn-dx

34 The five-day workweek. (2001, August 26). *Korea Herald*.

35 Dong, E. (2002). *Free time in Japan and China*. Unpublished paper, State College, PA: Pennsylvania State University.

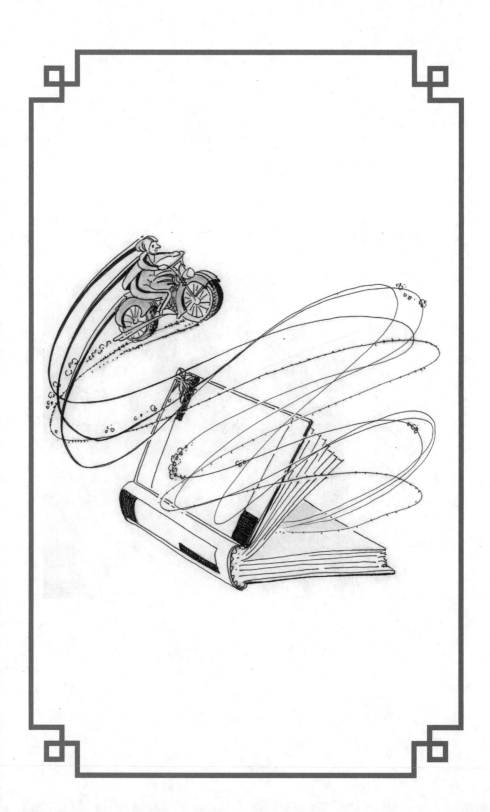

Getting Involved: From Killing Time to Central Life Purpose

How did you get involved in your current leisure behaviors? Who or what was responsible for you playing video games, loving to go mountain biking, or reading for pleasure? In this chapter we will examine not only how people get involved in leisure activities but also what prevents them from participating, how their participation in a given leisure behavior changes over time, and even why their cycle of involvement comes to an end.

Constraints to Participation

All of us are constrained from using leisure by a number of factors. At this very moment, you might wish to be swimming, watching television, or going downtown with your buddies but feel obligated to read this book. All humans are sometimes and in some ways prevented or hindered from doing what they want during their leisure. Actually, a world without constraints would make no sense. All of us are subject to constraints and limitations—That is the human condition.

We may conceptualize three different types of constraints to leisure behavior.[1] The first type of constraint is *structural*. In such situations, a person has a desire to undertake some leisure experience. He or she may, for instance, want to go skiing. A constraint then prevents the person from participating—perhaps a lack of snow or no transportation to a ski site. These barriers, like lots of structural constraints, are usually not absolutes. That is, if your desire to go skiing were intense enough, you might be able to travel somewhere and ski, perhaps by borrowing the money to do so. Many structural constraints such as "lack of time" often indicate that the individual didn't want or need to participate enough to give up some other activity to do so. For example, I may say that I "never have enough time" to go to the museum of art in my community even though I still have enough time to watch television several hours each day. In cases such as this, the individual may simply have decided that the costs of participating outweigh the benefits. Some structural constraints to participating in a leisure behavior, even if not absolute, are so imposing that the individual is stopped dead in his or her tracks. For example, you would like to take your flying lesson today, but the visibility is so bad that all aircraft have been grounded.

We are also hindered from participating in leisure activities due to individual psychological barriers which may be called *intrapersonal*. We may want to go for a hike but feel too depressed to go out of the house. We may want to write a poem but feel we just don't have the skill or inspiration. Stress, anxiety, religious belief, attitudes of our friends, and whether or not we believe the activity is appropriate for us all determine if an intrapersonal constraint exists which makes our involvement unlikely. Think about how many differences in the participation of males and females can be explained in terms of intrapersonal barriers. Females, historically, may have been taught that a wide variety of leisure behaviors, from automobile racing to conducting an orchestra to going to a poolroom, are not appropriate for them. This has produced very different intrapersonal constraints to participation between females and males.

Finally, there are some constraints which might be called *interpersonal*. Such constraints involve interaction with other people or relations between individuals. You might wish, for instance, to play racquetball but can't find anyone to play with. Perhaps you would like to start a coin collectors' club but no one else is interested. Since many leisure activities involve other people, there are lots of interpersonal constraints. Table 4.1 shows a series of statements that were used to measure various kinds of leisure constraints among teenagers.

> Here's the deal. She's not going out of this apartment at night by herself. There's too much crime around here. Sometimes I'll take her somewhere, but I'm scared myself. When her father lived here, it was different. He would go with her but now that he's gone, she just stays in on weekends. Now she doesn't even ask about going out in the evening.

Table 4.1 Leisure Constraint Statements[2]

Intrapersonal

I am too shy to start a new leisure activity.
I am more likely to do a new leisure activity that my family would think is alright.
I am unlikely to do a leisure activity that makes me feel uncomfortable.
I am more likely to do a new leisure activity that my friends thought was alright.
I am more likely to do a new leisure activity that is in keeping with my religious beliefs.
I am more likely to do a new leisure activity that doesn't make me feel self-conscious.
I am more likely to do a new leisure activity that doesn't require a lot of skill.

Interpersonal

The people I know live too far away to start a new leisure activity with me.
The people I know usually don't have time to start a new leisure activity with me.
The people I know usually don't have enough money to begin a new leisure activity with me.
The people I know usually have too many family obligations to start a new leisure activity with me.
The people I know usually don't have enough skills to start a new leisure activity with me.
The people I know don't have the transportation to get to a new leisure activity with me.

Structural

I am more likely to do a new leisure activity if the facilities I need to do the activity are not crowded.
I am unlikely to do a new leisure activity if I have other commitments.
I am more likely to do a new leisure activity if I have transportation.
I am more likely to do a new leisure activity if I know what is available.
I am unlikely to do a new leisure activity if the facilities I need to do the activity are not convenient.
I am unlikely to do a new leisure activity if I don't have the time.
I am more likely to do a new leisure activity if I have the money.

The three kinds of constraints we have discussed must be overcome in a given sequence for participation to take place. That is, one must first overcome intrapersonal constraints and decide it is appropriate to participate. Only when intrapersonal constraints are overcome will interpersonal constraints become a consideration. If the individual thinks it is appropriate to participate, then the issue of finding others with whom to participate becomes an issue. Finally, if this constraint is overcome, then structural constraints must be overcome. Perhaps an example is in order:

> When in sixth grade, my daughter wished to learn to wrestle. Most other girls did not "want" to wrestle because, perhaps, they had been taught that it was not an activity they "ought

to do." This *intrapersonal* constraint was the most powerful deterrent to participation. Having overcome this constraint, Tamara was then faced with the *interpersonal* constraint of finding people with whom to wrestle, an obstacle that was overcome with the help of the physical education teacher who identified a few smaller, lighter sixth-grade boys willing to wrestle with her. Finally, the *structural* constraint of location was overcome when a separate wrestling mat was provided after school for her (and eventually a few other girls) to practice wrestling.

People with a disability, some to a greater extent than others, have a unique set of constraints to participation. Such people may have a physical handicap, may be emotionally disturbed, or may be developmentally disabled. In addition, they may have the situational disability of residing in an institution, such as a hospital, shelter, prison, or other mass living arrangement. Individuals with such disabilities have not only the obvious structural disabilities, such as being confined to a wheelchair or finding the rules of a game beyond their comprehension, but also they have unique interpersonal and intrapersonal constraints. Other people may not feel it is appropriate for them to be involved in certain leisure activities. An individual with a disability may have to contend with his or her own depression, anxiety, or lack of socialization into specific leisure activities in ways that others do not. Changes in society's attitudes toward such individuals could help minimize both the interpersonal and intrapersonal constraints with which they must contend.

The following three concepts—leisure preferences, leisure constraints, and leisure participation—influence each other. Here are some examples. You live in a small apartment and have a set of drums you wish to play. The constraint to playing the drums is that the amount of noise they would make would lead to complaints and the possibility that you might be thrown out of the apartment. After six months, you begin to think less about playing the drums and decide to buy an acoustic guitar which you begin learning to play. Thus, the constraint changed your leisure preference. People, in most cases, gradually quit desiring to do the things they are prevented from doing. Suppose you are a teenage male and would like to learn ballet but fear you would make a fool of yourself. You nevertheless decide to attend just one introductory ballet class and find lots of males in the class, including a football player who sees nothing unusual about being there. Your participation in the activity begins to diminish the fear that you will make a fool of yourself by doing so. Gradually, the constraint disappears.

Finally, participation may change a preference. You may feel certain that you would not like wilderness camping but, once exposed to it, decide that it is worthwhile and that you want very much to participate. Changing a person's leisure preferences by exposing him or her to an activity is a very important issue to those who operate commercial sport facilities, manage resorts, or work for the U.S. Tennis Association or thousands of other organizations concerned with specific leisure activities. Thus, they develop lots of schemes to get people to try the activity or activities they are promoting—"Try it, you'll like it," they promise.

Whether or not a person tries to overcome the constraints to a given leisure activity may have to do not only with what constraints they anticipate but also their ability to overcome these constraints.[3] Thus, if you were interested in learning whitewater kayaking, you would have to consider not only your lack of equipment and skill at handling such a boat in swift water but also the likelihood that you could obtain a kayak and whether you were capable of developing the boating skills necessary. People's perceptions about their ability to overcome obstacles appear to be related to their self-esteem. Self-esteem, the degree to which one is satisfied with their feelings about how they see their "self," appears to be related to leisure constraints. Low self-esteem may be defined as follows: "self-rejection, self-dissatisfaction, self-contempt." An individual with low self-esteem lacks respect for the self he or she observes. The self-picture is disagreeable, and the person wishes it were otherwise. A study by Raymore, Godbey, and Crawford[4] found that, among teenagers, those with lower self-esteem identified more intrapersonal constraints during their leisure as well as total constraints. Since teenage females were more likely to have low self-esteem than males, they identified more of such constraints.

Some researchers have pointed out that, in many cases, individuals don't really overcome or negotiate a constraint to their leisure activity as much as they simply accommodate it.[5] Broad cultural beliefs and the assumptions of those in power define what is "normal." Because of this, many people never "overcome" or "negotiate" some conditions defined as undesirable in society. Rather, they simply accommodate the situation in ways which never lead to equal acceptance.

Getting Involved

Do you remember the first time you tried some leisure activity with which you are currently involved? There is some evidence that family, friends, and school are the most important sources of people's initial exposure to most leisure behaviors. Television increasingly exposes individuals to new activities and therefore suggests participation. In examining leisure behavior throughout the life cycle, various life stages are characterized by certain preoccupations that lead to certain interests expressed through participation in certain activities. As we will see in Chapter 8, preoccupations change greatly throughout the life cycle and, thus, so do leisure behaviors. Research by Brandenburg[6] found that conditions within four categories needed to be present for a person to begin participating in a specific leisure activity. There had to be *opportunity*—which included such factors as geographical accessibility, transportation availability, physical capabilities, financial considerations, time availability, access to resources, and changes in living circumstances. There also needed to be *knowledge*— in other words, in some way knowing enough about the activity that an interest is aroused. The *social milieu* in which the individual resides—family and friends—must approve of the activity or at least be accepting of it. Finally, there must be *receptiveness*—a willingness or desire to enter into the new experience.[7]

Sometimes, of course, beginning a leisure activity is a matter of key events but sometimes it is just an accident. We may actually be forced to undertake a leisure activity by circumstances and then find it worthwhile and continue it. Similarly, our involvement may occur by chance. Think of how you began some leisure activities. What key events led to your beginning participation?

> I'm the only white guy in the band—and I'm the drummer. Sometimes that puts me under a little more pressure. If we play clubs that have a mostly black clientele, I get dissed sometimes. Nothing terrible but you can see the change of expression on their faces when they see me behind my drums. So I get a little bit "in your face" with them. Watch this, Jack. Maybe take a solo when I shouldn't. When I went to high school, most of the kids were white and I didn't get it about being a minority... Now I'm starting to.

> My Dad was, like, you're going to play golf. I didn't want to—dumb game—old, white guys riding around in carts on a big lawn. My Dad can be a pain in the butt. He kept after me and then one day just said—we're going to the golf course, get ready. I didn't like it much at first, except for putting. Not sure what happened, but now I have an eight handicap.

Continuity, Growth, and Change

Once involved in a leisure activity, an individual may continue to participate only once or twice or may become involved for the rest of his or her life. Presently, we don't know a lot about how long individuals stay involved with given leisure activities because most studies dealing with leisure activity don't measure the participation of the same individuals more than once.

Continuing to be involved in a leisure activity, of course, does not mean that participation remains unchanged in terms of skill level or meaning. If you stay involved with some leisure activity, you may go through several stages of participation. Sociologist Hobson Bryant's[8] research indicates that people may go through several stages of specialization in regard to a leisure activity. In the *initial phase*, they are beginners with few expectations concerning the behavior. Some people are content to stay at this stage. Beginners who fish, for instance, want merely to catch a fish, any fish by almost any means. If the individual chooses to go further with the activity, a *learning stage* begins to take place. Bigger challenges are accepted, and documenting success becomes important.

In the third stage, *specialization*, the individual becomes specialized in some aspect of the activity, perhaps becoming a fly fisher. Technique, equipment, protocol, aesthetics, and association with other similarly specialized individuals become more important. Finally, in the *highest stage of specialization*, the individual may build his or her identity around the activity, loving the behavior for its own sake.

The idea of specialization in leisure may be applied to many activities. In regard to boating, for instance, Donnelly, Vaske, and Graefe[9] found that one form of boating—sailing—had a greater range of specialization than motor boating. Within both kinds of boating, they found that there was a hierarchy of specialization from day boaters to overnight cruisers to racers. The most specialized participants were those who raced sailboats.

The fact that there are stages of specialization doesn't imply that everyone who continues to participate will go through each stage. You may, for instance, have some cross-country skis in the closet which you remove once or twice a year to stumble around in the snow. That may be the only level of involvement you want. Someone else might get further "into" cross-country skiing, beginning a process of specialization. Furthermore, there is the question of whether or not everyone starts as a beginner. There may be some transfer of knowledge from one leisure activity to another. A beginning racquetball player, for instance, may not really be a beginner if he or she has played handball for several years.

Evidence also indicates some people don't want to become specialized in a leisure activity, even if they continue to participate for many years. A study of bridge players found that people who continued to play bridge for some time became either "serious" players or "social" players.[10] For social players, getting along with other players and being friendly was more important than knowledge and ability of the game. Bridge served primarily to strengthen their social ties with other members of their bridge club. The rules of the game were only loosely observed. Refreshments and conversation were an important part of the experience. If there were prizes given for winning, they were small and booby prizes were sometimes given. For the serious player, bridge ability was the primary basis upon which one got to play in a group. Socialization was minimum and unnecessary talking was not allowed during the game. The serious bridge player read books about strategy, tried to win Master points and basically viewed the game as a challenge that requires the constant development of their skill level. Thus, for a given leisure activity, some people, although continuing to play for many years, did not go through a process of specialization while others did.

Another way of viewing the process of specialization is that of the "amateur." Sociologist Robert Stebbins[11] has studied people who go through a progression of increasingly serious involvement in activities from which they do not make their living. When they voluntarily begin participation in some activity, they are immediately confronted by professional standards. As professionalism has grown, beginners in many leisure activities are confronted with standards of excellence that make their own accomplishments seem mediocre by comparison. The beginning tennis player may watch the U.S. Open on television, for instance. The beginning guitarist may hear recordings of Eric Clapton or attend a concert. At this point, the beginner must choose between starting a "career" as a participant in the activity, which will involve increased learning and identification with the activity, or remaining a "dabbler," restricting his or her identification with the activity and participating in a nonserious manner. If the participant begins the process of becoming an amateur, however, he or she moves away from play and toward serious commitment. The "amateur," a term that in its most basic sense means one who loves, is more and more prevalent in our society according to Stebbins because technology has closed most avenues of fulfillment in work. Work motivations, therefore, are sought outside of work through leisure activities which may lead to attractive identities. Amateurs, however, encounter some problems. They are serious about some form of leisure and are therefore misunderstood by their friends. While their friends, for instance, may play bridge for fun, amateur bridge players take the game seriously and study it. Their avocation may get out of hand, interfering with other duties. Amateurs get all wrapped up in their form of serious leisure. They also are outsiders in the professional world of their activity and must make their living elsewhere.

Amateurs provide many services to both the public and to the profession in regard to the activity in question. Amateurs often work with professionals in educating, coaching, advising, or supporting the public in regard to their activity. They may, for instance, run clinics, workshops, exhibitions, or classes where the public can learn more about tennis, modern jazz, coin collecting, or astronomy. The amateur serves the public using standards of excellence set and communicated by professionals. Although amateurs may not be as "good" at their activity as professionals, they often have a broader knowledge of the activity than the professional because the professional has to constantly polish technique to make a living at the activity.

The progression of participation in a leisure activity, however defined, is such that a given activity, whether bicycling or oil painting, can have a huge range of meaning, from something done merely as diversion to something which is a central source of self-definition. "Oil painting," therefore, or "bicycling" doesn't mean too much until one understands the activity's role in an individual's life. Those involved in the planning of recreation, park, and leisure services must increasingly recognize the level of specialization of those they plan for if their programs are to succeed.

Good Leisure

We may also think of continuity and change in leisure behavior in terms of what constitutes "good" leisure. Jay B. Nash[12] has provided a model (see Figure 4.1) showing a hierarchy of leisure participation in terms of what is the most desirable use of free time. Nash considered creative activity as the highest use of leisure, while criminal activity was deemed

> *Nobody seems to know that I raised three kids, worked at the bank, headed the Easter Seal campaign for eight years, and bake a mean key lime pie. I'm "The Bird Lady." Bird watching just slowly took over my life during the last ten years. I think I know where almost every bird is in this county. Know their habits. Know how to get close to them. When I'm in the mall, sometimes someone I don't even know comes up and says: "Oh, you're the Bird Lady." I am.*

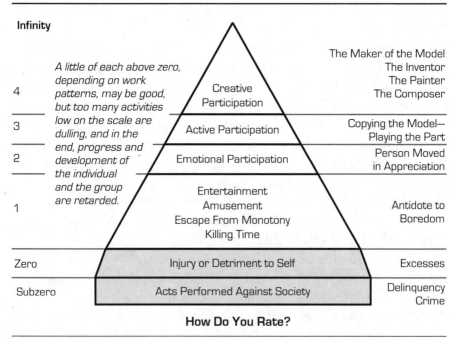

Figure 4.1 Man's use of leisure time participation broadly interpreted[13]
Reprinted with permission.

the lowest. This model provides a useful critique of the levels and kinds of involvement in leisure activity although, in theory, criminal activity as leisure could also be seen as creative participation or an antidote to boredom. Perhaps the levels 1 through 4 of the model are the most useful, since they specify a continuum for the use of leisure from the standpoint of the degree of self-investment and, presumably, growth. If we examine "creative" participation, it is evident that most participation in leisure is not creative. "The Maker of the Model" is unique in that he or she "advances" in the leisure activity in question by developing new and better ways of doing it. This new and better way in music, for instance, might be inventing a musical instrument, composing music, or developing a unique way of phrasing a song or playing an instrument. Thus, creative means "novel" and "better" as well as "appropriate."

Strangely enough, this is exactly how Bishop and Jeanrenaud described creativity in children's play: "Creativity is the production of novel responses that have an appropriate impact in a given context."[14] How insightful and amazingly simple. The painter who drops a balloon full of paint on a canvas has done something novel but not appropriate. The painter who reproduces the style of Cezanne has done something appropriate but not novel. When one engages in creative leisure by making a novel and appropriate response, it is assumed that he or she will be improved and, to some extent, so will society. Thus, there is a higher moral worth accorded such activity.

Leisure may also be judged in terms of moral growth by defining the source of pleasure derived from participating. Smith[15] has argued that pleasure-seeking may be divided into three types: sensory, expressive-cortical, and intellectual-cortical. The basis of difference among these three types is the importance of the cortex area of the brain in generating feelings of pleasure.

Sensory recreation or leisure, which includes activities such as eating, children's play, rock music, vandalism, hunting, sports, snowmobiling, and flirting all involve the pleasurable use of muscles which are sensed by the proprioceptors (nerves sensing muscular movement). Some of these activities involve physiologically pleasurable fear. Smith described some sexual activities as follows:

> A lot of so-called sexual activity also stems from a "playground mentality." Caressing, kissing and intercourse provide

many pleasurable stimuli, but not all apparent sexual activity is truly sexual. The first adolescent contacts between boys and girls generate great feelings of excitement and pleasure, but these are largely autonomic, arising from the pleasurable sensations in changes in the heart rate, respiration rate and the movement of the stomach and intestines. Because these early pleasures are primarily autonomic, they inevitably decline as the two people become more familiar with each other. The mystery and intrigue are gone; sex becomes routine; the flame has gone out of their romance. Some change is necessary to rekindle the feelings: having sex in more erotic or naughty places, in semipublic places, or with new partners. Truly sexual feelings intensify with familiarity as the couple begins to draw together emotionally and become more skilled in their caresses. In brief, much so-called sexual attraction is basically pleasurable fear—like a roller coaster ride. In fact, a roller coaster is a not unknown analogy in describing many love affairs.[16]

Expressive-cortical recreation activities are based upon a mingling of people's sensory and intellectual characteristics. The activities which use creative thought to produce something which gives sensual pleasure or adds a major intellectual dimension to a sensory experience might include wine tasting, painting, film making, or sex based upon emotional closeness.

> At first I drank light beer—whatever was cheapest. Also, I didn't know anything about beer or ale. I drank too much of it. Then John took me to a beer tasting and I began to learn a little bit—grain, hops, yeast, water. There are thousands of ways they can be combined and brewed, and the tastes produced are very different. I mean, a chocolate stout and a pilsner are about as different as day and night. Generally, draft beer is always going to be better than bottled beer, although you might get an argument from some people, because beer usually doesn't get better with age. Fresh is good. The temperature of the beer is also important. Lots of beer is served so cold you can't really taste it. Anyway, for me it's all about the flavor. You learn how to drink beer—I'm not just a drunk frat boy anymore.

Intellectual-cortical recreation activities involve pleasure obtained from intellectual activities that don't involve sensory stimulation. Participants in such activities form an elite group in any society which is regularly singled out for admiration or, as is much more common because of social values, ridicule. These are the philosophers, theologians, linguists, mathematicians, logicians, certain historians, theoretical physicists, mystics and, at times, politicians.

Smith[17] advocated a minimum of support for sensory recreation activities, which he termed *subhuman*. The human being is unique from other animals, Smith argued, and his recreation should stress this uniqueness. Thus, Smith has delineated a major question concerning leisure ideals. Do we seek our place with the other animals or seek our uniqueness, which is surely our more highly developed intellect, during our leisure? Should we seek to live, as Keynes advocated, increasingly in the mind? I find it hard to react to this proposition with anything but mixed feelings. Surely we must admire leisure activity which transcends the body, which rises above the unconscious, automatic responses of our physical selves. Rising above the physical, is, in many ways, rising above one more form of enslavement to the freely chosen, the God-like realm of the mind and spirit. Still, we are animals. We belong here no less than other animals, and we would be deceiving ourselves to ignore our bodies, our physical desires, or the pleasures of food and touch. Also, how alone from the rest of the world we would be! Smith's typology and his view toward it appear to be one more schema for our perfection. It is distressing to think that, as a species, we may have to come much closer to perfecting ourselves, and our use of freedom, to survive. The lessons of history seem to tell us this, though, particularly when technology has begun to give us greater power for harming ourselves. How can we act and enjoy with the other animals when we have tools, weapons, a self-consciousness, an awareness of death, which they don't have? Yet, how can we act differently without becoming lonely little gods?

Can we specify what "good" leisure is? Probably not. Nevertheless, here is an attempt to do so. What do you think about the following ideas?

1. *Good leisure evolves within selected frameworks.* That is, good leisure doesn't stay the same. It doesn't reach equilibrium—equilibrium is death. Instead, one must get better or worse,

more moral or less moral, etc. Good leisure continues to evolve, but not at random. It grows and changes in ways the participant provides for. Thus, playing the guitar is not a fixed activity; it continues to change and evolve in ways that the player shapes within her or his limitations and inspiration.

2. *Good leisure evolves toward complexity.* As we continue in a leisure activity and in our lives, our repertoire of responses in regard to the activity increases, our appreciations become more complex and our knowledge increases. This doesn't mean we give up joy, only that the joy increases due to a better understanding of what the leisure activity is all about.

> At first there was only mashed potatoes. I thought a potato was a single thing. All mashed potatoes were alike. Then I began to find out there was no such thing as "a potato."
>
> There are high-starch potatoes—Russets, which are great bakers and mashers; Long Whites, with very thin skin and tiny eyes, good for home fries; Round whites, low starch and just the thing for potato salad; Round Reds which are best if dug up before they reach full size; Yellow Flesh potatoes, such as Yukon Gold, which have kind of a buttery flavor; Blue and Purple Potatoes which were first grown in South America and have a kind of nutty flavor.
>
> Then, of course, you can make mashed potatoes with the skins on or off; you can sauté garlic and whip it in to the potatoes, or onion—lots of kinds of onions—or cheese—hundreds of kinds of cheese. You can use milk. You can smash the potatoes, whip them, or mash them with a hand masher. There are herbs that can be added—chives, parsley.
>
> There are. Of course, mashed potatoes made with dehydrated potato flakes—when I am king of the world all such mashed potatoes will be stuffed up the nose of the person who made them. Here's the deal, if you think mashed potatoes are a given commodity, your whole life is diminished—Do you think I overdid this?—I don't.

3. *Good leisure increasingly produces importance, meaning and love.* As you continue to ride your mountain bike, grow your garden or write your short stories, they should become more important in your life. They should produce more meaning and provide a shield for you against the chaos, which is always very near. So, too, should your leisure activity produce increases

in your capacity to love. The increased love of a few leisure activities will effortlessly transfer to increased love of life.

4. *Good leisure produces increased uniqueness, idiosyncrasy, and eccentricity.* Good leisure makes you distinct from other people, more recognizable, and distinct. This doesn't mean you are necessarily "better," but that who you are is more evolved. In some ways, being "eccentric" doesn't mean you are a crackpot; rather, it means you have your own way of doing things and of living. You are not automatically interchangeable with other humans because you have become who you are to a greater extent than previously. In some ways, the opposite of eccentric is neurotic, which is lack of certainty about who you are and what you possess. Good leisure makes you more of who you are, without doing any harm to other people who are "less" who they are.

5. *Good leisure involves joyful giving.* One doesn't take in good leisure—one gives. My father gave himself to the garden; my mother gave herself to the organizations she served as a volunteer; my friends give themselves to the game of squash or to hiking or a football pool. In good leisure, the idea is not that one takes from the experience but rather gives to it in a joyful way.

6. *Good leisure recognizes limits and rules.* There are boundaries past which one does not go. Even though growth and complexity occur in good leisure, the behavior has limits and rules. One need not go past those boundaries in order to escape boredom. When the limits disappear, so does good leisure.

7. *Good leisure moves toward the intuitive, the touched, and the trusted.* As leisure moves from bad to good, it moves from that which must be justified on some other basis—for instance, I do aerobic dance because it improves my body and my health, to the intuitive, I love to dance. In good leisure one feels touched— by God—as though one has received a gift and will accept it. Good leisure is trusted—for example, I know growing vegetables is good.

8. *Good leisure involves skill and challenge.* In all forms of good leisure, there is a challenge. This challenge may not be one of physical skill or mental acuity but rather one of simply carrying

the activity through the way it was meant to be—the way the participant has come to understand it. The skill and challenge change and dance around each other in a playful manner. The physical skills may decline even as the mental skills increase. The spiritual resources may increase. The understanding of the challenge may change—will change. Each time the individual goes back to the activity seeking meaning and pleasure, however, the challenge will present itself once again.

9. *Good leisure requires accepting one's life with joy.* For leisure to be good, one must believe his or her life is good; one must accept one's life with joy. Failure to be able to accept gifts is associated with an inability to accept good leisure. As discussed elsewhere, if one cannot celebrate his or her own life, his or her use of leisure is likely to reflect that failure.

Ceasing Participation

We can divide the reasons why individuals cease participation into reasons which are more or less voluntary and those which are not. Reasons which are not voluntary closely parallel the constraints discussed earlier. You may, for instance, participate in a basketball league but be forced to stop because of a severe pain in your shins (structural barrier). Structural, interpersonal, or intrapersonal constraints may make you cease participation since the costs of participating now outweigh the benefits.

Not all the reasons for ceasing participation are involuntary— sometimes we simply choose to stop. I, for instance, don't play basketball now, although I used to. I could still play, but I would rather play squash or tennis. Some people stop participating in an activity, either temporarily or permanently. As we will see in another chapter, many people, in the later stages of life, resume an activity, perhaps with some modifications, which they had stopped many years ago.

Ceasing participation in a leisure activity cannot be understood in isolation from an individual's total leisure pattern. As Jackson and Dunn[18] found, using data from a household survey in Alberta, Canada, when respondents were asked about their leisure behavior during the year, 51 percent of the sample said they had ceased participating in some previously done leisure activity during the year. Of that 51 percent, 23 percent were "Quitters" who did not replace that activity with a new one, and almost 28 percent were "Replacers," who added some new leisure activity during the year. Forty-nine percent of the sample had not ceased participating in any leisure activity during the year and of these, 20 percent were "Adders" who added one or more new leisure activities without dropping any. Around 29 percent were "Continuers," neither dropping nor adding activities. Respondents were more likely to drop exercise-oriented sports than others.

I really hated it. I simply couldn't bowl anymore even though I was in a league and had an average of 145 last year. My knees just won't bend that much. I thought nothing would replace it—and nothing will.

Valerie got me to go with her to a Red Hat Society meeting, but that's not for me. I liked the competition.

There's a pool table in our basement and I used to shoot nine ball with my kids. I practiced up and now I'm in a "senior" pool league—at the same bowling lanes where I used to bowl.

Study Questions

1. What current constraints exist in regard to your participation in leisure activities? Are such constraints intrapersonal, interpersonal, or structural?

2. Define an "amateur."

3. Identify three or four leisure activities you currently participate in and identify the circumstances surrounding your initial participation. Was your initial participation "voluntary?"

4. What leisure activities have you ceased participating in during the last few years? Why did you stop?

5. What, for you, is "good" leisure?

Exercise 4.1

Specialization in Leisure Activity

Review for a minute the concept of specialization in leisure activity as conceived by Bryant.[19]

Now think about your own leisure activities. In what leisure activity or activities, if any, are you most highly specialized? Describe the process of how you began participation in the activity and what constraints, if any, you had to overcome when starting to participate. Describe the circumstances under which, with continued participation, you became more specialized and how that has changed the way in which you participate, who you participate with, and the meaning of the activity to you.

Endnotes

1   Crawford, D. and Godbey, G. (1987). Reconceptualizing barriers to family recreation. *Leisure Sciences, 9*(3), 119–127.

2   Raymore, L. Godbey, G., Crawford, D., and Von Eye, A. (1993). Nature and process of leisure constraints: An empirical test. *Leisure Sciences, 15,* 104.

3   Jackson, E., Crawford, D., and Godbey, G. (1993). Negotiation of leisure constraints. *Leisure Sciences, 15*(3), 1–11.

4   Raymore, L., Godbey, G., and Crawford, D. (1994). Self-esteem, gender and socio-economic status: Their relations to perception of constraints among adolescents. *Journal of Leisure Research, 26,* 99–118.

5   Samdahl, D., Hutchinson, S., and Jacobs, S. (1999, May). *Navigating constraints? A critical commentary on negotiation in leisure studies.* Paper presented at the 9th Canadian Congress on Leisure Research, Wolfville, Nova Scotia.

6   Brandenburg, J. (1982). A conceptual model of how people adopt recreation activities. *Leisure Studies, 1*(3), 263–277.

7   ibid.

8   Bryant, H. (1979). *Conflict in the great outdoors.* University, AL: The University of Alabama.

9   Donnelly, M., Vaske, J., and Graefe, A. (1986). Degree and range of recreation specialization: Toward a typology of boating related activities. *Journal of Leisure Research, 18*(2), 81–96.

10   Scott, D. and Godbey, G. (1992). An analysis of adult play groups: Social versus serious participation in contract bridge. *Leisure Sciences, 14*(1), 47–67.

11   Stebbins, R. (1992). *Amateurs, professionals and serious leisure.* Montreal, PQ: McGill-Queens University Press.

12 Nash, J. (1953). *Philosophy of recreation and leisure* (p. 89). Dubuque, IA: William C. Brown.

13 ibid. Reprinted with permission.

14 Bishop, D. and Jeanrenaud, C. (1980). Creative growth through play and its implications for recreation practice. In T. Goodale and P. Witt (Eds.), *Recreation and leisure: Issues in an era of change* (p. 87). State College, PA: Venture Publishing, Inc.

15 Smith, S. (1980). On the biological basis of pleasure: Some implications for leisure policy. In T. Goodale and P. Witt (Eds.), *Recreation and leisure: Issues in an era of change* (pp. 50–62). State College, PA: Venture Publishing, Inc.

16 ibid., p. 57

17 ibid.

18 Jackson, E. and Dunn, E. (1988). Integrating ceasing participation with other aspects of leisure behavior. *Journal of Leisure Research, 20*(1), 31–46.

19 Bryant (1979)

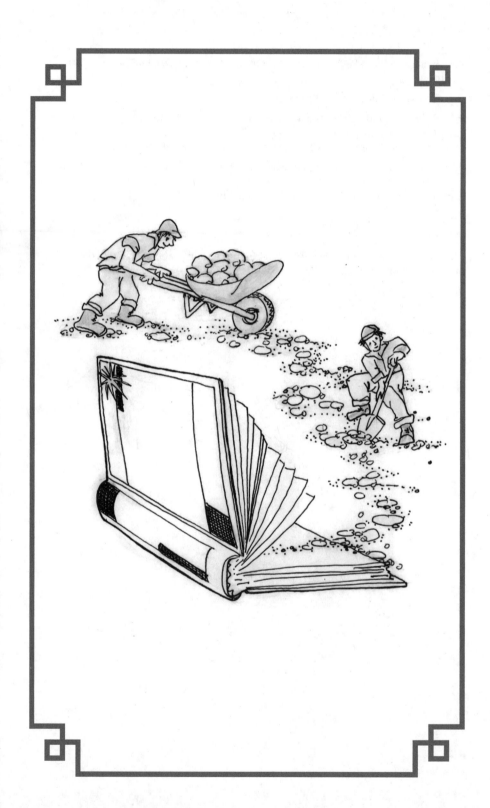

Work and Leisure and Work and Leisure

The Industrial Revolution changed methods of work so that the production of goods became more centralized in factories. The proportion of people engaged in agricultural occupations diminished and cities grew up around the factories. One effect of industrialization was to divide work and the rest of life into separate spheres. "Work" came to mean "disciplined and persistent activity devoted to achieving a goal, with the actual activity only instrumental to the accomplishment of the final goal of this activity."[1] Work is still often thought of as externally compelled activity rather than internally compelled—activity undertaken because other people require you to do it or because circumstances, such as lack of food, shelter or other things defined as necessary, require you to do it. This definition of work fits most factory workers and many service workers, such as those in the fast food industry, very well. Work is what you have to do, and leisure is what is left over. You punch the time clock and begin working; punch it again when you stop. People who run a drill press all day, or flip hamburgers, or sort vegetables on a conveyor belt have little doubt about when they are at work and when they are not. For them, the line of demarcation between work and leisure is very rigid. This rigid separation between work and leisure still holds true for the vast majority of people in the world.

It is hard for us to understand life in primitive societies, where work and leisure were inextricably related. Hunter-gatherer and agrarian societies involved a continuous fusion of work and leisure—the notion of being "at work" would be lost on a Bushman. So, too, the line between work and leisure is meaningless for the artist and craftsperson. According to C. Wright Mills, the simple self-expression of play and the creation of the ulterior value of work are combined in work-as-craftsmanship.[2] The artist is at work and at play in the same act.

One reason for this fusion of work and leisure is the activity. For the artist and craftsperson, the same activity which satisfies an inner compulsion also satisfies external compulsions, such as the need for food and shelter. That is, the same activity that satisfies an inexplicable inner urge to, say, create a painting also produces a painting which can be sold in some cases for money to buy food. Such fortunate circumstances, in which an individual can "earn" a living for an activity which he or she would "do for free," is historically rare.

Another set of traditions has made a distinction between work and leisure in terms of the relative worthiness of work or leisure. The ancient Greeks, as mentioned earlier, insisted that work could have nothing to do with leisure. Work was a necessary material evil to be avoided by the leisure elite. Only a fool would choose to work, and the only real justification for work would be to obtain leisure.

These traditions, however, are not those of most people. In North America, the Puritan Protestants who came to America from England had little of the fatalism and otherworldly asceticism which had been associated with Roman Catholicism since medieval times. Indeed, the hard life of these settlers meant that their very survival was dependent upon an ethic that admired work and distrusted idleness. As the sociologist Max Weber has pointed out, Calvinism was the Protestant sect most responsible for the formulation of a work ethic.[3] The Calvinists believed that people were predestined to heaven or to hell; those going to heaven would show some sign that they were among those selected while they were still on earth. By hard work, frugality, and accumulation of capital, an individual might show that he or she was saved from eternal hell. Thus, a harsh physical environment, economic necessity, and religious belief combined to produce an ethic of work. While some limited forms of recreation were acceptable to the Puritans, idleness, pleasures of the flesh, and many forms of celebration were distrusted.

More recently, it may be that the differences between work and leisure are not so much conceptual as social. Researchers have argued that the difference between work and leisure is not a conceptual one. In work, participation is coerced by necessity. Only a narrow segment of one's person is required, the selection of coworkers is made by necessity rather than choice, and the timing and sequence of action is usually

Idle hands are the devil's work-shop! I'll bet you think that sounds silly, but I work with juvenile delin-quents and, lemme tell you, if you don't keep them busy, they will definitely get into trouble. No doubt about it. Sometimes we arrange boxing matches so they beat themselves into being tired. We have all kinds of sports and games going on because if they just sit around for even short pe-riods of time, there's going to be trouble.

external to the worker (that is, set by seasons, tools, machines, materials, or work organization)—and finally, there is usually a tangible outcome.

Thus, we cannot determine whether activity "A" is work or lei-sure without understanding some-thing about its social organization. While many have speculated that the line between work and leisure is likely to disappear in the near future, it seems probable that leisure will still be distinguishable from work according to how it is orga-nized and with whom it is under-taken. The growing gap between rich and poor in the United States has meant that, for many poor workers, the line between work and leisure is even more sharply drawn. For middle and upper class professionals, however, work and leisure may be blended.

Viewing the World in Terms of "Work" and "Leisure"

If we attempt to understand "leisure" only by relating it to work, we will encounter a number of shortcomings. First and foremost, these terms may not apply to the majority of the population, who do not work for pay. Included here are most students, children, homemakers, the "unemployed," many who are seriously ill or possess a serious disability, those who are retired, those in prison, and others. Dividing our lives into categories of work and leisure thus reflects the lives of adult males in industrial society more than others and reflects their power to describe the world in their terms. There are serious questions as to whether measuring human behavior from these labels can capture much of the meaning they have. As Bella observed, studies of leisure activity are often blind to the meaning of many activities that are relational in nature:

As a result, the activities that are stereotypically associated with men have been studied, but those expressive and relational activities associated with women have not been. We find out about the activity, but not the relationship with the person who shares that activity…. As an example, one evening I simultaneously taught my teenage daughter how to iron her cotton shirts while we both watched television. I also ironed a number of my own shirts and we discussed the costume she might wear for a 1950s dance at school. I would hesitate to call this experience 'work' or 'leisure.' The closest I can come, without stripping too much meaning from the experience, would be 'parenting.'[4]

There is also the problem of finding work and leisure components interspersed in the same activity. Some entertainment of business clients may vary from having elements of work to having mainly leisure meanings. For a category like preparing meals or eating, there may be a range of meanings relating to freedom or necessity. Also, as Bella pointed out, "family leisure" activities, such as preparing for and celebrating Christmas, may require the organization of tasks by someone in the family in work-like fashion—usually the female.

Labeling the meaning of our lives based around paid work and forms of free time dominated by white males are still common. Thus, for instance, we find that there is less participation in "outdoor" recreation by certain groups such as African-Americans, women, high-school dropouts, and others. We do not start with categories of activities that correspond to the everyday life of, for instance, a teenage African-American female. When we say someone is "unemployed," the term relates only to paid work and denies the fact that they are, in reality, always "employed" in some behavior. Work and leisure are thus categories of life that reflect capitalism, industrialism, science, males, and Caucasians. In effect, these labels, and those used by all groups to describe human activity, reflect the exercise of power by defining what is real in their own terms.

Satisfaction with Work

There appear to be a number of indications that people are less satisfied with their work than in the past. One reason for this may simply be that workers have much higher expectations than they previously had. To the generation that went through the Great Depression, the chance to achieve a subsistence income was often enough to satisfy a worker. To a generation raised in a period of economic affluence, however, a subsistence wage is often not enough. Another reason is the work climate of ultra efficiency, downsizing, and rapid change that characterizes many companies where people work. Workers are more fearful of losing their job, being relocated, or the company doing anything it wants without regard for the worker.

Parker,[5] from a review of related research, found six main themes concerning work satisfaction. Work was satisfying when these six elements were part of the experience:

1. Creating something—a feeling that one has put something of oneself into a product;

2. Using skill—whether the skill is manual or not;

3. Working wholeheartedly and not being arbitrarily slowed down;

4. Using initiative and having responsibility—freedom to make decisions;

5. Mixing with people—social contact; and

6. Working with people who know their job—competent bosses and associates.

Work was *not* satisfying when the following five themes were in evidence:

1. Doing a repetitive job;

2. Making only a small part of something—making the worker an appendage of the machine;

3. Doing useless tasks;

4. Feeling a sense of insecurity; and

5. Being too closely supervised.

More recently, Csikszentmihalyi[6] found that complaints about work did not center around salary. Rather, they had to do with lack of variety and challenge. Additionally, complaints centered around conflicts with other people on the job, especially the boss. Finally, such complaints related to "burnout." Workers who experienced too much stress, too little time to think or too little time to spend with their family were dissatisfied. The more a job inherently resembles a game—with variety, appropriate and flexible challenges, clear goals, and immediate feedback—the more enjoyable it will be, regardless of the worker's level of development.[7]

For factory workers and others in blue-collar trades, sociologist Robert Schrank has argued that the opportunity to socialize on the job (he calls it schmoozing, which is Yiddish for chatting or gossiping) is more important to the happiness of workers than the satisfaction of accomplishment.[8]

Another important variable in explaining satisfaction or dissatisfaction with work may be the higher educational level reached by employees. Those with higher levels of education may have far higher expectations or needs about a job in terms of their ability to use skills, the opportunity to take part in decision making and in self-expression. Today many highly educated people are "underemployed," having little chance to use their knowledge, judgment, or skill.

While better-educated employees have fewer problems with their physical work environment, they have increased difficulty with working hours and excessive workloads. Also, as education level increases, the importance of challenge increases. Additionally, workers are satisfied to the extent that their educational attainments match the educational requirements of their jobs. The most dissatisfied workers are those who are too highly educated for their jobs.

We've got a big problem here. About half our employees are surfing the Web on company time. Big problem. I don't want to treat them like criminals but unless you really clamp down, the temptation is too great for them to resist. We shouldn't have, I guess, but we monitored their e-mail for a week. It was amazing. Maybe 30 percent of the messages were private—or at least they thought they were private. We are losing a lot of money because of this situation. What would you do?

Leisure as Compensation for Unsatisfying Work

Can leisure make up for work that is unsatisfying? Perhaps the best answer is that it can, but very often it does not. As Csikszentmihalyi determined, people at work are more likely to be in flow experience at work than at leisure. [9] About one-half the time they are working they are confronting challenges which are above average. This was far less true for leisure where people were more likely to express apathy, feeling passive, weak, dull and dissatisfied.

> Thus we have the paradoxical situation. On the job, people feel skillful and challenged, and therefore feel more happy, strong, creative, and satisfied. In their free time, people feel there is generally not much to do and their skills are not being used, and therefore they tend to feel more sad, weak, dull and dissatisfied. Yet they would like to work less and spend more time in leisure. [10]

While obviously not everyone is satisfied with their jobs, those who suffer from dissatisfaction may not compensate for it during their leisure because of the choices they make during leisure. If those choices do not provide for opportunities to exercise skill, accept challenges, undertake activity which leads to an attractive identity, leisure is unlikely to provide compensation for unsatisfying work. It would also appear, however, that if an individual chooses activities which produce meaning and offer the chance for major investment of the self, leisure has the potential to serve as such compensation.

> I have this lousy job—I stand and watch cans go by on a conveyer belt. Once in a while one of them doesn't seal properly, so I remove it from the line. Try that for eight hours—on your feet—by yourself. I become a regular zombie. Sometimes I daydream but you have to keep paying attention because if a can or two gets by you that didn't seal, you lose your job. When I get off the bus and walk up the stairs to my place, I always feel like I'll do something exciting—but the most exciting thing I do is watch *Desperate Housewives*. I think that my dull job has made me a dull person—and I need to do something about that.

Relations between Work and Leisure

How work and leisure relate to each other in one's daily life is also important. Whether a person's leisure and work are fused together or whether they are split apart as opposites will affect the role leisure plays in their lives. These two corresponding functions of leisure have been labeled as "spillover" and "compensation."[11] Work may be said to spill over into leisure to the extent that leisure is the continuation of work experiences and attitudes; leisure is compensatory if it seeks to make up for dissatisfaction felt in work.

Stanley Parker[12] carried the analysis of these two types of relationships further, and added a third. He distinguished between extension (spillover), opposition (compensatory), and neutrality. With the *extension* pattern, the similarity of at least some work and leisure activities and the lack of demarcation between work and leisure are the key characteristics. This pattern is typically shown by social workers, successful businessmen (perhaps they are successful because they have little or no time for leisure), doctors, teachers, and those engaged in similar occupations. The main aspects of the *opposition* pattern are the intentional dissimilarity of work and leisure and the strong demarcation between the two spheres. People with demanding physical jobs, such as miners and oil-rig workers, may either hate their work so much that any reminder of it in their off-duty time is unpleasant, or they may have a love-hate attitude toward it. The third pattern, that of *neutrality*, can be partly defined by a "usually different" content of work and leisure and an "average" demarcation of spheres. But it is not the intermediate pattern between the other two, because it denotes detachment from work rather than either positive or negative attachment.

Vigorous recent support for the spillover model comes from findings about how Americans spend time. This Newtonian theory says that "bodies in motion stay in motion, bodies at rest stay at rest." Those who stay busy with work also stay busy during leisure. For example, findings indicate

- more arts participation or organizational participation by people with longer work hours

- more survey participation by people with less free time

- greater gains in free time by those already having more free time

- more participation in outdoor recreation by those working longer hours
- higher "outputs" from those with fewer related time inputs

These findings challenge the notion that there is a "zero-sum" property of time—if people spend more time on Activity A, they must by necessity spend less time on some other activity to make up for it. Instead, with "more-more" behavior, busy people remain more active in several areas. The main exceptions to the more-more syndrome came from two activities that are very time-consuming and less active: watching TV and sleeping. In order to fit in all their daily outside activities, the more active people slept less and watched less TV.

In Exercise 5.1 at the end of this chapter, you can explore your own work-leisure relations.

Who Works and for How Long

Everyone does some work. In our own and other industrialized nations, however, work is usually considered to have another element—you get money for doing it. Much of the discussion in the mass media about how long we work or how much leisure we have is based upon information concerning the amount of time spent in paid work or in work-related activities. The most frequently cited statistic is workweek length. Many other types of information are used in analyses of work time, including percentage of the population in the labor force, percentage of those who hold two or more jobs (moonlighting), age of entry and retirement from the labor force in relation to life expectancy, unemployment rate, number of vacations and holidays, and time spent in continuing job-related education.

Changes in Work from 1900

There seems little doubt that from 1900 to 1950 there was a decrease in the amount of time individuals spent in paid labor. The workweek was dropping from close to 60 hours a week to 40. While some of this decline was due to technological advance and increased productivity, the rising power of labor unions was a major contributing factor. Labor unions were not only responsible for a shorter workweek but also for the increasing prevalence of paid vacations. Additionally, toward the end of this era, the creation of Social Security and private retirement funds enabled many people to "retire" from work at 65 years of age. The percentage of those who worked for pay within the population, however, was far less, because the number of women working outside the home was substantially smaller than today's 70 percent.

If we examine the workweek length during the second half of the twentieth century, we will find relatively little change. Actually, the workweek length has remained around 40 hours per week for full-time employees since the 1940s. Some decline in workweek length which has taken place since then is attributable to more and more part-time employees entering the job market—primarily women and teenagers.

Historian Ben Hunnicutt[13] argued that there has actually been no increase in leisure in our society during the last 50 years. From the early nineteenth century up until the Depression, he wrote, workers, through various labor movements, had steadily reduced their hours of work. Their notion of "progress" was tied to the idea that technology could slowly reduce the amount of toil needed for survival. Gradually, government regulations began to limit the hours that children and women could work and to provide for more leisure for government workers. Reducing the hours of work, it was assumed, would provide an opportunity for workers to deal with the more important cultural and spiritual issues of life—to improve their community and their own physical fitness. This way of thinking changed during the Depression, when more leisure came in the form of mass unemployment. The federal government, under Franklin Roosevelt, began massive programs to make work for unemployed adults, and work creation rather than work reduction became government policy.

Coinciding with the change in government policy was the increasing link between leisure and consumer credit and advertising. People became convinced that the successful use of leisure required lots of material goods and, with the advent of easy credit, began spending more money on leisure activity. Leisure became "commodity intensive" (you bought lots of stuff to use during leisure) and, when work productivity increased, people preferred more money rather than more time off the job.

In recent decades, "progress" has come to mean "full employment," and taken to its logical extreme, full employment means everyone works for pay all the time. Is this an ideal society? The idea that progress is associated with less work has been, temporarily, put on hold, even as free time is increasing.

Not only has workweek length not made any large overall declines during the last 45 years, but also the percentage of the population in the labor force has actually increased slightly. In 2007, about 74 percent of all males ages sixteen and over and 60 percent of females were in the labor force.

A higher percentage of the population working for pay might seem to indicate that our society has less leisure than a few decades ago. Today, however, we have earlier retirements and a longer life expectancy in relation to age of retirement. Only about one in four people work until age 65 before retiring. The total percentage of all our life's hours devoted to work declined from 23 percent in 1900 to 15 percent in 1960 and may continue to decline.

Changing Definitions of Where Work Should Be Done

Work is increasingly "portable;" that is, it can be done in many different places. As most workers become involved in services and the production of information becomes important to providing such services, the computer and other digital devices of communication make the location of many people's work more and more flexible. This has led to the "outsourcing" of work to people in other countries or other locations within a country. Examining insurance claims, word processing, writing airline tickets, and filling orders for a product are increasingly done by people in remote locations. Also, more people are now working from their homes.

From Specialist to Generalist: Changes in the Roles of Women and Men

In most preindustrial societies, everyone had some work role: children, old people, sick people—everyone contributed. Those of you raised on a farm are aware that this situation still exists on family-run farms. The idea that a child could or should do almost nothing productive is a rather recent one. The Industrial Revolution changed all this. Work became specialized, and when and how the work was done was planned to suit the needs of those who owned the means of production. Children at first worked incredibly long hours in the factories, right along with adults, but the inflexible work schedules and intolerably hard working conditions changed when child labor laws were passed. Similarly, peonage laws were enacted to protect the mentally retarded, emotionally disturbed, and others confined to institutions from being forced to perform what amounted to slave labor. During the 1930s, the retirement ages of 65 for males and 60 for females were selected by the federal government to serve as a base for paying Social Security. These ages were chosen for political expediency to curb unemployment among younger workers.

Today, the idea that a typical U.S. household contains a husband who is employed full-time and a wife who is not employed outside the home is false, as it is in all modern nations. Less than one out of five U.S. households conforms to this model. It is just as likely that the female will be employed and even more likely that a female will head the household.

A higher percentage of younger women are becoming full-time workers and millions of women are "attached" to long-term careers that pay well. Among the reasons for this are higher educational attainment of women, changing aspirations, and inflation which would all seem to indicate that the revolution in women's work is under way.

Another important reason for women's entry into the labor force and attachment to career has been the fact that there has been little financial gain for most households during the last few decades but higher material expectations. The financial gains during this period have gone to a narrow band of the population, perhaps one out of five, while the material desires of most of the population have increased dramatically.

The majority of the married couples in the Baby Boom Generation today (born between 1941 and 1960) would be poor if one of them did not work. For those born later, the situation is even more critical. Many couples in their twenties today cannot even consider either one being out of the labor force for long. Thus, economic necessity and the unwillingness to lower our economic standard of living or distribute economic resources more equitably in society has been a big part of the reason for the changes in the roles of both men and women.

Changes in Housework

As women have entered the labor force in record numbers, the term *second shift* has come to mean the work that is done before and after paid work. During the second shift, shopping, household cleaning and maintenance, childcare, meal preparation, and other duties are performed. While various studies lead to somewhat different conclusions, all evidence suggests that women put far more hours into the second shift than do men. Historically, of course, domestic life was promoted as the ideal for middle-class women. Home was the haven from a heartless world which the woman would manage. While most poor women worked for pay in whatever jobs they could find and many women worked for pay until they were married, the ideal promoted was one where the woman became specialist in domestic life and child rearing and the man became a specialist in some form of paid work.

Today, two trends are evident concerning housework. First, the total time devoted to housework is declining, and second, males are participating more than a few decades ago. While women spent an average of 27 hours per week on housework in 1965, in 1995 they spent only 15.6 hours.[14] Men's hours of housework increased from 4.6 hours per week in 1965 to 10.1 in 1985 and then declined slightly in 1995 to 9.5 hours. Not surprisingly, women still do more of the work inside the house. Males spent an average of only about 1.7 hours per week cooking in 1995 while women spent 4.5 hours.[15]

For many women, housework has simply become less important. More women are employed, and employed women spend eight hours less per week on chores than jobless women do. Women with higher levels of education

> Andrew does just about all the cooking—and vacuums the whole place every Saturday. I really don't know how to cook. Some of what he cooks is great—some isn't, but he's getting much better. I'm proud of him, and I think he is proud of himself. We both think my job is as important as his, so we share housework. A number of the couples we know say they share housework, but then you find out that means the husband clears the table after dinner and puts the dishes in the dishwasher. Andrew does half—I've calculated the time spent and we are about even. At work, I have a chance to take a more ambitious job—more stress, but more authority. I'm going to take it. If Andrew does half the housework, I should earn half the money.

rate housecleaning as less important than women with lower levels of education.

In all circumstances, however, females continue to do more housework than males. When an employed woman marries, her housework time increases by 2.5 hours to 15.7 hours per week—about seven hours more than her husband does. When kids come along, working mothers increase housework about 1.7 hours per week to 17.4 versus working dads whose housework time increases by less than one hour to 9.4. [16]

Consequences and Strategies

Partially as a response to the changes in work and household work roles, young females and males are deferring marriage, getting more formal education, having fewer children and placing more importance on career. The average female is almost 25 years old today when she marries. The average male is over 26 years old. More couples live together prior to marriage than do not. The average number of children a woman has in the United States is 2.0 and in many modern nations where women routinely work for pay, the birth rate is closer to 1.0 than 2.0. Almost no females with undergraduate degrees want to be full-time homemakers. The majority of undergraduate university students are female. These trends are likely to become more pronounced, since 40 percent of females are not in the labor force but are increasingly likely to be.

Just as women's work roles are in a state of change, so too are men's. Fatherhood is being taken more seriously by many men. A survey of fathers found that almost all fathers surveyed said they had changed baby diapers, had taken their children to the doctor and had left work to care for a sick child. [17] In most cases they reported their fathers had not done these tasks. Also, nearly seven out of ten said they would like the opportunity to stay home and care for their children while their wives worked. While twenty years ago it was very unusual for a father to be present at the birth of a child, it is now quite common. The "men's movement" has helped many males expand their consciousness not only about being a man but also what that means in terms of fatherhood.

Because males' roles are in the process of change due not only to changes in women's roles but also changes in who works for pay within the typical family and changes in men's consciousness about their roles and responsibilities, many new arrangements regarding work are being considered. However, paternity leave when a child is born, for instance, is much less likely to be granted by employers than maternity leave.

In the United States, jobs are frequently designed on the assumption that males don't have children or are married to a woman who does not work outside the home. Vacations come at different times for working men and women. Making jobs more flexible will be a key variable in adjusting to the new roles of men.

While no one can guess how much more men's roles will change, those men who have changed the most have tended to be those with higher levels of education. They are far more likely, for instance, to spend additional hours with their children than males with lower levels of education. Whether changes in men's roles come about for males with lower levels of formal education remains a critical question. Whether or not this happens will be tied to the issue of whether jobs are restructured in such a way as to encourage it.

A revolution has taken place to the extent that women have entered the labor force. The variety of jobs they take, and the extent to which they pursue careers and obtain formal education to do so have improved; however, the revolution, according to some sociologists, is now stalled. One reason for this may be the federal government's current lack of interest in making the necessary reorganization of society to facilitate women working. Most nations provide paid maternity and paternity leave for up to one year, allowing the new mother and father to rearrange their schedules, but no such opportunity exists in the United States. Similarly, daycare has been left largely to the private sector and is often too expensive for many couples to afford. While women typically work outside the home in today's society, that society has, by and large, not yet been reorganized in ways that facilitate this change.

Workplace Trends

In a world in which work is changing rapidly in terms of how it is done, what work is done, when it is done and who does it, identifying trends is difficult. Nevertheless, the American Society of Training and Development identified a series of trends at a conference in which experts from all over the world shared their ideas.[18] The trends identified were as follows:

1. **Money:** Increasing pressure from shareholders for short-term profits means that there is greater pressure on employees to produce results and on training to show a return on investment.

2. **Diversity:** The growing cultural diversity of organizations means a greater need for people with different backgrounds to work together and find better ways of balancing the "local" with the "global."

3. **Time:** The increasing expectation for just-in-time products and services is resulting in shorter time frames for learning, often facilitated through technology.

4. **Work:** With the rise of virtual work and virtual workplaces, people are increasingly physically disconnected and have to learn to work in new ways.

5. **World:** Changes in the distribution of the world's population—in geography, economic standing, age and race—pose new challenges for organizations as they seek the right human capital to succeed.

6. **Meaning:** In a world where things seem to be constantly changing, people are increasingly looking for work that has meaning and which nurtures them spiritually.

7. **Change:** As the pace of change appears to quicken, people become increasingly resistant to change and question whether technology has advanced too quickly.

8. **Knowledge:** As the knowledge sector accounts for even larger percentages of the world economy, what people know and do becomes more important.

9. **Technology:** Technology is increasingly used to automate work, changing the types of skills people need and transforming how they learn.

10. **Careers:** The changing relationship between employees and employers and the rise of the free agent worker challenge the traditional notion of career.

A recent study by the RAND Corporation found that work trends in the near future include the following:

- Employees will work in more decentralized, specialized firms, and employer-employee relationships will become less standardized and more individualized.

- Slower labor force growth will encourage employers to adopt approaches to facilitate greater labor force participation among women, the elderly, and people with disabilities.

- Greater emphasis will be placed on retraining and lifelong learning as the U.S. workforce tries to stay competitive in the global marketplace and respond to technological changes.

- Future productivity growth will support rising wages and may affect the wage distribution.

- The tie between employment and access to fringe benefits will be weakened.[19]

These trends have great implication for government policy in a variety of areas, from public health to social security to daycare.

> I work with about twenty people in this office—kind of. In reality, what I do is sit and stare at a screen all day and move my fingers. I really don't know the people around me, even though we talk now and then—when our supervisor isn't around. I'm kind of by myself all day—it's strange.
>
> At home, I have the same computer setup as at the office. I'm also alone when I use it. My mom wonders why I don't meet a guy at work. Really, I hardly meet anyone.

Offshoring: Will It Be The Next Revolution in Work?

While there may be a tendency to think that there are some jobs that are "American jobs," a revolution in work is underway in which jobs are sent offshore to other countries where they can be done more cheaply and, sometimes, efficiently. Basically, the rule of thumb is any job that can be run through computer wire or is repetitive can be offshored. While some people assume the critical variable in the labor market is between highly educated people and less educated people, economist Alan Blinder says, "The critical divide in the future may instead be between those types of work that are easily deliverable through a wire (or via wireless connections) with little or no diminution in quality and those that are not."[20] Such jobs include a very diverse cross-section, including security monitoring, typing services, airline reservations, reading of X-rays by radiologists, accounting, computer programming, and many others. Jobs that require face-to-face contact, whether high-paying jobs like physicians or lower paying jobs like waiters or the cop on the beat, cannot be easily outsourced. According to Blinder, an estimated 42 million American jobs could be offshored under current conditions! Leisure and hospitality jobs, however, seem highly immune from this situation.

The offshoring revolution means that education must be rethought, the "safety net" for American workers, the weakest of any modern nation, must be rethought, and creativity must be valued more as a critical job skill.

What does this list of changes mean to you? Learning, it would seem, is becoming more important, and the willingness and ability to learn must extend across one's life—not just until one graduates from college. Change is a condition of life and one must be able to recognize and cope with it. Time is perceived as scarce, but perhaps it may be more accurate to say that what one does with time is increasingly important in terms of one's success at work.

Work is changing in fundamental ways and such changes change us—and will continue to do so for the rest of our lives.

Careers and Retirement: Obsolete Concepts?

Due not only to the internationalization of the economy but also due to the accelerating rate of change in North America, our notions of "career" and "retirement" may have to be altered. Such concepts came out of the Great Depression and the period of unparalleled affluence after World War II. Mandatory retirement at age 65 with assistance from Social Security and sometimes pensions was a way of making room for younger people in the labor force. Our notion of career, in which one pursued a given line of work over a lifetime with continued advancement, income increases, and the acquisition of specialized work skills came about after the Second World War. However, neither of these concepts makes sense in our rapidly changing world.

Actually, both careers and retirement have already changed in our society. In regard to retirement, for instance, only about one worker out of four works until age 65 (or later) when they become eligible for

Social Security. The average age of retirement has continued to decline, although a minority of workers today retires later or not at all. Furthermore, many who "retire" actually go back into the labor force on a part-time or full-time basis.

Our notions of both retirement and career are being reshaped by the job advancement patterns and the incomes earned by the huge Baby Boom generation. While Baby Boomers have higher levels of education than any previous generation and while they have the highest expectations concerning both external and internal rewards from the job, the huge number of qualified workers from this generation outnumber the available middle-level and upper-level management positions which career advancement is thought to lead to. One recent estimate was that the number of these positions would grow only half as fast as the number of qualified applicants who expect to move into them. Thus, many workers' career advancement will be put on hold.

While there have been a huge number of jobs created between 1987 and 2007, many of these positions have been in low-paying, high-rotation, or dead-end jobs, such as restaurant workers or hospital aides. The fast-growing retail trade employment sector pays workers, on average, over one fourth less than service workers as a whole. While many high-tech jobs, such as microelectronics and computer analysts, operators, and programmers, were created in the last decade, the most frequent occupational positions people took were: (1) janitors, (2) nurses' aides and orderlies, (3) sales clerks, (4) cashiers, (5) waiters and waitresses, (6) general office clerks, (7) professional nurses, and (8) fast-food workers. Those who work in these low-paying positions are not very likely to be unionized or have benefit packages. Today, less than one out of six employees is in a union.

Many of these occupations do not provide for either "career" or for "retirement" in the sense we have come to think of them. As a result, many Americans may face a disastrous retirement. Many will need to continue working if they are to avoid severe economic constraint. More than one out of every five Americans ages 62 and older who expected to retire early is still working.[21] Also, since the average family size has been declining rapidly and since people are living longer, many retired people will have their own parents to take care of. Conversely, owing to decreased family size, there will be fewer sons and daughters to take care of them.

All these factors and more would seem to suggest that a higher percentage of older people will continue in the labor force in some capacity. In spite of immigration increases, we are likely to continue to experience a labor shortage. The generation of workers after the Baby Boom generation is so much smaller that many jobs will not be filled without changes in our retirement practices. Stated another way, the economy is projected to grow at two to three percent annually while the labor force growth will be only about one percent. The average worker's age has risen to 39 years and continues to rise. One reaction to this is to raise the mandatory retirement age, a process the U.S. Congress has already begun. There will also need to be changes in Social Security regulations, which currently serve as disincentives to work. This may be combined with a tax on Social Security payments for elderly who are well-off financially. Elderly people often make excellent workers, although many will need retraining. The next generation of elderly people will be in better health and have more education than today's elderly. They tend to have good work habits, and restructuring jobs to make them appropriate for elderly workers, such as changing the hours of work per day or the number of days worked each week, for example, will allow many elderly people to work again. Retirement, like work, will be spread around.

According to an analysis of the prevalence of unanticipated work in retirement and its consequences for the well-being of older adults conducted by sociologist Philippa Clarke,[22] almost 30 percent of respondents older than age 62 still were working for pay. Clarke identified three distinct patterns among those who still were working:

- About 37 percent of people, mainly older men, had expected to take early retirement. If they ended up working beyond age 62, their life satisfaction was lower than that of retired peers with similar recent labor force activities, health, and socioeconomic and demographic factors.

- About 59 percent of people, mainly older women, generally had expected to be working after age 62. Their life satisfaction also was lower than peers who had stopped working.

- The one group that seemed to benefit from later life work were younger, less educated respondents who tended to be ambivalent about the probability of retiring early. This group comprised only about four percent of the sample. Their life satisfaction was much higher if they stayed at work past age 62.

Older workers approaching retirement have faced notable and dramatic changes in the structure of state and corporate pension plans and benefits. With recent and future changes in Medicare and Social Security older workers who long have expected to retire early are being forced to reverse their decisions and work longer than they expected. The patterns are quite clear that the move towards a so-called "ownership society" in the U.S. has consequences for the well-being of older workers who may have been operating under a different set of assumptions when planning for their retirement.[23]

> I kept asking Al what he was going to do when he retired. He told me he would play golf, go fishing and that his wife had a huge list of things to do around the house.
>
> Well, he retired. You can't play golf for half the year in Michigan, he doesn't fish when it's cold, and the list his wife had wasn't very long—maybe because she doesn't want him in the house all the time. Now he's looking for a job. Oh, also, I don't think they could make car payments unless he gets some extra income rolling in.

The Changing Nature of Work

The kind of work done in a global economy is subject to rapid change. Companies cross national borders in search of profit. The basis of an economy can change very rapidly. The state of Vermont, for instance, went from an economy based primarily on agriculture to one based on tourism in only a few decades. The nature of work is shaped by the evolution of the economy and the economy is being driven by three factors which can't be controlled: demographic changes in the population, the growing desire for higher per capita income among people in underdeveloped nations, and technological change.

Globalization of the economy has been brought about by the revolution in communication (e.g., computers), transportation (e.g., jet engines, quick bulk delivery), and the liberalization of trade. Such technological innovations are now "built in" to the economic system, universities, government laboratories, and corporate research programs, indeed they are built into the economic process. Thus, many jobs can be eliminated, such as in sales, banking and travel agencies, and the decision of whether or not to do so is not a technical one, but a social one.

Technological change may be most important. The globalization of the economy should be understood as being caused primarily by major increases in information technology, which reduce the cost of communication. These reduced costs have helped globalize financial and production markets.

Digital technologies are in three distinct groupings: information appliances (e.g., computers, televisions, audio systems), communications (networks of information exchange), and content industries (e.g., entertainment, studios, news organizations). These three industries function together to bring about huge change. They result in a networked economy that uses information appliances and content. Working together, they can utterly transform the processes of an industry. These same technologies provide the critical tools for educating the future workforce. Because of this, "The key issue for every modern society is its ability to adjust, both psychologically and economically, to constant turmoil."[24]

Capitalism requires a constant process of tearing down and building. In the coming era of rapid change, the tearing down will be considerable. Globalization, technological change, and demographic change have altered the success criteria of the marketplace and the factors which determine if a company will succeed. Traditional work environments that relied upon order, structure, rules, regulations and a hierarchy will not function very well in the new economy. Today, organizations that succeed are likely to be lean, decentralized, have high levels of work participation in decision making and use leading-edge technology and well-educated and trained workers who receive positive financial and personal rewards. In a period of rapid change, organizations need to be able to act quickly and change quickly.

Such change has produced a growing gap between the haves and have-nots. (Or, in some cases, it has been used as an excuse for such a gap.) Those among the have-nots are: 23 million people who are either officially unemployed, discouraged and not seeking work; involuntarily working only part-time but looking for full-time; or in temporary or on-call work. Only 10 to 15 percent of the widening income disparity between the haves and have-nots, however, is due to imports from low-income countries. Less than one in ten of the jobs destroyed were due to imports. Productivity has been going up three times faster than wages of workers. During a period of sustained growth we see increases in poverty. This usually doesn't happen. What may be causing the widening gap between the haves and have-nots is more the power and greed of the haves than technological change.

There are some signs of progress in the movement toward equality of wages, however. Women's wages are within 18 percent of men's and closing. Black males earn about 70 percent as much as white males, up from 60 percent twenty years ago.

A 2007 survey found the top ten trends related to work centered around healthcare, work-life balance, and illegal uses of technology (see Table 5.1).

Table 5.1 Top Ten Work-Related Trends Overall[25]

1. Rising healthcare costs
2. Increased use of outsourcing (offshoring) of jobs to other countries
3. Threat of increased healthcare/medical costs on the economic competitiveness of the United States
4. Increased demand for work-life balance
5. Retirement of large numbers of baby boomers (those born between 1941 and 1960) around the same time
6. New attitudes toward aging and retirement as baby boomers reach retirement age
7. Rise in the number of individuals and families without health insurance
8. Increase in identity theft
9. Work intensification as employers try to increase productivity with fewer employees
10. Vulnerability of technology to attack or disaster.

New Meanings of Management

The management of work is also in a state of change. In modern nations, where much of the work is done by "information" workers, management is changing its meaning and function. While "management" may have meant "someone who is responsible for the work of subordinates" immediately after World War II, that meaning changed in the early 1950s to "someone who is responsible for the performance of people." Today, however, according to Drucker, it means one who "is responsible for the application and performance of knowledge."[26] Drucker explains that

Land, labor and capital are important chiefly as restraints. Without them, even knowledge cannot produce; even management cannot perform. But where there is effective management, that is, application of knowledge to knowledge, we can always obtain the other resources.[27]

Managers must also manage for change, which means the organization in question destabilizes. "The task of management in the knowledge-based organization is not to make everybody a boss. It is to make everybody a contributor."[28] Thus, employees must increasingly be convinced that what they are doing makes sense and is worthwhile. While those who do unskilled labor may still be treated as "subordinates," increasingly such jobs are being done by machines. For most organizations which do "work," the issue will be determining and obtaining the knowledge needed to do the job and then continuing to change as the requirements of the organization change. Over two centuries ago, Ben Franklin said that time was money, but today knowledge and cooperation are money. Managers will have to deal with this shift in many kinds of work. In some industries, such as the garment industry or the manufacturing of shoes, there continues to be a "sweat shop" approach to production, with managers operating as absolute bosses. In most forms of work, however, the use of employee knowledge by managers will separate organizations which succeed from those who do not.

Jobs as the Critical Issue of the Next Decade

Many analyses of work find that the same process of technological change which led to agriculture workers declining to two percent of the population has moved through manufacturing and is now producing a huge decline in the need for service workers and, shortly, for information workers. The majority of jobs may be technologically replaceable right now by computers, robots, or other technological means. As a vice president of Taco Bell said recently, the company's goal was to shrink the kitchen in its restaurants as small as possible and get rid of all employees except for point of sale. While Americans often think that jobs which are exported to third-world countries are not subject to re-engineering—they are. The phenomenon is worldwide. Additionally, some jobs are not deported; they just disappear.

Job sharing, with a corresponding reduction of hours worked, is an idea whose time has come and is beginning to be recognized in countries like Germany and France. Our choices may be either massive unemployment or shorter workweeks for many employees, more free time, less financial resources and more dependence upon the public and private, nonprofit (third) sector for leisure.

The ways in which work may be spread out are still being thought about and experimented with but include:

1. *Job sharing*—This usually involves two persons filling a single job, both dealing with the same customers, clients or files at the same time.

2. *Flextime and compressed workweeks*—Under flextime a person may choose the time he or she starts and finishes work. Compressed workweeks give employees the right to take time off on one day—often to stretch the weekend to include a Friday or Monday—if they make up the time by working slightly longer hours the other days of the week.

3. *Leading-edge employers*—Such employers have sought to attract and retain desirable employees by becoming much more flexible in the work patterns of their employees, in effect customizing the work schedule to fit the life of the worker.

4. *Four-day workweek*—This alternative, which has been recently initiated by Volkswagen in Germany and elsewhere, involves employees working only four days a week. There are many alternatives under this model, some in which workers work 36 hours over four days and others in which they work as few as 30. In some cases, employees may choose what additional day of the week they want off from work, but since most want either a Friday or a Monday to produce a three-day weekend, many companies may assign or limit the right to choose the additional day.

5. *Reduced work time and job creation*—Some recent union or other worker agreements have reduced the hours of current employees in order to create new jobs or to avoid layoffs. In some cases, these agreements have meant a proportionate reduction

in salary or other forms of pay; in some cases they have not.

6. *Limiting overtime*—Under such arrangements, the extent to which employees can work overtime is minimized, with overtime after a certain number of hours being compensated by additional time off rather than more pay.

7. *Early retirement*—Under this arrangement, employees are given financial incentives to retire from work at an earlier age than previously.

8. *Flexible and phased-in retirement*—This allows for workers to retire gradually; cutting back their hours, usually with attendant cutbacks of pay and benefits.

> It's pretty spooky. The company started flextime and also lets lots of people work from home. It's almost as if it doesn't matter when you work or where you work. There are a few meetings each month we have to show for in person, but other than that, when and where don't matter too much as long as you get the work done.
>
> At first I worried about putting in face time at work, but they really don't care if you're there or not. I tried working at home but it wasn't very functional for me—too many distractions. I'd watch ESPN and eat cookies or something. You know what? I think I'd like it better if we all had to show up at the same place at the same time. Am I nuts, or what?

None of these techniques, of course, guarantees that more jobs will be created or work shared. In any of these alternatives, the employers in question may simply use the technique to cut back on the number of full-time employees.

Not only is the distribution of work changing, so are the types of employment available. In the emerging economies, work may be redefined and redistributed as follows:[29]

- **The Professional Core**—Well-qualified people, professionals or technicians or managers. They get most of their identity and purpose from their work. They are the organization and are likely to be both committed to it and dependent upon it. They will work long and hard, but in return they want not only proper rewards in the present but some guarantee of their future. They think in terms of careers, of advancement, and of investing in the future.

- **The Contract Fringe**—Made up of both organizations and individuals who will do much of the work formerly done by core professionals. They will be paid for results, not for time, in fees, not wages. Work will be subcontracted to them.

- **The Flexible Labor Force**—Hired help which employers hire as needed for as little money as they can pay. Part-time and temporary workers, the flexible labor force will do low or no-skill jobs both to supplement income in a two worker family or because they have no choice.

- **Consumers**—Those who purchase products will increasingly be asked to do some labor as part of the purchase—pumping the gas they buy, assembling the furniture, clearing the table at a fast-food restaurant and recycling the products they use.

- **Volunteers**—Those who choose to do work for reasons other than pay. They will increasingly be recruited, trained, "hired," evaluated, promoted, fired, and in other ways serve the same functions as paid workers. As Drucker stated: there are no more "volunteers; there are only unpaid employees."[30]

> O.K. so first McDonald's taught us to clean up after we eat and put the trash in a can. Then the gas stations taught us to pump our own gas, then to swipe a credit card so we didn't even go inside the station, but now supermarkets want us to scan and bag our own groceries. I don't know why, but that's the limit for me. I'm simply never going to do that—sue me.

This new redistribution of work will have fundamental implications for how people experience different stages of life as well as their life chances.

The mix of jobs is in a constant state of change in our society, reflecting changes in technology, the characteristics of our population, the demands and conditions of the international market, and many other factors. There will be an increasing need for medical services, international trade will be increasingly important, more education and training will be necessary to get the best jobs, automation and expanded use of computers will reshape many jobs, and people will be increasingly likely to change jobs and careers. While Americans average about eight different employers between the ages of 25 and 64, that number is likely to increase, as will the number of different occupations a person has.

Most of the fastest-growing jobs are in the service sector, which accounts for almost four out of every five jobs. These jobs are in areas such as medical care, law enforcement and corrections, travel and hospitality industries, food services, data processing and social work. Many of these jobs are ones which replace or assist those in traditional professions, such as medicine and law.

In terms of jobs which require a college degree, Tables 5.2 and 5.3 show expected job growth from 2004–2014. As you can see, jobs in health, education, and leisure and hospitality are projected to grow sharply while agriculture and manufacturing will continue to decline.[31] CEOs look for technology-literate people capable of learning, critical thinking, and problem-solving skills; oral and written communication skills; and the ability to work in teams.[32] Thus, it may not be the college degree as such, or even the grades one receives which determine job success, but what he or she has actually learned: spoken and written communication, ability to analyze and solve problems, ability and willingness to work with others in teams, and perhaps most important, ability to continue learning. Students who think they have "completed their education" are in for a rude shock. A person's "knowledge about knowledge" or "information about information" will be critical. That is, how and where you find out what you need to know in rapidly changing circumstances.

Study Questions

1. Describe the extension, opposition, and neutrality relationships between work and leisure.

2. What kinds of "skills" will be needed for most workers in modern nations in the near future?

3. What changes are taking place in women's and men's paid work and housework patterns?

4. How do you think "careers" and "retirement" will change in the next twenty years?

Table 5.2 Fastest growing occupations covered in the *Occupational Outlook Handbook*, 2004–14[33]

Occupation	Employment change (%)	Most significant source of post-secondary education or training
Home health aide	56	Short-term on-the-job training
Network systems and data communication analysts	55	Bachelor's degree
Medical assistants	52	Moderate-term on-the-job training
Physician assistants	50	Bachelor's degree
Computer software engineers, applications	48	Bachelor's degree
Physical therapist assistants	44	Associates degree
Dental hygienist	43	Associates degree
Computer software engineer, systems software	43	Bachelor's degree
Dental assistants	43	Moderate-term on-the-job training
Personal and home care aides	41	Short-term on-the-job
Network and computer systems administrators	38	Bachelor's degree
Database administrators	38	Bachelor's degree
Physical therapists	37	Master's degree
Forensic science technicians	36	Associates degree
Veterinary technologist and technicians	35	Associates degree
Diagnostic medical sonographers	35	Associates degree
Physical therapist aides	35	Short-term on-the-job training
Occupational therapy assistants	34	Associates degree
Medical scientists, except epidemiologist	34	Doctoral degree
Occupational therapist	34	Master's degree
Preschool teachers, except special education	33	Postsecondary vocational award
Cardiovascular technologies and technicians	33	Associates degree
Postsecondary teachers	32	Doctoral degree
Hydrologist	32	Master's degree
Computer systems analyst	31	Bachelor's degree
Hazardous materials removal workers	31	Moderate-term on-the-job training
Biomedical engineers	31	Bachelor's degree
Employment, recruitment and place-ment specialists	30	Bachelor's degree
Environmental engineers	30	Bachelor's degree
Paralegals and legal assistants	30	Associate degree

Table 5.3 Occupations covered in the *2006–2007 Occupational Outlook Handbook* with the largest job growth, 2004–14[34]

Occupation	Employment change (in thousands)	Most significant source of post-secondary education or training
Retail salespersons	736	Short-term on-the-job training
Registered nurses	703	Associates degree
Postsecondary teachers	524	Doctoral degree
Customer service representatives	471	Moderate-term on-the-job training
Janitors and cleaners, excepts maids and housekeeping cleaners	440	Short-term on-the-job training
Waiters and waitresses	376	Short-term on-the-job training
Combined food preparation and serving workers, including fast food	367	Short-term on-the-job training
Home health aides	350	Short-term on-the-job training
Nursing aides, orderlies, and attendants	325	Postsecondary vocational award
General and operations managers	308	Bachelor's degree or higher, plus work experience
Personal and home care aides	287	Short-term on-the-job training
Elementary school teachers, except special education	265	Bachelor's degree
Accountants and auditors	264	Bachelor's degree
Office clerks, general	263	Short-term on-the-job training
Laborers and freight, stock, and material movers, hand	248	Short-term on-the-job training
Receptionists and information clerks	246	Short-term on-the-job training
Landscaping and groundskeeping workers	230	Short-term on-the-job training
Truck drivers, heavy tractor-trailer	223	Moderate-term on-the-job training
Computer software engineers, applications	222	Bachelor's degree
Maintenance and repair workers, general	202	Moderate-term on-the-job training
Medical assistants	202	Moderate-term on-the-job training
Executive secretaries and administrative assistants	192	Moderate-term on-the-job training
Sales representatives, wholesale and manu-facturing, except technical and scientific products	187	Moderate-term on-the-job training
Carpenters	186	Long-term on-the-job training
Teacher assistants	183	Short-term on-the-job training
Child care workers	176	Short-term on-the-job training
Food preparation workers	175	Short-term on-the-job training
Maids and housekeeping cleaners	165	Short-term on-the-job training
Truck drivers, light or delivery services	164	Short-term on-the-job training
Computer systems analysts	153	Bachelor's degree

5. What, in your opinion, are the advantages and disadvantages of a holistic approach to work and leisure?

Exercise 5.1

The purpose of this exercise is to examine your work activity and the relation between your work and your leisure. In this exercise we will consider work to be "disciplined and persistent activity devoted to achieving a goal with the actual activity only instrumental to the accomplishment of the final goal of the activity." It is activity that is externally compelled rather than internally compelled, and undertaken because people or circumstances require you to do it.

1. List some current activities in which you are involved which you consider to be work.

2. Look at your time budget for the week you kept it. How many hours of work did you do that week?

3. What was your most time-consuming work activity?

4. Using Parker's[35] conceptualization of work-leisure relations as extension, opposition, and neutrality, which work-leisure relationship do you think most closely describes you, or do you see no relationship at all between your work and leisure? Why?

5. What kinds of work do you expect to do when you leave this college or university?

6. Could this kind of work be offshored? Why or why not?

7. What relationship do you think your work and leisure will have in that job, if any? Why?

8. Do you think you could be happy if your primary opportunity for self-expression and achievement comes during your leisure and not from your work? Explain.

Exercise 5.2

The object of this exercise is to examine your reaction to having a job which might cause a "neutrality" or even "opposition" work-leisure relationship for you. Assume that after six months of searching for a job after graduation, you can find only a salesperson's job in a large department store. You accept the job.

1. Do you believe your leisure patterns would change from what they currently are? Why?

2. Do you believe you could find adequate means for self-expression and fulfillment during your leisure? Why?

3. Do you think any of your leisure activities could make a meaningful contribution to society? Why?

4. Could you be a "success" in the eyes of your friends and family with such a job? Why?

5. What kind of leisure behavior, if any, do you think would be denied you because of such a job? Why?

6. Could you be happy with leisure as a central life interest instead of work? Why?

Endnotes

1   Theodorson, G. and Theodorson, A. (1969). *Modern dictionary of sociology* (p. 466). New York, NY: Thomas Y. Crowell.

2   Mills, C. (1956). *White collar* (p. 222). New York, NY: Oxford University Press.

3   Weber, M. (1958). *The Protestant work ethic and the spirit of capitalism.* New York, NY: Charles Scribner's Sons.

4   Bella, L. (1989). Women and leisure: Beyond androcentrism. In E. Jackson and T. Burton (Eds.), *Understanding leisure and recreation: Mapping the past, charting the future* (pp. 157–158). State College, PA: Venture Publishing, Inc.

5   Parker, S. (1972). *The future of work and leisure.* New York, NY: Praeger.

6   Csikszentmihalyi, M. (1990). *Flow: The psychology of optimal experience.* New York, NY: Harper and Row.

7   ibid.

8   Schrank, R. (1979). Schmoozing with Robert Schrank. *Successful Business,* (Spr), 40–44.

9   Csikszentmihalyi (1990)

10   ibid.

11   Wilensky, H. (1960). Work, careers and social integration. *International Social Science Journal, 12,* 543–560.

12   Parker, S. (1972). *The future of work and leisure.* New York, NY: Praeger.

13   Hunnicutt, B. (1989). *Work without end.* Philadelphia, PA: Temple University Press.

14   Stapinski, H. (1998, November). Let's talk dirty—We won't clean, don't ask us. *American Demographics, 20*(11), 50–54.

15 ibid.

16 Robinson, J. and Godbey, G. (1999). *Time for life: The surprising ways Americans use their time* (Rev. ed.) University Park, PA: Penn State Press.

17 *Redbook* survey. (1993). Cited in M. Landsberg, In the footsteps of Supermom: Here's the new improved dad. The Associated Press, *Centre Daily Times,* June 20. State College, PA, June 20.

18 Wells, R. (2002, March 8). Workplace trends. Citing American Society of Training and Development Future Search conference, June, 2001, Chicago, Illinois.

19 Karoly, L. A. and Panis, C. W. A. (2004). *The 21st century at work: Forces shaping the future workforce and workplace in the United States* (MG-164-DOL). Arlington, VA: RAND Labor and Population. Retrieved August 14, 2007, from http://www.rand.org/pubs/research_briefs/RB5070/index1.htm

20 Blinder, A. (2006). Offshoring: The next industrial revolution. *Foreign Affairs, 85*(2), 118.

21 Swanbrow, D. (2006, August 14). *Early retirement: Is it better to spend it at work or at play?* Retrieved August 15, 2007, from University Record Online at http://www.umich.edu/~urecord/0506/Aug14_06/18.shtml

22 Clarke, P. (2006, August). Cited by Swanbrow, D., *Early retirement: Is it better to spend it at work or at play?* Retrieved August 15, 2007, from University Record Online at http://www.umich.edu/~urecord/0506/Aug14_06/18.shtml

23 ibid.

24 Cooper, R. (1998). Cited in D. Bollier, *Work and future society: Where are the economy and technology taking us? A report to the Aspen Institute's domestic strategy group* (p. 5). Washington, DC: The Aspen Institute.

25 Schramm, J. (2006). *SHRM workplace forecast.* Alexandria, VA: Society for Human Resource Management. Retrieved October 11, 2007, from http://www.shrm.org/trends/061606WorkplaceForecast.pdf

26 Drucker, P. (1997). Quoted by R. Lenzner and S. Johnson in "Seeing things as they really are." *Forbes Magazine,* March 10, 44.

27 ibid. (p. 45)

28 ibid. (p. 109)

29 Handy, C. (1990). *The age of unreason.* Boston, MA: Harvard Business School Press.

30 Drucker, P. (1997)

31 Bureau of Labor Statistics. (2007). *BLS releases 2004–2014 employment projections.* Washington, DC: Author. Retrieved November 21, 2007, from ftp://ftp.bls.gov/pub/news.release/ecopro.txt

32 Bollier, D. (1998). *Work and future society: Where are the economy and technology taking us? A report to the Aspen Institute's domestic strategy group* (p. 38). Washington, DC: The Aspen Institute.

33 Bureau of Labor Statistics. (2007). *Occupational Outlook Handbook,* Table 1. Washington, DC: Author. Retrieved October 11, 2007, from http://www.bls.gov/news.release/ooh.t01.htm

34 Bureau of Labor Statistics. (2007). *Occupational Outlook Handbook,* Table 2. Washington, DC: Author. Retrieved October 11, 2007, from http://www.bls.gov/news.release/ooh.t02.htm

35 Parker (1972)

Spending Money for Leisure: The Best Things in Life Are Free (or Fee)

Today, leisure costs money—almost one fifth of total household expenditures:

> As household incomes have grown during the last 26 years, the proportion of spending on some nonessential items has increased. Spending on food and nonalcoholic drink, as a percentage of total expenditure, has reduced from 25 percent in 1976 to 16 percent in 2002–03. Over the same period spending on leisure goods and services has increased from 10 percent to 18 percent. Spending on transport also increased over this period, from 13 percent to 18 percent, reflecting changing patterns in car ownership and the volume of travel undertaken. There have also been notable increases in spending on telephone communication.[1]

Leisure doesn't have to cost money. Children's games—hopscotch, climbing trees, running—cost little or nothing. So, too, do leisure activities such as contemplation, political dialogue, writing poetry, voluntary community service, and other activities the ancient Greeks considered to be leisure.

Hobos who rode the rails to wherever the trains took them had leisure but no money, and even if they stole, it was usually just something to keep them going to the next place. When most people long for leisure, De Grazia stated, what they really want is free time with ease and abundance.[2] What most of us want costs money, however, and money costs us work, which in turn costs us time. (Exercise 6.1 at the end of this chapter asks you to consider activities without financial cost.)

In many ways, leisure emerged in the modern world due to commercial enterprises:

> The energy of entrepreneurs, assisted by advertising, was an important influence…on leisure in general. Hence a curious and apparently contradictory situation: not so much the commercialization of leisure as the discovery of leisure, thanks to commerce. Beginning in the eighteenth century with magazines, coffeehouses, and music rooms, and continuing throughout the nineteenth century, with professional sports and holiday travel, the modern idea of personal leisure emerged at the same time as the business of leisure. The first could not have happened without the second.[3]

Personal leisure & Business leisure

Modern leisure was, in some senses, brought about to the extent to which people were offered opportunities to use it in ways that had mass appeal. The commercial sector supplied such opportunities far more than government, church or other institutions.

> Look, I like having money and the things I want to do during my free time cost money—sometimes lots of money. Jen couldn't be more different. She's happy hiking in the woods, watching birds, visiting friends and having herbal tea or something. I like to shop, every new style, every new version of a product. If a plasma TV comes out with a 60-inch screen, I have to have it or I'm not happy.

How Much Money Is Spent for Leisure?

It is difficult to determine how much money we spend for leisure. Many things we buy have some connection to our work as well as to our leisure. I might, for instance, buy a sports car to drive to work as well as to drive in road rallies during my leisure. Some "sports" clothing is also worn to work. The entertainment of business clients may be partly a leisure experience as well as work. Another reason for uncertainty about how much money we spend for leisure is that many expenditures are illegal and thus are never reported. We can only estimate how much money people spend on prostitution, drugs, or gambling because much of such behavior is illegal. (It may be argued, however, that compulsive drug use or gambling doesn't represent leisure behavior at all.)

Finally, it's tough to estimate what part of government expenditures go to further leisure activity. What part of the expenditures of the U.S. Forest Service, for instance, is counted as a leisure expenditure? In spite of these difficulties, we can obtain a reasonable estimation of your own leisure spending and get a rough estimation of leisure spending in the United States. In Exercise 6.2 at the end of this chapter, you will obtain some idea of your own leisure-related spending patterns.

While it is difficult to precisely determine how much is spent for leisure, if one examines the "favorite" leisure activities of the American public, it becomes clear that most involve spending lots of money.

The Scope of Leisure Spending

The Department of Commerce, which measures consumer spending, defines recreation spending to include home electronics, radio and television, music, entertainment, sporting goods, amusements, home gardening, toys, books and magazines, and recreation equipment like boats, motor homes, and bicycles. Measured in this limited way, spending on recreation has increased from $209.2 billion in 1990 to $702.4 billion in 2004—an increase of $412.2 billion.[4]

In studies of the economic impact of some specific forms of recreation, such as hunting, fishing, bird-watching, and other wildlife-related recreation, a national study found that participants spent $120.1 billion in pursuit of these pastimes and supported hundreds of thousands of jobs.[5] After losing ground in the early 1990s, wildlife-related activities, such as bird-watching and photography, increased 13 percent over the last decade. Wildlife watchers' spending also increased 19 percent, from 37.5 billion in 1996 to 44.7 billion in 2006.[6]

The majority of leisure spending, of course, is not measured in the previous statistics. For example, of the $458 billion consumers spent on transportation in 1990, more than one third involved leisure travel.[7] About a third of all automobile vehicle miles are for recreation trips while 60 percent of air passengers are on leisure, not business, trips. Because travel and tourism is a $3 trillion a year industry worldwide, with revenues of over $600 billion in the United States, the impact of leisure travel is huge.

If we deduct business travel from estimated spending for tourism and add the portion of leisure spending that occurs at home or in the local community, one gets a leisure spending figure in the neighborhood of one trillion dollars.[8]

Most of this increase is due to the fact that the economy has consistently grown over the last 50 years, as evidenced by the increase in GDP and per capita GDP over time:

> If similar arguments are used, considerable portions of consumer spending on housing, clothing, food, and education can be classified as leisure spending. Add all of this up and leisure easily accounts for over one trillion dollars or about a third of all consumer spending. In an economy driven primarily by consumer spending, this makes leisure America's number one economic activity.[9]

Since 1948, real GDP has grown at an average rate of 3.1 percent while real per capita GDP has grown at almost 2 percent per year. These increases have allowed individuals to buy better quality goods and services and also to change their definition of what is "necessary." As this has happened, a higher percentage of individual income has become "disposable." That is, income which need not be devoted to necessities such as food, clothing and shelter.

This trend is also evident in many other developed and developing nations. In South Korea, for example, annual leisure spending has risen to an average of US$1,047 per adult.[10] Trips and outings account for over half of this amount, with about 15 percent spent on improvement activities and less than 6 percent on cultural activities. It is expected that this amount will increase, because Korea has recently implemented a five-day workweek. About one-half of the population thinks this will increase their spending for leisure and about two-thirds say they plan to take an overseas trip in the future.

In Japan, the most popular leisure activities change little from year to year. They include eating out with family or friends, going for drives or trips during holidays, and taking domestic tourism trips that often include taking a dip in hot springs.[11] Next is karaoke with accompanying visual images, which has taken firm hold as an easy-to-enjoy pastime. "People sing karaoke in bars, in karaoke rooms rented out to groups, and even in their own houses using home karaoke sets." Following

> Everybody wants to play golf in Japan, but only a few can afford it. Outside Tokyo, there are many golf driving ranges which are three or four stories high. Many people practice driving balls out into a field. It must look strange to an American—lots of golf balls flying out of a building and landing in a field with distance markers. We don't have as much land for golf courses as you do—it's very, very expensive to play here. So many of these people hitting golf balls have never actually played on a golf course.

karaoke, renting videos, visiting theme parks, and participating in Japan's unique leisure business of pachinko (a pinball-like casino game) were most popular. According to the 2001 *White Paper on Leisure*, spending for leisure activities— expenses for eating out, durable goods, culture and entertainment, sports, traveling, and pocket money—was ¥85.57 trillion ($748 billion USD) in 2000. The number of domestic sightseeing trips involving overnight stays during 2000 was estimated at about 193 million, or an average of 1.5 trips per person, almost the same as the previous year. Such trips are estimated to have cost a total of ¥8.7 trillion ($76 million USD), or about ¥57,500 ($502 USD) per person.

As many countries modernize, leisure becomes a significant part of the economy.

Leisure-Related Jobs

While a comprehensive count of leisure industry jobs is hard to find, there are some leisure-related jobs in every industry, including defense. Crandall claimed that travel and tourism employs nine million people in the United States.[12] There are about 250,000 public sector jobs in federal, state, county and local recreation, park and other leisure agencies. There are nearly two million writers, artists, entertainers and professional athletes. No one has completely sorted out all of the jobs that are linked to leisure and converted these to full-time equivalents. The simplest way to get a total leisure job estimate is to convert leisure spending to jobs.

If about $40,000 in consumer spending generates a job (full-time equivalent), a trillion dollars in leisure spending translates into 25 million jobs—about a quarter of all jobs in 1990. If this isn't enough, figure that every leisure job generates another job in a supporting industry. This ties nearly half of all jobs to leisure.[13]

Depending on which measure used, leisure is between five and twenty times the size of the automobile industry in the United States. In 1990 there were almost twice as many full-time equivalent jobs in lodging establishments alone as in all of businesses, manufacturing, motor vehicles and parts. Leisure industries are generally far more labor-intensive than the auto industry and manufacturing. Ironically, this means that leisure industries provide more jobs.

Thus, Americans' use of leisure provides a huge portion of jobs in our country, although we rarely associate economic well-being with the use of free time.

At first my parents thought it was a terrible idea—my majoring in Recreation, Park and Tourism Management. It sounded funny to them. My Mom said she knew I liked to work with people but she was worried I would never make the big time.

I did my internship with Cleveland Metroparks—really first-rate outfit. Their park system can levy taxes so they have a secure base to operate. Also, people in Cleveland really support parks. When I graduated, I got a job as a recreation supervisor in Dayton. I really liked it although there were a lot of evening meetings to attend—neighborhood groups and such. When Waukegan offered me a job as Assistant Superintendent of Recreation and Parks, I took it. I love it. Good pay, a city car, good benefits—but mainly I'm helping this community.

Waukegan has lots of immigration. There is good cooperation from every group in the city. Brownfields are being reclaimed for retirement housing, a big new park being planned, ethnic festivals with good food. You have to be a bit of a politician to survive, but now I see how the system works. You've got to give and take.

My Mom and Dad visited last week and I took them all over the city. When they left, Mom said she was proud of me. So is Dad. He didn't say so, but I can tell.

Economic Significance of Free Time

The economic significance of leisure goes far beyond measures of spending and jobs. These figures account for spending *on* leisure. Also of economic significance is the fact that most consumer spending occurs *during* free time. A few leading industrialists, Henry Ford among them, long ago understood that if people did not have enough free time to shop, they could not buy up all the new products coming on the market. Holidays and festivals account for large upswings in retail sales, with Christmas sales making or breaking the year for many businesses. It has been suggested that shopping for pleasure has become our most popular leisure activity.[14] Compared to Europeans, Americans spend three to four times as many hours a year shopping. Megamalls cater to leisure shopping today, just as interstate highways stimulated the number one outdoor recreation activity during most of the 1970s—driving for plea- sure. Shopping centers have become a gathering place for teenagers after school, a place for seniors to get exercise, a location for various com- munity events and fairs, and a place to just browse and pass the time.

Shopping centers are not alone in using leisure to sell their products. The vast majority of advertising is directed at us during our favorite leisure pursuits. Try to watch television, listen to the radio, read a maga- zine, watch a rented video, attend a movie or sporting event, or just take a leisurely ride without being interrupted by some commercial message. Businesses sell to us during our leisure and in most cases directly use our interest in leisure to help sell their product.

The More Central Role of Leisure in the Economy

There is every indication that the products and services used during leisure constitute an increasingly important part of our economic well-being. Leisure activity, for instance, has become the primary economic base for many large cities. While cities have traditionally been created around manufacturing, their economies are being transformed in such a way that they are increasingly dependent upon a variety of forms of leisure expression. A great deal of decentralization has taken place both in manufacturing and in the service industries—almost anything can be produced almost anywhere. As the industrial base of cities has eroded, much of their economic well-being is dependent upon diverse forms of leisure expression. Such forms of expression can be seen in urban waterfront redevelopment as well as in the increased emphasis upon and competition for shopping, conventions, tourism, sport, entertainment, dining and drinking, historic preservation, festivals and celebrations, nonvocational adult education, and the fine arts.

Leisure also plays an increasingly important role in efforts at local economic development. Attracting desirable employers to a community today means considerably more than developing industrial parks and providing economic incentives. For many companies, whether or not they decide to expand into or move to a new community depends largely on whether or not the type of employee they need for their company to prosper would want to live in that community. This is sometimes referred to as the "quality of life" issue. If you examine quality of life, however, much of it has to do with leisure (e.g., parks, the arts, sport, entertainment, opportunities for tranquility, the qualities of the natural environment). The extent to which a community possesses or develops these amenities may have a central bearing on its future economic well-being. This realization has caused many communities to regard their recreation, park, and leisure services as an economic investment.

Commercial Leisure Service Organizations

If you think about your own community for a minute, you can probably identify several organizations directly related to recreation and leisure. The leisure service industry is primarily a twentieth century phenomenon that is growing and will continue to grow. These organizations have undergone tremendous structural differentiation during the last few decades and are now often quite specialized. One company, for instance, may manufacture only A-frame houses while another specializes in bowling equipment.

A classification of commercial recreation businesses by Chubb and Chubb[15] appears in Table 6.1. Any attempt to categorize recreation and leisure businesses will quickly become obsolete since new forms of such

Table 6.1 Commercial Recreation Businesses Classification[16]

Shopping Facilities	Food and Drink Services
Conventional stores	Food and beverage stores
Other retailers (e.g., catalog sales, markets)	Fast food establishments
	Cafés and coffeehouses
Participatory Facilities	Restaurants
Dancing establishments	Bars and nightclubs
Sports establishments	Refreshment services at events
Amusement Parks	**Shows, Towers, and Tours**
Traditional	Traveling shows
Theme	Overlooks and tours
Camps, Hotels, and Resorts	**Other**
Campgrounds and marinas	Museums, gardens, and parks
Hotels and boarding houses	Stadiums and racetracks
Self-contained resorts, seasonal	Farms and estates
Spas and beauty resorts	Native peoples' enterprises
Sports resorts	Camps and schools
Travel clubs	
Cruise ships	**Products and Services**
Mobile resources (river, lake, backcountry)	Recreation products
	Professional services
	Rental

businesses are being created every day. Let's look at a few commercial leisure services in a bit more detail.

Resorts

Over one third of all receipts in the lodging industry come from pleasure travel. This situation has not only contributed to the success of well-known resorts such as Sun Valley in Idaho, the Greenbrier in West Virginia, and French Lick Springs Hotel in Indiana, but it has also caused many hotel/motel operators to add to their properties such features as electronic games and pinball centers; tennis, handball, or racquetball courts; fitness rooms; and arrangements with nearby golf courses, ski areas, or theaters. For many urban dwellers, hotels and resorts increasingly are offering specific "programs" or "packages," such as getaway weekends for families. Also flourishing are "singles weekends," where the opportunity to meet members of the opposite sex and participate in various recreation activities is more important than the room itself. Resorts also are managed by the public sector. The

Kentucky State Parks, for instance, operate resort-type parks which have many of the features found in resorts in the private sector. Several other states are now taking this approach. In many other cases, resorts are situated near public lands which are the attraction that draws people to the resort.

Theme Parks

Theme parks, such as Disneyland and Disney World, Busch Gardens, Six Flags Over Texas, and many others, are a fairly recent form of recreation. Theme parks provide several hours to several days of recreation, primarily in the summer, for millions of people. Such parks provide passive entertainment in which customers are seated in a ride or an auditorium. Entertainment and thrill rides are the essence of such parks. They develop one or more themes, and often seek to appeal to all age groups. Restaurants have also carried out this theme concept.

More recently, the participatory or recreation-oriented theme park has grown rapidly. These include parks with waterslides, innertube courses and wave-making swimming pools, and those that offer imaginative playground equipment, such as huge climbing nets, go-carts, bumper boats, and miniature golf.

Theme restaurants, which may combine animated shows, indoor playgrounds, electronic games, gift shops, and oversized television screens, have also grown rapidly. Huge fast-food chains such as McDonald's have already incorporated some of these approaches, such as providing children's playgrounds at selected restaurants.

Theme parks often cannot rely on making a profit by charging admissions for rides, but must sell patrons other products or services. Remaining revenues come from food, gift items, souvenirs, and other merchandise.

Today, theme parks are beginning to provide recreation programming, such as special events, and to institute daily and weekly changes in their operation. They are also increasingly found in countries

> At first, you don't understand where the profit is. At the movies, it's the popcorn, big candy and soft drinks; in most restaurants, it's the alcohol. In lots of theme parks, it's the souvenirs and concessions; for most tour guides, it's the tips; for teaching golf pros, it's the equipment sales. You have to know where the profit is, then you have to milk it.

outside North America. Disney, for example, now has theme parks in France and Japan.

Sport Facilities

Commercial enterprises that offer specialized sport facilities are becoming increasingly popular. For some activities, such as bowling, the commercial sector is almost the sole provider of opportunity while in others, such as tennis, the commercial sector sometimes overlaps the public and private nonprofit sectors or may provide more specialized, elaborate facilities for the true tennis "nut" who is willing and able to pay for superior resources. Such operations may include swimming pools, tennis courts, fee fishing ponds and lakes, hunting preserves, golf courses, marinas, bowling lanes, skateboard centers, billiard parlors, ski centers, hot tub centers and spas, ice-skating rinks, racquetball centers, and many others. In some cases, such as racquetball and aerobic dance, the phenomenal growth of interest brought about a boom in commercial facilities almost overnight.

Many commercial sport centers, which were originally developed around a single activity such as racquetball, have found it to be in their best interest to diversify their offerings with aerobic dance classes, karate lessons, sauna or steam baths, weightlifting, exercise machines, and other equipment or activities. In some cases, this has led to their functioning like a commercial community recreation center. Some sport operations even offer restaurants, cocktail lounges, daycare programs, equipment sales, and related services.

Lifestyle Centers

While shopping malls have always had a leisure component, "lifestyle centers" are beginning to challenge shopping malls. The International Council of Shopping Centers defines a lifestyle center as "an open-air, higher-end, leisure-oriented development of 150,000 to 500,000 square feet that includes a mix of stores from conventional mall tenants to specialty fashion retailers and home-goods outlets. They are also likely to include dining and entertainment options."[17] Such centers represent the reinvention of the mall with more emphasis on leisure activity as well as shopping.

Vacation Homes

Over two million Americans own vacation homes. Many large corporations are involved in recreation real estate, not merely developing the land but also offering the leisure amenities which have become necessary to make such complexes successful. Ski trails, tennis courts, golf courses, swimming pools, and riding stables must be developed as well as boutiques, night clubs, hotels, lodges, and other amenities. Developers typically are not interested in offering these facilities themselves. The object is to raise the value of the surrounding land so that houses or condominiums may be built and sold at a profit. Some well-known recreation real estate developments, such as Sun Valley, Idaho; Sea Pines Plantation, South Carolina; New Seabury on Cape Cod, Massachusetts; and Big Sky in Montana are not nearly as large as those that are currently being planned.

Today, instead of buying a vacation home outright, many people are entering time-sharing arrangements, which guarantee them the use of a house, apartment, or other accommodations for a certain number of days or weeks each year at a specified time. Usually time sharing is done under condominium-type arrangements, with those who buy time owning a portion of the building and the common ground surrounding it and agreeing to pay a monthly fee for maintenance services. Some organizations now act as brokers for those who own a "time share." For a fee, individuals may enter their time at a vacation home into a "bank" of other time-share listings and trade their time share for a vacation somewhere else. Thus, an individual may swap vacation sites

> Yeah, there is tension among the people who come here. At first, everyone just wanted a summer vacation getaway in the Poconos. Then, as their kids grew into teenagers who didn't want to come here, some couples came alone. If they divorced, one or the other would own the place and they wanted to rent it out by the week—usually to loud party animals. When couples got older, they would use the place in winter— that meant snow removal, winterizing the rec center—lots of costs. Now some of them have left New York City or northern New Jersey and are retiring here. They want a supermarket, hospitals, and a year-round community; they don't want any big expenditures for swimming, golf, or skiing. The younger people want to go first-class and have lots of excitement. Yeah, we have some battles here.

from region to region or country to country. Such arrangements are complicated, however, and require that participants develop a good information base before getting involved.

Leisure Components of Business and Commerce

In addition to the previously mentioned forms of commercial recreation, many businesses and commercial ventures may be said to have an important leisure component. Mass media, for instance, such as television, radio and prerecorded music, have transformed our use of leisure in fundamental ways. Television viewing continues to be the most time-consuming form of leisure behavior, and the videorecorder and cable networks revolutionized how television is used and how much it costs.

Gambling also constitutes a huge business. If both legal and illegal forms of gambling are considered, one study concluded it should be considered "the major American business." One out of three Americans gambles at least once a month, and they are more likely to gamble on athletic teams and sporting events than anything else. The widespread involvement of states in lotteries has meant that states now have an ambivalent position with regard to gambling: If it is immoral, why does the state sponsor it? If it is not immoral, why does the state continue to ban many forms of gambling?

While eating food can't always be considered a leisure experience since we must eat to survive,

The wait staff can't really make the meal—but they can screw it up. We eat out a lot, and you can tell the difference between waiters who know what they're doing and those who don't. First, they are unobtrusive. Don't get in the way. Second, they don't rush you. Third, if they don't know something— for instance, if there's chicken stock in the soup or cilantro in the pasta, they find out immediately. Also, they listen to what you say, glance at you as they go past. Lots of diners are pretty impatient these days and wait staff have to keep watching to see if they're needed but not stop by when they're not. It's complicated. The best wait staff are friendly, but not familiar. They also know what they are serving—most don't. When I get a good one—which is rare—I tip them big.

increasingly it appears that eating constitutes a leisure experience. We eat more than we need to for survival purposes; we eat "fun" food and other foods that we select based upon the pleasure of eating them rather than nutrition; we eat in leisure environments; and we eat as part of leisure experiences, such as going on a vacation. Finally, we eat meals with friends and associates as a leisure experience in itself.

One area of life related to leisure in which the economic signifi-cance is underestimated is the arts. Although twenty years ago people spent twice as much on sports as they did on the arts, today there is more spending on the arts than sports—and the gap is increasing. Most spending in the arts continues to be in the private sector.

Even the use of alcohol and other drugs may be considered a lei-sure experience. While some use may constitute addiction, just as over-eating, gambling, or other compulsive behaviors may be thought of as addictions, much of the use of alcohol and other drugs is voluntary and pleasurable.

Leisure as a Commodity

What are we to make of the fact that most of us, during our leisure, are involved in activities that involve spending money either as a necessary condition to participate or as the primary means of leisure expression, such as shopping at the mall? As sociologist John Kelly pointed out, some political theorists begin with a contrast between leisure that is participation in the marketplace and leisure that is part of individual self-definition and self-development or of creating community.[18] Marx, for example, thought the social system could be divided into those who owned and controlled the means of production and those who were required to labor by selling their time for wages: "Since power is in the hands of those who provide investment capital, the prime aim is to yield an adequate return on such investment over a period of time."[19] The entire social system is subservient to this elite group, and the system is directed toward maintaining this power relationship regardless of the consequences. Leisure is a critical dimension in binding the worker to the political system. Since the worker is cut off from any sense of production, production comes to be accepted primarily because it gives access to the marketplace. The things that people can buy are thought to provide pleasure and freedom. Alienated from their work, yet supportive of the system, the worker becomes a consumer of leisure as a means of escape and maintains a false consciousness of the world.

For Max Weber, too, the worker was trapped within an economic system. According to Weber, the drive toward productivity in society trapped the worker in an "iron cage."[20] As the workplace became rationalized, a system of penalties and rewards was instituted which facilitated the economic process. The worker had no escape from these penalties and rewards.

It could be argued, therefore, that the worker had no choice but to accept an economic system which made commodification of leisure happen in very diverse ways. To some, it represents the development of the happy slave whose consciousness about the system is false. To others, it is a sign of economic progress that is the envy of the rest of the world.

Leisure and Materialism

How shall we judge the materialistic lifestyle reflected by the leisure behavior of many of us? While on the one hand we may be distressed by the commercialism of many of our leisure experiences, the overwhelming evidence is that we prefer it that way, although these preferences have been molded by advertising.

The ability of the common person to obtain increasingly higher amounts of disposable income during the last century has triggered multiple revolutions, dealing with expectations as well as with behavior. A primary change has been the ability of the (mythical) average citizen to participate in activities once reserved exclusively for the rich. Many sports and physical recreation activities, such as golf, tennis, sailing, tourism, roller skating, and bicycling, were the almost exclusive province of the rich less than 150 years ago. Bicycles, for instance, cost from $100 to $125 in 1880 and, at that time, that amount of money represented a small fortune.

Diversity of leisure experience is also a consequence of increased discretionary income during the last century. The range of leisure experiences available to us has increased dramatically. Because of this, we are experientially richer than we would be otherwise. My daughters, for instance, have been to Britain on vacation and already have some understanding about how our culture differs from our British neighbors, which could not have been obtained without the trip.

A third benefit has been the quality of certain leisure experiences. If you hear or play the same song on a Martin guitar which you previously heard on an inexpensive one, you can tell the difference. Some high-culture art forms, such as opera, cannot be produced without significant financial investment. But money does not automatically improve the quality of a leisure experience, and a person with very little money can lead a rich leisure life—take Socrates, for example. If we are to delight in the world rather than devour it, then many leisure pursuits are free, or nearly so: singing, walking through a forest, running, writing stories or telling them to children, talking with a friend, watching the moon climb over tall buildings, or just resting.

Our materialistic lifestyle has harmed our leisure experiences in many ways. Our desire for things often makes us live in an unleisurely manner, or trade away opportunities for leisure for more money. Materialism also has sometimes caused us to equate leisure with a time for the consumption of products at the expense of our own imagination and inner resourcefulness. The desire to sell leisure goods and services has led to the creation of artificial needs. Children are sold endless toys on television. Adults become convinced that their tennis game is inadequate without expensive equipment and accessories. Further, those who are poor are often taught to believe that they cannot use their leisure in satisfying ways because of their limited incomes. Leisure products and services may serve to distract us from that which is important, may complicate our lives, and may ruin any chance for inner peace or serenity.

In spite of all this, materialism appeals to most of us and, given a chance, there is considerable evidence that it appeals to much of the rest of the world.

Exercise 6.1

Stop and think about your own recreation and leisure activities for a minute. Do you participate in leisure activities that don't cost any money? Think about this a minute before you answer. List any leisure activities which qualify in the space provided here and be prepared to report them or write them on the board if requested by your instructor.

I participate in the following leisure activities which have no monetary costs:

1.

2.

3.

4.

5.

Exercise 6.2

The purpose of this exercise is to gain a better understanding of your own leisure monetary spending patterns and the relationship of such expenditures to your leisure time and leisure activity patterns, and to compare such information with similar data from other students.

To complete the assignment, refer to the leisure monetary expenditure sheet (p. 169). Each student will be asked to keep a record of his or her leisure monetary expenditures for a one-week period beginning on Monday and ending Sunday. In keeping this record, each student should observe the following rules:

1. Record only those expenditures you actually make during the period or expenditures you agree to make—for example, charging the cost of a pair of skis.

2. Record all items you purchase regardless of whether they are for your own use—for example, record the cost of a toy you bought for your little sister.

3. Do not record the cost of a leisure item that was bought for you—for example, your date pays your way to the movies.

4. Do not "prorate" any expenditure except leisure travel. For example, if you receive a daily newspaper, but have a subscription which you have not paid for during the seven-day period, don't record any portion of it. If you have paid the subscription during the seven-day period, however, record the entire amount. All leisure travel in an automobile you own or have financial responsibility for should be prorated at 48.5¢ per mile traveled.

In regard to expenditure categories, please note the following. Sporting goods and clothing should include all clothing purchases used primarily for a leisure activity, even if there is some limited use for everyday wear (e.g., tennis shoes which you occasionally wear to class). Food should not include any expenditure for your normal breakfast, lunch, and dinner. Only dining out where the meal constitutes a leisure experience and a break from routine and snack food (e.g., soft ice cream, pretzels, hoagies) should be recorded. Licenses and dues refer to any payment you have made to be eligible for participation in a leisure activity (e.g., hunting, ham radio operator) or have paid to become a member of a club which will further your leisure interests (e.g., dues to an outing club). Fees and admissions refer to payment for tickets, cover charges, and other payments you have made to be a spectator or participant in a leisure activity not covered under licenses and dues. Reading refers to all reading matter of your own choosing which you purchased during the seven-day period. Leisure travel and vehicles include all payments for travel that was undertaken by choice during the period and not made necessary by your status as a student or by other obligations. Prorate car travel expenditures at 48.5¢ per mile, and record the amount of bus, train, air, or taxi fare. Also include the cost of any leisure vehicles (e.g., snowmobiles, motorcycles, or other travel vehicles used primarily for leisure activity). Do not include any automobile costs other than the 48.5¢ per mile expenditure.

Sample Leisure Monetary Expenditure Sheet

Expenditure	Mon	Tues	Wed	Thu	Fri	Sat	Sun
Games, toys							
CDs, DVDs, etc.							
Sporting goods, clothes							
Food							
Licenses, dues							
Pets, pet food							
Photos							
Fees, admissions							
Hobbies							
Alcohol, tobacco							
Travel, vacations, vehicles							
Reading							
Other							
Totals							

Exercise 6.3

Tomorrow morning you receive a fax message that your Aunt Mert, whom you met only once as a child, has died. Aunt Mert, somewhat of an eccentric, had more money than anyone knew. She has left you $1 million dollars and has arranged to have the taxes paid on it. The will is uncontested, and the lawyer who has settled matters for dear Aunt Mert wants to know where you want the money deposited. Within a few weeks, the money has been deposited in your bank account and, after some professional advice, invested in government bonds and other no-risk or low-risk ventures.

This change, according to Thorstein Veblen, would inevitably change your use of leisure. That is, you would not be capable of avoiding such a change. Perhaps, however, he was wrong. Try to answer the following questions as honestly as you can. Use your imagination.

1. Would your current leisure activities change? If so, how?

2. Would your style of participation in leisure activities change? If so, how?

3. Is it inevitable that you would increase your material standard of living? Would you buy an expensive car? travel to exotic places? move into a bigger apartment or house?

4. If you did exchange your material standard of living and your use and style of leisure, how do you think your friends would react?

5. Would you, consciously or unconsciously, begin to use your newfound wealth to show that you are somehow different from your friends?

6. Would you do things during your leisure which purposely displayed your wealth?

7. How do you think your friends would react if your leisure patterns changed and your style of participation became such that they could not behave in the same way?

Study Questions

1. Why is it difficult to determine how much money is spent for leisure?

2. Discuss some trends in our use of the mass media.

3. Why is the operation of many forms of commercial recreation more financially risky than other businesses?

4. Is it accurate to say that our leisure behavior reflects a "materialistic" lifestyle? Why or why not?

5. What was your reaction to the results of the monetary spending exercises? Were you surprised? Why or why not?

Endnotes

1 Expenditure on selected items as a percentage of total household expenditure: *Social Trends, 34.* Retrieved June 14, 2007, from www.statistics.gov.uk/STATBASE/ssdataset.asp?vlnk=7479

2 De Grazia, S. (1961). *Of time, work, and leisure* (p. 9). New York, NY: The Twentieth Century Fund.

3 Rybczynski, W. (1991). *Waiting for the weekend.* New York, NY: Penguin Books.

4 U.S. Census Bureau. (2007). Personal consumption expenditures for recreation: 1990–2004. In the *Statistical abstract of the United States 2007: Arts, entertainment and recreation.* (p. 761). Washington, DC: Author.

5 U.S. Fish and Wildlife Service. (2007). *2006 National survey of fishing, hunting, and wildlife-associated recreation: National overview preliminary findings* (p. 4). Washington, DC: Author.

6 U.S. Fish and Wildlife Service (2007, p. 2)

7 Arthur Andersen, LLP. (1996, December). *Macroeconomic impacts of the casino gaming industry.* Washington, DC: American Gaming Association.

8 ibid.

9 ibid.

10 *Consumer Newsletter Survey.* (n.d.). Retrieved June 15, 2007, from http://safe.cpb.or.kr/textdata/HOMEPAGE/200205/0600001/2001.html

11 Institute of Free Time Design (2001). Reja hakusho (White Paper on Leisure), and Ministry of Land, Infrastructure, and Transport (2001) Kanko hakusho (White Paper on Tourism). Tokyo.

12 Academy of Leisure Sciences (developed by D. Stynes). (1993). *Leisure—The new center of the economy.* Denton, TX: Academy of Leisure Sciences.

13 ibid.

14 ibid.

15 Chubb, M. and Chubb, H. (1981). *One third of our time.* New York, NY: John Wiley & Sons.

16 ibid.

17 Kerch, S. (2002, November 1). *Malls getting a run for the money: Upstart retail designs threaten shopping icons.* Retrieved August 31, 2007, from CBS.MarketWatch.com at http://www.marketwatch.com/news/story/malls-dethroned-array-new-shopping/story.aspx?guid=%7B0262B28E-BA93-4474-A779-936C91DF9912%7D

18 Kelly, J. R. (1986). Commodification of leisure: Trend or tract? Revised manuscript for *Loisir et Société,* 12(1), 107–121.

19 Marx, K. (1967). *Capital.* London, UK: Lawrence and Wisharrt.

20 Weber, M. (1958). *The Protestant ethic and the spirit of capitalism.* New York, NY: Charles Scribners Sons.

Holy Days, Holidays, and Celebrations

Religion and leisure have always been related in ways which may not be readily apparent. Before considering these, let's examine a conventional definition of religion:

> Concern over what exists beyond the visible world, differentiated from philosophy in that it operates through faith or intuition rather than reason, and generally including the idea of the existence of a single being, a group of beings, an eternal principle, or a transcendent spiritual entity that has created the world, that governs it, that controls its destinies, or that intervenes occasionally in the natural course of its history as well as the idea that ritual, prayer, spiritual exercises, certain principles of everyday conduct, etc., are expedient, due, or spiritually rewarding or arise naturally out of an inner need as a human response to the belief in such a being, principle, etc. [1]

From this definition, religion is seen as an attempt to make sense of the world in matters which are beyond our observation, proof, or understanding. In this sense we all have religion, since we all have shown concern for what exists beyond the visible world in a number of ways. Each of us has addressed the question "Why?" to the universe. Each of us has also considered the beliefs of a body of people with a similar set of beliefs. Whether or not we are members of an organized religion, we have been influenced by religious beliefs and are likely to have given them serious consideration at some point in our lives.

Similarities Between Leisure and Religion

How we attempt to make sense of the universe and our part in it will shape our leisure values, behavior, and the extent to which we experience leisure as a state of mind. In considering these relationships, perhaps we should begin by examining some ways in which religion and leisure are similar.

Celebration

Of all the links between leisure and religion, the common root of celebration is most important. Religious belief leads to a sense of celebration of the universe and one's place in it, and celebration also springs from religion in more formal ways. Christmas, for instance, celebrates the birth of Christ, although it also serves as a time for celebration not connected with Christianity. "To hold a celebration," stated the Swiss Catholic philosopher Josef Pieper, "means to affirm the basic meaningfulness of the universe and a sense of oneness with it, of inclusion within it."[2] This sense of celebration, then, means that we accept our very lives and our places in the universe with joy. Such a sense of celebration, Pieper believed, is at the heart of true leisure:

> Leisure, it must be clearly understood, is a mental and spiritual attitude—it is not simply the result of external factors, it is not the inevitable result of spare time, a holiday, a weekend or a vacation. It is in the first place, an attitude of the mind, a condition of the soul....[3]

Leisure occurs, in other words, only when and if we are capable of spiritual celebration. We cannot "force" leisure to happen any more than we can force ourselves to have religious faith. The celebration which is necessary for leisure and religious expression can't be brought about by "working" at it. For example, think of those times when you have gone out to celebrate, even planned and prepared for it carefully, but not found such a feeling within yourself. The most careful planning for a party, the most frantic fun-seeking, according to Pieper, will not automatically result in leisure. At certain times, and in some lives, the ability to accept and celebrate our lives in the greater scheme of things is simply lacking. Leisure, according to this conceptualization, is something that occurs from the inside out. Pieper believed that we cannot "force" this sense of celebration to occur; we cannot experience leisure just because we wish to. The state of leisure, however, is more likely to be attained by those who are quietly contemplative, those who are open to experience. Individuals who quietly observe what the world has to teach them are more likely to obtain leisure—not because they gain power over the world, but because they delight in it.

> *It was an amazing thing. We were at the football game. Did a little tailgating but nothing crazy. The stands were packed. It was twilight and the sky was beautiful over the stadium— We were doing that silly cheer—We Are.... and I started thinking: We are a team but also a university, a town, a country, a world floating in the air, a universe—we are everything— and the cheer was more like a prayer that I'm happy to be alive. Does that make any sense? No? Well, I guess it doesn't have to.*

Free Will

Both religious belief and practice and leisure behavior and values spring from the individual will. As Charles Brightbill has stated, "Each places us at the center of our own destiny and each recognizes the supreme worth of the individual."[4] In matters of religious faith as well as the use of leisure, there are no experts. While some individuals may study religion or leisure behavior all their lives, they cannot determine what you should believe or how you should use your leisure. You cannot be advised successfully as to what you should put your faith in, or how your leisure should be spent. This is not to say that our religious beliefs and leisure values and behavior are not influenced by many different forces in society, but only that without individual acceptance or selection neither religion nor leisure come about. A person cannot be forced to have faith any more than he or she can be forced to engage in pleasurable activity voluntarily.

> *My parents pushed and pushed me to take Catholicism seriously. I just couldn't. It wasn't for me. We had fights about it. For awhile, I would just go to Mass and keep quiet but finally, at sixteen, I told them I wasn't going anymore. They accepted that but my Mom took it as a personal failure on her part. Now, at 35, for whatever reason, I find myself drawn to the Church. Most of my friends aren't into religion, so I go by myself. It's really not like my Mom is pulling my strings or anything. I want to do this—I'm kind of amazed.*

Integration

Religion and leisure, in a broad sense, are both integrative and inclusive. Gordon Dahl has referred to leisure as "man's synthesizing factor in a component civilization."[5] Leisure can provide an opportunity to express the whole self rather than only one part or facet of the self. Leisure activity may also serve the same integrative function as religion. Recreation, which is often used as a synonym for leisure, may be considered as "re-creation," a therapeutic process of repairing the wear and tear resulting from paid and unpaid work and its process. Thus, by recreation we mean to restore, to reestablish, to return to an original or ideal state. In other words, recreation may serve to make us whole again.

In some cases, we may not believe that a recreation or leisure activity can be integrative because we are often taught that such activities are secondary in importance. It is individual faith and perception, however, that determine such things rather than the characteristics of the specific activity. Recently, for instance, a man visited me who was interested in finding ways to make tennis more accessible to older people who had never played before. The man, who was in his sixties himself, had been an excellent player all his life but was now hesitant to devote his energies to a game when there were so many "serious" problems in the world. After giving the matter much thought, however, he concluded any activity can be a mechanism that gives meaning to a person's life or serves as an integrating mechanism. What is important, in the end, is "faith" in the activity.

Certainly those who have found a sense of wholeness or inte-

> I'm 74. I have high blood pressure, arthritis in my knees and hands— actually almost everywhere. My husband died three years ago. I'm just beginning to realize I'll never get over it. Thank God I've got this garden. I'm using raised beds so I don't have to bend so far. Also, sometimes I take this little stool out to sit on while I'm weeding. There is still something magic about this. Putting little dry seeds into the ground and then, after nothing more than watering and the soil warming, a tiny plant emerges and then it grows and flowers. Then you get a vegetable or, if it's broccoli, you can eat the flowers before they blossom. Did you ever read Dylan Thomas? You should. He wrote this line: "The force that through the green fuse drives the flower drives my green age." I can't improve on that. When I'm in the garden, the world makes sense and is worth living in.

gration in specific recreation or leisure activities exhibit an attitude toward the activity that could easily be identified as religious. Many people "believe" in camping or rock climbing or gardening or smoking pot as an integrating experience which transcends everyday life and is worthy of celebration.

Personal Well-Being and Self-Realization

Both religion and leisure also express the desire for personal well-being and self-realization if we make certain assumptions. Leisure here is considered as a state of mind or as the opportunity to engage in worthwhile activities. Its function is that of personal development. In our present society, which contains increasing numbers of people who are concerned with how leisure is spent, religious thinkers of many faiths tend to accept free time as a period of potential spiritual growth. The spirit of leisure, according to Robert Lee, is the spirit of learning, or self-cultivation. "Leisure is the occasion for the development of broader and deeper perspective," Lee wrote, "and for renewing the body, mind and spirit…. leisure provides the occasion for learning and freedom for growth and expression, for rest and restoration, for rediscovering life in it entirety."[6] Such a conception of leisure brings it close to a conception of the religious life in both its active and contemplative aspects.

Search for the Authentic

A basic part of religious expression, particularly in modern societies, is the search for what is real or authen-

China interests me greatly. Both Mary and I started reading about China for no particular reason other than interest. Then we read some Confucius because you can't understand China unless you know the thinking of Confucius. Finally, we decided we were going to plan a trip there. Of course, you can't see China in one trip. The first trip was mostly Shanghai and then down to Hang Zhou. The Chinese say: Above is heaven, below is Hang Zhou. It's a lovely city with a lake and big trees. We have started to appreciate the complexity of their food and just how differently they think.

On our next trip, we will be a little more adventurous. We will get to the western part of the country— Yunan Province. Conditions are pretty primitive and it won't exactly be a fun trip but we are starting to understand one of the oldest cultures in the world. In some way, understanding more about China is changing both of us. We maybe have a little more perspective about the world— and our lives.

tic. While we may think of "modern" societies in terms of advanced urbanization, expanded literacy, generalized healthcare, rationalized work arrangements, geographic and economic mobility, and the emergence of powerful nation states, the underlying idea of "modernity" is a "mentality that sets modern society in opposition both to its own past and to those societies of the present that are premodern or underdeveloped."[7] These underdeveloped societies and our own country's past are viewed as being more real, more authentic than our own. This belief that the real and authentic are found elsewhere or in other times where life is purer and simpler is part of a unifying consciousness of individuals in modern societies. Because

> Sometimes I envy people who live in places that seem a little more—real. Where I live is all malls, big box stores, McMansions and highways—but there's nowhere to go that seems very authentic. When I was in the old part of Tampa and saw the Cuban men sitting in the sun playing dominoes—or when I was in a diner in Homer, New York, where the locals all gather and shoot the breeze over coffee and pie—it's just different. How do you get a real life? I guess, for openers, you don't live in a housing development. Maybe it's just romantic thinking on my part. I mean, I want to go where there are no cars, but I would plan to get there in a car.

of this, according to MacCannell, the expansion of modern society is linked to modern mass leisure, especially international tourism and sightseeing. The citizens of modern societies may use leisure expression, particularly tourism, to search for the real: "…the religious impulse to go beyond one's fellow man can be found not merely in our work ethic… but in some of our leisure acts as well."[8]

Ritual

Both religious expression and many forms of leisure behavior involve ritual. Ritual may be defined as a "perfunctory, conventionalized act through which an individual portrays his respect and regard for some object of ultimate value to its stand in."[9] Most of the rituals of formal religion came from the premodern era, but many of the rituals we express through leisure are modern. Certainly many forms of tourism, such as making a "ritual" visit to the Statue of Liberty in New York City or to Westminster Cathedral in London, constitute ritual. So, too, do we

There are four of us. We're all university professors or retired from it—The Doggies. Each of us has a dog name. I'm Big Dog. We have been doing this for about eighteen years now. We meet in June for about four days. We have a pool tournament, pretend we can cook, drink beer, lots of kidding and guy humor. We have doggie shirts and masks and a lot of other paraphernalia. We drove through town with our doggie masks on and thought we were very clever. Dan wore his doggie mask while getting off the plane but, since 9/11, that kind of stuff is out. Winning the tournament is important but the rituals of the four days, setting the tournament rules, exchanging presents, and having one unexpected event planned—last year we had a string quartet playing Vivaldi in the garage—that's why we do it.

find ritual in athletic team mascots, the ceremonial aspects of karate, or the crowning of Miss America.

Holy Days and Holidays

Special days of celebration are nothing new. They are found in all cultures and do not always have a religious basis. In 321 AD, for instance, Constantine the Great ordered Sunday to be a public holiday, but not in reference to Christianity.[10] While some holidays originated as religious ceremonies, others came about as festivals celebrating spring or the harvest. In primitive cultures, it was believed that gods manifested themselves in many ways through the weather, or the forces of nature, or the success or failure of crops. Holidays in such cultures were often used to observe various "taboos" or restrictions which, it was believed, would ensure good treatment from the gods or would at least appease their anger.

In medieval Europe, however, holidays became increasingly associated with religion. The Catholic Church declared about one day in three to be a holy day of some kind, but many of those days which honored a saint were abandoned after the Reformation. As civilization became more complex and more urbanized, empires arose and, along with them, feelings of patriotism and national ties. Holidays then took on the added function of celebrating military victories, honoring military and religious leaders, or marking important events in the development of the nation. In urban areas, holidays began generally to be less a celebration of a specific event and more a termination of work and an opportunity to play.

In Europe during the eighteenth century, while the workweek ended on Saturday evening, there were a variety of holiday periods which were observed. In England, for instance, work was halted to partake in the annual feasts of Christmas, New Year and Whitsuntide (the days following the seventh Sunday after Easter). While everyone observed such holidays, the period of observation varied from town to town. Work might stop for a few days or a few weeks.[11] Villages also observed their own festivals and wakes, involving mainly sport, dancing and other public amusement. There were also communal holidays with special events such as prize-fights, horse races, and other competitions. Additionally, when circuses came through town or fairs were held, work generally stopped.

There was also, for some men, a holiday called "Saint Monday." This was the custom of staying away from work on Monday that existed not only in England but also in France, Sweden, Belgium and elsewhere. Perhaps as a reaction against the loss of medieval saints' days due to changing rules of employers and the Protestant Reformation, many workers, in effect, created their own holiday. Saint Monday was also a way that those who remained drunk through Sunday could have a day to sober up. By the end of the eighteenth century, heavy-drinking workers often stayed drunk for days at a time, sometimes working no more than four days a week. Part of the Saint Monday tradition was a reaction against the longer workdays demanded by factory owners. Because of the widespread observance of Saint Monday, most sporting events such as cricket matches, prize-fighting, animal baiting, and horse races took place on Monday since the organizers of such events knew most workers would take this day off.[12] Attendance at botanical gardens and museums also were at their peak on Monday. This "small holiday" helped prepare society for the two-day weekend. It also helped to popularize tourism because it provided two days in a row for travel rather than one.

Holidays in the United States and Canada evolved from a variety of sources and have changed greatly in their meanings and how they are celebrated. Such holidays may be considered either patriotic (e.g., Washington's Birthday in the United States, Dominion Day in Canada), seasonal (e.g., New Year's Day), or religious (e.g., Christmas). In addition, there are unofficial holidays, such as Super Bowl Sunday and local or regional holidays which are sometimes officially recognized. The first day of deer hunting season is also a holiday in some parts of rural America—public school is closed, and many employers don't expect their employees to report for work. Think about your own region and local area for a minute. Are there any holidays unique to them? How do you suppose they came about?

For many holidays in North America, the occasion is increasingly marked by celebrations which have little relation to the origins of the holiday. There is also the feeling that Americans don't give sufficient attention to such holidays, but this is by no means new. In 1876, President Grover Cleveland observed, "The American people are but little given to the observance of public holidays."[13] While many people feel that Christmas is much too devoted to Santa Claus, presents, and parties; Thanksgiving to eating; and New Year's Eve to drinking, a holiday in a democracy provides the choice of celebrating or not as well as choosing how one will celebrate. The observance of holidays in the United States also varies tremendously because of our diverse ethnic and experiential backgrounds. It is not surprising that Leif Ericson Day (October 9) is more likely to be celebrated by Norwegian-Americans than by Italian-Americans, that Rosh Hashanah is a New Year's celebration for those of the Jewish faith but not for others, and that Veterans' Day may mean more to the American Legion or the Veterans of Foreign Wars than to others.

While there are many holidays recognized by various groups in our society, Congress has declared nine federal legal public holidays: New Year's Day, Washington's Birthday, Memorial Day, Independence Day, Labor Day, Columbus Day, Veterans' Day, Thanksgiving Day, and Christmas Day. Since January 1971, five of these have been officially celebrated on Mondays (Washington's Birthday, Memorial Day, Labor Day, Columbus Day, and Veterans' Day), thus creating three-day weekends for millions of federal employees and others.

Many holidays have been transformed from their original significance as religious holy days to holidays with little or no religious meaning. Groundhog Day (February 2), for instance, is the American version of Candlemas Day, which originated in Europe as a religious observance centered around the purification of the Virgin Mary. The belief that if Candlemas Day were sunny, winter would continue, was somehow brought to this country and changed to involve the shadow of a groundhog.[14]

Major holidays and celebrations have also shifted in importance and meaning. Prior to the 1900s, civic festivals and the Fourth of July were more important occasions for celebration and strong emotion than "family" holidays such as Thanksgiving or Christmas. Christmas was more a time for attending parties and dances than for celebrating family solidarity.[15] Only during the twentieth century did the family come to be the center of festive attention.

A number of other national/political holidays have fluctuated in popularity, including the birthday of Martin Luther King. Minor holidays include:

- Inauguration Day (January 20, the day of the President's inauguration)
- National Freedom Day (February 1, celebrating the Emancipation Proclamation)
- Alamo Day (March 6, celebrating the standoff at the Alamo by Davy Crockett's boys)
- Pan American Day (April 14, to foster intercontinental solidarity and cooperation among members of the Organization of American States)
- Patriots' Day (third Monday in April, to celebrate the American Colonies breaking free from the British)
- Loyalty Day (May 1, to stimulate patriotic displays in the United States to counter May Day celebrations in the Soviet Union)
- Cinco de Mayo (May 5, to commemorate the efforts of Mexicans to retain their national independence)
- Armed Forces Day (third Saturday in May, a chance for the Armed Forces to display their readiness)
- Bunker Hill Day (June 17, a celebration of the American colonists' victory in that famous battle)
- Citizenship Day (September 17, a celebration of the immigration of foreign citizens to the United States)
- American Indian Day (fourth Friday in September, in honor of Native Americans)
- United Nations Day (October 24, to honor the United Nations)

- Election Day (Tuesday after first Monday in November, a day for casting a vote)

- Bill of Rights Day (December 15, a day to reaffirm our national purpose, proclaimed by President Franklin Roosevelt in 1941), and

- Forefathers' Day (December 21, in celebration of our founding fathers)

In addition to these holidays, manufacturers and special-interest groups have promoted a huge number of "special" days, such as National Cheese Day or Aviation Day.

As the population of many countries changes due to immigration, holidays seem less and less likely to be nationally celebrated. Cinco de Mayo means more to a Mexican-American than a Vietnamese-American. Muslims and Jews each have their own holy days. As populations within a country become more diverse, such holidays and holy days are likely to be celebrated only by small portions of the society.

Thus as the population of the United States grows more diverse, determining what days are "holidays" will become more difficult. For Muslims, the month of Ramadan is all-important but Cinco de Mayo is not. The celebration of patriotic holidays will become more difficult as Indians, Filipinos, and Russians migrate to the United States. Chinese-Americans have different ideas about when the "New Year" occurs and how it should be celebrated. Like other parts of U.S. culture, holidays will become increasingly "decentralized."

Sunday or the Sabbath

Sunday, in our society, serves as a day of Christian religious observance and also as a day of leisure for most of us. However, the concept of a special day for rest and religious observance is a tradition that predates Christianity. The Jewish Sabbath evolved as a special day, to be set aside from other days as a sign of the covenant between God and Israel. No work was to be done on that day, travel and business transactions were not allowed, and even food had to be prepared on the preceding day. Even though these regulations were restrictive, the Jews regarded the

Sabbath with joy and pleasure.[16] This holiday affirmed Israel's faith in God.

For early Christians, the origin of Sunday was obvious; Sunday, the first day of the week, was the day of Christ's resurrection from the dead. For some time, however, these Christians continued to celebrate the Jewish Sabbath too. The actual designation of Sunday as a day of worship and rest evolved gradually. The New Testament in no way provided any authority for such a designation, nor is there any indication that either Jesus or the early Christian leaders thought of Sunday as a continuation of the Jewish Sabbath into the next day. It was not until the Puritan movement of the sixteenth century that the Lord's Day began to be referred to by Christians as the Sabbath, and laws were enacted to make it a day of rest, quiet, and religious observance.

During the fifteenth century, the disagreement between Puritans and non-Puritans concerning appropriate behavior on Sunday grew quite bitter in England. Compulsory church attendance was the rule in early seventeenth century England, and it was not of the Puritans' doing. However, the rest of the day was given over to sports, dancing, and other forms of recreation. The Puritans objected to this, believing that no recreation whatsoever was appropriate on Sunday. Such attitudes were based upon the Old Testament interpretation of the Sabbath which King James challenged by issuing a pronouncement, the *Book of Sports*, in 1618. It was the King's pleasure, the pronouncement stated:

> That after the end of Divine Worship, our good people not be disturbed, letted or discouraged from any lawful Recreation, such as dancing, either men or women, archeries for men, leaping, vaulting, or other harmless Recreation, nor from having of May-games, Whitson Ales, and Morris dances, and the setting up of Maypoles and other sports therewith....[17]

Unlawful pastimes, however, such as bull- or bear-baiting, were prohibited, as were "interludes."

The bitterness of the dispute in England concerning Sunday recreation was so great that, when the Puritans took power, they had the *Book of Sports* burned by the public hangman. The Puritans took this attitude to America and continued to try to prohibit all forms of recreation on Sunday. While attitudes toward Sunday recreation slowly changed, the issue was widely debated; change did not come without bitter fighting. Rural areas were slower to change their customs than urban ones. In South Carolina, for instance, church attendance was compulsory until 1885. While some members of the clergy began to support Sunday recreation, others preached against it: "You cannot serve God and skylark on a bicycle," one minister told his congregation.[18] A number of "blue laws" were enacted by local governments, which specifically forbade individuals from participating in a wide range of leisure activities; made it illegal for movie theaters, dance halls, taverns, and other places of amusement to open; and tried to enforce a general halt to pleasure-seeking on Sundays.

In spite of such ordinances, Sunday gradually became a day devoted to social and recreational activities as well as to worship. As commercial recreation opportunities expanded, Sunday blue laws began to have a negative effect on the local economy as well as on people's enjoyment. Today, although a few blue laws continue to exist, many traditions of Sunday have been lost in both the twenty-four hour economy and a more diverse society. The extent to which Sunday is differentiated from other days varies. While in some modern nations, such as Holland, a movement is underway to reinstitute Sunday as a time to "shut down the system," such movements will fight an uphill battle. As the pace of life has sped up and as a higher percentage of the population enters the labor force, however, Sunday is increasingly a day for catching up on shopping and household maintenance.

Growing up in a little town, Sunday shut the whole system down. Stores weren't open; Main Street was almost empty; the majority of people went to church. Even the drug store was shut but it had a pharmacist "on call," in case someone needed an emergency prescription.

Sunday felt different too. You knew it was Sunday, not Saturday. Sometimes we took a ride in the family car and found the one place that was open—a dairy that sold great ice cream—butter brickle for me!

Gradually Sunday opened up to shopping, the malls began to encroach on the privacy of the day, then the downtown stores fought back and opened at 1 p.m., then noon, then 11:00 a.m.— Sunday was no longer special. Church attendance dropped off. TV began kind of reorganizing Sunday. Sunday basically disappeared. Something really important was lost. Calling a halt to life for one day a week seemed to be a great thing—and I'm not even religious.

Leisure and Organized Religion

Organized religion shapes leisure behavior in a number of ways. The ideals and beliefs of a religion define, to some extent, the relation of humans to a supreme being and delineate those human qualities and behavior which are worthy and those which are sinful. All these beliefs will shape the leisure values and behavior of those who are followers of the religion and, often, those who are not. Additionally, organized religion usually addresses the question of what forms of pleasure are worthwhile. Since, in the United States, six out of ten adults are members of an organized religion, the potential for religion to shape leisure is great.

Established religions are also able to exert a restrictive influence on how the general public is able to spend its leisure, although this influence is generally less today than it was in the past. One example is restrictive Sunday legislation, which has affected people in many countries during many periods in history. In England, for instance, the Lord's Day Observance Act of 1780, drawn up by the Bishop of London, severely limited Sunday trade.[19] All places of commercial entertainment were to be closed. Subsequent legislation closed public houses on Sunday and prohibited the sale of newspapers, tobacco, and even implements for shaving.

A very different example of religious influence on leisure patterns may be seen in the Mexican institution of bullfighting. Kluckholn and Strodtbeck have described the typical Mexican's passive dependence upon the saints and his or her submissive and accepting attitude toward the supernatural.[20] These attitudes are reflected in many of their leisure pursuits, such as bullfighting. The domination of the bull by the matador and the submissive behavior the matador expects from his assistants may be said to symbolize the attitudes of fatalism and submission.

In America and Europe, the Church's traditional attitude toward games has been one of condemning them outright, or at least controlling them, with the strongest opposition usually reserved for games of chance. Kaplan argued that this is because, in such games, one's luck is uncontrollable whereas, according to the church, God is not at all fickle.[21] He establishes an order with cause and effect. Religious belief, based upon reward for good behavior and punishment for bad, opposes a view of life in which luck is a powerful factor.

In specific terms, then, organized religious institutions have sought to ban some forms of leisure behavior and to promote others. While it is impossible to generalize about these forms of leisure behavior, those activities which historically have been condemned most widely include: (1) theatrical productions, (2) consumption of alcohol and other drugs, (3) games of chance and gambling, (4) dancing, (5) sexually related activity, (6) idleness, and (7) violence or cruelty.

The Puritans who settled in America were opposed to most forms of recreation, and even today not all of their attitudes have disappeared. We have come to use the term *puritanical* to describe someone who is against pleasure, or one who is a prude. The Puritan attitude toward leisure and recreation actually came about for a number of reasons. True spiritual values, the Puritans believed, could only be realized if one refused the pleasures of the world.

There was also a reflection of class conflict in the behavior of the Puritans. These people, who were from the lower classes, resented the pleasures of the rich, which they could not afford. Resentment towards the privileged "leisure class" easily led to a condemnation of the pleasures of which they partook. As Dulles has pointed out, "These two influences, spiritual reform and economic envy, can never be disentangled."[22] Additionally, the Puritans who settled in New England had little time for pleasure, as they were struggling to exist in a hostile land. Their work ethic and their disdain for pleasure and idleness were, to some extent, necessary to ensure survival. Those who wish to improve themselves economically often take on some of the traits we associate with Puritanism. The Chinese, under Mao, adopted many behaviors that were similar to Puritanism in order to make the "great leap forward" economically. Interestingly, in times of economic plenty, Puritanism has nearly always declined.

Many of the Puritans who settled in North America believed in original sin. Believing that mankind was inherently sinful, and maintaining an Old Testament attitude toward sin, they came to the logical conclusion that man was in need of punishment. They believed that humans were not worthy of pleasure. Belief in original sin may have been the biggest religious barrier to the pleasurable use of leisure in North America and, perhaps, in other countries as well.

Many Purtians also subscribed to the notion of predestination. It was believed to be predetermined at birth that some people would go to heaven while others would not. Those who were among the "elect" would show some sign of their good fortune while on earth—such a sign usually being economic well-being.

It would be incorrect, however, to assume that the Puritans were successful in halting recreation and leisure activity. The rules of conduct were so strict for church members that only 4,000 out of 16,000 arrivals in the Massachusetts Bay Colony belonged to the church. Taverns sprang up in New England, and drinking became an outlet for many. As Dulles has stated, regarding the Massachusetts Bay Colony as being devoid of all amusement ignores the fact that large numbers of its settlers were not sympathetic to Puritanism and could not be convinced to equate pleasure with sin. "Puritanism failed to eradicate the early Americans' natural urge of play. It brought on the inevitable revolt against attempted suppression of human impulses."[23]

While organized religion continued to exert pressure for prohibiting certain forms of recreation and leisure, it also gradually came to promote many forms of such activity. Slowly the church came to understand that objecting to idleness or drinking did little good if the substitute was always more work. Since factory workers were usually working 10 to 12 hours a day, the church's warnings against strong drink and idleness often fell on deaf ears.

Gradually the church began to realize that it could not impose its will upon an increasingly urban population without some accommodation to prevailing conditions. If the church disapproved of commercial recreation, it had to provide some alternatives. As the *Northwestern Christian Advocate* stated: "If amusing young people aids to save them, then the work is fully and gloriously worthy of the church."[24] During the close of the nineteenth century, the churches made increasing provision for recreation and social activities. Libraries, gymnasiums, auditoriums, and other facilities became part of the facilities at churches. Activities such as potluck suppers, strawberry festivals, raffles, charades, fairs, and athletic events have become standard offerings of many churches.

Religious reformers of this era were also responsible for the development of formal organizations "which purported to provide wholesome, moral and character-building experiences that would prevent the evils of the adult world from tempting young people into partaking of sinful pleasures."[25] Organizations such as the Young Men's Christian

Association, Young Women's Christian Association, Young Men's Hebrew Association, Young Women's Hebrew Association, Catholic Youth Organization, Salvation Army, B'nai B'rith, and the Christian Service Brigade/Pioneer Girls are examples of groups that evolved as alternatives to saloons, pool halls, and idleness.

Today, agencies affiliated with major religious orders are among the most active voluntary organizations addressing leisure needs. The "Y," for example, has assumed a large responsibility in many communities for meeting public recreation needs. In a number of smaller cities and towns, it provides the best facilities for indoor sports and games, physical fitness activities, and social and cultural programs. These agencies are more and more inclusive in terms of who may participate.

Leisure Experience as Religion

Much of the dissatisfaction with religious institutions today centers around the great extent to which they have become rational, serious bureaucracies devoid of celebration. Congregations are often bored, and churches have become filled with a commercial spirit. The sense of mystery, so necessary for faith, is gone for many. Ceremony and ritual are sometimes missing, or are mere reflections of past cultures to which we can barely relate. To the extent that spiritual expression is nearly lacking or unsatisfying in existing organized religion, three kinds of alternatives have emerged to try to fill the void.

First has been the return to fundamental Christianity, and to ways of practicing religion associated with former times. If modern religion has lost its way, then for many the solution has been to return to religion as it was practiced in previous times, when it had more meaning. Such religious practice is characterized by a new emphasis upon the importance of faith, a greater dedication to the teachings of Christ, a missionary approach to nonbelievers, and emotional celebrative worship. Along with these beliefs has been an attempt to reemphasize the concept of sin as well as religious joy.

A second approach to finding new meaning in spiritual terms has been widespread interest in new cults, such as Scientology or the Hare Krishna sects. Such groups, which require total dedication from their members, are characterized by secrecy, individual devotion to and dependence upon other members of the group, and personal sacrifice for the goals of the organization. Such behavior may serve to shield the individual from the meaninglessness of society at large.

A third approach in seeking more satisfying spiritual expression is to use some leisure experience or activity as a means of finding satisfaction. While any leisure activity may serve as the means for such spiritual expression, certain activities such as wilderness camping, growing plants, taking drugs, and jogging seem to be more obvious in their contributions to some individuals' spiritual needs. In wilderness camping and other outdoor recreation activities that isolate the individual from others, as opposed to mass outdoor recreation, one may gain, according to Aldo Leopold

> the perception of the natural processes by which the land and the living things upon it have achieved their characteristic forms (evolution) and by which they maintain their existence (ecology).[26]

Another leisure experience which has served as a religious experience for many is jogging. One survey of joggers, for instance, found that over one-half of the respondents reported experiencing a spiritual high while running. Higdon saw the following parallel between the born-again Christian and the "born-again" runner:

> There is the phenomenon of the born-again runner, akin to the born-again Christian; the individual, often middle-aged who might have been active athletically in youth, but then lapsed into sinful ways; eating too much, drinking too much... allowing the body, described by the scriptures as the "temple of the spirit" to degenerate to the point where the temple appeared threatened by destruction (i.e., occluded coronary arteries). When that person decides to run, it is a form of spiritual as well as a physical awakening, a conversion to a new discipline which will result in a rebirth of the spirit.[27]

Running may represent the form by which many practice their religious beliefs. Running itself is for many no less an act of purification than prayer or confession. Running expert George Sheehan has said that the runner's spiritual experience occurs in what he calls the "transpersonal stage" of running. According to Sheehan, this stage often comes after 30 minutes into the run when "meditation becomes contemplation; what has been a measure of things becomes awareness of the sacred."[28] For the jogger, running can become a mystical experience which transports the normal ego into deeper transpersonal spaces. For the transpersonal runner, life may begin to revolve around running, which represents an encounter with the sacred.

In many countries, as diverse as Brazil, Korea and Britain, the game of soccer has many features similar to a religion. A soccer field can possess the aura of a church. Soccer fans, when giving traditional cheers and responses, participate in ritual and ceremony. Soccer not only provides identification with a particular group or nation but also the capacity to generate a wider, more universal sense of shared humanity, or what may be called "the ultimate." Unfortunately, soccer fans sometimes share the tendency, which throughout history has characterized those who are fanatic members of religious organizations, of doing great harm to those whose beliefs are different. In fact, the soccer riot has something in common with a holy war.

Religion, Leisure, and the Emerging Postmodern Culture

The emerging postmodern society is one where truth is anything people can be made to believe. All problems of organizations will therefore have a public relations and image component.

The postmodern era pits not so much those with one set of beliefs against another but believers against nonbelievers. The collapse of belief is all around us. The concept of relative truth and multiple truths means that many who live in modern nations are very different from their ancestors and those in developing nations who willingly kill each other over absolute beliefs about god(s) and the universe.

Amidst the chaos, there is progress toward a future in which people will live free of belief as we have known it, at home in the symbolic universe. We can see, if we look closely, at the ideas and events of the postmodern world, a new sensibility emerging—a way of being that puts the continual creation of reality at the heart of every person's life, at the heart of politics, and at the heart of human evolution.[29]

The modern world has brought us into an awareness of multiple and conflicting belief systems. It has heightened our concern with what is real. There is a growing suspicion that all belief systems are social constructions. The nature of truth is multiple or simply a social construction. This has led us to a kind of freedom which can hardly be thought of as leisure:

> Today we are all "forced to be free" in a way that Rousseau could not have imagined when he coined that famous phrase. We have to make choices from a range of different stories— stories about what the universe is like, about who the good guys and the bad guys are, about who we are—and we also have to make choices about how to make choices. The only thing we lack is the option of not having to make choices—although many of us try hard, and with some success, to conceal that from ourselves.[30]

Thus, scientists and religious fundamentalists may find themselves on the same side—both may have absolute views of what is true. For the majority, a number of things may be true and the basis for deciding what is true cannot be attributed to any single method, belief system or variable. (Historically, the various rationales of recreation movements, of course, were based on absolute belief in what was and was not worthwhile in terms of leisure.)

In the postmodern world, creating image will become critical for organizations in both the public and market sectors. We are entering the postscientific era. No wonder almost all large organizations treat public relations as a critical part of their mission.

The postmodern era corresponds to the "saturated self." As psychologist Kenneth Gergen observed, new technologies have made it possible to sustain relationships—either directly or indirectly—with an ever-expanding range of other persons.[31] This has led to a state of "social saturation" in which the very ways we perceive and characterize ourselves are changed.

Emerging technologies saturate us with the voices of human-kind—both harmonious and alien. As we absorb their varied rhythms and reasons, they become part of us and we of them. Social saturation furnishes us with a multiplicity of incoherent and unrelated languages of the self. For everything we "know to be true" about ourselves, other voices within respond with doubt and even derision. The fragmentation of self-conception corresponds to a multiplicity of incoherent and disconnected relationships. These relationships pull us in myriad directions, inviting us to play such a variety of roles that the very concept of an "authentic self" with knowable characteristics recedes from view. The fully saturated self becomes no self at all.[32]

Thus, the fax machine, call waiting, e-mail, the Web, cell phones, text messaging, improved air travel and other technological changes not only complicate our lives but also put our very identity at risk. In such a situation, as others are incorporated into self-concept, their desires become ours. "...[T]here is an expansion of goals—of 'musts,' 'wants,' and 'needs.'"[33] While our use of time may not be changed by this condition, our sense of the necessary is, with the attendant result of making time psychologically more scarce and the truth more individual.

Postmodern life may make some people more susceptible to cults which offer absolute assurance about what is true, what is real and the nature of god. For others, use of leisure will increasingly be an arena for defining what is real and

> It just seems like there is so much you are supposed to do. Read the labels on everything you buy in the supermarket and then figure out if carbs are really so bad—or maybe complex carbohydrates are a good thing to eat. Do you eat beef when the cattle have been fed sludge and chicken manure? How much should you exercise? What charities are really worthwhile? I get 50 e-mails a day and it sometimes seems like the people who send them are all talking to a different person. I need to find out about how to interview for a job. Should you take birth control pills for more than five years? I just found out about Google Scholar so maybe that's where I'll check it out. There is a whole lot that you need to find out, and I always seem to be behind.

what is important at an individual level. Leisure behavior may become synonymous with religious experience: the making of meaning and the celebration of the unknown.

The Rise of Religious Influence in Developing Nations

While many of the residents of "modern" nations experience "post-moderism," for the rest the world, where the vast majority of people live, both Christianity and Islam have an increasing impact on daily life and both religions are likely to develop a more fundamentalist approach. In the process, leisure activity will likely be more restricted. Jenkins recently explained:

> If we look beyond the liberal West, we see that another Christian revolution, quite different from that being called for in affluent American suburbs and upscale urban parishes, is already in progress.... In the global south (the areas that we often think of primarily as the Third World) huge and growing Christian populations—currently 480 million in Latin America, 360 million in Africa, and 313 million in Asia, compared with 260 million in North America—now make up of what Catholic scholar Walbert Buhlmann has called the Third Church, a form of Christianity as distinct as Protestantism or Orthodoxy, and one that is likely to become dominant in the faith.[34]

While Christianity will be changed, so too will the influence of other religions. Globalization takes place in a post–Cold War era in which "Power is shifting from the long predominant West to non-Western civilizations."[35] Global politics have become multipolar and multicivilizational. Today, the most important countries in the world come from civilizations that are vastly different, and "modernization" of such countries does not mean that they will "Westernize." Although during the last 400 years relations among civilizations "consisted of the subordination of other societies to Western civilization..."[36]—this pattern has been broken:

> The West won the world not by the superiority of its ideas or values or religion (to which few members of other civilizations are converted), but rather by its superiority in applying organized violence. Westerners often forget this fact; non-Westerners do not.[37]

While it is often assumed that English has become the international unifying language, the percentage of the world's people who speak English is declining, constituting about 7.6 percent of the world's population. Indeed, all Western languages combined are spoken by only about one out of five people in the world.

In terms of religion, Christianity accounts for slightly less than 30 percent of the world's people. Islam, which accounts for a bit less than 20 percent of the world's population, will continue to increase in numbers since "…Christianity spreads primarily by conversion, Islam by conversion and reproduction."[38] How various religions react to globalization will be diverse and unpredictable. Additionally, the share of the world's population under the political control of various civilizations will shift so that the long dominant "West" will account for only about 10 percent of the world's citizens. Allegiance of more people may be to the religion into which they were born rather than to the country in which they live. As Table 7.1 shows, the percentage of the world's population under the political control of Hindu, Islamic and Orthodox civilizations is about 40 percent.

Table 7.1 Shares of World Population under the Political Control of Civilizations, 1900 and 2025

	Western	African	Sinic	Hindu	Islamic	Japanese	Latin	Orthodox	Other
1900	44.3	0.4	19.3	0.3	4.2	3.5	3.2	8.5	·16.3
2025	10.1	14.4	21.0	16.9	19.2	1.5	9.2	4.9	2.8

Adapted from Huntington, *The Clash of Civilizations and the Remaking of World Order*, 1996, p. 85

Thus, leisure may be shaped more directly in the many regions of the world where a more fundamentalist Christianity and Islam are practiced, even as the postmodern era in many modern nations means religion plays less of a role. This gap may produce huge disputes about what forms of leisure expression are appropriate and for whom.

To conclude this chapter, you will be asked to examine your leisure activities as they relate to religious experience in Exercise 7.1.

Study Questions

1. What makes celebration a common link between religion and leisure?

2. Give an example of how holy days became a holiday and discuss how the change took place.

3. Why might a soccer riot and a holy war have something in common?

4. How did the tradition of observing Sunday come about? How has its observance changed?

5. What are some major ways in which organized religion shapes leisure behavior in our society?

Exercise 7.1

Write a brief essay on a leisure activity in which you are involved or have been involved which has some elements of religion. Specifically, comment on the extent to which this activity was

(a) characterized by celebration,

(b) undertaken of your own free will,

(c) provided the chance for integration and expression of the whole self,

(d) provided a sense of personal well-being and self-realization,

(e) represented a search for the authentic, and

(f) involved ritual.

Tell why you felt each of these elements was or was not present.

Endnotes

1   Stein, J. (Ed.). (1966). *The Random House dictionary of the English language* (p. 1212). New York, NY: Random House.

2   Pieper, J. (1952). *Leisure: The basis of culture* (pp. 43–45). New York, NY: New American Library.

3   ibid.

4   Brightbill, C. (1960). *The challenge of leisure* (p. 38). Englewood Cliffs, NJ: Prentice-Hall.

5   Dahl, G. (1972). *Work, play, and worship in a leisure-oriented society* (p. 74). Minneapolis, MN: Augsburg Publishing.

6   Lee, R. (1964). *Religion and leisure in America* (p. 33). New York, NY: Abingdon Press.

7   MacCannell, D. (1976). *Tourism: A new theory of the leisure class* (p. 8). New York, NY: Schocken Books.

8   ibid. (p. 10)

9   ibid. (p. 42)

10   Lee (1964, p. 33)

11   Rybczynski, W. (1991). *Waiting for the weekend.* New York, NY: Penguin Books.

12   ibid.

13   Greif, M. (1978). *The holiday book: America's festivals and celebrations.* New York, NY: Universe Books.

14   ibid.

15   Coontz, S. (1991). *The way we never were—American families and the nostalgia trap.* New York, NY: Basic Books.

16   Lee (1964, p. 33)

17   Dulles, F. (1965). *A history of recreation: America learns to play* (p. 151). New York, NY: Appleton-Century-Crofts.

18   ibid.

19   Godbey, G. and Parker, S. (1976). *Leisure studies and services: An overview* (p. 52). Philadelphia, PA: W. B. Saunders.

20   Kluckholn, F. and Strodtbeck, F. (1961). *Variations in value orientations* (p. 235). New York, NY: Row and Peterson.

21   Kaplan, M. (1960). *Leisure in America* (p. 150). New York, NY: John Wiley & Sons.

22   Dulles (1965)

23   ibid. (p. 151)

24   ibid.

25   Farrell, P. (1978). Recreation youth-serving agencies. In G. Godbey (Ed.), *Recreation, park, and leisure services: Foundations, organization, administration* (p. 188). Philadelphia, PA: W. B. Saunders.

26   Leopold, A. (1949). *A sand county almanac* (p. 19). New York, NY: Oxford University Press.

27 Higdon, H. (1978, January). Running and the mind. *Runner's World*, 36.

28 Sheehan, G. (1979, May). Dr. Sheehan on running. *Runner's World*, 35.

29 Anderson, W. T. (1990). *Reality isn't what it used to be* (p. xiii). San Francisco, CA: HarperCollins.

30 Anderson (1990, p. 8)

31 Gergen, K. (1991). *The saturated self — Dilemmas of identity in contemporary life.* New York, NY: Basic Books.

32 ibid. (pp. 6–7)

33 ibid.

34 Jenkins, P. (2002, September). The next Christianity. *Atlantic Monthly*, 290(2), 54.

35 Huntington, S. (1996). *The clash of civilizations and the remaking of world order* (p. 29). New York: Simon and Schuster.

36 ibid. (p. 51)

37 ibid.

38 ibid. (p. 65)

Leisure Throughout the Cycle of Life

A child, given a toy drum for Christmas, may first bang on it for fun, hearing rhythms which delight. She may learn to play a snare drum in a school band, take lessons, purchase a whole set of drums, practice in the garage, form a rock band, then store the drums for a few years after having children. Later in life, she may teach her children to play, play drums in an amateur Dixieland group, learn to play conga drums, and finally, perhaps in a nursing home or with old friends, play a tambourine during a group singing program.

The life journey may be compared to seasons. Childhood is a time of learning and growing, of acquiring competence, accepting protection and absorbing the traditions of one's elders. Children learn much about the world and themselves through play.

Adolescence is marked biologically by female menses and male puberty. It represents what has been called a coming of age, a flaming up, or a ripening. "The coming of age period is also when youths learn to substitute the approval of their friends for that of their parents—a substitute that helps forge a generational identity."[1]

In young adulthood, one launches families and careers, seeks to convert dreams and ideas into reality, and may become a soldier. At this stage, individuals are still caught up in the conflicts and emotional involvements of childhood, but must cope with the demands of family, community and of work. During this stage, much of leisure expression becomes relational—activity whose meaning is tied up with relating to children, spouse, parents, fellow workers, and neighbors. Leisure activity may also become much more planned and organized. As a college student, one might have played racquetball or gone for "power walks" with little advance planning, but after marriage and children such activity may become more limited and carefully planned.

At midlife, individuals feel the first signs of aging and begin to realize they are past their biological prime. In many ways, this phase is the heart of life. Plans are realized, young adults are mentored, and standards are set (or should be) for children. It is a phase of life in which individuals assume dominance within their society. Leisure activity begins to be modified here and, if one is to get a chance to do what they want during their free time, it likely happens now—a trip to China, a boat on the lake, a course in gourmet cooking. While there may be some crisis in this period, it is much less compelling than the often unrecognized crisis of the teenager.

In elderhood, most people gain leisure—both in terms of time and in terms of tranquility. Life slows down noticeably. The obligations of family and career subside and the reins of power are passed on, often a little at a time, to younger people. Yet this is also a time for setting standards, passing on wisdom, making endowments, and taking advantage of society's highest leadership posts.[2] Leisure experience, for the fortunate elderly, is maintained, usually appreciated more, and further modified to meet the limitations of health. Nature is appreciated more, as is order and simplicity. Doing things one wants becomes more important than doing things others want you do to or for which you are rewarded.

The final phase of life, for those who reach it, means testing whether the other people in one's life were trustworthy—one becomes dependent. Expectations about life are lowered and, for those who adjust successfully to this phase of life, appreciation levels are increased dramatically. A ride in a car, a cup of tea, a conversation with an idealistic young person is better understood to be of significant importance. In late elderhood people often become more "selfless" because, perhaps, their self is in the act of disappearing.

Although all these periods of life are subject to individual variation, the life cycle is now understood as a developmental sequence that most people pass through in the same order. Entry into each "season" of life is usually preceded by a period of transition that is troublesome. Each season of life is defined by developmental tasks rather than specific events, such as marriage. Human development is viewed as a relatively orderly sequence of stable (structure-building) and transitional (structure-changing) periods. Developmental tasks are crucial to the evolution of the period. Firm choices must be made, and behavior must be modified in ways that allow for new ways of living.

Today, most social scientists no longer believe that life unfolds in highly identifiable "stages" and instead bring a "life-span" perspective to aging in which the central belief is that change is an unpredictable but continuous process involving multiple causes and multiple outcomes. This way of thinking assumes that there are transitions in life which individuals all go through. As people do this though, "individuals develop characteristic modes of behaving, interacting, problem solving, and preparing for the future that provide continuity across career sequences and through time."[3] In spite of change, then, each of us has some characteristics that are fairly predictable. These characteristics define how we adjust to change.

As many researchers have noted, adaptability is a major theme in women's development. This continuous adaptation which women make means that they may adjust to changing circumstances more easily but may not be able to make long-range plans as easily. One practical consequence of this, for example, is that women may often not be as highly specialized in many forms of leisure expression which require the setting and carrying out of long-range goals. A married man might more easily decide to become a highly expert tennis player over the next several years than his wife, since the wife likely has major responsibility for child rearing, meal preparation, and other domestic duties.

Women who do not have careers outside the home are often

> I had this dream long ago. In high school I imagined that all the seniors in my class were lined up on a starting line to race. Some knew they were faster or slower than others. What they did not know is that each had an invisible, undetectable rope tied to one leg. The ropes were of different lengths. Some were very short. Others were hundreds of miles long.
>
> At the gun, they began to run a race with each other. Some of the runners, sometimes those who were apparently faster, were almost immediately jerked to a halt and fell flat on their faces. Others kept running or walking, aware now that a few had fallen. Still others, seeing that people had fallen, stopped running for a minute to consider whether such racing was worthwhile or whether to go back to help. A few did.
>
> Even after all these years I can recall this image, can sense the ropes tied to people's legs. So far, I have kept running—but I know about the rope.

> It was O.K. with Carlos that I played golf. He would even drive me to the course sometimes. But when I got really serious about it and didn't worry about having the apartment clean or making sure the fridge was full of food, he seemed to think that meant I didn't love him.
>
> It was O.K. for him to put the guys first. If they wanted to watch three football games and suck up a lot of beer, that was cool. So it became an issue, and we split up.
>
> My new boyfriend understands right off the bat that golf is critical to my happiness.

seen as always available to help others in the family, neighborhood, and community. Their commitments also may be, as Henderson and associates noted, perceived as lacking in structure and legitimacy.[4]

Females even appear to derive their identity differently from men. For males, the formation of individual identity may come prior to intimate relationships, while resolution of female identity may be held in abeyance since identity is found in merging with others or in intimacy. The female may come to know herself through relations with others. Many females, therefore, develop a sense of independent identity in their thirties, and women who don't seek new or additional roles during this period may have trouble later. While the male identity is often contingent upon separation from the mother, female identity is often based more on an ongoing relation with the mother that doesn't involve separation. Women, therefore, according to Henderson and colleagues, may not differentiate themselves from others as much as men and may feel a diffuse guilt for the welfare of their families and others.

Today, however, as most young women enter the labor force and as the number of children born to a female in modern nations averages less than two, there may be increasing similarity between the development of males and females.

The Effects of One's Generation

If we are to understand the relationship between leisure behavior and age, we must examine not only the life stage of individuals, but also the generation they were born into. Each succeeding generation faces different circumstances and events that shape their behavior. This means, for example, that one generation of teenagers will behave differently from another since they have had different life experiences.

The oldest generation in our society, born before 1920, survived the Great Depression. Most members of this group have been through two world wars. Many were immigrants or sons and daughters of immigrants and lived in an era when half the country was rural. They married late and had small families.[5]

The next generation, born between 1921 and 1940, entered adulthood during a period of affluence and optimism about the future. They married early, bought large houses and cars, pushed for civil rights, and had larger families. Today, many are divorced.

> See, kids today don't get it. They don't understand you can starve. Not have enough food or money to pay for heat. In the Depression, I sold apples on the street, sometimes went behind restaurants to find what had been thrown out. I even stole a few things.
>
> Kids today think you automatically get a car when you're sixteen. You automatically get a house at 30 or so. One of these days they're going to get a big surprise and then we'll see how tough they are. Maybe what we need is another Depression.

A younger generation, born during the "boom" years following World War II, began to settle in central cities and small towns, the areas deserted by their parents. More women of this generation have put independence and work before marriage and childbearing. Many married later or not at all.

The generation born between 1961 and 1980, sometimes called the Thirteenth Generation, Generation X or Baby-Buster Generation, often is more politically conservative and concerned with career. Although socialized into a psychology of entitlement in regard to material goods, this generation is economically poorer than the previous. Often the children of divorce, their educational attainment, in spite of more years of formal education, often lags behind their peers in other industrializing countries. The Thirteenth Generation faces a tough job market in an era of large government debt and corporate "downsizing."

Finally, the Millennial generation—born between 1981 and 2000—is nearly as large as the Baby Boom (1941–1960). They're also called the Internet Generation, Echo Boomers, the Boomlet, Nexters, Generation Y, the Nintendo Generation, the Digital Generation, and, in Canada, the Sunshine Generation. Generation Y is generally considered to be the last generation wholly born in the 20th century, whose birth years have now concluded. Using the broadest definition commonly cited, Generation Y (as of 2008) includes Americans in their mid and early 20s, teenagers and children ages 8 and older.

Gen-Xers (1961–1980) sometimes complain that Millennials are another indulged generation like the Boomers—that they're self-absorbed and Pollyanna-ish, while Millennials charge that Gen-Xers are cynical and aloof—that they throw a wet blanket on fresh ideas and idealism. Millennials are "the 'Babies on Board' of the early Reagan years, the 'Have You Hugged Your Child Today' sixth graders of the early Clinton years, and the teens of Columbine."[6]

During the post–World War II era, children were all the rage. It was a popular time to be having children and to be a kid for Baby Boomers. Then, when the Gen-Xers were growing up, the spotlight shifted. Latchkey kids, children of divorce, and kids with two working parents found themselves growing up on their own, in the shadow of the Baby Boom.

One Gen-Xer stated, "The Boomers took so much and left us so dry."[7] The early nineties saw the spotlight swinging back. Las Vegas and Club Med went family. Parents and grandparents took the kids along on trips across the country and to destinations all over the globe. Eating out—once an adult thing—became a family matter. Ninety percent of fathers attended the birth of their children. National attention to children was at an all-time high—The earlier peak was in the 1960s when the Boomers were kids. Older parents—the average age to become a mom was now 27—brought more maturity to their roles as caregivers, teachers, and coaches.

Trends in the 1980s and 1990s that have shaped the Millennial generation include:

- *Focus on children and family.* In the decades right before and after the turn of the Millennium, Americans moved the spotlight back onto children and their families.

- *Scheduled, structured lives.* The Millennials were the busiest generation of children we've ever seen in the United States, growing up facing time pressures traditionally reserved for adults.

- *Multiculturalism.* Kids growing up in the 90s and 00s have more daily interaction with other ethnicities and cultures than ever before.

- *Terrorism.* During their most formative years, Millennials witnessed the bombing and devastation of the Murrah Federal Building in Oklahoma City. They watched in horror as two Columbine High School students killed and wounded their classmates, and as school shootings became a three-year trend. And their catalyzing generational event—the one that binds them as a generation, the catastrophic moment many witnessed and were old enough to understand during their first, most formative years—is, of course, the terrorist attacks on September 11, 2001.

- *Heroism.* Emerging out of those acts of violence, Millennials witnessed the re-emergence of the American hero. Police officers, firefighters, and mayors were pictured on the front page of the newspaper, featured on television specials, and portrayed in art and memorabilia. In the ten months following 9/11, the word *hero* was heard more than it had been in the entire ten years before.

- *Patriotism.* During the post-Vietnam and Watergate era, patriotism was at an all-time low. Displaying the American flag— always and forever the right thing to do for members of the World War II Generation—had become less and less common, particularly among disillusioned Boomers and skeptical Xers. September 11 changed all that.

- *Parent advocacy.* The Millennials were raised, by and large, by active, involved parents who often interceded on their behalf. Protective Boomer and Xer parents tried to ensure their children would grow up safely and be treated well. Parents challenged poor grades, negotiated with the soccer coach, visited college campuses with their charges, and even went along to Army recruiting centers. Millennials actually like their parents.

- *Globalism.* With pen pals in Singapore and Senegal, Millennials grew up seeing things as global, connected, and open for business 24/7.[8]

Because this generation grew up in a time of increasing income disparities, many Millennials grew up in households of "working poor," whose wages were insufficient for even lower middle class living.

> I think you have to take care of yourself. Government shouldn't have to — they really can't and, if they do, it produces a lot of lazy people. Politics stinks. It doesn't float my boat. I like business. That's where the action is. I'm preparing myself to succeed in business. I mean, I read about the War on Poverty when the Liberals were in office. Poverty won and the money mostly went to people who weren't poor. I'm not going to be poor.

The Cycles of Lives— Four Turnings

If there is a cycle of life, there may also be an historic cycle of growth and decay that can be measured and predicted. If the ancient notion of a "saeculum" is used, which means a period of eighty to one-hundred years, roughly the length of a long human life, then it may be that the cycles of life come in fours: growth, maturation, entropy and destruction.[9] These historic cycles may be described as "turnings" of seasons of history. Just as an individual life is a season, so is a period of four lifetimes:

The first turning is a *high,* an upbeat era of strengthening institutions and weakening individualism, when a new civic order implants and the old values regime decays. The second turning is an *awakening,* a passionate era of spiritual upheaval, when the civic order comes under attack from a new values regime. The third turning is an *unraveling,* a downcast era of strengthening individualism and weakening institutions, when the old civic order decays and the new values regime implants. The fourth turning is a *crisis,* a decisive era of secular upheaval, when the values regime propels the replacement of the old civic order with a new one.[10]

To the extent that such historic cycles take place, leisure may be directly affected. In the first turning, leisure may occur through organizations that promote patriotism, such as the Girl Scouts or fraternal organizations such as the Lions Club. In the second turning, leisure may be used as a means to counter the old order, such as bands playing alternative rock music or poets writing poems of protest. In the third turning, recreational drugs may serve one group while a new order uses leisure to promote a new set of ideals. In the fourth and final turning, leisure activity is often limited both by financial disaster and a redefinition of morality and acceptable behavior.

To the extent that the history of a culture follows this circular pattern of evolution, leisure activity often signals the transfer from one turning to another.

The Changing Role of the Family

The family is the primary social unit in which individuals become socialized, learn about the world, and develop values and behavior. Evidence suggests that the role of the family, like other social institutions in our society, is undergoing a crisis of reorganization. As discussed elsewhere, divorce is more common as is deferring marriage to a later age. There are more single-parent and gay and lesbian families. It is no longer possible to define what the duties and obligations are for husbands, wives, mothers, fathers, grandparents, or neighbors. These roles have to be worked out on an individual basis.

While the family is in a state of change, the impact of such change depends on the types of adjustments and arrangements to them that are made by the individuals in question and by society.

When I read about the four turnings, I think we are at number four. No one even mentions that we killed hundreds of thousands of Iraqi civilians when we started the war. Everyone has an excuse for their addictions. People sue each other like crazy. We seem to be blind to global warming. I mean, kids who don't even have a job are walking around with credit cards. I think we are living in a big bubble that's about to have a pin stuck in it.

My parents were so great when they started to understand that I was gay. I think at first they just put it out of their mind—but my Dad said, one day it hit him like a ton of bricks. That's how I am and I shouldn't have to suffer for it. Even though it was hard for him—he welcomed Nancy into the house.

Surprisingly, Mom took a little more time. Nan and I slept in separate beds in the house for quite a while but then, on one trip back home, that changed. My folks have made such a difference. Both Nan and I have good jobs now. We may go to New Jersey and get married.

You know—you find out who your friends are if you turn out to be gay. I lost some friends—but I found a bunch more.

While adjustment to divorce does not have to mean children will be less healthy or do less well in school, some evidence argues that divorce more often than not has significant negative effects on children. Divorce

> ...is best understood not as a single event but as a string of disruptive events: separation, divorce, life in a single-parent family, life with a parent and a live-in lover, the remarriage of one or both parents, life in the breakup of one or both step-parent families. And so on.[11]

Children who live in single-parent families are two to three times more likely than children in two-parent families to have emotional and behavioral problems. They are more likely to drop out of high school, to get pregnant as teenagers, to abuse drugs, and to get in trouble with the law. Thus, while divorce need not produce such problems, it disproportionately does.

Perhaps the post–World War II era, in which individuals married early and had large families, has given us a mistaken idea about the "commitment" of individuals today. Social psychological research demonstrates that "commitment" is a process rather than a product; it is also inherently unstable and "something which grows and changes over time."[12] While we may imagine a past in which people made commitments to each other for life, in reality such commitments were more uncommon than common, unless people had no option in the matter. Divorce, for example, was not common in the nineteenth century, but marital desertion was a very serious problem.

There is often a mistaken belief that families were more secure or held more sacred in the past. Families would almost always depend upon others to help them. The expectation that the family would be the main source of personal fulfillment was not traditional in the eighteenth and nineteenth century.[13] Divorced fathers were not forced to pay child support until 1920. As many as 20 percent of children lived in orphanages in the early 1900s and even by 1940, 10 percent did not live with either parent. Families were generally not the center of leisure and recreation; alcohol, drug and child abuse were more rampant than today; and the age of sexual consent in the nineteenth century was nine or ten.[14] The idea that romantic love could be the all-encompassing foundation for a lifetime marriage was also foreign:

The hybrid idea that a woman can be fully absorbed with her youngsters while simultaneously maintaining passionate sexual excitement with her husband was a 1950s invention that drove thousands of women to therapists, tranquilizers, or alcohol when they actually tried to live up to it.[15]

Families were always dependent upon neighbors, community, relatives and government to get them through. While divorce is more common today, those marriages that do survive are more likely to be described as happy by the couple than in the past.

Changes that have occurred in the family in recent times have meant that leisure has played a more central role in determining family cohesiveness. The modern family has shifted its primary functions away from meeting instrumental needs (things which are done as a means to an end) toward meeting expressive needs (things which are done for their own sake). Leisure has become, increasingly, the arena in which family members relate to each other. This is an era in which many children have little idea what their father, and increasingly their mother, does at work. Few families work together, unlike agricultural societies, and instead every family member, sometimes from the age of two years, goes out into the world every day to work or school or daycare. Leisure has become the arena in which family relations are established and maintained.

> When my parents split up, I thought my world was coming to an end. My sister was stronger about it than I was, although she started dating a real loser. My Dad and I were close but it seemed like he forgot about me. He would show up sometimes and want to take me out for pizza. He got a younger girlfriend, and I didn't like her. My grades dropped a lot but then I saw that nothing was going to change. I quit holding my breath and got on with things. Still, I'm bitter about it and probably won't get over it. I guess the big things you don't get over—just kind of store them in your system and get on with your life.

DAUGHTER

In a scrub-grass area
down the bank from the turnpike
I pushed you in a swing
until it got so dark
I could barely see your shoes
rising into the air.

I carried you back
to the apartment in silence.
You were limp with wonder.
Someday nothing will mean
more than that.

As we walked through
the parking lot
you pointed
at the evening star;
its distant light swimming,
and I held you
the way I imagine
it is held
by the universe.

—GCG

Life Seasons and Leisure's Functions

If we examine various life seasons, it quickly becomes apparent that leisure fulfills different social functions. Some leisure activities typically are done alone; some are done only with members of the same (or opposite) sex; some are done only with peers (others whose status is roughly equal to ours); and some are usually done with parents, spouse, children, or relatives.

Many leisure activities are undertaken not because of an individual personal preference or because a particular leisure activity is uniquely appealing. Rather, they are undertaken because they permit the strengthening or maintenance of social bonds with friends, neighbors, or kin. Thus, while at an individual level, an adult male or female might prefer a game of tennis to Monopoly, the family's group decision may be to play Monopoly in order to be with one another, enjoy each other's company, or show each other respect.

The extent to which leisure activity is undertaken with these various motivations appears to vary throughout the life cycle. Among adults, particularly males, such participation is more likely to become compensatory-recuperative, relational, or role-determined. When an individual reaches old age, involvement once again is likely to become unconditional.

Childhood

For preschool children, it may not make sense to use the term *leisure*, since there is little division between work and leisure for children. Their freedom to choose what they want to do (or know how to do) is greatly restricted by lack of money, transportation, parental control, and their lack of experience in the world. Children are constantly involved in the magical world of play.

Even though play may not be done for any purpose outside itself, many social scientists believe that play serves as a way that children take on the culture they are raised in. It is also sometimes considered to be a way for children to resolve conflicts without serious consequence. Sutton-Smith has suggested that through play children may "test out" their curiosities without experiencing repercussions in the event of failure:[16]

> There is a growing body of research that shows a link between play and the development of cognitive and social skills that are prerequisites for learning more complex concepts as children get older. For example, play is linked to growth in memory, self-regulation, oral language, and recognizing symbols. It has been linked to higher levels of school adjustment and increased social development. Play has also been linked to increased literacy skills and other areas of academic learning.[17]

Shapers of Children's Play

Several variables are important in helping to shape a child's play patterns, including the child's sex, age, social class, style of upbringing, and the culture in which the child is raised. The social class of a child's parents, for instance, may greatly determine how much space a child has in which to play. In an apartment, particularly a high-rise, parents may not let a child play on the grounds surrounding the building because they cannot watch the child like they could in a detached house with a yard.

Parents' style of upbringing will also affect play. Many of you, for instance, were taught as a child that play was worthwhile, but only after your chores had been done. "Sure, you can go out and play. But first, clean your room." Thus, you were taught the importance, or, more precisely, the centrality, of work. Other children may not have been taught this and were left more or less free to do what they wanted, when they wanted. It is worth noting that those who have been taught to do their work first are better prepared to function in an industrial society where work is of prime importance.

The culture in which a child is raised will also influence play. In societies that stress individual success as a goal, children are more likely to play physical skill games and to use success in these games to relieve their anxiety about achievement. Failure, of course, will increase that anxiety, as I recall from my Little League days. In a society such as that of the Hopi Indians, however, children play games that imitate the activities of adults in a noncompetitive way, and little achievement anxiety is instilled.[18] In our own highly competitive society, parents often look for an "end product" from children's play which demonstrates achievement or success; therefore, parents structure play to achieve these aims. Beauty pageants or competitive swimming meets for young girls or Cub Scout merit badges for young boys are examples. Perhaps it can be said that all societies demonstrate important aspects of their culture by how their young play.

Adolescence

It was not until recently in the Western world that adolescents or teen-agers achieved a separate status from adults and children. The term *teenager* did not appear in the American vocabulary until the 1930s. It has been argued that increased technology, urbanization, and special-ization of society have produced problems which are either exclusive to this age group or affect them more intensely than others. Perhaps because of this, the associations made in adolescence are more compel-ling than in other periods of life; friends and peer groups become all-important. This, of course, has both good and bad consequences. If all of one's friends smoke at this stage of life, for instance, it is difficult for the teenager to avoid smoking. Indeed, teenagers experience a great confusion of values. While there is a strong trend toward social con-formity with their peer group, there is also a shifting back and forth from childish to more adult behavior. In some ways, teenagers suffer from the same lack of clearly defined roles, as do the elderly, in our society.

Many of these situations serve to bring teenagers closer to each other, sometimes through gangs or social groups that develop leisure-activity patterns which are not accepted by the rest of society. The high crime rate, prevalent use of drugs, and high rate of alcohol-related and distraction-related (e.g., cell phone, text messaging, radio) automobile accidents among teenagers may all, to some extent, reflect this situation.

As children enter adolescence, they begin to increase their independence from their parents and are affected more by the influences of others their own age. Some take part-time jobs, their mobility often increases, and thus they begin to have a greater range of options in regard to the use of leisure.

In adolescence, the individual must internalize the knowledge and attitudes appropriate to certain adult roles. Most adolescents in our culture, for instance, must learn the appropriate driving regulations to pass a state driving examination. Similarly, they must learn safe and legal driving techniques or risk fines, injury, or even death.

During this period teenagers also go through small successive shifts in status and roles, which often make them uncertain about how they should behave. With increasing age and education, generally, comes increasing freedom and access to resources. Adolescents also appear to have more time for leisure and higher participation rates in leisure activities than their older counterparts. Teenagers are more likely to participate in most forms of outdoor recreation than those who are older, unless automobiles are involved.

It is often argued that at this stage of the life cycle a separate "youth culture" emerges, complete with separate values, music, clothing, hair styles, social concerns, language, attitudes, and sexual mores. Members of such a culture are, in some ways, segregated from the rest of society, particularly in the case of male adolescents. Hanging out on street corners, in cars, at the local amusement arcade, and even Internet chat rooms, teenagers often appear to withdraw into a separate society— one which has the status of neither children nor adults.

During this period of life, there is experimentation with how to relate to the opposite (or same) sex. Dating and socializing produce the opportunity for commitment between two individuals. The factors that may produce commitment to a relationship include love for the partner, the status that comes with the relationship, and feelings of obligation to sustain the relationship. Commitment is reduced by anxiety about the relationship, the attractiveness of alternative relationships, or internal and external pressures to try other alternatives, such as loneliness, family and friends.

Dating couples appear to be happier when there are equitable relations. Couples who are in relationships that are not equitable report more feelings of guilt and more distress, as well as higher amounts of anger. They are also less likely to think that the relationship will last.[19] Thus, it appears that commitment in relationships is more likely to occur where there are equitable relations between the partners. Leisure behavior is often the arena in which such equity is tested.

Today, the period of "adolescence" often extends into a person's mid-twenties or even to age thirty, rather than just their teenage years. The majority of teenagers go to college or take a job which will not support their material desires, so many, if not most, continue to be supported by their parents. Many continue to live at home, or leave home and then return for several years. Most are not economically self-supporting. Thus, being an adolescent extends for a significantly longer period of life than it did a few generations ago.

Adulthood

Becoming an adult in our society is something that doesn't happen all at once at a given age. Leisure options also develop at different ages: being eligible to drive for pleasure at one age, enter a nightclub at another, buy a snowmobile on credit at another. In one sense, when teenagers long for adulthood in our society, they are longing for leisure—freedom to do what they want when they want.

Rather than consider adulthood a single period, it makes more sense to envision it as several periods with different preoccupations, interests, and changing patterns of leisure. While earlier theories of aging assumed that adulthood was characterized by either stability or decline, more recent concepts recognize the potential for age-related gains as well as losses in adulthood. While adulthood has often been considered to be merely the continuation and eventual decline of skills developed in childhood, it is now thought of as a time of continued and distinct development. This continued development of adults is sometimes referred to as "plasticity."[20] That is, there are differences among individual adults that provide the potential for different behavior and development. There are many kinds of influences on adults: historical, psychological, biological, cultural, and community-related, and these influences interact with each other to produce adults who develop along very different paths.

Although not all researchers accept the notion of plasticity among adults, there seems to be evidence that individuals play an important role in shaping their plasticity. An individual adult's lifestyle, for example, may shape biological plasticity. Something as simple as jogging regularly may influence maximum oxygen intake, muscular and skeletal development, weight control, and production of lipoproteins and lower serum cholesterol level. Even the intelligence of an old-age individual can be improved through training.

While plasticity can occur at almost any point in the life span, the potential for plasticity decreases with age.

Early Adulthood

During the years of young adulthood the leisure pattern that an individual adopts depends upon the lifestyle he or she assumes. The major preoccupations at this stage of life are identification with social institutions, intimacy, and commitment. The commitment at this stage of life may be to beginning a career, marriage, a given field of study, certain leisure activities, or a social cause of students, social club, gang; or for the involuntarily unemployed and those in the alternative lifestyle, it may be finding a way of life which relies little upon industrial technology or which involves pursuing some art form.

This stage of life is increasingly characterized by both males and females preparing for a career, often living together but not married. It is now more common for young males and females to live together prior to traditional marriage than not to. In an increasing number of cases, there is tension in the relationship of young couples concerning living arrangements that can accommodate the careers of both partners. A common characteristic of this stage of life is a constriction of leisure activities as young people focus on one major interest, such as an occupation, finding a mate, or friendship with peers.

These dudes are family. I ain't got nothing else. We're tight. I would run through a wall for one of these brothers. The folks around here give us a hard time— but they don't care nothing about us—just scared. Without the boys, I don't got nothing. Nothing. I ain't going nowhere and might as well just hang and be cool. We don't want trouble, but if it's there, we going to handle it.

Parenthood brings about changes not only in the responsibilities of couples but also in their leisure. Having a baby often makes two kinds of shifts in regard to work and leisure—the mother will do considerably more in terms of her work role and will make small gains in terms of her leisure preferences. It should be pointed out, of course, that there is increasing variation among cohabiting males and females in terms of division of labor and leisure pursuits. Just as our "mass" society is fragmenting, the meanings of institutions like marriage are becoming more diverse as well. Marriage may mean the most important lifetime commitment an individual makes or something one does every few years. The roles within such marriages are increasingly defined at the individual level rather than by society at large.

Changes in marital roles and leisure patterns do not necessarily produce difficulties. To a great extent, problems are caused when individuals within a marriage (or other relation) have particular ideas about who ought to do what with regard to housework and childcare. Role theorists assume that people who are highly "sex-typed" in personality may find themselves uncomfortable doing things that they think "should" be done by members of the other sex. A wife who believes there should be equality between the sexes in terms of child rearing may be unhappy if her husband believes the traditional division of labor is preferable. A father who wants equality in relations and duties toward children may similarly be unhappy if the wife has traditional attitudes, believing she should be the primary parent. The process by which children learn these roles, then, is critical in how they adjust later in life to their role as marriage partners and parents.

Middle Adulthood

There has been a tendency to think that middle age is associated with loss and trauma. The "midlife crisis" has become an idea that is fixed in the minds of many people. There is a feeling that it is necessary to go through a process of traumatic adjustment to later life. For women whose primary commitment has been to a career, awareness of limited time left for childbearing or mixed emotions about not having had children may produce psychological problems. It appears that for women who formed their identity and sense of self in their younger years based entirely around finding a suitable mate and motherhood, the potential for crisis is great in the middle years.

While the midlife crisis of females may revolve around work and identity, for the male the crisis may be described as follows:

...The hormone production levels are dropping, the head is balding, the sexual vigor is diminishing, the stress is unending, the children are leaving, the parents are dying, the friends are having their first heart attacks, the past floats by in a fog of hopes not realized, opportunities not grasped, women not bedded, potentials not fulfilled, and the future is a blur.[21]

The most recent research concerning midlife, however, suggests this is not generally true:

Instead of being a time of turmoil, unbearable stress, hormonal change, loss of control, failing health, bad backs and crumpling marriages, for most people middle age turns out to be the most fulfilling time of life...[22]

Midlife, while it possesses challenges, as do all other seasons of life, is perhaps less a time of trauma than both earlier and later periods of life.

Later Adulthood and Retirement

Life span developmental psychologists have theorized about the process of aging and now argue that development occurs throughout the life span in both continuous and discontinuous ways, and in a multidimensional manner. Although aging has been associated largely with decreases in functioning, development is characterized by both gains and losses throughout life and the potential for change and new learning remains in old age. This concept, as mentioned earlier, has been called *plasticity*, the malleability

Am I old? Don't know. I don't think of it like some people do—you go up a hill, get to the top and then you start going downhill. If that were correct, how do you know when you are at the top of the hill? I'm a lot smarter now than at 25, when I didn't know my butt from a hole in the ground. But I'm also slower—forget people's names—like yours. That doesn't mean I don't know a lot about you— I just have trouble with names. You have many "selves" and these selves get older at different ages. Intellectually, my understanding of the world is still growing. You pick and choose more carefully as you age—the ones who don't are very often dead by now. Everything matters more. The choices you make about food, exercise, travel, friends, everything. When I was younger, it's almost as though I was getting ready for life—now I'm living.

of people to contexts and interventions.[23] That is, individuals have some potential to change positively or negatively and their behaviors help determine how they change. As pointed out in Chapter 11, some researchers find that older people's intelligence is improved by playing games such as bridge or doing crossword puzzles. Thus, our behavior continues to shape our development.

What the previous approaches have in common is to stress the various pathways aging can take and the possibilities for prolonging involvement in life and to recognize the plasticity and the room for growth that remains even in later life. This period of life is one characterized by the male and, increasingly, the female ceasing full-time employment. Later adulthood has been divided by some researchers into three stages—preretirement, retirement, and old age. Some gerontologists refer to the "young-old" (ages 65–74) and the "old-old" (75 and older). Since "old age" covers a span of life from 65 to 85 or 90, it has become necessary to think of it more as stages or seasons.

> O.K. I read these fancy theories. My Grandmother knew all this stuff long before these theories. She told me: "You make the most of what you've got." She also told me that you have to keep adjusting to what life throws at you and try to be happy about it. So I guess Grandmom was a gerontologist.

The very term *retiree* indicates the centrality of work in our society. It also indicates how much we take our self-definition from our work role. People who describe themselves as "retired" identify only the role they don't have, and say nothing of the roles they do have. In our culture retirement brings a preoccupation with realigning commitments but it need not bring a retirement from commitments. From the standpoint of leisure, this period of life brings change rather than retirement.

There is a great tendency to misjudge the situation of retirees. The majority of those 65 years of age or older live as a dyad (husband and wife) in their own home. Most older adults continue to live where they did before they retired. Older adults, while often living just above the poverty level, are no more likely to be poor than any other age group. In terms of accumulated assets, they are often one of the wealthiest groups in society. Thus, for many retired people, the potential to use leisure in meaningful ways is great.

Part of the reason for the previous generation of older adults often being limited in their leisure choices was a combination of poverty, low levels of formal education, and lack of acquired leisure skills. Today, many people ages 65 and older have higher in level of education and income and have been socialized into a number of leisure skills which retirement gives them the time to pursue.

It is easy to overestimate the impact of retirement on recreation and leisure behavior. The vast majority of Americans continue to reside at the same place they did previously and to pursue the same leisure activities after retirement that they had formerly undertaken. Older adults are "aging in place."[24] That is, the vast majority do not move south or west or anywhere. Of those 65 and older, only one percent left their home state in a given year. Suburbs are becoming inhabited by older adults (and young singles) even though they were designed largely for families with children. "Most suburbs lack housing, transportation and healthcare options for an aging population likely to move from being active adults to wanting assisted living to requiring intensive medical treatment.[25]

Just as the ancient Greeks believed the life of leisure required extensive preparation, so, too, does retirement. Since those with a broad range of recreation and leisure skills seem to adjust best to retirement, those who have limited leisure interests and skills need to awaken old leisure interests and learn new leisure skills prior to retirement. Similarly, those whose self-definition is based almost exclusively on their work, or whose leisure activity represents an extension of their work, will have a more dramatic reorientation. This often is true not only because those leisure activities undertaken by individuals whose work is of central importance are often of a relaxing or diversionary nature, but also because such activity is frequently undertaken as a spillover from their occupations. When work ends for these people, not only do many of the leisure activities that spilled over from work end but also the relaxation and diversionary activities are not satisfying replacements for work. The successful retiree must have leisure skills, and such skills, like work skills, are learned.

Trends in Retirement. As Baby Boomers retire, the 50-year-old trend toward earlier retirement is coming to an end. "Rather than retiring abruptly and at earlier and earlier ages, as many in their generation did, Boomers will stretch out their working lives, moving in and out of new and varied careers."[26] Retirement will be viewed as a process rather than as a single event.

For years, federal laws provided incentives for people to stop working at earlier and earlier ages. The average age of retirement fell steadily after World War II. Now antiwork incentives are being replaced by provisions which are age neutral or encourage people to work longer. The age at which Social Security payments are made is rising from 65 to 67 years of age, and will likely continue to rise further. This may produce a long-term trend toward later retirement. Later retirement may not mean people staying in the same job longer but rather working part-time after retiring from their career jobs. Some people may continue working full-time while others work part-time and still others serve as volunteers.

Not all observers agree that later and later retirement will become a reality. Some researchers think that Boomers will retire when they can afford it regardless of their age. Some Boomers will have to work longer to finance the style of life they are accustomed to.

The extent to which Baby Boomers choose to keep working may be considerable. While some of those who plan to keep working are motivated by the collapse of the stock market during 2000–2002 or declining healthcare benefits, others want to maintain the social interaction they had and a reason to get out of bed. As older adults choose to stay in the labor force, every industry providing leisure services will be affected because retirees have often been the backbone of many parts of the tourism industry, golf courses, and other leisure services.

The progression of our lives has been described in so many ways. To me, the journey through life that each of us makes is, in some ways, like falling snow.

SIX QUESTIONS FOR SNOWFLAKES

1.
From whose dreaming fingertips did you drop?

2.
Are you leaving home with strangers or arriving home with blind friends?

3.
Have you finished speaking or not yet begun?

4.
If you land in the river will you fall asleep or awaken?

5.
If you land on the ground will you disappear or get bigger?

6.
When I let go as you have through whose kingdom will I fall?

Trends in Leisure Activity in Later Life. As the huge Baby Boom segment of the population moves toward retirement, what retirement means will be redefined. Many Boomers have had stable careers and no children later in life. They will have higher expectations for use of leisure during retirement. Eight out of ten plan to work, at least part-time, so their leisure activity will need to accommodate a working lifestyle.[27]

"People will begin living a cyclical life: plan, go back to school, cease their major and reinvent themselves in new work," said Ken Dychtwald, an author of books on health and aging issues, including *Age Wave*. "People will pursue freedom, not retirement."[28] They will not simply passively retire, but rather take new risks, explore and sometimes have big adventures.

The following account illustrates this desire for adventure. A friend of mine, Tom Goodale, at the age of 64, climbed Mount Kilimanjaro, the highest point in Africa, with his two sons. Here are excerpts from his diary:

Mt. Kilimanjaro Trip: 2/6/02 – 2/20/02

Wed, 2/6 — Dulles, Gate C-19. Just finished 1½ hours of "9-5-2" with Greg and Daryl. We checked in nearly 3 hours early for our flight to Brussels. We're en route to Moshi, Tanzania, by way of UA to Brussels, KLM to Amsterdam, KQ to Nairobi, and the Davanu Shuttle bus from Nairobi, crossing the border, to Moshi via Arusha, Tanzania. With luck we'll be in Moshi mid-afternoon Friday, not quite 48 hours from now. If we miss the morning bus, the only tight spot on our schedule, we won't get in until 8 or 9 p.m. We land in Nairobi at 6:10 a.m. The bus leaves from a downtown hotel at 8, and we have to clear customs, get transit visas to allow a second entry into Kenya without the added expense of a multiple-entry visa, then catch a cab to catch the bus. And we've already heard of "Africa time." It could be friend or foe. The boarding process has begun. I have to find my tickets, boarding pass, passport, and shoes.

I'm nursing a small raw patch on my right heel. I have small feet and often wind up buying women's shoes or boots for want of alternatives. But they tend to be narrow and my feet are wide as well as short, and the right foot is between ¼ and ½ inch longer heel to arch than my left foot. So getting a pair of good hiking boots that fit is difficult at best. I ruined a couple "little" toes, one toe-nail gone and the other soon, trying to break in a pair of La Sportivas, a heavy but excellent quality hiking boot. Now I have a pair of Scarpas, which I think will be OK but at the moment I have a slight heel-lift problem with the right boot, resulting in a blister, but the toes are OK and I can manage the blister with Tuff-Skin, Mole-Skin or some combination of those plus getting the socks and lacing just right.

A 65-km hike is challenge enough without having to worry about boots and feet, quite literally every step of the way. When the first half of the trek is uphill, the last portion very steeply uphill, there is much else to think, and sometimes worry, about. We're headed for Uhuru Peak, the highest point on Mt. Kilimanjaro, thus also the highest point in Africa. At 19,340 feet above sea level, it is commonly 20 degrees below 0 early in the morning this time of year, not counting windchill.

It's all Greg's idea, but also Daryl's as those two have talked about this off and on for a couple of years, but Greg was the main promoter. Daryl bought in early and then Dad. That was in October '01. Mom and I were preoccupied with a November trip to China, and I was struggling with a public lecture to give at UNC—Greensboro. I said "sure" when invited, not knowing what I was getting into and not altogether convinced the trip would come off, given the boys' different but busy lives. I returned from China to find the planning well underway, so decided I had better get about some of the essential prelims. I had to get a replacement passport since mine delaminated near the photo and couldn't be repaired since the passport agency changed to a digital technology. So I had to get a new one, and went through Senator Warner's office to get an expedited passport, knowing it may take a while to get visas for Kenya and Tanzania. The anthrax scare had slowed official mail in DC to a crawl. The extra time put me, relatively at least, at ease, and the postal service and respective consulates came through.

I also got the necessary immunizations. Documentation was required for the visas, Yellow Fever in particular. So I had five shots in all, and was disappointed that none of them hurt. I was determined to be a man about all this, and there was nothing to be manly about. The bill hurt a little ($320), and the additional medications hurt more, especially the anti-malaria pills, Malarone, 22 of them at $10 a piece. To my pleasant surprise, my health insurance covered most of it. I also wound up with 8 Diamox for altitude sickness, though my doctor said they may or may not do any good and some side effects could be a nuisance. But if they might help fend off pulmonary and especially cerebral edema, I figured it wouldn't hurt. Change in barometric pressure and oxygen concentrations when at altitude results in water seepage through capillaries, allowing fluids to build up in the lungs and the brain. It's serious business, requiring the climber to get to a lower altitude quickly. I also have three levels of stuff to combat diarrhea; Pepto-Bismol chewable tablets, Immodium, and Cipro, and a bunch of other stuff in the medicine bag: tape, gauze, Band-aids, bacitracin, Iodine, water purification tablets, Advil, sunblock, insect repellent, tweezers, clippers, *a Swiss Army knife, even safety pins and rubber bands—everything but duct tape and WD 40.*

A majority of the people who undertake to climb Kili make it, I think, but many of them, it seems, stop at "Gilman's Point" and don't complete the final 200-meter climb, presumably because they are really tired from the climb by that point, stop to rest, and decide to head down rather than further up. The Lonely Planet guide says it's two hours from Gilman's Point to Uhuru Peak, thus another two hours back, and that, along with tiredness must be deterrents for many folks. And no one escapes completely the effects of climbing at altitude.

I have been doing a bit of jogging the past few weeks. Not nearly enough, I'm sure, but I hate jogging. And I've messed up my feet with blisters and have had to back off because of pushing too hard. Between old work boots (worn because they're heavy), the La Sportivas and now the Scarpas, I've had a blister or two for the past two months. I climbed three days with Greg out in Strasburg, twice up Signal Hill and once up Old Rag, not far from Culpepper. They're 1,900 and 2,400 feet vertical, respectively, I think, unless these are the above sea level numbers, making the climb less depending on the starting altitude. We also hiked the hills in Strasburg twice, 5 laps up and down two steep hills, carrying 4 liters of water and some odds and ends, imitating what we expected once at Kili. Daryl joined us one day that I couldn't answer the bell due to crushed toes from the previous day. That day I picked up the Scarpas. He and Greg did the steepest route up Old Rag.

Unless felled by altitude sickness, Daryl should do Kili easily. He is in super shape, having trained for the Marine Corps Marathon. He was up to 18 miles before a bad knee made him withdraw. Plus, while coaching two soccer teams, he gets in more aerobic work. Plus he lifts weights a couple noon hours a week. Greg isn't far behind, if at all, because he has done a lot of climbing over the past few months since his move to Strasburg. I've worked out some and am in good shape for 64, but that doesn't really count. The Mountain doesn't make allowances for age....

After eight hours in the Amsterdam airport and eight on the flight, the next seven hours were hard on my butt. The bus was almost at capacity, meaning that some of the seats that fold out into the aisle were full. Most people got off in Arusha as that is a major transfer point and also a base for those going to Kilimanjaro, although it is more than 60 miles from Moshi, which is a lot closer to the town of Marangu and to the park gate. Only four continued on to Moshi, three of them Goodales. I stretched out across four seats, including the fold-down aisle seat, and slept most of the 1½ hours to Moshi. What little we saw of Nairobi as we headed out of town was about what we expected. Dusty and thus dirty. More litter than most cities I've been in. Lots of vehicles, with a high percentage of trucks and buses of all sizes, including lots of diesel and thus lots of emissions particulate and gases. A few human drawn carts, none drawn by other kinds of animals. Bright colors in paints and apparel, heavy loads balanced on heads in both city and countryside, but mainly in the countryside. Nairobi is a government town as well as commercial center. Mostly Masi people in the area between Nairobi and Arusha. Children and tall, slim men tending goats and cattle along the roads....

Tomorrow we hike slowly. Today we started like a house on fire and wore ourselves down on a not very demanding route. Here, everyone says, go slowly. Tomorrow we go to Horombo Hut, about 11 km and 1,000 meters (3,280 feet) in altitude. No rush. Take five or six hours. Don't waste energy on a pace that isn't necessary. Slowly, slowly. Horombo is at about 12,500 feet. We'll stay an extra day there for acclimatization....

The slow pace not only saves energy but also aids in acclimatization. With all the time in the world, no one would suffer from going to altitude, at least not 19,000 feet. Even at our slow, plodding pace, we were the first to arrive at Horombo, except for one couple that literally blasted past us. We gained a thousand meters altitude (3,280 feet) and are literally in the clouds. From Marangu Gate to Mandara Hut we climbed through pretty dense foliage in near rainforest like conditions—except this is the dry season. Today we climbed through an alpine meadow after the first few kilometers out of Mandara....

Found Greg and Daryl watching a rescue team of trained Park Service employees taking a middle-aged Spanish man down to a rescue vehicle on a litter designed for mountain use. One wheel in the middle on a good shock absorber, with handles front and back for the two men who literally run him down the hill, a distance from here of about 15 kilometers, past Mandara Hut to the last road access point. From there a vehicle will take him to the hospital in Moshi....

The climb to Gilman's Point is very, very steep. We'll gain 1,000 feet in elevation in less than 4 km, and that is with switchbacks. You can't go straight up this hill. The word is that the first 300 meters of elevation aren't bad, the next 200 tough, and next 500 make the tough part look like kindergarten nap time. Lack of oxygen starts having an effect almost immediately, as even the first 300 meters are as steep as anything we've climbed these past four days. And there is no let up, no flat spot until you reach Gilman's Point—if you reach Gilman's Point....

There are four rooms at Kibo Hut, each accommodating about a dozen people. Ours held 14, on seven bunk beds. The rooms are co-ed so there is a lot of squirming around changing clothes inside sleeping bags. And you can't just "step outside and take a leak" as we central New Yorkers say. I managed to sleep a bit this afternoon but this evening will be tough due to the Diamox and to the large quantities I have been drinking faithfully, besides having a weak bladder, and going in and out of the cold....

On Wednesday, February 13, at 6:30 a.m., Gregory, Daryl and Thomas Goodale stood on Uhuru Peak, the highest point on Kilimanjaro and on the continent of Africa. I have tears in my eyes as I write these words (and as I am typing them now, 10 days later). I'm writing in the dining hall at Horombo Hut. I would be crying if there were not so many others around.

Five of those 6½ hours of climbing were the most physically and psychologically challenging thing any of us have experienced. It doesn't help when you pass people vomiting by the side of the trail, or especially when a climber was calling out for help because his guide was sick....

Everyone needs something to keep them going. For me, it's determination to not be the weakest link. OK, maybe I am, but this link isn't going to break. For Daryl, it is the need to complete a challenge since the knee problem made him withdraw from the marathon. For Greg, it is the fact that he was the impetus and sure as hell wasn't going to be the one we worried about....

At Gilman's we started down the steepest part of the climb and saw for the first time what we had come through, in the dark, on the way up. Good thing it was dark, it was just short of frightening, just barely believable. The bobbing headlamps above and below told us only that the pitch was steep. It did not tell us what might have happened had we lost our balance or stubbed a toe in the wrong place. Only then did we realize how great a responsibility the guides had. Later, Elian told us that in his 25 years or so on the mountain he has "lost" 15 people, but none from falls or accidents. Heart attacks, people thinking they can battle through edema, etc....

Thursday morning the 14th. We are up at 6:15 a.m., breakfast a bit before 7, and then the ceremony of photos with the whole crew that supported our climb. Last night we figured out tips. Elian asked us to prepare a list of amounts to go to each of the crew. He distributed the money. It seems we did OK, not great but good enough. To Tanzanians, all Americans are rich, and they're right, especially those that get to Marangu Gate. But a few of the really rich throw money around needlessly, skewing expectations. We did OK. Now it's handshakes all around and lots of "thank you"s and "thank you very much"s. "Asante. Assante sana."

As this diary shows, many older adults are going to refuse to act old when it comes to leisure.

Leisure Interest of Older Adults

Leisure is undoubtedly changed by retirement. In particular, the following forms of leisure are uppermost in the plans of Baby Boomers who plan to retire according to Fraser:[29]

1. **Traveling:** Baby Boomers already travel for pleasure more than any other age group, often taking multiple vacations throughout the year. Traditional activities such as antiquing and bed and breakfasts are popular, but so too is "adventure travel."

2. **Family activities:** Many Baby Boomers are becoming grandparents and spend more money on dinners and parties involving family. Family cruises and camps are also gaining popularity.

3. **Hobbies:** From stamp collecting to cooking to painting to wine making to playing a musical instrument, many adults are pursuing hobbies.

4. **Gardening:** Growing flowers and vegetables outdoors has grown in popularity and will likely to continue to grow. So has canning vegetables, making jams and jellies, and drying herbs from herb gardens.

5. **Fishing:** More people fish than play golf or tennis combined.[30] Specialized anglers do fly fishing, bass fishing, and many other forms, often as part of a vacation.

6. **Golfing:** Golfers are likely to be older adults and, increasingly, golfers who can afford it are retiring to communities built around playing golf.

7. **Volunteering:** Socially aware Baby Boomers look for opportunities to volunteer, donating both their time and their money.

8. **Reading:** Buying books increases as people get older. Those over age 55 account for about one-third of book purchases.

9. **Exercising:** People ages 55 and over are actually more likely to exercise than younger people and much of this exercise involves special equipment, shoes, fitness clubs, and sports equipment.

10. **Home improvement:** With the kids gone, many older adults take on home improvements and renovation projects.

As every modern nation's population ages dramatically, the ability of older adults to live independently in their communities will become the single most important variable in determining not only their quality of life but also the ability of the current healthcare system to survive. Independent living may promote higher levels of physical and psychological health[31] and living in the community may help maintain a sense of identity and independence, and allow the continuance of meaningful leisure activity that enhances quality of life.[32]

> I'd rather die than go to a retirement home. I'm not kidding. Don't let that happen to me. Don't.

Independent living refers to an individual's ability to perform activities of daily living (ADL) and instrumental ADLs, which require self-maintenance and independent community residence.[33] Additionally, independent living implies the ability to maintain satisfying forms of leisure behavior that maintain or enhance abilities needed for living without assisted care. Use of leisure is becoming part of government policy on aging since there is no way that retirement villages and nursing homes can become economically affordable for the greatly increased elderly population. Also, the evidence is clear that nursing homes are not where people prefer to live.

> Barbara, dear, I guess I'm better off here. The food is good and I have my flowers and the TV. I know I wouldn't have lasted much longer at home—and all of you come to see me so often. Also, I love the videocam so I can see my grandchildren in California.

In the United States, people are beginning to experiment with "virtual continuum of care residential living." This means that, for a fee, an older person who stays in their home in spite of some disability may receive various types of assistance, from visits by a nurse to yard work or delivery of groceries. Will any leisure services be "delivered" to such people? Perhaps they soon will.

Conclusions

While one's place in the life course is an important determinant of leisure attitudes and behavior, we should remember that this varies with different generations. Those who are retired now, for instance, are likely to behave differently than retirees of a previous generation. Those who reach retirement in the next generation will likely differ from those now retired. In fact, many of them may not "retire" at all in the traditional sense, unless forced to by poor health. Because those in the middle stages of life are more likely to participate in sports than the last generation of middle-agers, it is likely that they will also participate at higher rates during retirement.

As human beings, we are constantly evolving. Not only do the values and preoccupations which shape our leisure behavior change throughout various stages of life, the impact of these stages changes from generation to generation. What being a teenager meant to your parents is different from what it meant (or means) to you. Thus, the forces which limit and shape our leisure are not only our life stage but also the unique conditions of the generation with which we share that stage.

It would also be wrong for us to conclude that people are happier during their youth than in middle and old age. Bernice Neugarten, a scholar of adult development, has summarized three important points concerning the development of adults:

1. It makes no more sense to think primarily in terms of "prob-lems" or "losses" for middle age or old age than it does for youth.

2. As lives grow longer and we make more choices and commit-ments, more different from each other. Most people do not lose this uniqueness until their death.

3. Most people who have reached the ages of 40, 50, or 60 do not wish to be young again. Instead, they wish to grow old with the assurance that they have had a full measure of life's experience.[34]

These conclusions would seem to indicate the wisdom of an old adage— Every age has its rewards.

Study Questions

1. Briefly describe leisure activities in which you participate, including one which is unconditional leisure, one which is compensatory or recuperative leisure, one which is relational leisure, and one which is role-determined leisure.

2. What does it mean to say that play is "arousal-seeking" behavior?

3. Why is one's "generation" an important factor in shaping leisure behavior?

4. Are younger people "happier" than middle-aged or old people? Why or why not?

5. What leisure activities do you think you will be involved in at age 50?

Exercise 8.1

Preoccupations, Interests, and Leisure

Discuss the relationship of your use of leisure to your current preoccupations and interests. How does your choice of leisure activities, your style of participation, and the people with whom you participate relate to your major preoccupations and interests?

Endnotes

1 Howe, N. and Strauss, B. (1997). *The fourth turning—What the cycles of history tell us about America's next rendezvous with destiny (p. 55)*. New York, NY: Broadway Books.

2 ibid., p. 57

3 Kelly, J. R. and Godbey, G. (1991). *The sociology of leisure*. State College, PA: Venture Publishing, Inc.

4 Henderson, K., Bialeschki, D., Shaw, S., and Freysinger, V. (1989). *A leisure of one's own: A feminist perspective on women's leisure*. State College, PA: Venture Publishing, Inc.

5 Masnick, G. and Banes, M. (1980). *The nation's families: 1960–1990*. Cambridge, MA: Joint Center for Urban Studies of Harvard and MIT.

6 Howe, N. and Strauss, B. (2000). *Millennials rising*. New York, NY: Vintage Books.

7 ibid.

8 Raines, C. (2002). *Managing millennials*. Retrieved September 7, 2007, from http://www.generationsatwork.com/articles/millenials.htm

9 Howe, N. and Strauss, B. (1997). *The fourth turning—What the cycles of history tell us about America's next rendezvous with destiny*. New York, NY: Broadway Books.

10 ibid., p. 3

11 Defoe-Whitehead, B. (1993, April). Dan Quayle was right. *Atlantic Monthly*, 271(4), 47–84.

12 Brickman, P. (1987). *Commitment, conflict, and caring*. Englewood Cliffs, NJ: Prentice-Hall.

13 Coontz, S. (1991). *The way we never were—American families and the nostalgia trap.* New York, NY: Basic Books.

14 ibid.

15 ibid.

16 Sutton-Smith, B. (1971). Children at play. *Natural History, 80*(1), 55.

17 Bodrova, E. and Leong, D.J. (2007). Why children need play. Retrieved June 15, 2007, from *Early Childhood Today* at http://www.scholastic.com/ect

18 Queen, S. and Haberstein, R. (1974). *The family in foreign cultures* (p. 59). Philadelphia, PA: J. B. Lippincott.

19 Winn, K., Crawford, D., and Fischer, J. (1991). Equity and commitment in romance versus friendship. *Journal of Social Behavior and Personality, 6*(2), 301–314.

20 Baltes, P. (1987). Theoretical propositions of life-span developmental psychology: On the dynamics between growth and decline. *Developmental Psychology, 23*(5), 611–626.

21 Mogul, K. (1979). Women in mid-life: Decisions, rewards, and conflicts related to work and careers. *American Journal of Psychiatry, 136*(9), 1142.

22 A new look at middle age. (1999, March 20). *Centre Daily Times.*

23 Baltes (1987)

24 Satullo, C. (2002, February 24). Aging in place. *The Philadelphia Inquirer*, C4.

25 ibid.

26 Lewis, R. (1998, March 22). Boomers to reinvent retirement. *USA Weekend*, 6.

27 Fraser, C. (2002, March 1). *The big chill: A look at Boomers' top 10 desired retirement activities.* Retrieved June 15, 2007, from http://www.moneysbestfriend.com/default.aspx?id=89

28 Dychtwald, K. (2002). Quoted by Fraser, C. (2002, March 1). *The big chill: A look at Boomers' top 10 desired retirement activities.* Retrieved June 15, 2007, from http://www.moneysbestfriend.com/default.aspx?id=89

29 Fraser (2002)

30 American Sportfishing Association (2002). Quoted by Fraser, C. (2002, March 1). *The big chill: A look at Boomers' top 10 desired retirement activities.* Retrieved June 15, 2007, from http://www.moneysbestfriend.com/default.aspx?id=89

31 Searle, M. S., Mahon, M. J., Iso-Ahola, S. E., Sdrolais, H. A., and van Dyck, J. (1995). Enhancing a sense of independence and psychological well-being among the elderly: A field experiment. *Journal of Leisure Research, 27*(2), 107–124.

32 Mack, R., Salmoni, A., Viverais-Dressler, G., Porter, E., and Garg, R. (1997). Perceived risks to independent living: The views of older, community-dwelling adults. *The Gerontologist, 37*(6), 729–736.

33 Fillenbaum, G. (1995). Activities of daily living. In G. Maddox (Ed.), *The encyclopedia of aging* (pp. 7–9). New York, NY: Springer Publishing.

34 Neugarten, B. (1979). Time, age, and the life cycle. *American Journal of Psychiatry, 136*(7), 891.

Traveling to Leisure— Traveling as Leisure

When was the last time you took a trip for leisure purposes? Probably it occurred during the last few days. In modern societies, traveling is a part of everyday life, not only to work but also to a wide variety of leisure experiences—to dinner or the theater, to the beach, theme park, campsite or to any of an almost unlimited number of locations of leisure experiences. In such situations, as Clawson and Knetsch[1] pointed out, there are five stages: anticipation, travel to, participation, travel from, and recall. That is, we think about some leisure activity outside our home and make a decision to go. We also may make a few or many arrangements. We then travel, most frequently by car in North America. Next we participate in the leisure experience, return home, and then are left with some memories about what we did.

Much of this travel is a part of "ordinary life." We ordinarily go, on Thursdays, to the racquetball club or choir practice. The extent to which this kind of travel is increasing is suggested by the fact that the number of automobile miles traveled is increasing four to six times faster than the population. The growth or decline of such travel, of course, is related to a number of factors such as availability and cost of fuel; cost, safety, and convenience of public transportation; weather; level of traffic congestion; and availability of parking.

While much of our leisure-related travel is part of ordinary life, some of it is outside our daily routine. The vast majority of trips that may be thought of as being outside ordinary life (100 miles or more away from home) are for visiting friends or relatives or other pleasurable purposes, rather than for business. Tourism may be viewed as a subset of travel which has a profound impact on our economy. About one third of all automobile vehicle miles are used for recreation trips.

You really have to want to go to the Met. I love opera, and the Met is the best. From here, we drive from West Chester to the train station, try to find a place to park, take the train, then the subway, then walk. After the opera we repeat the process, even though we are already tired. Sometimes you see some scary folks on the subway. I don't like driving all the way into the City because the tunnels can get backed up for a half-hour and, when you finally do get there, you're tense and irritable. If the trip gets any tougher, I'll just listen to the opera at home on the stereo. I mean, it is a thrill to hear the diva hit that impossible high note that just sends you to heaven, but if it's hell to get there, the price is too high.

Sixty percent of air passengers are on leisure, not business trips.[2]

Tourism has emerged as one of the world's largest composite industries so rapidly that its consequences cannot yet be understood. It is decreasing cultural diversity in the world much the same way as agribusiness is decreasing biodiversity by limiting production to the food sources that best add to profit margins.

The scope of international tourism may be seen in Figure 9.1. China, for instance, had six million international tourists visit during the three-month period from April through June, 2006.

Careers are diverse within the tourism industry and include those with airlines, bus companies, cruise companies, railroads, rental car companies, hotels, motels and resorts, travel agencies, tour companies, food service, tourism education, tourism research, tourism journalism, recreation, attractions, tourism offices and information centers, conventions and visitors bureaus, meeting planners and others.

Some of the factors which account for the rise of tourism on an international level include rising disposable incomes, increasing urbanization, increasing mobility, increases in free time, higher levels of education and a greater global media network.[3] This has resulted in huge gains in the number of international arrivals during the last forty years. It is anticipated that growth in international tourism will continue worldwide during the next several years, with the largest percentage increases caused by travel to Asia and Oceania.

What exactly is tourism? According to tourism experts McIntosh and Goeldner,

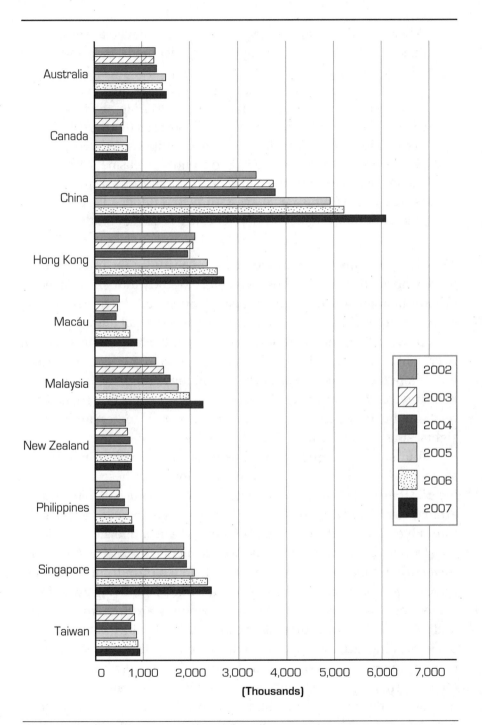

Figure 9.1 Visitor arrivals, 2002–2007[4] (Note: Excludes specific crossborder flows)

When we think of tourism, we think of people who are visiting a particular place for sightseeing, visiting friends and
relatives, taking a vacation, and having a good time. They
may spend their leisure time engaging in various sports,
sunbathing, talking, singing, taking rides, touring, reading,
or simply enjoying the environment. If we consider the subject further, we may include in our definition of tourism
people who are participating in a convention, a business conference, or some other kind of business or professional activity
as well as those who are taking a study tour under an expert
guide or doing some kind of scientific research or study.[5]

"Tourism" is defined very differently depending on the interests of
those who are defining it. Those who wish to study tourism as an economic phenomenon, or as an "industry," often define a tourist, in its
broadest terms, as "anyone away from his or her usual place of living
and/or work."[6] Some definitions specify that the tourist must stay
overnight and/or that the travel must be at least fifty or one-hundred
miles from their home. When such a definition is used, the tourist may
have traveled for a wide variety of reasons, such as visiting friends or
relatives, business/convention, outdoor recreation, entertainment/
sightseeing, personal, shopping, or other reasons.

Tourism, considered as an industry, is made up of a number of
segments, each of which offers career possibilities. These segments
include transportation, accommodations, food service, shopping, travel
arrangements, and activities for tourists that might involve history, culture, adventure, sports, recreation, entertainment, and related activities.

I would define tourism, in its most elementary sense, as voluntary
travel to a destination that is more novel than the place from which one
traveled. All tourism, while it may be motivated by moving away from
something, such as cold weather, or moving toward something, such
as the Grand Canyon, is ultimately chosen freely by the individual. The
distinguishing factor of all tourism destinations is that they are novel,
unique, unknown, or new to the individual than the place from which
the trip originated. Most tourism actually involves several trips, first
traveling to the primary destination and then taking many smaller side
trips once there. These side trips are also tourism, however, since the
destination for such side trips will still be more novel than the place

from which the individual traveled. If you go, for instance, from New York to London and arrive at a hotel where you stay for a week, your side trips from London to Brighton, Windsor Castle, or Yorkshire will still be tourism, since Yorkshire will be more novel than your London hotel. As we will see, there are many other elements used to explain tourism.

It is hard for us to imagine how much of a change has taken place historically in the orientation of human beings that has caused them to travel long distances for pleasure. Sociologist Eric Cohen commented on this change as follows:

> Whereas primitive and traditional man will leave his native habitat only when forced to by extreme circumstances, modern man is more loosely attached to his environment, much more willing to change it, especially temporarily, and is remarkably able to adapt to new environments. He is interested in things, sights, customs, and cultures different from his own, precisely because they are different. Gradually, a new value has evolved: the appreciation of the experience of strangeness or novelty. This experience now excites, titillates, and gratifies whereas before it only frightened.[7]

Thus, tourism represents a new orientation to the world. At its extreme, it is an attempt to literally be at home in the world. Those who are most able and interested in doing this often find that they begin to think of themselves more as a citizen of the world and less of a particular country.

They also begin to gain more understandings about the reasons for differences from country to country. There are reasons why China has a strictly enforced policy of limiting family size. There are reasons why the English still have a monarchy. There *are* reasons *why*.

I went to an international sociology conference in Nigeria. All the sociologists who attended from all over the world thought it would be a great experience. It was in some ways, but it's hard to remember how different the developing world is—extreme poverty produces desperation—and a lot of lawlessness. Many of the people at the conference just wandered around the city with their suits on, their name tags in place—there were over twenty robberies and muggings. I guess it was a good lesson in sociology. I wonder where we will go next year?

Those who have the opportunity to travel frequently often begin to see the world in more culturally relative terms rather than assuming that everything in their own country is superior. Gaining this understanding may be one of the best hopes humans have to chart a peaceful future.

Time Spent Traveling

If time is a defining and limiting factor in terms of the use of the informal educational infrastructure within a community, time spent in travel is of particular interest because much of the infrastructure cannot be used without travel. One of the reasons that learning about science and other topics has been largely assigned to public schools is that where children travel in the amount of time available for them to travel often limits them to school. The same can be said for adults. Americans have moved further away from each other in the last few decades, even as we have "urbanized."

There is a remarkable consistency in terms of the amount of time spent traveling, the duration and number of trips taken in daily life, and the number of minutes left over for exploring is both fixed and constant. While there are a few outliers, such as Californians, who spend 109 minutes per day traveling, most of the world spends about one hour in daily life going from point A to point B.[8] On average, people make three to four trips per day, whether they are rich or poor. Hupkes found a law of constant trip rates.[9] People tend to take a main trip per day, averaging 40 to 50 minutes. "Thus, what most people use or access daily is what can be reached in 20 minutes or so."[10] It should be further noted that about four out of every five miles traveled in the United States is by automobile.[11] Thus, access to automobiles, parking and cost of parking are important variables in terms of what educational sites people will visit within a community. Americans walk an average of only about one kilometer a day; which may be about 12 minutes worth of walking.[12] These statistics show how limited the potential is, on average, for people to walk to educational resources within their community.

While people average three or four shorter trips per day, they also average three or four trips per year outside their territory. These longer trips may be ones where the potential for educational use of community infrastructure is greatest, even though it is often the infrastructure of a city which is a tourist destination. Vacations constitute a larger block of time, television is viewed much less, and many side visits from the original destination take place, often of an educational nature.[13] In everyday life, however, the competition for every community-based institution where voluntary learning could take place, such as museums, historic sites, planetariums, arboretums, recreation and park departments and others, is not each other but rather television.

Tourism Theory

What accounts for tourism? Why do people brave the inconveniences and uncertainties of travel to places they often know little about? No single theoretical explanation is satisfactory to explain all tourist behavior. Nevertheless, there are several commonly accepted explanations for tourism. Tourism has been explained as novelty-seeking behavior, as play, as the seeking of the authentic, as relations among strangers, as a form of imperialism, and as pleasure seeking (sometimes called the four S theory of tourism—sun, sand, surf, and sex). It also may be motivated by the desire for anonymity or to fulfill fantasies. A study by Crompton of motivations for a pleasure vacation found that such motivations included: escape from a mundane environment, exploration and evaluation of self, relaxation, prestige, regression, enhancement of kinship relations, social interaction, cultural motives, and novelty.[14] Most certainly, many tourist experiences are undertaken due to a variety of motives.

As discussed, tourism always involves a destination more novel than the place where one resides. This novelty, uniqueness, or newness is viewed as a positive thing—a "pull" factor. For example, I have never seen the Grand Canyon; experienced Carnival in Rio; been to the Kentucky Derby, Australia, Alaska or Knott's Berry Farm—and I would like to. Novelty, according to this theory, is a key determinant in the individual decision to travel. While all tourists seek novelty to some extent, the degree to which they seek novelty varies greatly. Those who seek the most novelty, according to Plog,[15] are adventuresome and want to engage in individual exploration. They are small in number and make little use of the services of the tourism industry. Tourists who seek a middle range of novelty are likely to travel to areas with some developed tourist facilities and a growing reputation. To accommodate them, there is increasing commercialization of the tourist (guest)–host relationship. Finally, tourists who seek the least novelty use organized package tours to destinations that have become popular. The hotels and restaurants they use are more similar to their home area.

How much novelty a tourist seeks provides a basis for analysis not only of tourists but also the evolution of a tourist site and the type of appeal which is made to potential tourists. Butler,[16] for example, thought that tourist sites often go through six stages. The first stage is an exploration stage, where a small number of tourists arrive, making individual arrangements. Exploration is followed by an involvement stage, in which local residents begin to provide accommodations for tourists and a "tourist season" emerges. Then comes a development stage, in which the area has become a well-defined tourist market shaped by heavy advertising. In the consolidation stage, tourist visitation continues to increase but at a slower rate. Tourists now outnumber the residents. Then comes stagnation, when a peak number of tourists has been reached and the tourist infrastructure is at capacity. Finally, the site either experiences a decline in visitation because it cannot compete with newer attractions, or it enters a rejuvenation period in which the tourist attractions are changed and improved. These stages in the

We had been to Ottawa a few times and, at first, we stayed in a big chain hotel. High-rise. Those hotels are all the same and they seem to produce the same kind of visit—no matter where you are. This time I booked a bed and breakfast—against Chuck's better judgment—right near the canal.

We had a great time and actually learned some things about Ottawa: The first inhabitants were Indians. It became New France, then came under British rule. Their wonderful canal was designed to establish a waterway link between Montréal and Kingston, which used to be Canada's capital. A large part of the city burned down in 1900. They have an awesome farmer's market. Am I starting to sound like a tour guide? Sorry.

It's just that the woman who ran the bed and breakfast was tired of Americans who knew nothing about her country. She is French-Canadian and tried to give us all sides of the story. We also learned about "The Group of Seven"—Canada's best-known artists—and saw some of their paintings at the National Gallery. I love Jack Pine, a huge painting by the artist Tommy Thompson.

Our host helped us understand the city. She also made the best bacon and eggs I ever ate!

life cycle of the tourist site relate directly to the type of tourists who come to the site and how much novelty they seek.

Novelty is also tied to another framework within which we can analyze tourism-play. As discussed in Chapter 1, psychological theories of play assume that the individual has an innate need to process information—to be stimulated. Objects or environments that are novel and intense drive the individual into exploration of the object or environment to determine its interesting properties. Next, this process is repeated several times with minor variations. Finally, when the novel object or environment has been assimilated, creativity may occur—a response that is both novel and appropriate in its outcomes.

> When we go on a cruise, the thing I like is that you can see little bits of other places but still get back to the ship without any trouble. It's kind of like sampling different kinds of chocolate in a box but you can close the box easily. I guess I should be a little more adventurous. My daughter certainly is.
>
> She's been in the Peace Corps—in Sri Lanka. She lived like the Sri Lankans—eating that spicy food, enduring the tremendous heat without air conditioning and even dressing like they dress. I could never do that. At some point, I would want air conditioning, a cheeseburger, and CNN news. That's just how I'm wired.

Certainly, this progression describes many tourist experiences. An individual or group of individuals is attracted to a tourist destination (e.g., the Grand Canyon) at least partly because it stands out from the rest of the landscape. It is novel and intense. The individual or individuals in question then travel to the Grand Canyon and, to some extent, explore it—see what its properties are, what it has to distract or excite. Most tourists actually develop a routine of behavior at their tourist destination: the routine is then varied slightly each time as they learn about the new environment and as it becomes less novel. This routine allows them, in some sense, to master the site, and then gain some level of understanding of it that they didn't previously have. The area becomes more familiar, perhaps less stimulating. At this point, visiting even the Grand Canyon may start to seem more like ordinary life. Now the tourist may withdraw from the environment, start to treat it more like ordinary life, or make a creative response—react to the tourist site in a way which is both novel and appropriate. At the Grand Canyon, this might mean getting up before dawn to experience the earliest morning colors.

Tourism would seem to correspond to virtually every character-istic of play as identified by Huizinga[17] (see Chapter 1). Tourism, like play, is outside ordinary life, limited in time and space, surrounded by an air of mystery, utterly absorbing yet recognized as being somewhat make-believe, has something at stake, an outcome in doubt, and may promote the formation of social groups.

Tourism shapes the lives of those who reside in areas that become tourist sites, often in fundamental ways. This is particularly true when the hosts and guests are different in terms of their culture, technology, or economic resources. Native Hawaiians, farmers in Ireland, the Amish in Pennsylvania or elsewhere, or the residents of the Costa del Sol region of Spain may find that tourist visitation has gradually led to changes in the variety and price of food sold in local stores or restaurants, the language or languages spoken in their community, definitions of what is or is not ethical or important, and the types of occupations available to them. Tourism may bring changes the host culture desires, such as the creation of jobs, improvement of transportation and new technologies.

Tourism may also be conceived of as relations between strangers. Machlis and Burch have argued that tourism can be best understood as such relations. "Tourism is an intense, specific case of that which reg-ularly occurs in the daily life of modern society—the ordering of rela-tions among strangers."[18] According to this line of reasoning, travel is done for the same motives which drive our everyday life, such as "greed, curiosity, adventure and status."[19] The difference is that, for the tourist, daily routines which we take for granted, "eating, sleeping, bathing, talking, observing, thinking, sex and so forth," take on a differ-ent significance that is larger than life and is shaped by how we relate to strangers.

Finally, tourism may be thought of as a search for the authentic. The huge increase in tourism that has occurred throughout most of the "modern" world during the last fifty years may be associated not only with the rise of inexpensive travel and mass communications but also with the characteristics of modern life. MacCannell[20] said that modern life was characterized by advanced urbanization, expanded literacy, generalized healthcare, rationalized work arrangements, geographical and economic mobility, and the emergence of the nation-state. Modern

If you have done a lot of business travel and stayed in hundreds of hotels all over the world, you sometimes get tired of hotel people always trying to change things that don't matter much—putting a mint on your pillow or turning down the blankets in the early evening. When you have stayed in hundreds of hotels, they all seem the same. The bathroom is on one side of the room as you enter. There is a cabinet with a TV in it. A bed and a window, which is usually locked. There is a phone—which I never use—my cell is much less expensive. A lot of printed information. Maybe a fitness center—or a lounge. But they never get to the biggest problem that experienced business travelers have when they are in hotels. They never seem to catch on—The biggest problem is loneliness.

life is also characterized, he thought, by a mentality among citizens of modern countries that sets the modern society in opposition both to its own past and to underdeveloped nations. People in the modern nation develop a completely different set of beliefs and ideologies than their ancestors or those in less developed nations. Tourism, MacCannell believed, is uniquely suited among many leisure alternatives to draw the individual into a relation with the entire modern world. As leisure has displaced work from the center of social arrangements and as "culture" has been removed from everyday "work" activities, the emerging modern mind becomes interested in expanding its leisure experiences and continuously searching for alternatives and novelty.

Tourism represents the search for the authentic, for the real. The tourist, according to MacCannell, seeks to make sense of the world through his or her travels. To do this, the tourist must get past the phony tourist sites that have been set up just to lure the tourist and get to what is real or authentic about an area. The tourist may be ashamed of being a tourist since he or she can't always tell the real from the "tourist trap." The longer one is a tourist, however, the better he or she is able to understand what real life is like in an area and to avoid the commercialized areas that exist just for profit.

Tourism among those in the modern world, then, is a search for meaning—a search to try to make sense of the entire world. While this idea seems to have some merit, it may be argued that many tourists are not interested in such broad meanings. They may, for instance, seek merely to find a warm beach or a good time in a new location. MacCannell's explanation, then, may apply more to those with higher

In England, it seems nobody likes Manchester. When I tell people in London that I'm going to Manchester, they say: "Whatever would you want to go there for? There's nothing there!"

For me, there is. Manchester is where the Industrial Revolution happened. You can see it. The whole factory system that was imported by the United States. The whole mass production, division of labor, dark satanic mills—all that stuff. Manchester is real in a way London isn't. London is just a modern, multicultural city— but Manchester...

And when you get up in the Yorkshire Dales, there are these little villages that are still removed from the giant plastic whiz-bang commercialized world. Where people walk down to the greengrocer to buy their produce for the day. Pubs where old men spend an hour or three with a pint of bitter; not doing much of anything and not feeling any need to. I like the middle of Britain because it's real.

levels of formal education. There is also the question of what "authentic" means. As Cohen[21] and others have pointed out, some tourist sites seem to acquire a sense of the authentic *after* they have been developed. We may, for instance, have come to think of Disney World as "the real thing."

Regardless of whether or not tourism represents the search for the authentic, it does seem that tourism has emerged as a form of leisure expression that is of critical importance. There is every indication it will continue to grow and become increasingly important in shaping our view of the world.

While no one theory of tourism can explain the whole phenomenon, some general factors determine the attractiveness of a tourism site and help determine its success. These factors include natural beauty and climate; cultural and social characteristics; accessibility of the region; attitudes toward tourists; infrastructure of the region; price levels; shopping and commercial facilities; and sport, recreation and educational facilities.[22] If one of these items is noticeably lacking, it may be difficult for mass tourism to succeed.

Ecotourism

People are drawn to nature. Today, more and more people are drawn to a variety of exotic and unusual natural places. One may observe mountain gorillas in the jungles of Rwanda, colorful fish in the reef off Belize, or howling monkeys and singing birds in the Costa Rican rainforest.

Tourism produces change. It changes the tourist, the tourist site, and the economy of the host community. While these changes don't always occur in the same way, many researchers have found identifiable stages in various processes relating to tourism. Plog[23] found that tourist sites are attractive to different visitors at different stages of their evolution. Initially, a small number of adventuresome tourists visit an area. As the area becomes more accessible, better known, and better served, those tourists seeking less adventure and contrast begin to dominate. Finally, as the area becomes older and less different from the visitor's area of origin, a declining number of tourists who seek even less variation and novelty will visit.

The changes that are often produced by tourism are such that some who manage and study tourism have promoted what may be called ecotourism. *Ecotourism* is

> …tourism that consists in traveling to relatively undisturbed or uncontaminated natural areas with the specific objective of studying, admiring, and enjoying the scenery and its wild plants and animals, as well as any existing cultural manifestations (both past and present) found in these areas. The main point is that the person who practices ecotourism has the opportunity of immersing himself/herself in nature in a manner generally not available in the urban environment.[24]

Ecotourism assumes that the changes brought about by tourism will be less harmful and the tourist experience more meaningful if mass tourism can be avoided. Under various forms of ecotourism, tourists are more highly integrated into the existing host culture and they live more like the natives during their stay. Krippendorf[25] stated that such tourism is based upon planning with regional coordination of district plans before development takes place. Tourism schemes spring from a concept and use concentrated development within existing settlements rather than developing new ones. Green tourism protects the fine landscapes of the area, reuses existing buildings, and sets limits on the amount of development in an area. Only natives of the area serve as developers. The economic, ecological, and social issues surrounding tourist development are all considered rather than just the economic ones. Traffic plans favor public transportation. Developers are required to bear the social costs of their development, and the architecture, historical sites, and natural sites are retained even if they serve as an obstacle to tourism growth.

This vision of alternative tourism has much to recommend it. In effect, through alternative tourism the "integrity" of a community is more likely to be protected. Those who live in the area are likely to play a more central role in controlling their own destiny. As Butler observed, however, alternative tourism may actually cause a greater impact on the area in question:

> *We just got back from Costa Rica. It was a great trip! They are really trying to make ecotourism work. You go through this jungle area, but you are walking on wooden pathways, which are sometimes hanging in the air, so you won't disturb the animal and plant life. They actually limit what you can do or see. When we left, it was like we had never been there. No footprints. Minimum impact. I like that. I mean, I like being a tourist, but I hate tourists. Tourists usually destroy what they love, but in Costa Rica, maybe they can't.*

> ...at least potentially, alternative forms of tourism penetrate further into the personal space of residents, involve them to a much greater degree, expose often fragile resources to greater visitation, expose the genuine article to tourism to a greater degree, proportionally may result in greater leakage of expenditures, and may cause political change in terms of control over development.[26]

Many problems may occur. While local people can work as guides for tours, for instance, they may not possess appropriate language skills or hospitality training to lead foreign tourists. They also may not fully understand the delicate nature of their own environment and may cause environmental damage in spite of good intentions.[27] In many cases, the money earned from ecotourism does not go to indigenous people. The World Bank estimates that more than half of tourist spending in developing nations leaks back into industrialized nations due to foreign ownership of hotels and tour companies. Other studies suggest the figure could be as high as ninety percent.[28] In short, these criticisms of alternative tourism assume the negative effects of tourism may be minimized if it is kept at arm's-length from the local culture.

Whether or not alternative tourism is superior to mass tourism may depend upon on how one views the process of interaction between strangers. If you assume that there is a great potential for good to result from such visitation, then alternative tourism would seem superior. If, however, you assume that close contact between guests and hosts is likely to have negative results, then mass tourism may actually be superior. There would seem to be evidence of both good and evil resulting from such close contact. There is evidence of tourism being used as a means of actually protecting existing cultures. In Sweden, for instance, "cultural preservation tourist areas" which consist of villages and surrounding landscapes, have been used as ways of keeping the culture of Lapplanders alive. Tourists become patrons and sponsors.

> Sponsoring patron tourists should first of all be offered opportunities to learn the area thoroughly; courses should play an important part for patron tourists, as well as for the culture-preserving tourist areas. Traditions of different kinds in handicrafts, culinary arts, music, dance, folk costumes and such could be given as courses. There could be opportunities to learn about the flora, fauna, geology and languages of the area, and about methods of traditional farming, hunting and architecture.
>
> In the culture-preserving tourist areas, all tourists are considered guests, while at the same time being part of a team. The social function of the old village community demanded involvement in different matters, as well as giving security.
>
> Thus, sponsoring patron tourists would have the opportunity to take part in traditional life. For example, they could cut hay with a scythe in the meadows, milk the cows, go hunting, go fishing and even arrange folk-dances. The intention would be that the sponsoring patron tourists would come back year after year, and identify with the area. They should also have the opportunity to come at different times of the year and take part in various seasonal activities.[29]

This approach makes the local people teachers who present their own civilization to tourists. It also means that the tourist becomes "specialized," in effect becoming somewhat of an expert about the culture they are visiting. Such schemes mean that the tourism process must be planned locally.

Alternative tourism takes the tourist seriously and, in reality, trusts that the tourist will come to respect the area visited. It also assumes that local people will be less likely to "sell out" for short-term profit than outsiders. Whether or not this is true is difficult to judge.

The Development of the Tourism Industry

While the origins of tourism are uncertain, the term *tour* gained widespread social use in Europe in the eighteenth and nineteenth centuries. There is significant evidence of travel for leisure purposes long before this. Even some of the things we associate with tourism are centuries old, such as souvenirs. Ousby[30] documented the growth of a souvenir industry at Stratford-on-Avon, England within a century of the death of Shakespeare. A mulberry tree, under which Shakespeare reportedly had done much of his writing, was carved into snuff boxes and other trinkets and sold to tourists.

While a few privileged people were able to take the "grand tour" of Europe or elsewhere in search of culture and education, it was not until the Industrial Revolution that technological advances, such as the invention of the steam engine and the emergence of a larger middle-class, produced an upsurge in tourist activity. Thomas Cook in 1855 initiated tours to the Paris Exhibition—the first modern package tour. By 1864, more than one million people used his services, and he opened offices in New York and Rome. The tourism industry has grown tremendously since that time, and today, according to Blank,[31] it includes all those economic activities that take place because tourists travel. These

> There has to be something to bring back to show that you've been there. Postcards, t-shirts, little replicas of the Eiffel Tower or a Budda statue or a koala bear. It just doesn't seem like the trip is complete if you don't document where you've been—with stuff.
>
> While it's just "stuff" to me, my aunt still displays the fan I brought her from China on her coffeetable. Maybe she imagines what China must be like when she sees that fan. She's way too fragile to travel anymore. Maybe that fan was worth bringing back.

include food, lodging, transportation, recreation, attractions, tourist promotion and marketing.

From its inception, tourism has been planned so that tourists would see things in certain ways. "The character of places has been reinterpreted in the social imagination in sufficiently comprehensive ways as to change the dominant perceptions of them at various historic periods."[32] Tourism "toys" with history, often reshaping it to fit the needs of tourist entrepreneurs or state government officials. Rather than produce a multitude of images, mass tourism is dependent upon a few images which are often stereotypes or inaccurate. People forget that Florida is often humid and rainy, that New Orleans is dangerous and has high rates of poverty, or that London is essentially a modern city with huge traffic jams. Rather, they concentrate on what has been promoted: Disney World or the Miami waterfront hotels, the excitement of Mardi Gras or the French Quarter, and the history and culture of London. Mass tourism, then, has brought about not only a concentration of tourists traveling to one place but also a concentration of images of the place they visit. What they sometimes see are what Boorstin[33] called "pseudo-events." Attractions are made suitable for the masses by reconstructing them, removing elements which are unacceptable, etc. Thus, for example, Hawaiian dancing girls have to be dressed "decently" in accordance with what "decency" means to tourists. Traditional festivals have to be more colorful and respectable. "As a result, they largely lose flow of life and natural texture of the host culture."[34]

The travel and tourism industry, as mentioned earlier, is probably already the largest in the world, and it is only going to get larger. In the United States, the travel industry is the third largest retail or service industry, behind automobile dealers and food stores. Tourism is the largest employer in several states, including Alaska, Arizona, Colorado, Florida, Hawaii, Idaho, Maine, Nevada, New Hampshire, New Mexico, Utah, Vermont, and Wyoming. In spite of this, the tourism industry is risky. Tourist "demand" may change quickly and dramatically over a five- or ten-year period. One bit of bad publicity may change the visitation patterns of millions of tourists. At the same time, tourist investment projects such as hotels have life expectancies of 25 years or longer. While good feasibility studies may help control such risk, there is no guarantee that the tourist will continue to visit.

Tourism growth, however, has caused a variety of problems, particularly those associated with mass tourism. There may be scattered development or development without planning that harms the finest landscapes in an area or hurts the sense of community. Tourism development may be done primarily by outside developers who have little interest in anything but short-term profit. Farming may decline, and people may be forced into low-paying jobs related to tourism, many of which are seasonal rather than year-round. Transportation patterns may begin to favor the automobile and the travel needs of the tourist. Butler[35] categorized the following negative changes associated with tourism: price increases (e.g., labor, goods, taxes, land); changes in local attitudes and behaviors; pressure on people; crowding; disturbance; alienation; loss of resources, access, rights, and privacy; denigration; prostitution of local culture; reduction of aesthetics; pollution in various forms; lack of control over the destination's future; and specific problems such as vandalism, litter, traffic, and low-paid seasonal employment.

These problems are, according to Butler, ones associated with many forms of development and which can be minimized or avoided with appropriate planning. In countless cases, however, they are not.

Tourism may also be thought of as a process by which those from a more powerful culture slowly change and control the culture they visit. If the tourism process is thought of as hosts and guests, then the guests may slowly reshape the life of the hosts, particularly if there is a great difference in the stage of development in the guest and host cultures. In such cases, there is a cycle set in motion in which, at first,

> I live in a tourist city. I mean, San Antonio wouldn't be here without tourism or without the River Walk area. It's over half the economy of the city.
>
> Do I like it? I don't know. We get all kinds of tourists spending big bucks on food and booze so it's hard for the locals to go out to a nice restaurant. Sometimes, prices in stores are high because the tourists will buy anything. They rent cars and always seem to be lost. There are lots of car wrecks. Also, we have prostitution. Some of them have AIDS. You can't get rid of them because there's money to be made. Still, the area is well-managed. We have good policing and it's generally safe. I go there with my kids sometimes and take a water taxi around the area. It's actually beautiful. People are generally enjoying life. You win some and you lose some. Probably our quality of life would suffer without it—a lot.

the hosts are dominant in power over the guests. Gradually this changes to equality, then dependence of the hosts on the guests, and a final stage in which the needs of the host culture become secondary to the needs of the guests. As this happens, the way of life of the host culture is harmed or destroyed.

Some of these effects may be seen in Hawaii and other islands that have become popular tourist sites. Gradually, the beaches are crowded with high-rise hotels, and agricultural land is converted to tourism. The customs of natives are slowly replaced by the way of life of those who visit. Certainly there are advantages to this as well. The guests' culture may bring technological advancements as an improved material standard of living. It may bring contact with the outside world with resulting educational benefits. Thus, the outcome of guest-host relations can only be assessed after judgments are made about how desirable life was in the host culture before the arrival of tourists.

> I'm a Taiwanese aboriginal. We live below Kauhsiung in a hilly area where we have lived for centuries and centuries. I make my living by being a kind of actor in a presentation for tourists. We wear traditional dress and sing songs of my ancestors for them—the songs have been changed to suit the tourists. It is like we are stuck between two cultures. We can either try and keep our way of life or blend in with the mainstream and disappear. You can't hunt and fish anymore and make a decent living. You need to know how to sit in front of a machine and type messages. I'm proud of my heritage but that only gets you so far—I don't exactly know what to do—I don't exactly know who I am.

For such tourism projects to succeed, the guest culture must not be changed more than those of the visiting culture. The tourists cannot ask that the area be changed to accommodate their normal preferences in food, transportation or other aspects of everyday life.

Tourist entrepreneurs often present distorted images of those who live in tourist destinations both because they don't know much about their cultures or because such stereotypes are profitable. In terms of the portrayal of American Indians to tourists, for instance, there has been a tendency toward stereotypes that simply aren't true.

But it is this fictional construct that inevitably virginal tourists from abroad (and many mainstream traveling Americans) now carry in their head. It is a fusion of a thousand images of Geronomo, of the magnificent John Wayne, the sterling Gary Cooper, of intrepid forays in enemy scrub, of lone forts, of smoke signals from afar and of sinister ambushes in rocky and barren deserts.... It is the relative absence of the portrayal of female figures, for the Westernized parody being composed had to be masculine.[36]

Thus, while tourism can inform visitors about other cultures, it can also present distorted views in which little real learning takes place. Alternative tourism may help keep such distortions at a minimum by increasing the intensity and complexity of the ways that guest and host interact with each other and empowering the host culture to present itself.

Government's Critical Role

Tourism is not simply "an industry;" it is an important function of government. As an example of this, look at California's top tourism attractions for 2005[37] as shown in Table 9.1. While it may not shock you that Disneyland had 14.5 million visitors, you may be surprised to learn that Golden Gate National Recreation Area, managed by the National Park Service, had almost the same number of visitors. Yosemite National Park had about the same number of tourist visits as Knott's Berry Farm. Some state park locations had visitor numbers that equaled or exceeded many of the top amusement/theme parks and many national parks.

Not only does government manage many sites that are visited by millions of tourists, the existence of much of the commercial tourism industry is completely dependent upon government-managed tourist sites.

Government shapes the policies that either favor or do not favor tourism as an economic development strategy. Government promotes tourism within its borders and uses taxes as a way to promote or discourage tourism. In addition, government environmental regulations and their enforcement or lack of enforcement are critical in determining if ecotourism can succeed.

Table 9.1 California's Top Attractions, 2005[38]

Top California Amusement/Theme Parks (based on 2005 attendance)

Disneyland, Anaheim	14,550,000
Disney's California Adventure	5,830,000
Universal Studios, Hollywood	4,700,000
Sea World, San Diego	4,100,000
Knott's Berry Farm, Buena Park	3,470,500
San Diego Zoo	3,100,000
Santa Cruz Beach Boardwalk	3,000,000
Six Flags Magic Mountain, Valencia	2,835,000
Paramount's Great America, Santa Clara	2,070,000
Monterey Bay Aquarium, Monterey	1,884,000
Six Flags Marine World, Vallejo	1,537,000
Legoland, Carlsbad	1,430,000
San Diego Zoo's Wild Animal Park	1,400,000

Top 10 National Park Facilities (based on 2005 visitation)

Golden Gate National Recreation Area	13,602,269
San Francisco Maritime Museum	3,976,056
Yosemite National Park	3,304,144
Point Reyes National Seashore	1,988,585
Fort Point National Historic Site	1,682,041
Joshua Tree National Park	1,375,111
Sequoia National Park	1,004,843
Cabrillo National Monument	826,615
Death Valley National Park	800,113
Whiskeytown-Shasta-Trinity National Recreation Area	740,275

Top 10 State Parks (based on 2004/2005 fiscal year visitation)

Old Town San Diego State Historic Park	4,578,683
Huntington State Beach	3,062,714
Sonoma Coast State Beach	3,059,141
Seacliff State Beach	2,916,181
Bolsa Chica State Beach	2,695,594
San Onofre State Beach	2,551,463
Doheny State Beach	1,984,200
Oceano Dunes State Vehicle Recreation Area	1,871,162
New Brighton State Beach	1,674,889
Malibu Lagoon State Beach	1,546,979

Tourism in the Post 9/11 Future

The travel and tourism industry continues to be the second-largest employer in the United States, and there is every reason to believe tourism will grow in importance during the next few decades. As the economies of the world become more dependent upon each other, it will become increasingly important to understand each other's culture. International tourism is therefore likely to expand. The vast changes sweeping the former Soviet Union and Eastern Europe may also positively affect tourism because travel restrictions are being lifted and western currency is highly valued.

Certainly, the tragic events of 9/11 in the United States made tourism more difficult. History seems to indicate, however, that tourists have a short memory. While one plane being blown up over Scotland a few years ago brought North American tourism to Britain to a screeching halt for the next several months, the incident is almost forgotten and North American tourism to Britain is thriving. Terrorists do indeed pose a threat to tourism, but acts of terror are nothing new—only relatively new to the United States. Tourism, and the rest of life, will go on in spite of such acts of cowardice.

Domestic travel may show relatively little growth in the next few years. Part of this slowing down of domestic travel may have to do with saturation of travel desire. Domestic air travel in the United States, one of the most fully developed markets in the world, is close to maturity— a condition in which the growth rate will approximate that of the economy or the population. Whether other sectors of the travel industry will reach such saturation is a critical question in terms of tourism growth.

In international terms, tourism will likely increase due to greater interdependence among nations. All nations are being pushed into the modern world and tourism is an integral part of that world. Certainly tourism must be better managed and more effectively planned than much of it has been in the past. At all political levels, tourism will become an issue.

Whether tourism slowly emerges as a means of regional, national, and international understanding or merely as a business that often exploits for short-term profit remains to be seen. What seems certain is that it will increasingly shape our cultures, our economies, and our personal lives.

Study Questions

1. What are some of the theories that explain why people become tourists?

2. What is *alternative tourism*? Do you think it is a theory that can be put into practice successfully? Why or why not?

3. Have you ever been a tourist? If so, what was your motivation for becoming one?

4. Would you like to see tourism become a larger part of the economy of your local community? Why or why not?

Endnotes

1   Clawson M. and Knetsch, J. (1966). *Economics of outdoor recreation*. Baltimore, MD: Johns Hopkins.

2   Stynes, D. (1993). *Leisure—The new center of the economy*. Denton, TX: Academy of Leisure Sciences.

3   Griffin, T. and Boele, N. (1993). Alternative paths to sustainable tourism. In *American Express' annual review of travel* (2nd ed.; pp. 13–23). New York, NY: American Express.

4   Tourism Futures International. (2007). January to March visitor arrivals, 2002–2007 [Figure]. Retrieved August 15, 2007, from http://www.tourismfuturesintl.com

5   McIntosh, R. and Goeldner, C. (1990). *Tourism principles, practices, philosophies* (6th ed.; p. 3). New York, NY: John Wiley & Sons.

6   Blank, U. (1988). *Community tourism imperative—The necessity, the opportunities, its potential*. State College, PA: Venture Publishing, Inc.

7   Cohen, E. (1972). Toward a sociology of international tourism. *Social Research, 39*(1), 164–182.

8   Zahavi, Y. (1981). Travel characteristics in cities of developing and developed countries. *World Bank Staff Working Paper No. 230*. Washington, DC: World Bank.

9   Hupkes, G. (1988). The law of constant travel times and trip rates. *Futures, 14*(1), 38–46.

10   Ausubel, J., Marchetti, C., and Meyer, P. (1998). Toward green mobility: The evolution of transport. *European Review, 6*(2), 137–156.

11   Robinson, J. and Godbey, G. (1997). *Time for life: The surprising ways Americans use their time*. University Park, PA: Penn State Press.

12   Ausubel, Marchetti, and Meyer (1998)

13   Robinson and Godbey (1997)

14   Crompton, J. (1981). Dimensions of the social group role in pleasure vacations. *Annals of Tourism Research, 8*(4), 550–567.

15   Plog, S. (1977). Why destination areas rise and fall in popularity. In E. Kelly, (Ed.), *Domestic and international tourism*. Wellesley, MA: Institute of Certified Travel Agents.

16   Butler, R. (1974). The concept of a tourist area cycle of evolution: Implications for management of resources. *Canadian Geographer, 24*(1), 17–36.

17   Huizinga, J. (1955). *Homo ludens—A study of the play element in culture*. Boston, MA: Beacon Press.

18   Machlis G. and Burch, Jr., W. (1983). Relations between strangers: Cycles of structure and meaning in tourist systems. *Sociological Review, 31*(1), 669.

19   ibid.

20   MacCannell, D. (1976). *The tourist: A new theory of the leisure class*. New York, NY: Schocken Books.

21   Cohen, E. (1988). Authenticity and commoditization in tourism. *Annals of Tourism Research, 15*(3), 371–386.

22   Ritchie, J. and Sins, M. (1978). Variables influencing the attractiveness of a tourism region. *Annals of Tourism Research, 5*(2), 251–260.

23   Plog (1977)

24   Boo, E. (1990). *Ecotourism: The potentials and the pitfalls, Vol. I and II* (p. 79). Washington, DC: World Wildlife Fund.

25   Krippendorf, J. (1987). *The holiday makers*. London, UK: Heinemann.

26   Butler, R. (1989). Alternative tourism: Pious hope or Trojan Horse? *Journal of Travel Research, 28*(3), 40–45.

27   Good, J. (1998). *Ecotourism*. Unpublished paper. University Park, PA: Penn State University.

28   Markels, A. (1998). Guide to the guides: Is ecotourism an oxymoron? *Audubon*, September/October, 66–69.

29   Grahn, P. (1991). Using tourism to protect existing culture: A project in Swedish Lapland. *Leisure Studies, 10*(1), 33–47.

30   Ousby, I. (1990). *The englishman's England: Taste, travel, and the rise of tourism*. Cambridge, England: Cambridge University Press.

31   Blank (1988)

32   Hughes, G. (1991). Tourism and the geographical imagination. *Leisure Studies, 11*(1), 31–42.

33   Boorstin, D. (1961). *The image*. New York, NY: Antheneum.

34   Cohen (1972)

35   Butler (1989)

36   Hollinshead, K. (1991). The disidentification of 'Indians' in cultural tourism. *Leisure Studies, 11*(1), 47.

37   California Tourism. (2007). *California fast facts 2007* (p. 6). Sacramento, CA: Author. Retrieved September 11, 2007, from http://www.visitcalifornia.com/media/upload/files/FastFacts-06FINAL2.pdf

38   ibid.

Leisure and Sexuality

If leisure behavior is thought of as activity that is voluntary and/or pleasurable, then many kinds of sexual and sexually related activity are an increasingly important component of leisure behavior. In spite of this, sexuality isn't often studied from the standpoint of leisure behavior. When subjects such as the Sociology of Leisure and Recreation Education began to be offered in colleges and universities in the 1940s, it was hardly considered respectable to study leisure, let alone to study the sexually related uses of leisure. Undertaking research concerning sex also was, and continues to be, extremely difficult.

If you think about human sexual behavior for a minute, it's very easy to understand its potential for leisure. First, all sexual behavior, even intercourse, is learned. Human beings are not born knowing how to kiss or have intercourse, we don't have highly fixed definitions of what is erotic, although we do develop sexual needs without being taught. Also, we learn how to express these needs by seeing other people (or other animals), by experimentation, by reading or observing pictures, or by formal instruction. If none of these learning devices are utilized, the individual remains ignorant. Researchers at sex clinics have found that many childless couples who visited the clinic were not able to have children because they didn't know how to have sexual intercourse. They hadn't learned how. "Going to bed" had not been sufficiently explained.

Not only do humans "invent" and reinvent forms and meanings of sexual expression but most sexual activity is for purposes of expression rather than procreation. Comfort has distinguished sexual behavior as either *procreational* where the intent is to produce offspring, *relational* where the intent is expression of serious emotional involvement, and *recreational* where pleasure-seeking is the main motivation.[1] Since the incidence of sexual intercourse to childbirth was reported by Kinsey[2] in 1953 to be approximately 1,000 to 1 (and there may be an even greater ratio today due to more prevalent use of birth control), most sexual behavior must be thought of largely within the realm of leisure or free time activity. Perhaps Italy best exemplifies this—a country whose Roman Catholic religion views birth control as sinful yet possesses one of the lowest birth rates in the world.

While it is widely assumed that modern nations have undergone a "sexual revolution" during the 1960s and 1970s, it is difficult to determine what the dimensions of this revolution have been. Sexual historian Vern Bullough[3] has argued that there has been basically no change in the sexual behavior of men in the twentieth century. Premarital sexual rates for women, however, more than doubled between the 1930s and 1971, and sharply rose again to a peak in 1976. Since 1976, however, there was no further increase. Thus, the "sexual revolution" may have been a revolution among women and it now seems to have run its course. More conservative sexual attitudes may stem largely from increased awareness of AIDS and other sexually transmitted diseases.

Sexual activity is one of the most important aspects of daily life. It is rated as the most enjoyable of daily activities in time-diary studies.[4] Anecdotal studies indicate it is the thing most college students think about during lectures.[5]

> AIDS changed everything. If you were just hooking up in bars, it meant you could get killed. It meant there was a big risk, even with condoms. I met a lot of dudes who didn't know that—or didn't care or were just stoned or wasted; they would follow anybody home. You gotta be smarter than that these days.

Pursuit of sex has forced politicians from office, terminated promising careers, and probably been the most-often topic of public gossip.

Indeed, as historian Theodore Zeldin observed:

Over the centuries, it [sexual desire] has been extraordinarily flexible and versatile, serving opposing causes, playing many different roles in history, like an actor, both tragic and comic, sometimes simple roles, reproducing hackneyed stereotypes and sometimes experimental, complex ones, deliberately mysterious.[6]

Sexual behavior requires more explanation than it provides. It is the "ultimate dependent variable."[7] In the emerging postmodern world, sexualities have become stabilized, decentered and de-essentialized— "sexuality is no longer seen as harboring an essential unitary core locatable within a clear framework... there are only fragments."[8]

Also, as sociologist Nelson Foote[9] has observed, the stimuli which cause sexual desire among males and females are primarily symbolic rather than physiological. That is, the things that stimulate us sexually are not fixed by our body's chemistry as much as they are learned symbols. In some societies, for instance, a woman's breast may be considered sexually arousing, while in another society women may go bare-breasted. Large biceps and a "beefy" chest may make a man more sexually appealing in one era but not another. Consequently, we are not compelled by heredity to respond in fixed ways to certain sexual stimuli (although we may be highly conditioned by our culture). A related circumstance is that the human female, unlike other mammals, potentially will accept intercourse at any time. Therefore, humans develop longings for or aversions to sexual activity quite apart from instinct. Anthropologists have observed that in societies in which children are permitted to observe the sexual intercourse of adults, they may become active participants in full sexual relations several years before puberty. Freud[10] contended that sexual energy (libido) was not a product of puberty but a basic life force from birth to death. How this energy is expressed is determined more by family relations and social experiences than by biological factors.

> Almost every unhealthy change women have made in how they try to look has been to attract men. Corsets used to be so tight they cut off your blood supply. High heels were to make your butt stick out, which really harmed your feet—your spine. Then the Paris fashion show decided thin was cool, so many women starved themselves. Well, I guess men do some things to make themselves attractive to us—pumping iron— and shaving. But they don't do nearly as much. Not even close!

Historical Perspectives

Sexual activity has always had the potential to be a form of leisure behavior, and the beliefs of various societies and the degree to which they struggled for survival have greatly influenced that potential. The earliest influences upon attitudes toward sexual behavior in the western world were the Talmud and the Old Testament.[11] Marriage and children were of the greatest importance to the ancient Hebrews, and all men, including priests, had to marry. A woman could be divorced for failing to have children.

In Greece's Classical Period, the main function of women was still childbearing. The Greek gods and goddesses were believed to have active sex lives and, perhaps because of this, many prohibitions against sex were absent in Greek society. The double standard was accepted in regard to sexual behavior; it was expected that married men would have sexual relations with women other than their wives, but this freedom did not apply to women. Marriage in Greece, Rome, and other ancient societies typically was not based upon love, especially not upon romantic love. Since love was not part of marriage, men sought amorous activity outside of marriage. Women, other than prostitutes, were prevented from doing so by their home-based existence and second-class status in society. Finally, since homosexuality was more acceptable than in many other societies, it was common for older men to have sexual relations with young boys, and provisions were made for them to meet, both in temples and in private residences. The Greek island of Lesbos, birthplace of Sappho who is recognized for her homoerotic poetry about love between women, gave rise to the term *lesbian*.

The Influence of Christianity

The emergence of Christianity reinforced women's second-class status. Man was considered superior, and woman was thought to be the cause of his downfall and misfortune since Adam and Eve. Even the institution of marriage was not made one of the seven sacraments until the sixteenth century. The worship of the Virgin Mary in the Middle Ages was responsible for the development of the code of chivalry by the aristocracy. According to this code, women were to be idolized for their character and, originally, sexual relations had no place in this concept. It was the beginning of romantic love, full of emotion and longing.

Virginity was a virtue and a sign of women's moral superiority. As with many ideals, the reality of sexual relations during this period was far different; rape was common, and adultery flourished among both the nobility and the peasantry. While the Church may have had strict prohibitions against many forms of sexual expression, priests themselves often used their religious authority to seduce women. Also, as historian Tuchman has observed: "While the cult of courtly love supposedly raised the standing of noble ladies, the fervid adoration of the Virgin (Mary), which developed as a cult... left little deposit on the status of women as a whole."[12] Women were commonly considered inferior to men; this belief was reinforced by the all-male clergy.

> ROMANCE
>
> Night wind
> in the tall trees
>
> The trees think
> they have
> somewhere to go
>
> The wind thinks
> it has somewhere
> to stay
>
> —gcg

During the Reformation, Martin Luther and other religious leaders began to recognize the sexual needs of men and women, declaring that intercourse between man and wife was normally permissible, and that frigidity and impotence were grounds for divorce. As the concept of chivalry spread to the middle classes, love became the basis for many marriages.

The Puritans who arrived in the New World were trying to keep their own way of life, which included the belief that sex was sinful. The Calvinist belief in thrift and hard work, and the distrust of pleasure and idleness became part of the American character. Even in the mid-1800s there was shocked criticism concerning the introduction into society of dances such as the waltz and the polka. Members of the clergy complained of "the abomination of permitting a man who is neither your lover nor your husband to encircle you with his arms, and lightly press the contour of your waist."[13] Nevertheless, these dances became popular. Even prejudice toward mixed swimming gave way, although very slowly.

Victorian England maintained a double standard in regard to sex. While a proper lady was expected to be ignorant about sex, acting as if she did not even know of its existence, Brewer has referred to her male counterpart as "the boozing, whoring, one standard for me, another for my wife, typical Victorian male."[14]

Such attitudes are still found in our society, reflected in our beliefs and in the laws concerning what we may do during our leisure time. There are still laws against adultery in some states today, although they are increasingly unenforceable. In the early 1900s, such laws brought severe consequences to offenders, as the *Chicago Code of Ordinances of 1911* demonstrated:

> If any man and woman live together in an open state of adultery or fornication or adultery and fornication, every such person shall be fined not exceeding $500, or confined in the county jail not exceeding one year. For a second offense, such man and woman shall be severely punished twice as much as the former punishment, and for a third offense, treble, and thus increasing the punishment for each succeeding offense. Provided, however, that it shall be in the power of the party or parties offending, to prevent or suspend the prosecution by their intermarriage, if such marriage can be legally solemnized, and upon the payment of the costs of such prosecution.[15]

The revolution in sexual mores and behavior which has occurred, however, has blunted our distrust of sensual pleasure. Fewer laws exist governing sexual behavior, and those which do exist are often not enforced or are not enforceable.

Sex-Related Games and Contests

Many popular songs observe that love is a game or has elements of games. If games are considered to be forms of play that have specific rules and require skills, knowledge, or endurance on the part of the players, then many forms of behavior relating to love and sex can be considered games.

Many such games and contests are related to courtship. Traditionally, adolescent males have engaged in competitive games and contests with each other for the right to court or receive the affection of a female of their choice. From the jousting of knights to high-school football games, in which young men butt heads while female cheerleaders watch admiringly, such events are based upon the traditional notion of the aggressive man and the submissive woman.

An early New England custom of bundling represented a kind of courtship contest in which a girl and her suitor were allowed to get into a bed together, keeping their undergarments on, after the girl's parents had retired for the night. Although the practice of bundling came about so that the courting male would not have to walk home through a freezing night, the sexual overtones are obvious. In some cases, parents provided obstacles such as a board fitted into a slot that divided the bed in two, encasing the lower parts of their bodies in tight garments, or even tying the girl's legs together. The degree of freedom parents gave such couples was often related to their desire for their daughter to be married.

Pornography

Many forms of pornography constitute a use of leisure time in our society. Most of us have at some time been exposed to reading matter, pictures, movies, or other forms of material that our society (or some members of our society) consider to be obscene, although that which is considered lewd or obscene, of course, is culturally determined. The art that is sacred in one civilization may be considered lewd in another; one society may require women to cover their breasts, while another requires that they cover their faces in public. Not all obscene displays that serve as leisure activity are so considered because of their sexual aspect. Our own society, for instance, bans certain forms of entertainment that were popular in other times or other cultures. Such pursuits as bull-baiting or bear-baiting, in which large dogs were set on a bull or bear with a bloody fight ensuing, are not permitted because the cruelty and violence to the animals are considered to be obscene. It should be noted, however, that our society does not seek to ban fictionalized violence as it prohibits fictionalized sex. Thus, a child watching television may watch one person murder another but may not watch them have sexual intercourse or even swim in the nude.

Leisure activity that could be considered pornographic may take many forms. *The Obscenity Report*[16] has classified types of pornography in contemporary society as (a) books and manuscripts; (b) film and plays; (c) the spoken word; (d) art, pictures, and music; and (e) advertising. The *Yale Law Review* has provided a listing of 68 methods of dissemination that have at one time been banned or prohibited by the courts of some states when they were thought to transmit obscenity.[17]

Such methods include dancing, photographs, records, statues, and drawings.

Books and magazines cover a wide range of written material of various quality, style, and intent. Serious literature, such as James Joyce's *Ulysses*, has sometimes been held to be obscene. Other books are intentionally written without "socially redeeming value," primarily to arouse the sexual interest of the reader. (Sexual arousal is generally not considered a socially redeeming value, although some social scientists feel it has a positive effect upon behavior.) Many such books seek to use the frankest possible language. Some magazines, such as *Playboy*, have enjoyed huge success by combining sexually oriented material with other articles and features not related to sex.

Films and plays may also be classified as "skin flicks," "porno films," and plays which exist primarily in order to exhibit sexual activity, as opposed to those in which such activity is a natural and necessary occurrence in the development of the story line. As movies have become more explicit, the film industry has developed a code to distinguish the degree of sexual frankness or level of maturity for which the film is appropriate. This, of course, has also made it easier for those who want to attend sexually explicit films to do so by looking for the X-rated ones. Television, which is now presenting more sexually explicit material, has also begun to inform viewers about the "mature" nature of certain shows. The issue of how far television should go in presenting sexually explicit material is an explosive one, since it is difficult to prevent children from viewing such programs. To some extent, rental of X-rated movies, which have become available in most communities, allows adults to view sexually oriented programming without allowing children to do so.

Most societies consider certain words to be obscene, and therefore seek to curtail or limit their use. Part of the negative reaction presumably caused by such words is based upon linguistic custom and tradition. A word such as "shit," therefore, has a different value than a word such as "feces," even though they are synonymous. Such linguistic values are constantly changing; it is hard for us to imagine how Clark Gable shocked the nation in *Gone with the Wind* by uttering "…I don't give a damn." One form of leisure activity that often uses words considered to be obscene is graffiti, written slogans and risqué or obscene comments in public places. In many ancient cultures, there is evidence of graffiti of the same type found today on the walls of public restrooms and covering our urban areas.

In some societies, the visual arts may be considered lewd simply by revealing the human body. *The Obscenity Report* bemoaned the "disturbing tendency of religious greeting cards to expose areas of cherubim's bodies which are best left private."[18] Erotic art is found in most societies, and attitudes toward it vary; some consider it to be of religious significance, while others imprison those who produce it. Music and advertising usually are considered pornographic only in a subliminal manner. Such music motifs or rhythmic patterns are considered to be sensual or suggestive. Advertising often implies sexual rewards for those who use a certain product or associates its use with sexually attractive people.

What is pornographic and what is not are often analyzed in our society on the following bases: Is it offensive? Does it incite lust? Is it repulsive and without redeeming value? In a multicultural society such as our own, the range of opinion concerning what is offensive, repulsive, and without redeeming value is extremely broad. This has made it quite difficult to interpret the test of pornography as stated by Chief Justice Alexander Cockburn in England in 1868, which was used in this country until the late 1950s. The test was "whether the tendency of the matter charged as obscenity is to deprave and corrupt those whose minds are open to such immoral influences, and into whose hands a publication of this kind may fall."[19]

The relationship between exposure to material considered obscene and the committing of sex crimes is not yet clearly understood. There is evidence that viewing sexual material does cause an erotic response in some people, but so does daydreaming. The effect of this erotic response, which is more prevalent in males than in females, is subject to question. Some scholars have argued that pornography acts as a substitute for antisocial sexual behavior; others have contended that it stimulates such behavior. Perhaps the most disturbing finding concerning pornography, particularly sexually violent pornography, is that it tends to desensitize those who view it.

Today the Supreme Court leaves judgments concerning obscenity as a matter to be interpreted according to local community standards. Two difficulties arise from this approach: (1) there may be great variation of opinion and attitude among those of the local community, and (2) many materials in question are distributed nationally through the mail or produced for a national readership or viewership. Differing local standards make such undertakings difficult.

Pornography in all its forms is primarily a product of the male imagination. There is little history of pornography designed for females, except that produced for lesbians. The current Women's Liberation Movement, which has sought to make the roles of men and women in our society more equal, may be partially responsible for the beginnings of a pornography industry designed for women. Many magazines and calendars now portray the male in photographic displays in much the same manner that magazines aimed at males have traditionally treated females. Also, the female stripper has been joined by the male exotic dancer who performs in bars for a female audience.

Some would argue that pornography should be distinguished from erotica. Erotica is merely material that is sexually explicit. Pornography is the *perversion* of the erotic and involves degradation or violence. Understood in these terms, it is natural that many women's groups have fought pornography since women are the target of most degradation or violence depicted in pornography. The fear is that viewing pornography may desensitize the viewer to the acts viewed. While women are the "victims" of most degrading or violent pornographic material, men are the victims of most violence depicted in the media. How are we harmed by viewing countless televised murders—both real and fictitious? Today, there is evidence that society is, in many cases, becoming more concerned with the depiction of violence and degradation than with the erotic.

A bigger issue may be the easy access most children have to pornography on the Internet and on television. While many schemes have been proposed to limit access to such content, no solution has been found which prevents children from viewing pornography on a home computer or TV.

There is also the issue of the blurring line between pornography and popular entertainment. Rap music is all about casual sex and females who are portrayed as nothing more than sexual outlets. Female pop singers dress and act very much like soft porn movie stars. MTV is mostly about sex. As the line between pornography and popular music and entertainment blurs, it becomes more difficult to identify what pornography is. While expressing sexual desire and pleasure publicly is often thought of as part of the liberation of women, it is also part of the re-enforcement of women as sex objects.

It is difficult to predict the future of pornography. There is some evidence that after the initial exposure to pornographic films, many viewers do not attend others. Pornography is ultimately repetitious, since the number of sex acts and displays is limited. Some observers believe that the widespread availability of pornography is one more indication of the extent to which sex has become shallow or meaningless in our society, with a corresponding loss of the capacity for deep love. Others, however, feel that pornography may help free us from our Puritanical inhibitions and disgust with our own bodies, and may actually enhance our capacity to love. In nearly all forms, though, pornography represents sex as a consumable item.

> *I really don't see that it's a big deal. Every guy I know has checked out on a porn website—so have most of the women. Some of it is really funny. When you see a naked woman cold it doesn't always make you horny. It's kind of weird. Sometimes, you can see the women in those pictures are being taken advantage of—even I can figure that out. On the other hand, why don't they know better? Every now and then I check out a porn website—and I'm a minister.*

Prostitution

Prostitution, which has been called the world's oldest profession, has always been dependent upon men choosing to use their leisure time for sexual activity outside of marriage. In early Greece, where the double standard existed for men and women, two types of prostitution flourished. Since the Greek male believed that sexual intercourse not only was his right but also was essential to his health, prostitutes were considered necessary and were expected to accompany men in public where wives were forbidden. Such prostitutes were usually intelligent and well-educated. The second form of prostitution began as a means of worship because money paid to certain prostitutes was used for the upkeep of the temples. Some of these "love goddesses" were slaves in supervised brothels, while others were women who voluntarily sacrificed their virginity to the gods and goddesses. Male prostitution also existed, since homosexuality was more accepted.

Prostitution was evident in Christian societies in the Middle Ages. Although Christian emperors tried to abolish it, prostitution was finally accepted as a necessary evil in order to control adultery and rape. Prostitutes were sometimes organized into guilds and lived in designated houses in special districts. Unlike the Greek courtesans, however, they were often abused by their masters and clientele.

In industrialized nations, prostitution became a byproduct of urbanization. It was reported that there were 80,000 prostitutes in London in 1861, even though the entire male population only numbered 1,300,000. In the United States, every large city had its red-light district, where men could gamble, drink, and hire the services of prostitutes.[20]

Increasing sexual permissiveness is thought to have caused some decline in prostitution during the last few decades. Today, however, prostitution is legal in several counties in Nevada, and illegal "freelance" prostitutes are making a comeback in American towns and cities. Additionally, male homosexual prostitution is flourishing, valuing novelty and youth above all else.

Prostitution is a way of life for many who are forced to live on the streets of our urban centers, whether they are runaway or "throw-away" children, drug addicts, or the mentally ill. Such prostitution exploits the powerless and is dangerous for all concerned.

Prostitution is also being used as a basis for tourism. Many organized tours to southeast Asian countries, often aimed at businessmen from Japan, Germany, and elsewhere, feature prostitution as the main attraction.

The advent of AIDS has made all forms of prostitution extremely risky for all concerned. This is made an even bigger problem due to the link between prostitution and drug addiction.

If we consider prostitution to be engaging in sexual behavior to gain some reward other than the experience itself, then prostitution may be extremely common. Engaging in sexual activity to be popular, to obtain a favor, to get or hold a job, to achieve power over an individual, or to become a member of a certain social circle appears to be common. The joys of sex, in other words, are "prostituted" in many ways.

Biological Perspectives

While the expression of sexuality has a strong historical and cultural component, our biological evolution has shaped many aspects of sex and reproduction. There is a tendency for issues surrounding gender to become politicized. Those on the political left tend to think of gender issues in terms of the environment and the way that gender is defined and reinforced by society. Those on the political right tend to think in terms of biological differences between the sexes and to assume that such differences define the destiny of males and females. The answer from many geneticists is that both biology and environment combine to shape maleness and femaleness. Both interact with each other. Genes, for example, interact with the environment, weather, and nutrition. As a leading science writer, Deborah Blum asserted:

> Perhaps our best chance...of narrowing the (gender) gap is to understand it. The sexes are unlike each other because humanity—as well as the vast majority of species—evolved that way. Earth-based biology likes a two-sex system. Evolution has conserved it, probably for billions of years, because it works.[21]

The denial of difference, in other words, may actually hinder the chances for the gender gap to close.

There is solid consensus among scientists that, in humans, if there is no introduction of testosterone, a girl will be born. In terms of behavior, steroid hormones are the critical ones in terms of gender differences. Among males, these include androgens, made primarily in the testes, the best known of which is testosterone. Estrogens are made in females, primarily in the ovaries. None of these hormones, however, are exclusive to gender. Females have testosterone and males estradiol, the best known androgen. The balance of these hormones changes based on environmental situations. While males average ten times as much testosterone as females, males in a marriage they define as a good one usually experience a decline in testosterone level. In both males and females, testosterone levels rise and fall with stress-related factors.

Males and females also vary in terms of their roles and strategies in sexual reproduction. Sexual reproduction has great costs to our fitness and is the arena for intense competition to pass one's genes on to future generations. Our genes, of course, don't care about us; they want only to reproduce themselves. Intellectually, sexual reproduction could be viewed as God's little joke on humans. There is, for example, the issue of orgasm:

> ...orgasms are not only uncoordinated, they are systematically sooner for men than women. This bias is one of the more unfortunate illustrations of the principle that natural selection shapes us to maximize reproduction, not satisfaction. Imagine the reproductive success of a man who tends to come to orgasm very slowly. He might please his partner, but if the sex act is interrupted or his partner has been satisfied and does not want to continue, his sperm will sometimes not get to where they will do his genes any good. The same forces shape the timing of the female sexual response. A woman who rapidly has a single orgasm may, on occasion, stop intercourse before her partner ejaculates and thus will have fewer offspring than the woman with a more leisurely sexual response.[22]

Things are not equal when it comes to sexual reproduction, and cannot be made so. The investment a female makes in the egg is many times the investment a male makes in the sperm. If a female can induce males to fight over her or otherwise pick from a larger pool of males, she increases her odds of picking the best mate. This ability of females to choose (while violated sometimes by rape) gives females enormous power over males. Such power may lead to male mammals adopting traits which make them more attractive to females, even if they are harmed by doing so. As Helena Cronin reported, if the huge colorful feathers of male peacocks or large antlers of male Irish Elks attract females, these traits may become so pronounced that the peacocks can barely fly or that Irish Elks become extinct.[23]

Humans are mammals and, among mammals, when a female is impregnated, the female is sure the baby is hers but the male is not sure the baby is his. This uncertainty means that male expenditure of time and energy caring for the offspring will generally have a more dubious payoff than similar investments by females.[24] Males and females therefore develop different reproductive strategies. Males are more interested in fertility and sexual loyalty. Females are more interested in good genes and resources.

Since biology operates on the principle that difference is better, "The point of having two parents is to combine dissimilar sets of genes."[25] Thus it should not surprise us that women appear to be attracted to the scent of men, through their sweat, who have different genes from their own.[26]

Many issues pertaining to sexual reproduction are largely shaped by our biological evolution. Effective birth control, however, has meant that our genes don't get their way with us as easily as before. Females in most modern countries give birth to an average of less than two children, as opposed to seven a few centuries ago. The timing and selection of fathers are controlled to a greater extent both by modern birth control and safer and more readily available abortions. In terms of abortion, however, nature controls us more than our own actions. The estimated rate of miscarriage for one-week old human embryos is approximately fifty percent.[27] We are, in summary, highly shaped by our biology in terms of sexuality.

Perhaps because we are so highly shaped by our biological makeup, it is not surprising that many aspects of sexuality, such as pornography and prostitution, which exist in almost all societies, are primarily the product of the male imagination rather than that of the female.

> Look, every female prof at this school keeps telling me that women are the victims and there's not much difference between males and females when there is. It's how we were raised. It seems to me that kind of thinking is outdated. There are differences that are wired into us. To me, as a woman, the issue is that those differences shouldn't put me at a disadvantage. But—it depends on how you look at it. You can watch a football game and point out that female cheerleaders are chosen mostly because they are attractive. Or you can point out that the male football players will, in many cases, end up with permanent injuries they got entertaining the crowd.

The Impact of Women's Changing Roles on Sexuality

As women's roles began to change and as the drive for women's rights intensified in the United States, a number of changes occurred which influenced sexual behavior and relations. The gap between accepted ways of behaving for men and women began to close in regard to sexual behavior, although such differences are still generally identifiable. Women's rights groups have sought ways of putting an end to women being treated as sex objects, even as television and other mass media, even comic strips, treat women (and men) more as sexual objects. Specific concerns have dealt with the right to abortion, rape prevention and more humane ways of dealing with rape victims, dissemination of birth-control information, ending sexual harassment on the job, and prohibiting degrading sexual displays and exhibitions involving women. Also, they have worked toward increasing sexual freedom for women and minimizing or eliminating the double standard for men and women in sexual matters.

To accomplish such aims, the notion of a woman being more "passive" than a man had to be changed. In sexual matters, as in others, males historically have been more likely to be the initiators of behavior while females have been more likely to be in a position of responding. Effecting change in matters of sexual and other behavior, therefore, has involved either seeking to protect the passive behavior of females through legal and other means and/or restructuring social behavior in ways to make the female less passive.

Think about this active-passive or actor-receiver division as it relates to males and females you know. Let's examine this active-passive dichotomy with regard to their sexually related behavior. Keep in mind that medieval chivalry established as ideals of behavior a passive, virtuous (and virginal) woman, ignorant of the ways of the world, who was to be worshipped and won over by the heroic deeds and courteous attention of a pursuing male. Such roles, in which women were both idealized (as an extension of the worship of the Virgin Mary) and considered as objects to be won, may still be with us today. In Exercise 10.1 at the end of this chapter (page 287), you will be asked to explore this idea to see if it is part of your life.

While the changing roles of women have not meant that they participate in leisure activities in the same patterns as do men, it does mean that differences in men's and women's participation continue to decline.

The Gay and Lesbian Revolution

Today there is increasing recognition that individuals are diverse in their sexual orientations. One part of this recognition is the revolution going on with regard to gay and lesbian men and women. Attitudes toward homosexuality have varied from culture to culture and during different historical periods. As mentioned previously, in ancient Greece homosexuality was not generally condemned. During the Middle Ages, having sexual relations with someone of the same gender was considered sinful, but those who did so were not thought of as a type of person different from others. During the sixteenth to eighteenth centuries, such behavior became a crime, but those who committed it were still not thought of as a separate class of human beings.

The notion that all of one's passionate attachments should go toward a member of the opposite sex was absent in the middle-class Victorian family. Romantic friendships existed between men, although for a short period, arising in the late teens and ending at marriage. Physical caresses and emotional intimacy characterized such relations, which were considered normal.[28]

Lesbian relations and deep friendships between women were treated differently from those of men. Since marriage, for many women, has historically meant literally "taking a master," close friendships between women, often with open displays of physical affection, were not only tolerated but sometimes encouraged. Part of this was due to the male notion that women could not satisfy each other sexually or that sexual relations between women were merely a prelude to relations with men.

> There were in several eras and places many instances of women who were known to engage in lesbian sex, and they did so with impunity. As long as they appeared feminine, their sexual behavior would be viewed as an activity in which women indulged when men were unavailable or as an apprenticeship or appetite-whetter to heterosexual sex.[29]

Many deep friendships between women, even women who live together, however, are not primarily sexual in nature. While the male imagination has produced pornographic literature depicting lesbianism as completely sexual in nature, "...even the sexologists' evidence seemed to suggest that homosexuality was generally no more appropriate a term to describe lesbianism than it was to describe romantic friendship."[30] What characterized such relations, in which sexual relations might be a part or might not, is that two women's strongest emotions and affections were directed toward each other. While such relations were accepted by society in previous times to a great extent, open love relations between women ceased to be possible after World War I, due in great part to the medical profession's emerging belief that such relations were a form of mental illness. Lesbianism was condemned and lesbians were sometimes forced to submit to hysterectomies and estrogen injections due to the ignorance of psychologists and physicians. These negative views were internalized by many lesbian women, whose own self-image was greatly harmed by them. During the 1960s, however, the sexual openness of the era produced more tolerance. Additionally, the feminist movement and the mass movement of women into the labor force meant that lifelong relations between women were more possible.

For gay males, who had found less tolerance for their sexual orientation in society than lesbian women, conditions became worse in the nineteenth century. Those in modern medicine, particularly psychiatry, began to view homosexuality as a form of mental illness. By the 1940s, homosexuality was discussed as a form of psychopathic, paranoid and schizoid personality disorder.[31] Having defined it as an illness, there were futile attempts to "treat" it. Gay men were sometimes subjected to lobotomies, castration and aversion therapy, none of which changed their orientation. Sex researcher Alfred Kinsey[32] was startled that he could not find one homosexual whose sexual orientation had been changed by any medical procedure. Not only did homosexual orientation not change as a result of the efforts of the medical profession, it was also not possible to document that homosexuals were mentally ill. The administration of various psychological tests showed time and again that homosexuals and heterosexuals could not be told apart by their personality or psychological make-up. Today, while evidence is inconclusive, there is increasing reason to believe that sexual orientation is largely genetically determined. How society responds to this understanding remains to be seen but sexual orientation is a civil rights issue just as race, age, gender and other statuses.

Use of leisure is greatly shaped by sexual orientation. Even in childhood, play may signal sexual orientation. Some research concludes play that is not gender typical in young boys prior to puberty, such as dressing in women's clothing or playing with dolls, or taking the role of the mother in playing house, indicates a homosexual orientation in 75 percent of the cases. This demonstrates how deeply rooted sexual orientation is. As boys and girls with homosexual orientations go to school, it quickly becomes apparent that most of society has been designed in ways that don't meet their needs, particularly their leisure needs. School dances assume heterosexuality. School sports assume males should be aggressive and females the admirers of that aggression. The explorations of sexuality which teenagers often brag about to each other can be cause for severe persecution if such explorations are with a member of the same sex. The romantic poems read in English class are almost always about the romances of "straight" people. No wonder gay and lesbian teenagers have far higher rates of suicide and emotional problems. No wonder, too, that they sometimes seek to form separate groups or institutions which allow them to be themselves during their free time. In adulthood, gay and lesbian subcultures are often formed in urban areas that are largely segregated from the rest of society. The decision of whether or not to acknowledge one's homosexuality has implications not only for one's work life but also for one's leisure pursuits since much leisure activity revolves around close social relationships. In some cases, those in various gay and lesbian communities develop their own recreation and leisure institutions. In other cases, they attempt to use the resources available to the general public, with mixed success. To an extraordinary extent, gays and lesbians

> Look, I always knew I was gay. Always. Even as a little kid I was drawn toward toys that were intended for girls. I wasn't attracted to girls as a teenager— but I pretended for a while. It was terrible to go to a dance, want to dance with a guy and know that it wasn't going to happen. I'm gay. That's the way it is. I've had counseling and endless discussions with other gay guys and I am, now, O.K. with myself. My parents are mostly O.K. with me. I'm 25. Yes, I've had a string of casual encounters, but I have a partner now. We are talking about a permanent relationship. Who knows, by the time we decide, maybe we'll actually be able to marry legally—but I wouldn't bet the ranch on it.

contribute to theater, art, music, literature and other forms of leisure expression enjoyed by the public. The constraints on their use of leisure, however, remain massive. In spite of this, there is more disposable income for homosexual couples for leisure pursuits since most remain childless and have dual incomes.

Leisure and Sexuality Today

In many senses of the word, it would be a mistake to think of our society as a "sexual" one. Compared to many preindustrial societies, our own provides little opportunity for physical gratification, touching, or bonding between individuals. Indeed, in many situations, we are encouraged not to touch each other since all touching is assumed to be sexual. This is not true in many preindustrial cultures. In Bali, as Berman[33] pointed out, during the first six months the child is always in someone's arms except when being bathed, and the parents typically play with the male child's genitals while he is in the bath. In the Middle Ages, public physical contact with children's private parts was considered an amusing game, forbidden only when the child reached puberty. While this attitude changed during the Renaissance, it is still widespread in Islamic cultures.

In much of our culture, however, sexual and sensual aspects of everyday life have been removed or segregated from the rest of life. We may, said another way, have more sex but be less sexual. The awareness of this on the part of many in our society is leading to changes in the way we bring children into the world, the importance we place on physical touch, and our attitudes toward our bodies.

Certainly, change is taking place. Fathers are usually with their wife during the delivery of a baby—sometimes recording the event. The importance of touch is being recognized in some quarters, even if it has to be labeled as "therapeutic touch" to be legitimate. Sensuality is surely emerging even as the frequency of sexual intercourse is declining.

As mentioned earlier, sex today has three important uses in our society, according to Alexander Comfort: (1) sex as parenthood (procreational sex); (2) sex as total intimacy between two people (relation sex); and (3) sex as physical play (recreational sex).[34] While organized religion in our society hasn't traditionally accepted pleasure as a legitimate motive for engaging in sexual activity, it recently has tried to head off the movement toward recreational sex by asserting that worthy sexual activity must be relational.

Recreational sex is, of course, nothing new. In even the strongest kin-based cultures, the gap left between relational sex and sex designed to produce offspring has been filled by recreational sex. While some forms of sexuality expressed total involvement between two people, others reflected "an old human pattern in which sexual contacts were permitted between a woman and all her husband's clan brothers or a man and all his wife's titular sisters."[35]

Today, many in our society are beginning to believe that procreational, relational, and recreational sex all have a role to play. What do you think?

Sexual Behavior

A number of trends have dramatically influenced sexual behavior during the last few decades. Many of these trends are similar to those that have influenced other forms of leisure behavior.

There is little doubt that technology has been responsible for the leisure potential of much sexual activity. Effective means of contraception have drastically reduced the incidence of procreation in sexual intercourse. Kinsey and associates reported that the ratio of sexual intercourse to pregnancy in a sample of over 2,000 women was approximately 1,000 to 1.[36] Other significant findings included

- Increased premarital intercourse among females to levels nearly comparable to those of males;
- An increasing percentage of marital copulations leading to orgasm decade by decade;
- A steady approach to equivalence of males and females in premarital petting and marital sex-play techniques;
- An increase in extramarital intercourse; and
- Declining insistence by males on premarital female virginity.

Psychiatrists at some universities report that students who are still virgins feel insecure and hurt because of their lack of sexual experience and because of peer-group pressure to become sexually active. Other students embrace a "secondary virginity" in which the individual becomes celibate after a disillusioning period of sexual promiscuity.

Whatever people think, young people are increasingly sexually active. Among America's young women, 1 in 5 has engaged in sexual relations by age 16, two-thirds have done so by age 19, and over 9 out of 10 have had sex prior to marriage. The teen pregnancy rate and abortion rate is currently twice that in the United States compared to most European countries. White females are more likely to use legal abortion while African-American females are more likely to give birth out of wedlock. In summary, sex before marriage has become a normal way of behaving for American youth, even if such ways of behavior are not fully acceptable to many.

Recognizing Sexual Needs

One of the most far-reaching trends affecting current sexual behavior is the increasing recognition of the sexual needs of many segments of our population for whom it was frequently assumed that sex was inappropriate. These include the elderly, the physically handicapped, prisoners, the mentally retarded, and single adults. Because sexual behavior has traditionally been legitimized in terms of childrearing, for instance, the elderly were thought of as somehow asexual (think about your grandparents for a minute). It often was assumed that old people's interest in and ability to undertake sexual relations had ceased.

Age does induce some changes in sexual performance, chiefly in males for whom orgasm becomes less frequent and more direct physical stimulation is needed to produce an erection. Barring disease, however, most older people are capable of sex and, as sexual attitudes among the elderly become more liberal, they will increasingly insist on using that ability. This has tremendous implications for many areas of life for the elderly. Old-age homes, for example, often segregate their room arrangements by sex and make no provision for elderly males and females to be alone with each other.

The availability of Viagara and other similar products, which enable sexual performance for many males who were impotent, is beginning to redefine sexual relations among the elderly. Such drugs have restored sexuality to many older marriages, with a wide variety of results. In some cases, it has made for happier couples, but in others it has meant that a female who was content not being sexually active was suddenly put in the position of responding to her husband's sexual advances. In a few cases, older males have left home, armed with a supply of Viagara, seeking new conquests.

Society is increasingly recognizing that the physical or mental condition of a person does not and should not cause the removal of sexual expression. Seeking to suppress sexual expression of such individuals, in fact, is likely to compound problems. The same may be said for many special groups who are institutionalized. Pretending that those removed from society have no sexual needs is quite likely to compound existing problems. This is being realized by some authorities responsible for the management of some prisons, schools for people with retardation, hospitals, etc., but not by others. Even in a supposedly sexually liberated society, the recognition of sexual needs is slow.

> *I was quite happy not having sex with Harry anymore. I mean, we're both in our seventies and are bodies are not what they used to be—not at all. Harry found out about Viagra. How could he not? So he dashed out and got a prescription for it. We had made this adjustment in our marriage to a loving partnership—no sex— and I was happy with that. But now Harry thinks he's a stud muffin again—and we've got problems—or maybe I should say I've got problems.*

The treatment of sexual matters in recent fiction and nonfictional writing reflects a number of diverse themes, including sexual politics, sex education, pornography for women, sexual therapy, and the sexual capacity and needs of groups such as the elderly and institutionalized populations. A number of novels (and nonfiction as well) have dealt with the liberation of women from the standpoint of sex. Women's magazines are also more frankly interested in sexual behavior.

Marriage and Divorce

Another trend affecting the sexual patterns of Americans is the continuing popularity of marriage, despite its increasingly temporary nature.

Serial marriage, to the extent that it replaces lifelong marriage, will further break down the idea of maintaining one sexual partner throughout adult life. It also will result in more one-parent families and greater exposure of children to parents in dating and courtship situations. As mentioned previously in Chapter 8, however, marriage for life has historically not been as prevalent as we may think, and where it has been, people often have far shorter life expectancies.

The increasing acceptance of living together before marriage, which is often a trial marriage, and the increasing prevalence of serial marriage mean that marriage is less important in our society in terms of its impact on our sexual behavior.

Perhaps another reason for divorce stems from the assumptions our culture makes about marriage. People marry because they are "in love," full of a dependent feeling we associate with romance. As George Bernard Shaw put it:

> When two people are under the influence of the most violent, most insane, most delusive, and most transient of passions, they are required to swear that they will remain in that excited, abnormal and exhausting condition continuously until death do them part.[37]

Scientists studying the chemistry of the brain often argue that romantic feelings are largely a product of hormones released when people are in love, including acetylcholine, which produces a feeling of excitement; dopamine, which induces a feeling of well-being; norepinephrine, phenylethylamine, serotonin and others which, in combination, produce a wonderful feeling which lasts, on average, about eighteen months.[38] It is hypothesized that this chemical release occurs historically in order to propagate our species. "Monogamy is definitely not what nature intended man and women to be doing. The more genetic diversity we have, the better able the species will be to survive."[39] While propagation of the species is not a big issue in today's society, our brain chemistry has not changed. People vary in the extent to which they are affected by the chemical releases and our behavior is shaped in some way by our body chemistry and notions of romantic love. If marriage cannot have a basis other than feelings of romance, it is not likely to be permanent.

Time-Deepening and Sexual Behavior

Current sexual activity often shows great emphasis upon time-saving behavior. Time deepening, mentioned in Chapter 2, applies to sexual and nonsexual behavior alike. Linder[40] has argued that the amount of sexual activity in our society may actually be decreasing, if measured from the standpoint of the amount of time devoted to it. What is often thought of as promiscuity on the part of today's females, Linder suggested, may only be an acceleration aimed at saving time for both male and female. Furthermore, he suggested that conjugal fidelity may be increasing, in fact if not in mind, simply because it takes too much time to establish new contacts. This notion is borne out by the fact that many of today's prostitutes meet their customers in cars in indoor parking garages for "quickies." Certainly, one reason for the success of singles bars is their ability to provide an attractive place for males and females where they could quickly make "pickups" for sexual purposes.

The increase in pornography may also be considered evidence of the desire to save time in sexual relations. Pornography may offer a convenient way of providing some of the sensations of other forms of sexual activity in a less time-consuming manner. In addition, it may serve as a kind of compensation for the frustrations produced by a lifestyle in which one's love life is reduced to a series of brief and impersonal encounters.

Many sexual institutions and customs have almost been eliminated from our society owing to time consciousness. Taking a mistress, for instance (the practice of a married man establishing a long-term relationship of an emotional and sexual nature with another woman), requires considerable time, which many of today's males simply do not have. The rigid scheduling and planning of all activity also makes it difficult to obtain the social freedom needed to prepare the groundwork for such a sustained affair. The love affair has often been replaced by the "one-nighter"—an impersonal, hurried sexual liaison between near strangers.

Blurring Distinctions between the Sexes

A final trend in leisure-related sexual activity is the blurring of distinctions between sexual roles, resulting in an increase in the range of acceptable behavior of male and females. Since many forms of leisure behavior are directly related to gender, changes in the concepts

Hooking up is the ultimate time-saving device. You don't know the person, won't know them afterward—or usually not—and it's all about sex. Takes only a couple of hours and there's no "commitment" baggage. Is it a bad thing? I don't know. It's like scratching an itch only there's another body involved.

of masculinity and femininity may alter future leisure patterns radically. A number of factors have changed the images of male and female from polar extremes to a continuum, with very few individuals at either end. Much of this change has resulted from a new societal permissiveness and emphasis upon achieved status rather than ascribed status. Furthermore, today's society is more accepting of deviant sexual patterns. Indeed, with the development of effective means of contraception, movements such as gay liberation and women's liberation, bisexual social functions, sex-change operations, sex therapy, and increased pornography, it has become increasingly difficult to determine what sexual patterns are truly deviant. There has been, however, increasing recognition that some people are addicted to sex just as others are addicted to alcohol. As Peele pointed out, the instant gratification, ritual and gradual deterioration of self-image associated with addiction may be associated with sex.[41] Self-help groups have been formed for sex addicts, much like those for people addicted to alcohol.

As the potential of sex to become leisure activity has increased, its practice has become more diverse. In such a period of change, the link between politics and sexual behavior is becoming stronger and stronger. The Gay Liberation Movement, for instance, has concentrated on increasing the protection of homosexuals' rights under the law and developing a political power base. In cities such as San Francisco, this political power is already a reality.

In issues such as abortion, providing birth-control devices and information through the schools, allowing massage parlors or porno bookstores in downtown areas, no-fault divorce, and other issues, change is being effected through the political system; this period of testing is likely to continue.

The sexual revolution has reshaped our lives, but today the search is for ways to integrate sex into our lives, and to do so in ways that are healthy, rather than to approach it with the mentality of a consumer.

> You can see that the TV networks want sensitive guys—Metrosexuals—to play a role in reporting the news. The women who are getting hired are drop dead beautiful and they can read a teleprompter, but some of the guys are now not the father figures who used to read the news. Metrosexuals aren't gay, but they don't have any macho in them either—none.

Study Questions

1. Should a book dealing with leisure behavior contain a chapter dealing with sexual behavior? Why or why not?

2. Why do you think there has been little pornography over the ages designed for females?

3. What kinds of problems do you suppose gays and lesbians face in terms of recreation and leisure within your community?

4. In what ways does human sexuality diminish with age? Do the aged continue to have sexual needs?

5. How has "time deepening" influenced leisure behavior during the last decade?

Exercise 10.1

Among your friends, which of the following are true?

1. T F Males are more likely to initiate dates than females.

2. T F Males are more likely to pay for expenses during dates than females.

3. T F Females are expected to be less sexually aggressive than males.

4. T F Females are less likely to read "dirty" books and magazines than males.

5. T F Males are more likely to propose marriage or living together than females.

6. T F Males are more likely to perform courtesies, such as holding doors open, for females than females are for males.

7. T F Males are more likely to seek to attract the attention of females by "showing off" than females are likely to show off to attract males.

The higher the number of "true" statements, the more the "actor-receiver" roles are divided between males and females. If the majority of your answers are "true," discuss whether or not you consider these divisions between males and females to be a problem. If you do think these divisions create problems, what are they? Why?

Endnotes

1   Comfort, A. (1973). Sexuality in a zero-growth society. *Current, 148*, 29–34.

2   Kinsey, A., Pomeroy, W., Martin, C., and Gebhard, P. (1953). *Sexual behavior in the human female* (p. 60). Philadelphia, PA: W. G. Saunders.

3   Bullough, V. (1984, April 9). The revolution is over. *Time Magazine, 123*(15), 75–83.

4   Robinson, J. (1993). Round midnight. *American Demographics, 15*(6), 44–49.

5   Leonard, G. (1982, December). *The end of sex.* Esquire, 72.

6   Zeldin, T. (1994). *An intimate history of humanity* (p. 128). New York, NY: Harper Perennial.

7   Simon, W. (1996). *Postmodern sexuality.* New York, NY: Routledge.

8   ibid.

9   Foote, N. (1954). Sex as play. *Social Problems, 1*(4), 159–163.

10   Freud, S. (1938). Three contributions to the theory of sex. In A. Brill (Ed.), *The basic writings of Sigmund Freud* (p. 128). New York, NY: The Modern Library.

11   Juhasz, A. (1973). *Sexual development and behavior: Selected readings* (p. 84). Homewood, IL: Dorsey Press.

12   Tuchman, B. (1978). *A distant mirror: The calamitous fourteenth century* (p. 215). New York, NY: Alfred Knopf.

13   Dulles, F. (1965). *A history of recreation: America learns to play* (p. 151). New York, NY: Appleton-Century-Crofts.

14   Brewer, L. (1962). *The good news* (p. 95). London, UK: G. P. Putnam's Sons.

15   Worthington, G. and Topping, R. (1925). *Specialized courts dealing with sex delinquency* (p. 11). Montclair, NJ: Patterson Smith.

16   *The obscenity report—The report of the task force on pornography and obscenity.* (1970). New York, NY: Stein and Day. (pp. 27–34, 80)

17   *Yale Law Review.* (1966), pp. 1409–1410.

18   *The obscenity report* (1970, pp. 27–34, 80)

19   *Yale Law Review* (1966)

20   Juhasz (1973, p. 193)

21   Blum D. (1997). *Sex on the brain—The biological differences between men and women* (p. 5). New York, NY: Penguin.

22   Nesse, R. and Williams, G. (1996). *Why we get sick—The new science of Darwinian medicine* (p. 196). New York, NY: Vintage.

23   Cronin, H. (1991). *The ant and the peacock.* New York, NY: Cambridge University Press.

24 Nesse and Williams (1996, p. 186)

25 Blum (1997, p. 15)

26 ibid.

27 ibid.

28 Faderman, L. (1991). *Surpassing the love of men—Romantic friendship and love between women from the Renaissance to the present.* London, UK: The Women's Press.

29 ibid.

30 ibid.

31 D'Emilio, J. (1998). *Sexual politics, sexual communities* (2nd ed.). Chicago, IL: University of Chicago Press.

32 Kinsey, Pomeroy, Martin, and Gebhard (1953, p. 60)

33 Berman, M. (1984). The re-enchantment of the world. New York, NY: Bantam Books.

34 Comfort (1973)

35 ibid.

36 Kinsey, Pomeroy, Martin, and Gebhard (1953)

37 Shaw quoted by O'Connell, L. (1993). Love: It's all in your mind, says chemist. *Orlando Sentinel*, July 29, p. 23.

38 O'Connell, L. (1993). Love: It's all in your mind, says chemist. *Orlando Sentinel*, July 29, p. 23.

39 Bowers cited in O'Connell, L. (1993). Love: It's all in your mind, says chemist. *Orlando Sentinel*, July 29, p. 23.

40 Linder, S. (1970). *The harried leisure class* (pp. 77–93). New York, NY: Columbia University Press.

41 Peele, S. (1989). *Diseasing of America: Addiction treatment out of control* (p. 5). Lexington, MA: Lexington Books.

Leisure and Education

Most uses of leisure involve learning. For some leisure activities, the learning is very limited—a small part of the experience. For other activities, however, learning is a central part of the experience. In this chapter we will examine the importance of education for leisure, some ways in which education for leisure may come about, and the relationship between the quantities and qualities of one's education and use of leisure.

Use of Leisure and Intelligence

The levels of various kinds of intelligence we possess are related to our use of leisure. What is less well-understood, however, is that our use of leisure appears to be related to the development and retention of various types of intelligence. The experiences we undergo and the intellectual demands they make on us may literally change our brains in ways which increase or decrease intelligence. Psychologist Donald Hebb noticed that his children's pet rats consistently outperformed animals raised in the laboratory in complex learning tasks. The children's rats, which lived in an "enriched" environment with opportunities for play and for more stimulation, excelled in learning mazes and other tasks that bore no direct relationship to the mental stimulation they had previously received.[1] Physical differences in the brains of the enriched environment rats gave evidence of their greater abilities. The cortexes of their brains were heavier than the laboratory rats, with more dendrites and synapses. "Stimulation thus manifests itself in the wiring of the brain, which in turn improves the brain's ability to learn."[2] While similar results have not yet been produced with people and the cellular mechanisms of learning are not yet understood, it would appear that, to a great extent, the stimulation the brain receives alters the brain physically in ways that shape our intelligence.

The human brain may be said to be plastic; that is, it changes over time and our behavior plays some role in how it changes. A newborn baby's brain is not yet finished or totally functional:

> It has more neurons than an adult's, but weighs only one fifth as much because these neurons have not yet connected with each other. Each neuron rapidly extends its transmitting fiber (axon) from the cell body toward its final destination. The mechanisms by which the axon reaches the correct location are not yet known, but they are almost flawless... The initial development process... is thus one of proliferation followed by selection. It permanently fixes the general structure of the brain, but not the details of the wiring.... That wiring, as it turns out, is at least partly the product of experience.[3]

Thus, to some extent, our experiences and behaviors appear to shape our brain's capacities.

Think about the extraordinary implication of these ideas—and how they relate to leisure. If your experiences and behaviors result, to some extent, in how your brain physically develops, then what you freely choose to do given the opportunity would seem to be of critical importance to your intellectual development. Our minds and bodies are not separate but part of the same thing. While our genetic makeup may set the limits of our abilities, how close we come to reaching such limits is based partly on what we do in time and space. If during our leisure, our environments are "enriched" (like those of the pet rats), we will come closer to reaching our intellectual potentials. Children who have the opportunity for challenging forms of play develop differently from those who receive little stimulation. People who use leisure to engage in challenging experiences develop intellectually in ways those who use leisure merely to relax do not. Our work, of course, is a critical factor in our intellectual development but, increasingly, use of leisure must be thought of as an important arena for shaping human intellectual potential. Interestingly, the ancient Greeks thought that over 2,000 years ago.

It also appears that use of leisure is an important way in which adults, particularly older adults, maintain intelligence. As Sherry Willis, a noted researcher on aging and intellectual functioning put it, with regard to maintaining various forms of intelligence among older adults: "Use it or lose it."[4] Research by Willis and colleagues found that elderly people who did crossword puzzles and jigsaw puzzles were found to be higher in verbal knowledge than those who didn't. Higher fluid reasoning was related to doing crossword puzzles.[5] Other studies have found that playing bridge among those 55 and older was positively related to working memory and reasoning.[6] These findings and others show various kinds of intelligence being related to leisure choices among older adults. While it seems that people with higher levels of intelligence choose to do more intellectually stimulating activities during their leisure (e.g., play bridge) than others, it also appears that the choices older individuals make during their free time enhance or detract from their ability to maintain, and increase, various types of intelligence.

> When I started crossword puzzles, I was so bad I thought—this is not for me. But I kept doing them, started using a dictionary and sometimes got a little help from my wife, who's pretty good at them. Little by little I got better. Now I'm doing the *New York Times* crosswords and, many times, believe it or not, I can fill in almost the whole thing. Not bad for a good ol' boy from Carbondale.

One implication of these findings is that it may be possible to "intervene" with individuals in order to help them change their leisure behaviors in ways that help increase their intellectual functioning. Some studies, for instance, have found that individuals with senile dementia increased their cognitive abilities through programs of dance, music, pets, and visitation.[7] This intervention, whether done by friends, local government or private long-term care workers, may be thought of as education for leisure.

Education for Leisure

As we have previously seen, leisure has become an important part of our lives. Rather than merely the leftover part of life, it has become more central in determining our happiness. It has also become an area of life in which we may do great harm not only to our bodies but also to our potential for individual development and growth. To avoid doing such harm, one must be prepared for leisure just as one is prepared for work. Just as "skilled" workers generally have better prospects in the workplace than "unskilled' workers, so too do those who are "skilled" in their uses of leisure have better prospects for happiness and personal growth than those who do not. Consider the thoughts of psychologist Mihalyi Csikszentmihalyi:

> Unless a person takes charge of them, both work and free time are likely to be disappointing. Most jobs and many leisure activities—especially those involving the passive consumption of mass media—are not designed to make us strong and happy. Their purpose is to make money for someone else. If we allow them to, they can suck out the marrow of our lives, leaving only feeble husks. But like everything else, work and leisure can be appropriated to our needs. People who learn to enjoy their work, who do not waste their free time, end up feeling that their lives as a whole have become much more worthwhile. "The future," wrote Charles K. Brightbill, "will belong not only to the educated man, but to the man who is educated to use his leisure wisely."[8]

Leisure, in other words, must be planned for and must involve the acquisition of skills—and such a process is educational. Leisure must ideally be developmental, a continuing process of giving oneself to activity and learning and changing from it:

> To fill free time with activities that require concentration, that increase skills, that lead to a development of the self, is not the same as killing time by watching television or taking recreational drugs. Although both strategies might seem to be different ways of coping with the same threat of chaos, as defenses against ontological anxiety, the former leads to growth, while the latter merely serves to keep the mind from unraveling. A person who rarely gets bored, who does not constantly need a favorable external environment to enjoy the moment, has passed the test for having achieved a creative life.[9]

A creative life, then, will mean that we must become self-entertaining rather than continually needing external sources to entertain us. This involves the exercise of the human will. It means we must act rather than be acted upon. Many of our interests are developed through learning rather than being an innate part of us. People who develop such interests, who have goals, are generally happier than those who do not. People who lead meaningful lives tend to have challenging goals that take up their energies, goals that give their lives significance. They achieve some purpose. They are resolved to pursue their goals and they acquire skills to do so. This, according to Csikszentmihalyi, can bring harmony to our consciousness.[10]

Bringing such harmony to our consciousness may be particularly difficult in our world of "over-choice." The mass media is overly convenient. Drugs, food, and alcohol are readily available. Every form of entertainment competes for our time. It may be that we choose simply to distract ourselves from life. Ironically, the evidence is mounting that such direct pleasure seeking without the opportunity to learn, acquire skills and grow personally is not very pleasurable after all. As leisure is viewed more and more as a mere commodity that can be purchased for a price, our society may be increasingly unhappy, even as we crave more free time.

> At a certain point, I decided to pick and choose what to do with my free time. Now I don't go to many movies because most of them are a waste of time. There is an old restored theatre near here that shows really worthwhile movies, lots of them from other countries. I go once in awhile; partly just to be in the theatre. Also, I have started making jewelry and look for antique beads to match the patterns in my mind. The mass produced stuff is usually not very interesting. Maybe that's also why I started cooking my own food and growing a lot of it in the backyard. Michael didn't like it at first but now he does. When it comes to leisure, I'm going to be who I was supposed to be; not some stupid consumer being jerked around by advertising. Not some mindless babe looking only for approval. Me.

These ideas are very similar to those of the ancient Athenians, who assumed that education for a life of leisure was imperative if free men were to avoid disaster. Our own systems of formal education, while largely concerned with the world of work and necessity, have increasingly begun to pay attention to leisure and its uses. Robert Frederick[11] traced the status of leisure time (extracurricular) activities in American public schools through at least four stages of development. During the Colonial Period an attitude of restraint prevailed: children were expected to attend to their lessons. With the lessening of formal religious influences in different parts of the country, there was tolerance for children organizing their own dances, parties and so on. Early in the twentieth century, schools developed their own extracurricular programs, with expanded plans and staff. The contemporary period, actually an extension of the third, is one of formalization, including the assigning of academic credit to leisure subjects. Thus, one might take a course in acting, creative writing, music appreciation, or learn a sport in a physical education course.

The education needs of a society reflect the situations and conditions under which its members live. While the ancient Greeks, with their slave culture, assumed that educating for leisure was imperative if the free man was to avoid disaster, our own formal education systems have been centered around work, both in respect to teaching methods and with the use made of various areas of study. Until we reach our mid-teens, schools are places we attend because we are obligated by law, where we do school*work*. Students usually attend colleges or universities to aid themselves in the pursuit of a career (although their reasons for going are, of course, diverse and complex). Although education for leisure has been one of the seven aims of the National Education Association, it is only recently that it has begun to achieve this goal.

In the following sections we will examine some different conceptualizations of education for leisure.

> My mom's boyfriend said he had learned a lot about using leisure in high school. Classes in drama, literature, art, music, physical education. I'm not getting any of that. The grade school kids don't even get recess. Our school is full of TVs and computers—I guess that's what we're getting trained to do in our free time. So what am I going to do the rest of my life after work—stare at a screen?

Stressing Leisure-Related Content

Charles K. Brightbill,[12] an American scholar of recreation and leisure, has been influential in developing a concept of education for leisure that is based upon exposure to leisure activities. He began by inviting us to think of education not in the narrow, fact-cramming, diploma-directed sense, but rather in its deepest and best meaning—in terms of thinking and learning processes. If we are to have leisure, we must educate ourselves for it. If we do not learn how to use the new leisure in wholesome, uplifting, decent, and creative ways, said Brightbill, we shall not live at all. This does not mean that leisure should be regimented. It is not as important that people use parks, beaches, and libraries as it is that they learn to use their leisure time in personally satisfying and creative ways—either with or without society's organized resources.

Brightbill stated that "education for leisure" means exposing people early and long—in the home, the school, and the community—to experiences that will help them develop appreciations and skills to use in their increasingly available leisure time. He stressed that education for leisure is a slow, steady process, involving the imparting of skills and the readiness to exercise them. Leisure can contribute to the aims of education such as comprehending the world, attaining health and emotional stability, and appreciating and expressing beauty. In this sense, leisure is not an escape from the toil of education; it is a revitalizing element in the process of education itself.

Responding to the
Needs of Special Populations

Leisure education has another set of meanings for those individuals who are sometimes termed *special populations*. People who have developmental disabilities, emotional disturbance or physical handicaps face unique problems using their leisure in satisfying ways. Education for leisure has unique implications for individuals who have mental or physical disabilities. A leisure education program for individuals with disabilities may involve the opportunity to: (1) increase social skills necessary to develop friends, strengthen relationships, gain interpersonal acceptance and strengthen role relations; (2) develop a sense of awareness and appreciation concerning leisure that will be useful in self-development; (3) express his or her individuality; and (4) develop philosophical positions.[13] Strengthening these skills may make it more likely that an individual will experience success in specific leisure activities.

For adults with mental retardation, the ability to live independently in a community may be as much a function of their ability to use leisure in satisfying ways as their ability to find employment. While such an individual might, for instance, find employment for which he or she had received training and learn the process of taking a bus to work, what happens when the individual returns from work, gets off the bus, and walks back to his or her room or apartment? Dattilo identified the following as necessary components in an effective leisure education program for people with mental retardation: (a) awareness of self, (b) perception of leisure competence, (c) awareness of leisure, (d) knowledge of leisure resources, (e) decision-making skills, and (f) social interaction skills. Thus, adults with mental retardation would need to learn to make appropriate choices about recreation participation that realistically recognized their abilities as well as limitations. They would need to learn and make choices concerning leisure based upon an awareness of numerous different possibilities. They would also need to enhance their ability to make choices based upon a greater knowledge of leisure resources. Finally, it would be necessary to develop or improve social interaction skills. Education for leisure for individuals with mental retardation would thus be not only challenging but also could be a central determinant of the extent to which individuals in question are capable of living independently. Historically, many citizens with mental retardation have been prepared for a job in society but not in how to use their leisure in appropriate ways.

Donnie works at the hotel and he lives there as well. He's in his late thirties—mildly to moderately retarded. Single. Whenever I go there for dinner with friends, Donnie comes over and we have the same conversation. He learned to bowl. He also, somehow, learned to score bowling. Then he got into a league for adults with mental retardation. After that he got into a league that was just a regular league. His team won a trophy. I'll bet I've seen that trophy seven or eight times but still—I like seeing it. Donnie learned a leisure skill—and he got good at it.

To some extent, the same may be said for those who are emotionally disturbed, physically handicapped, ex-prisoners, and many others who have a disabling situation. In many ways, their ability to use leisure in satisfying, appropriate ways determines their fate as surely as their ability to do useful work does.

One simple answer concerning what schools should do to educate for leisure is that teachers must devote considerable attention to the "liberal" arts as well as to the "servile" arts. The servile arts deal with those skills that are related to work and to survival, to those activities that are primarily means to economic ends. If one wishes to be a computer programmer, carpenter, accountant, or nurse, there are skills that must be learned to perform these occupations. The liberal arts, however, deal with areas of human endeavor that are not, strictly speaking, necessary for survival or for work, but which help to define and fulfill us as human beings. Such areas of study might include a range of activities, including drawing, singing, playing sports, writing short stories, and studying history. In short, the school curriculum should reflect a balance between subjects which are useful to us in an economic sense and those which are intellectually, physically, and aesthetically "useful." During the early 1990s, there was a tendency to cut back on such course offerings due to lack of funds.

Recreational activities, nevertheless, often occupy an accepted place in the curriculum of educational institutions. Subjects and activities of a recreational nature were initially incorporated into school life because it was believed that healthy recreation could produce beneficial moral effects and because some influence over pupils' recreation made it easier to control their behavior. Today, however, in

> I'm going to run for the school board. I'm really POed about how they are handling the elementary schools. First they got rid of phys ed. Then they got rid of art. Then they cut back recess. Then they banned playing tag. Lunch is twenty minutes—and it's fast food. What the hell is going on?
>
> Kids have to play. It's what they are supposed to do. You can't expect them to sit at a desk all day. I mean, they may get better at taking tests but turn out to be really dull human beings. Also, they're not going to learn if they don't get some breaks from it. What the hell is going on? You also learn from playing, but the school board doesn't seem to understand that either. I'm going to let them know.

spite of cutbacks at some schools, recreation is recognized as being desirable for its own sake, and many schools employ specialists to deal with this increasingly broad aspect of the curriculum. Apart from learning sports, pupils in many schools can be introduced to literature, art, different types of music, crafts, and various other potentially satisfying leisure activities.

Making the Educational Process More Leisurely

A second way of regarding education for leisure is to view it in terms of the educational process rather than the academic content. If a school is to reflect a leisure ethic and prepare students to live in a society with such an ethic, the school must do this by example. The school building, for example, should not look like a factory. Students should have some experience with high autonomy situations in which they "practice" exercising freedom. There should be periods of time which are not rigidly scheduled, during which contemplation can take place. There should also be times to play, to celebrate, to volunteer, and even to loaf. Now, all this is easier said than done, but certainly some changes can be made, in the physical layout and design of a school, in procedures of instruction, and in other factors involved in teaching.

Let's take a single example of this—a classroom. Classrooms are often pathetically ugly, devoid of color, decoration, and any attempt at warmth, cheerfulness, or personality. In some cases, chairs are actually fastened to the floor so that the placement of the students is established in advance. If there is any furniture or equipment in the room, it is likely to be standardized; such furniture is justified as being "functional" as a means to an end. The room is eminently forgettable—an environment to be "endured."

If classrooms are to be more in keeping with a leisure ethic, they should not be standardized. Artwork, plants, fish, music, warm colors, sunlight wherever possible, displays and exhibits, and many other things can be used to make a classroom more leisurely. Such changes, however, would be suspect in many schools.

Many of you reading this book are students enrolled in a college or university. If you are, this book is used in connection with a course

> Our school looks a lot like a prison. The rooms are ugly. There is a buzzer system that tells us when to go to the next class. We have a rent-a-cop standing outside. Our lockers get searched. You have to go every day or you get in trouble. Everything is by the numbers and it just feels like—and looks like—a prison. So, that makes me a prisoner.

you are taking that is probably held in a classroom. If so, Exercise 11.1 (page 312) at the end of this chapter asks you to examine ways of making your classroom more leisurely.

Making the education process more leisurely does not mean that every classroom experience can be fun or that discipline should be abandoned; it means that the discipline is ideally imposed by the learner rather than the teacher. Self-discipline was a key part of the ancient Greek notion of leisure. The learning process should be one in which externally imposed discipline is gradually replaced by the discipline and curiosity of the learner. While this transformation cannot always take place, the most profound kinds of learning generally take place only when it does.

The process of achieving self-discipline is more likely to occur if the need of the individual to play (i.e., information-processing and stimulation) is considered in the learning process.

Learning about Leisure Alternatives

A third way of thinking about education for leisure might be called "consciousness expanding." The student would be presented with information about such matters as recreation and leisure in our society; its relation to work; its importance in relation to life, satisfaction, leisure opportunities in the community, or society at large; and the consequences of leisure behavior.

We may consider learning about leisure alternatives in a highly specific sense—finding out about what recreation, park, and leisure services actually exist in a community. There is a great tendency to assume that people have a greater information level about what exists in their community than they actually do possess. Once a given leisure service is established, some individuals in the population will participate, visit, register, use, or involve themselves in the service. Others will not. If we examine those who do not, these nonusers can be divided into those who are unaware of the existence of the service, those whose awareness level is very low or who are uncertain the service exists, and those who know it exists but don't have enough information to use it. Those who know about the service or who have a "functional" awareness level may be divided into those who wish to participate; those who don't wish to participate; those, if any, who are ineligible to participate; and those for whom participation would be inappropriate.

> We got this brochure from the Champaign Park District, and I couldn't believe all the opportunities for recreation. I mean, it was amazing. Sports, special events, picnic areas you can rent for almost nothing. Swimming. Special interest clubs. I didn't know about any of this stuff—and I've lived here three years!

In terms of nonparticipation in public leisure services, lack of knowledge or awareness is found to be quite common. Even some of those who know about a leisure service may not know enough about it to be able to use it. One obviously important aspect of exploring leisure alternatives, then, is finding out what exists. Those who educate for leisure must help in this process.

Leisure Counseling

Leisure counseling has been viewed in a number of ways. According to McLellan and Pellet:

> The object of leisure counseling is to determine the patients' leisure interests and then to assist in locating activities in the home community to meet their interests. The leisure counselor also helps the patients to examine the feasibility of their activity choices in terms of cost, accessibility, and personal skills and capabilities. Many different techniques are used in leisure counseling. These include individual or group counseling, the use of interest-measuring instruments, and referral services to community resources.[14]

Dickason[15] has stressed that leisure counseling must focus upon the feasibility of participating in an activity. Feasibility variables include (1) financial resources; (2) social, physical, and mental abilities; (3)

accessibility; and (4) related background experience. Counseling programs could include

- community field trips to gather information concerning available activities,
- individual and group discussion programs about what is available in the community,
- referral services where counselor and individual clients discuss and decide what type of introductory procedure would best help the client become acquainted with the services of a particular leisure service agency,
- follow-up programs in which clients report individually or in a group on their involvements in avocational activities within the community, and
- family counseling in which a leisure education program involves relatives of the client to better provide the client with support.

Basically, leisure counseling appears to be aimed at two groups: (1) those who are institutionalized and/or have a special disability, such as the emotionally disturbed, physically handicapped, or prisoners; and (2) the general public. In regard to leisure counseling with psychiatric patients, for instance, O'Morrow defined leisure counseling as

> The technique in the rehabilitation process whereby a professional person uses all information gathered about a patient prior to discharge to further explore interests and attitudes, with respect to leisure, recreation, and social relationships, in order to enable the patient to identify, locate, and use recreation resources within the community.[16]

In all these conceptualizations, leisure counseling seems to be (1) expanding consciousness and clarifying values, (2) providing information about leisure resources and otherwise "enabling" the client, and/or (3) changing values. A number of leisure counseling projects have been initiated during the last few years that have sought to expand consciousness, clarify values, and provide information about leisure.

It is in regard to changing values that leisure counseling may be controversial. In many cases, such change is aimed at making the individual more "productive" during their leisure or making things happen that will presumably be pleasing to them. Contrast these assumptions about the wise use of leisure with those of the philosopher Josef Pieper:

> Leisure is not the attitude of mind of those who actively interview, but of those who are open to everything; not of those who grab and grab hold, but of those who hold the reins loose and who are free and easy themselves—almost like a man falling asleep, for one can only fall asleep by 'letting oneself go.' Sleeplessness and the incapacity for leisure are really related to one another in a special sense, and a man at leisure is not unlike a man asleep.[17]

A person at leisure, then, might be one who watches things happen or who, if asleep, doesn't know what's happened (in some sense). One begins to see the problem here immediately. Who is to say that people should try to cram as many leisure activities into 24 hours as possible? Robert Bly's poem *Driving to Town Late to Mail a Letter* shows us what a beautiful experience wasting time can be:

> It is a cold and windy night. The main street is deserted.
> The only things moving are swirls of snow.
> As I lift the mailbox door, I feel its cold iron.
> There is a privacy I love in this snowy night.
> Driving around, I will waste more time.[18]

Who is to say what leisure should be in a multicultural society such as our own? Leisure counselors inherently must assume that their own values are superior to those of the person being counseled; this would often seem to require some unwarranted assumptions on the counselor's part. Certainly we can find some extremes in values where counseling would be warranted, such as cases where people break the law during their leisure, but generally such counseling is suspect. If this function of leisure counseling is proselytizing (seeking to convert others to your values), then we find a huge number of counseling "sources" in our society—parents, schools, commercial advertising, the scouting movement, Trout Unlimited, the lyrics of rap songs, the Bible, and many other sources. Perhaps leisure counseling which seeks to change values is best done by organizations that seek to change behavior. It is doubtful that public recreation, park, or leisure service organizations can undertake such a function or that they *should* undertake it even if they could.

After all, such organizations must seek to reflect the current leisure values of their clientele, which are often quite diverse.

There does, however, seem to be great value in helping individuals seek to clarify their values concerning recreation and leisure, and in giving them ideas and information about what they could do in their own communities. Many people haven't thought much about their leisure activities or even considered what they seek during leisure. Similarly, people are often unaware of things they can do and places they can go that are right under their noses. If leisure counseling can identify those leisure resources that people desire, then it may increase happiness.

If leisure counseling can play a role in the adjustment of a prisoner who is being released into the community, it can benefit both society and the individual. But, if leisure counseling is merely one more way of trying to sell a given leisure lifestyle that the leisure counselor happens to prefer, it is of limited use and has no place in public projects. We all have been counseled about our leisure, even if we did not recognize it as such. As a teenager, I was counseled by a policeman about my use of leisure to race cars. I have also received advice from teachers, girl-friends, poolroom proprietors, a tennis coach, poets, parents, sales-people, and many others. Leisure counseling is most difficult to give wisely, since it involves guiding another person's freedom in ways that (hopefully) result in their increased happiness. What an extraordinary responsibility! Perhaps we ultimately counsel by example.

A Holistic View of Education for Leisure

Some scholars of educational policy have sought to promote leisure in the educational process in form, content, and purpose. In examining education for leisure from the standpoint of educational policy, Robert Bundy,[19] an education consultant, stated that the modern problem of leisure has been defined in two very different ways. The modern or industrial notion for creating a leisure society is to increase free-time activities and keep people occupied constructively. The postmodern view, however, is that people must be helped to find self-defining work so that they can find leisure as a state of existence. Today's educational policy, Bundy believed, has concentrated more on the former version.

In formal education today, young people are segregated from society and have practically no responsibility for the welfare of others. In school the intellect is trained to control the emotions, and only pathways to knowledge that involve hard work are considered legitimate. Quantitative measurement and "useful" learning are stressed, job preparation and manpower planning dominate, little money is spent on the arts and humanities, and knowledge is fragmented into specialized areas.

For educational policy to help create a society of leisure in the postmodern sense, educational policy would need to undergo many changes. According to Bundy, "There would be a strong emphasis on the long-term educational objective of helping people find a self-defined work to do in life as well as a strong case for style and craft in one's work." The arts and humanities would occupy a central place in the curriculum. Learning would seek to interrelate different fields of knowledge. The basic thrust of education would be to fully develop the senses, the emotions, the intellect, the psyche, and the spirit. There would be a reduction on quantitative measures of evaluation. "More play, spontaneity, and festivity, and the capacity to be enchanted would be evident in the schools."[20] The notion of free time would make no sense. These changes are beginning to come about, Bundy has stated, both because public education can no longer afford our present methods of operation, and also because the eastern and western worlds are drawing closer together, creating a desire to synthesize knowledge in new ways.

A related critique of higher education has been made by Allan Bloom. Part of his complaint with modern universities is that they have abandoned the traditional mission of educating the whole person from some agreed upon perspective of what was important and worth knowing. To a great extent, universities have become merely vocational training centers. Within the university, Bloom stated:

> Each department or great division of the university makes a pitch for itself, and each offers a course of study which will make the student an initiate. But how to choose among them? How do they relate to one another? The fact is they do not address one another. They are competing and contradictory, without being aware of it. The problem of the whole is urgently indicated by the very existence of these specialties, but it is never systematically posed. The net effect of the

student's encounter with the university catalogue is bewilderment and very often demoralization. It is just a matter of chance whether he finds one or two professors who can give him an insight into one of the great visions of education that have been the distinguishing part of every civilized nation. Most professors are specialists, concerned only with their own fields, interested in the advancement of those fields in their own terms, or in their own personal advancement in a world where all the rewards are on the side of professional distinction. They have been entirely emancipated from the old structure of the university, which at least helped to indicate that they are incomplete, only parts of an unexamined and undiscovered whole. So the student must navigate among a collection of carnival barkers, each trying to lure him into a particular sideshow. This undecided student is an embarrassment to most universities, because he seems to be saying, 'I am a whole human being. Help me to form myself in my wholeness and let me develop my real potential,' and he is one to whom they have nothing to say.[21]

This rather extraordinary indictment, to the extent it is true, would mean that universities educate, essentially, for occupations, without regard for the broader kinds of understanding about life's meanings which the ancient Athenians assumed were necessary to successfully use leisure. Further, according to Bloom,

If the focus is careers, there is hardly one specialty, outside the hardest of the hard natural sciences, which requires more than two years of preparatory training prior to graduate studies. The rest is just wasted time, or a period of ripening until the student is old enough for graduate studies.[22]

If we accept this as true, it is no wonder that so many undergraduates feel alienated. No wonder they talk so frequently about "getting out into the real world." No wonder so much of their leisure activity seems to be escapist. While education for leisure certainly requires the acquisition of specific leisure skills, which many colleges and universities do provide, it also requires that the student grow intellectually. It requires that the student gain knowledge in the liberal arts, not just the arts which may be called "servile" (centered on work). Education must move beyond the realm of the specifically useful. As the philosopher Josef Pieper has stated

> Education concerns the whole man: an educated man is a man with a point of view from which to take in the whole world. Education concerns the whole man... capable of grasping the totality of existing things. This implies nothing against training and nothing against the official. Of course specialized and professional work is normal, the normal way in which men play their part in the world; work is the normal, the working day is the normal day. But the question is: whether the world, defined as the world of work, is exhaustively defined; can man develop to the full as a functionary and a worker and nothing else; can full human existence be contained within an exclusively workaday existence?[23]

For Pieper, it clearly cannot. If higher education is guided only by the desire to prepare for work and by the drive for efficiency, if everything it does is judged in terms of its usefulness, it cannot prepare students for leisure. To have leisure, to repeat, the educated person must have a point of view from which to take in the world. A point of view which allows that person to answer the central life question for those whose material needs have been met at some minimal level: "Given a minimum of constraints, what is worth doing?" A university that cannot help the student find new and better ways to answer that question cannot educate for leisure or educate the whole person.

Who Should Educate for Leisure?

We have discussed education for leisure so far primarily in terms of the role of the school. Actually, the public schools may not be the most important agents for education for leisure. Research by Kelly has found that youngsters were initiated into

My kid goes to college and the tuition will knock your socks off. He better be learning things that will help him have a good career. Basically, college is there to help him earn money. What he does in his spare time isn't important. You don't need help for that anyway. The idea is to make money—The idea is to be a success. Sure, it sounds a little cynical to be saying this but—look—that's the story.

leisure activities more often by their parents and friends than through the schools.[24]

The schools, as Ken Roberts[25] has pointed out, have a number of limitations that make it difficult for them to have an impact on their students' future lives. Many forms of recreation cannot be fully appreciated until people have attained physical, emotional or social maturity. Developing an appreciation of literature among children, for instance, is extremely difficult. It is not easy for the educational system to impart a set of values that pupils will use continuously to structure their leisure lives as they mature into adulthood. Technological and social developments are modifying the range of available leisure activities, making it difficult for the schools to prepare young people for their future leisure lives. Schools tend to emphasize organized competitive team games, but few adult leisure activities are of this kind. Finally, just as industrial recreation is shunned by many employees because it reminds them of work, so are extracurricular activities shunned by many students (particularly the less successful ones) because they remind them of school.

These limitations are rather important, particularly the ones dealing with changes in people's leisure interests as they age. Our leisure values change with age. This limits the schools not only in their ability to provide leisure experiences that can serve as models for the future years but also in their ability to provide leisure counseling. In regard to the first point, I can remember as a child watching my father grow a vegetable garden year after year. I had not the slightest interest in it. In my mid-thirties, however, I became interested enough to have a large garden, complete with parsnips, a compost pile, and an occasional Japanese beetle. I doubt that school could have interested me in gardening at the age of 14—I was a different person. In regard to the second point, leisure counseling in the public schools is limited to the extent that it deals with specific values or activities because the individual is likely to change leisure values and some activities as maturity is reached. (These problems are not unique to leisure, of course. Vocational counseling has the same problems. Students change their ideas about what careers they want to pursue and what they want to do with their lives.)

Because of these limitations, it may be appropriate to consider giving many other kinds of organizations responsibility for education for leisure. Many kinds of local leisure service agencies—from municipal recreation and parks departments to voluntary youth-serving agencies to commercial organizations—are involved in education for leisure. Such educational undertakings include (1) formal instruction in a leisure skill such as oil painting, golf, or flower arranging; (2) providing information about available community resources for leisure; (3) lectures, exhibits, seminars, displays, trips, festivals, and other methods that provide new ideas, information, and experiences; (4) research findings about what people do in the community and what they want to do, such as special populations' leisure needs; and (5) unique learning in programs such as urban gardening, camping, cultural exchange programs, and Outward Bound–type experiences.

In all these ways and others, leisure service organizations are involved in leisure education.

Level of Education and Leisure Behavior

What people do during their leisure and the leisure values they have are influenced by their level of education. Education not only stimulates interest in many forms of leisure activity but it also enables participation in some forms of leisure by providing necessary skills and developing appreciation. Many leisure activities cannot be enjoyed without some skills that are gained through formal education. Additionally, formal education develops appreciation for many forms of leisure expression that may not be instantly appreciated, such as many forms of "high culture"—poetry, opera, ballet—whose enjoyment is enhanced through repeated exposure. The same may be said of flyfishing.

Because higher levels of education tend to stimulate participation in leisure activities, it is not surprising that many studies have found a broader range of participation in leisure activities among those with higher income levels. Also, those with higher education are more likely to participate in most forms of outdoor recreation, sports, high culture, tourism, continuing education, reading, and volunteer activities. While part of this greater participation reflects the fact that those with higher education levels are likely to have higher incomes and be younger than their counterparts with less education, education itself often has a distinct bearing on such participation, even after the effect of income and age are taken into account.

> Here's the problem. We did a survey and asked parents in tough sections of LA what kinds of programs they wanted for their kids. Almost nobody checked camping. Does that mean the parents know about camping and decided it was a bad thing for their children? I don't think so. Most of them have never been camping so they didn't really have any experience upon which to judge it. It would like asking—"Do you like Martians?" Unless you have a met a few Martians, you don't know—they might be pretty nice.

The Increasing Need for Education for Leisure in Other Countries

The portion of life devoted to work is not only shrinking in the United States. In China, three holiday periods in May, October and February are giving more than one-fourth of the world's population extended periods of free time not dreamed of a decade ago. In South Korea, the five-day workweek and two-day weekend has arrived. In Taiwan, workers can now apply for two "golden weeks" free from work when they want them. In country after country, free time is increasing. The burning question this presents is what to do during that time. There is the danger that, in many of the countries where free time is expanding, the market sector will be the primary or even sole provider of leisure activity. Thus, shopping, tourism, and entertainment may dominate. There is nothing wrong with any of these forms of leisure, but they are not enough. As we have seen in previous chapters, the most satisfying leisure involves either (a) the skill-challenge variety that may produce flow, (b) socialization, or (c) contact with nature.

Unless people with more free time are taught leisure skills, applications and have the chance to try out various forms of leisure expression, they may simply live a life based around television and consumption. What will they tell their children? "I had freedom to choose and free time to do as I pleased, and I spent it watching TV." Education for leisure will become more critical as the potential to spend all of one's free time consuming becomes greater.

> I'm seventeen and I'm Korean. Many of my Korean friends follow every American trend that comes along, from rap music to wearing your jeans with your underwear sticking out. In Korea, what you do during your free time determines if you are a "banana" or not. A banana is yellow on the outside but white on the inside—I don't want to be a banana.

Study Questions

1. What generalizations can be made about the relationship between leisure and educational level?

2. What are some various meanings of "education for leisure?"

3. Do you think leisure counseling is a good idea? Why or why not?

4. What agencies and individuals should be involved in "education for leisure?"

5. Will participation in adult education increase during the next 20 years? Why or why not?

Exercise 11.1

1. Name three specific physical changes that could be made to provide your classroom with a more "leisurely" atmosphere for learning, and explain why each suggestion would improve the leisure quality of the environment.

   a.

   b.

   c.

2. If your suggestions were undertaken, would there be any negative consequences in making these changes?

3. Do you think your college or university would be receptive to making these changes if your class suggested them? Why or why not?

Endnotes

1   Paepke, C. (1993). *The evolution of progress.* New York, NY: Random House.

2   ibid.

3   ibid.

4   Diamond cited in Willis, S., Maier, H., and Tosti-Vasey, J. (1993). Correlates of crossword and jigsaw puzzle playing in the elderly. *Journal of Gerontology, 48*(4), 12–48.

5   Willis, S., Maier, H., and Tosti-Vasey, J. (1993). Correlates of crossword and jigsaw puzzle playing in the elderly. *Journal of Gerontology, 48*(4), 12–48.

6   Clarkson-Smith, L. and Hartley, A. (1990). The game of bridge as an exercise in working memory and reasoning. *Journal of Gerontology, 45*(6), 233–238.

7   Coyle, C., Kinney, W., Riley, B., and Shank, J. (1991). *Benefits of therapeutic recreation: A consensus view.* Washington, DC: National Institute on Disability and Rehabilitation Research.

8   Csikszentmihalyi, M. (1990). *Flow: The psychology of optimal experience* (p. 32). New York, NY: Harper and Row.

9   ibid.

10   ibid.

11   Frederick, R. (1959). *The third curriculum* (p. 72). New York, NY: Appleton-Century Crofts.

12   Brightbill, C. (1960). *The challenge of leisure* (p. 32). Englewood Cliffs, NJ: Prentice Hall.

13   Dattilo, J. and Murphy, W. (1991). *Leisure education program planning—A systematic approach.* State College, PA: Venture Publishing, Inc.

14   McLellan, R. and Pellet, L. (1975). Leisure counseling: The first step. *Therapeutic Recreation Journal, 9*(4), 161–166.

15   Dickason, J. (1978). Approaches and techniques of recreation counseling. In A. Epperson, P. Witt, and G. Hitzhusen, (Eds.), *Leisure counseling—An aspect of leisure education* (pp. 55, 59). Springfield, IL: Charles C. Thomas.

16   O'Morrow, G. (1968). *A study of recreation service to psychiatric patients in relation to predischarge planning and after care* (p. 17). Doctoral dissertation, Columbia University, New York.

17   Pieper, J. (1952). *Leisure—The basis of culture* (p. 41). New York, NY: New American Library.

18   Bly, R. (1972). *Silence in the snowy fields* (p. 38). Middletown, CT: Wesleyan University Press.

19   Bundy, R. (1977). Leisure: The missing future's perspective in educational policy. *Journal of Education,* May, 93–104.

20   ibid.

21   Bloom, A. (1987). *The closing of the American mind* (pp. 339–340). New York, NY: Simon and Schuster.

22   ibid.

23   Pieper, J. (1952). *Leisure—The basis of culture* (p. 41). New York, NY: New American Library.

24   Kelly, J. (1972). Socialization toward leisure: A developmental approach. *Journal of Leisure Research, 6*(3), 181–193.

25   Roberts, K. (1970). *Leisure* (pp. 16–119) London, UK: Longmans.

Leisure and Healthy Lives

Are you healthy? How do you know? What would indicate to you that you are very healthy or not so healthy? Would you merely ask a doctor to find out and, if so, how would she know? If you tried to answer this question yourself, you might decide to take an inventory of any ailments you have, how you feel, or how well or fit you are. Perhaps, also, you would think about many aspects of your life: your friends, personal habits, or the environment in which you live. Personal happiness might also be considered. "Health" is a highly complicated and often debated issue that we only partially understand. In this chapter, we will examine what health is and some of the ways leisure and its use are centrally related to individual and group health.

"Health," "wellness" and "illness" are concepts that are in a state of change in our society and, to a remarkable extent, there is little agreement as to what they mean. While our modern, scientific approach to disease is often one in which disease is thought to be caused by an outside agent invading the body, many notions of disease view it as imbalance or disequilibrium. In the traditional Chinese view of illness, while the outside agent idea is not ignored, sickness is "due to a pattern of causes leading to disharmony and imbalance."[1]

However, this view also assumes that the nature of all things, including the human body, is one of homeostasis. In other words, there is a natural striving to return to equilibrium. Going in and out of balance is seen as a natural process that happens constantly throughout the life cycle, and their traditional texts draw no sharp distinction between health and illness. Both are seen as being natural and as being part of a continuum, as aspects of the same fluctuating process in which the individual organism changes continually in relation to a changing environment.

Illness, then, may be thought of as attack by outside agents, or it may be an imbalance in the individual. This imbalance may be thought of as only between the physical, psychological, and social aspects of the organism, or it may be extended and thought of as imbalance between the individual, society, and the ecosystem. Such imbalances may be thought of as stress. As futurist Hazel Henderson noted:

> I have this vision of stress as a ball being pushed around the system. Everybody is trying to unload the stress in somebody else's system.
>
> For example, take the economy. One way to minister to the sick economy would be to create another percentage point of unemployment. That pushes the stress back on to the individual. We know that one percentage point of unemployment creates about seven billion dollars' worth of measurable human stress in terms of morbidity, mortality, suicide and so on... Another way of doing this is that the society can shove the stress onto the ecosystem, and then it comes back [30] years later, as in the case of the Love Canal.[2]

Why Do People Become Ill?

Health means more than how long one lives. It also means the qualities of one's life, for instance, "Are you feeling well or ill this morning?" Illness means lots of different things and occurs for many different reasons. While no absolute answers exist, physicians Nesse and Williams conclude that people get sick for the following reasons:

- Defenses
- Infection
- Novel environments
- Genes
- Design compromises
- Evolutionary legacies[3]

Some illnesses are really not illnesses but are mistakenly thought to be. A cough, for instance, is designed to expel foreign matter from the respiratory tract. Infections occur because some bacteria, viruses and fungi "treat us mainly as meals."[4] As we find new ways to fight these invaders that attack the body, they change in response, creating in an infinitely escalating battle. Some illness occurs because of our genes. Many terrible afflictions are the result, simply, of the genetic endowment passed from parents to children. Half the genes in a child are identical to those of the mother and half to those of the father. One fourth of the genes in grandparents are identical to those in the grandchild. Thus, illnesses are passed on by our genes, who care little about us, wanting only to reproduce themselves. Illness may also be the result of compromises in the design of human beings. Walking upright, for example, allows us to carry our babies and see where we are going, but it also predisposes us to back problems. In essence, if our system were perfectly designed for one function, it would not be well-designed for another.

Some of the illnesses or physical problems of humans are simply legacies of our evolution. If we were going to redesign the body, we would not want food and water passing through a tube in front of our windpipe since it exposes us to the danger of choking. That, however, is the way we are "wired." In terms of leisure, it is the last reason for illness that may be the most important.

Our bodies were designed over the course of millions of years for lives spent in small groups hunting and gathering on the plains of Africa. Natural selection has not had time to revise our bodies for coping with fatty diets, automobiles, artificial lights, and central heating. From this mismatch between our design and our environment arises much, perhaps most, preventable modern disease. The current epidemics of heart disease and breast cancer are tragic examples.[5]

This is where we see the most implication for leisure. Basically, we have evolved faster than our bodies could adjust. In many ways, our bodies are still back on the Serengeti plain in Africa. To the extent this is true, we are better off living more in nature than less—better off walking, eating foods that are not heavily processed, using natural light, and other ways to become less insulated from nature.

Even the landscapes we find preferable go back to this period of our evolution. Of all the variations possible in landscape, the African savanna type—grassy plains punctuated by mature trees wider than they are tall, usually with water present—is the most popular.

> So well do we love the savanna that we have recreated it all over the globe in the wide tree canopies and lack of undergrowth found in the Japanese Zen garden, the English landscape, and the American city park. Similar landscapes are found in the winelands north of San Francisco and the hill country of Kashmir, the Tuileries of Paris and the Poet's Walk of New York's Central Park. The widely spaced palms of Caribbean beaches and the open montane-type forests of the Colorado Rockies—two perennial favorites among travelers—also have savanna-like characteristics.[6]

Such landscapes may answer some old longing we have but don't quite understand. It may be a longing in our genes—to exist as our ancestors did. There is increasing evidence, then, that closeness to the natural environment is healthy. At the same time, a higher and higher portion of the world's exploding population lives in cities with few contacts with nature. Living closer to nature may also mean relying less on doctors and medicine every time we experience any discomfort.

Why Do People Die?

In many cases, people assume any behavior that keeps you alive longer is healthy and any behavior which causes you to shorten your life is unhealthy. To understand health and its relation to leisure, therefore, we must ask the question "Why do we die?" This question, of course, is one for which we have no ultimate answer without turning to religion, philosophy or understandings past science. An anthropologist, however, can tell us about the changes in the causes of people's deaths.[7] Historically, major causes of death have changed as follows:

Disaster > Disease > Decay

Our ancestors, who lived in trees, then in caves and huts, were more likely to die from a disaster than anything else. An individual froze to death, starved, fell out of a tree, or was killed in a battle.

Slowly, as humans gained a little more control over some aspects of their environment, disease became the most prevalent way in which people died. Bubonic plague, for instance, killed about one third of all people in Europe in the fourteenth century. Cholera, typhoid, malaria and other diseases ravaged many civilizations—and sometimes still do. It is hard to imagine how common death from disease was. While we may think that the Europeans who invaded what is now the Americas killed most of the indigenous population with their weapons, far more native people were killed by European diseases such as smallpox and influenza.

As humans developed defenses against these killers in the form of better sanitation, purer water, better means to preserve food, penicillin and other antibiotics, the leading cause of death for those in modern nations became decay—the wearing out of the body. This shift in reasons for death is shown in Table 12.1. As you can see, while diseases like pneumonia, tuberculosis and diarrhea and enteritis were leading causes of death at the turn of the twentieth century, today heart disease,

Table 12.1 Ten Leading Causes of Death in the United States (1900 and 2004)[8, 9]

Rank	Cause of Death	Percentage of All Deaths
	1900	
1	Pneumonia and influenza	11.6
2	Tuberculosis	11.3
3	Diarrhea and enteritis	8.3
4	Heart disease	8.0
5	Stroke	6.2
6	Nephritis	5.2
7	All accidents	4.2
8	Cancer	3.7
9	Senility	2.9
10	Diphtheria	2.3
	2004	
1	Diseases of the heart	27.2
2	Malignant neoplasms (cancers)	23.0
3	Cerebrovascular disease	6.2
4	Chronic lower respiratory disease	5.2
5	Accidents/Unintentional injury	4.6
6	Diabetes mellitus	3.0
7	Alzheimer's disease	2.7
8	Influenza and pneumonia	2.5
9	Nephritis	1.8
10	Septicemia	1.4

cancer, and stroke have replaced them. Almost all of the causes of death by 1990 were ones in which human behavior played some role. Almost all these causes are, if not "preventable," as we say, they are "delayable." While your genetic makeup is often the most important factor in determining things like heart disease, in many cases, your behaviors, habits and attitudes are critical in determining the likelihood of heart attack, cancer, or stroke.

Figure 12.1 shows a simplified web of causation applied to heart disease. Notice how many of these causal agents are partially shaped by our own behavior. Does the person engage in physical activity on a regular basis? What does their diet consist of? Do they smoke? Do they experience high levels of stress in their daily lives?

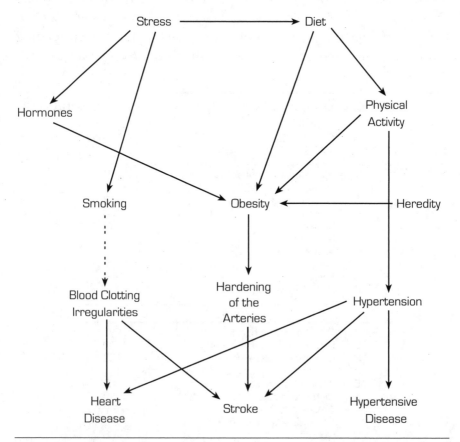

Figure 12.1 Simplified Web of Causation Applied to Cardiovascular Disease [10]

What the progression of causes of death means is that your daily habits, behaviors, attitude, beliefs and relations with others play an important role in your health and longevity.

Why Many People Die Before They Decay

None of the previous means that disasters or disease no longer cause substantial numbers of deaths. Many people die before they wear out, and most do so needlessly. If you are a young adult in North America, you are more likely to die from the disaster of an automobile wreck or the self-inflicted disaster of suicide than any other cause. Additionally, you may have self-inflicted yourself with a variety of diseases which will kill you at a later point in your life by smoking. Smoking tobacco is the leading cause of preventable death in the United States and Canada. Thus, we need not be rocket scientists to figure out that improving chances of survival into old age are critically linked to some simple decisions:

- Quit smoking now (please)
- Wear a seatbelt
- Don't drink and drive
- Seek help immediately if you think about suicide

You have probably heard these suggestions before. One reason some young people ignore them is a failure of their imagination. It may be difficult to imagine that you can die; young people expect to live forever. It may be impossible to

As a board-certified physician in gerontology, over the years I have come to the conclusion that people have to make intelligent tradeoffs. You can't live your everyday life based strictly on what behaviors are the healthiest.

First, in many cases we don't know what is healthiest. Is glucosime condritine effective? We probably won't know for another decade. Low-fat diets are believed to protect against breast cancer, but they may not help. There may be no link between a low-fat diet and rates of coronary disease. Dietary fiber may or may not help prevent colon cancer.

Also, what is pleasurable and what is healthy are often opposites. Sometimes you have to go with pleasure: Maybe a big plate of nachos grande. Sometimes pleasure and health are not opposites: Getting into a hot tub is usually good for you and it feels good too.

I guess that other than understanding there are a few incredibly stupid things you shouldn't do, such as smoke, healthy people have to live with uncertainty and have a little fun.

imagine that you are not in control of your destiny when you are driving a car—for even if you are driving carefully, someone else is not. That someone else may be driving drunk, not paying attention, talking on a cell phone, may simply make a mistake, or experience a mechanical failure.

It may also be difficult to imagine the effect on the lining of your lungs from accumulated tar in tobacco smoke. Such failures of imagination allow disasters and disease to account for millions of needless deaths.

> I'm afraid of a lot of things—flying, spiders, swimming in the ocean, taking exams—but for some reason I wasn't afraid of being in the car when Vince was driving after he'd been drinking. Then a month ago, Vince hit a student who was crossing the street downtown on our way home from a party. It was about 2 a.m. She has permanent injuries. Her parents are suing Vince. Now there's one more thing to add to my list of things to be afraid of.

Emerging Trends of Death and Disease

In the latter part of the twentieth century, some unexpected changes have occurred in regard to health. In the United States death rates from heart disease have declined significantly, particularly among middle-age and old people. This trend has also occurred in other developed nations throughout the world. At the same time, however, there has been a reemergence of infectious and parasitic diseases. This reemergence may have many explanations. First, the number of people with compromised immune systems is growing due to an aging population, people with AIDS, and people whose immune systems are compromised due to pollution exposure. In addition, a number of genuinely new diseases have emerged as a result of human actions that promote pesticide-resistant parasites, antibiotic-resistant diseases, and 'new' viral diseases.[11] Whether this represents a new stage in the evolution of disease or merely a return to what has been historically normal remains to be seen.

Three Disease Transitions

The transitions of diseases may be explained in three stages, just as causes of death may:

The first era of human disease began thousands of years ago with the acquisition of diseases from domesticated animals, such as tuberculosis, measles, the common cold—and influenza. The second era came with the Industrial Revolution of the eighteenth and nineteenth centuries, resulting in an epidemic of so-called "diseases of civilization," such as cancer, heart disease, stroke and diabetes. We are now entering the third stage of human disease, which started around thirty years ago—described by medical historians as the age of "the emerging plagues." Never in medical history have so many new diseases appeared in so short a time. An increasingly broad consensus of infectious disease specialists has concluded that nearly all of the ever more frequent emergent disease episodes in the United States and elsewhere over the past few years have, in fact, come to us from animals.[12]

Wellness

What does it mean to be well?

The concept of well-being or optimal health involves a delicate balance among physical, emotional, spiritual, intellectual and social health. Physical health may be thought of in terms of fitness, nutrition, control of substance abuse, medical self-help, and so on. Emotional health may refer to such areas as stress management and care for emotional crises. Examples of spiritual health are those themes dealing with love, charity, purpose and meditation. Intellectual health encompasses topics in the realms of education, achievement, career development, and others, while subjects concerned with social health may include relationships among friends, families and communities.[13]

Dunn first introduced the concept of "high-level wellness" as an alternative to traditional medicine in 1961 when he redefined health as more than just the mere absence of disease. Dunn described optimal health as a state of existence where one feels they have energy to burn.[14] Travis and Ryan[15] expanded on this concept of high-level wellness

I am writing because you are a friend. What I am going to tell you could be insignificant or could save your life. During the last month I have read quite a bit about avian flu—some of it at the prompting of my younger daughter, Tamara, who is a clinical veterinarian at the University of British Columbia.

Avian flu is predicted to produce a world pandemic by top scientists from CDC, NIH, WHO, and many other respected health organizations. This flu, which has already been in Pennsylvania, kills about 50% of humans who become infected. Some estimates are that the flu pandemic, which may come first from Guandong Province in China and spread here by tourists and other visitors to China, is carried by domestic chickens raised in conditions of such filth and density that outbreaks of flu are certain (or so everything I have read predicts). Very level-headed scientists say that this flu could kill one billion people. While killing all infected chickens could stop the epidemic, this is unlikely to always work, since many countries—our own included—are reluctant to harm the poultry industry. The current U.S. government plan to contain avian flu is to quarantine entire cities after an outbreak—or perhaps it is better to say they have no plan. When there was a rumor of quarantining Shanghai during the SARS epidemic (a very mild form of flu) 50,000 people evacuated the city on the first night.

While a severe outbreak would end life as we know it for some period of time, staying alive is highly dependent on one drug—Tamiflu, 75mg—a product made by Roche company. While many other countries have stockpiled Tamiflu, the United States—recently a disaster in disaster preparedness—has not. There is quite a bit of counterfeiting of the drug; the United States supply is estimated at 2% of the population. You need to take ten pills, two a day for five days within twelve hours of flu symptoms. My physician would not prescribe it at first because he was concerned about counterfeiting. I talked to the local pharmacist and he was "100% certain" that their supply was not counterfeit. They are a huge chain and made a bulk buy from Roche.

How to Identify Authentic Tamiflu vs. "Copycats"—Tamiflu comes in a white cardboard box, which contains a single blister package with 10 capsules. Each capsule is a distinctive yellow and light grey color, and is printed with the words "Roche 75mg." They will last up to ten years in the blister pack if kept in a dry place with no temperature extremes.

It is my hope that you will arm yourself with facts about avian flu. Life will change if it strikes, and Tamiflu is certainly not the total solution. It may, however, save your life. Prevention will include masks, serious hand washing, rubber gloves, and staying home.

The "Spanish" Flu of 1917 killed 50 million people worldwide, and its kill rate was only about 15 percent. It "probably" originated in Kansas.

If poultry producers raised chickens in less confined, more sanitary conditions, the flu might not be an issue, but huge battery-cage chicken factories not only torture the animals but also produce conditions that foster avian flu. If you think this issue merits your attention, read Bird Flu: A Virus of Our Own Hatching by Michael Greger, M.D.

by developing a model wherein both health and disease are situated at opposite ends of a continuum. As awareness, education and growth increase (a function of self-responsibility), a move toward high-level wellness is achieved. Conversely, a move in the opposite direction results in a progressive state of premature death as signs, symptoms, and disability are treated only after a patient is aware of his declining health. At the center of the continuum is a neutral point where no discernible signs of illness or wellness are present. Our current medical system is flawed in that it perceives this neutral point as a desirable state of health.

This concept supported the move toward individuals taking more responsibility for their own healthcare based on the following conclusions:

> Every time I get a cold it seems like it's when I'm stressed out. When my Dad told me he and Mom were separating, I had colds all that winter. Big exam—cold. Fight with Troy—cold. Big credit card bill—cold. I guess when you aren't well in one way, it affects everything else.

- Wellness initiated in one area of your life will reinforce health-enhancing behaviors in other areas.

- It is possible to be "well" even in the midst of illness and dying. A terminally ill patient may be in a state of physical decline, but if his spiritual disposition is optimistic, he can be said to be moving in the right direction on the health/illness continuum.

- A state of high-level wellness is within the reach of all. It will provide for a life of greater satisfaction, increased serenity, and expanded interest in the future.

- Attention to lifestyle and environment offers the most rewarding paths to improved levels of health. It is the most logical way of reducing healthcare costs, as well as reducing the chances of premature aging and unnecessary suffering from degenerative disease.[16]

Fitness

If wellness is a broad concept, "fitness," which usually means "physical fitness," is a more limited, but not easily defined, concept. From time to time in our history, there has been great concern about physical fitness. In the mid 1800s, as more people worked in factories or in offices, many influential people, such as Oliver Wendell Holmes, complained that lack of exercise was turning young people into "a pale, pasty-faced, narrow-chested, spindle-shanked, dwarfed race—a mere walking mannequin to advertise the latest cut of the fashionable tailor." [17]

While concern for obesity or lack of physical strength or endurance has been a periodic concern among the public, what we have considered to be physically "fit" has changed and been subject to swings in fashion. Fitness may simply be thought of as aerobic capacity—the ability of the body to take in and use oxygen. It might also have to do with the body's ability to metabolize food for nutrition. Some definitions consider fitness to be whatever physical condition facilitates the activity at hand—that is, in effect, being able to do what needs to be done. Therefore, in a given society, we might not really know what fitness was until we understood what had to be done.

Fashion and style have often reshaped our ideas about fitness, sometimes mistakenly promoting the notion that good physical fitness results in a single body type or physical ability. This mistaken belief has produced great harm. Exercising or gaining strength does not make everyone start to look like the people leading aerobic dance on television or lifting weights in "fitness" clubs. During the 1960s, for example, the introduction of very skinny fashion models at a Paris fashion show put great pressure on many females to change the way their body looked. While the initial reaction to the unusually slender fashion models was not a positive one, "Twiggy" and other very slender models slowly introduced the idea that females should have a certain type of body—a type which most females do not have. Many

> All these muscle guys, they think they're healthy. I'm not sure swelling up your muscles makes you healthy. What is healthy anyway? Maybe what's healthy for you isn't healthy for me.
>
> You eat like a pig and nothing happens. I have a salad and roll with water—water—and I don't lose weight. On the other hand, you get sick a lot more than I do. I have routines. My weight doesn't change much—even though I'd like it to. Who's physically fit, for that matter? Fit for what? How do you know what fit is unless you know what the person has to do in their daily life? I mean, exercise is good and all, but fit—I don't know what that means.

attempts on the part of females, involving dangerous crash diets and exercise programs, were really not so much issues of fitness as of fashion. The same may be said for the attempts of males to "bulk up," or develop muscle mass and "build" their bodies. Such behavior is as much about appearance and imitating a single model of fashion as about health. In many cases, such attempts to model one's body after another have negative health consequences. Improving fitness does not result in everyone looking alike—fortunately.

One method of changing people's behavior so that they will voluntarily come to prefer some new behavior is through the use of "nonaversive conditioning." Psychologist B. F. Skinner[18] theorized that if you wished to change someone's behavior you could use aversive conditioning, punishment, or penalties if they failed to change. Such threats of punishment aren't always very effective, however, since the individual may be willing to change only temporarily when the threat of punishment is imminent. A more effective way to produce change is "nonaversive conditioning," reinforcing the desired behavior with praise, encouragement and other rewards. To change people's leisure behaviors to ones which are healthier is also likely to require learning and practice, since people are likely to do in their leisure what they have been taught to do and what they are, to some extent, "good at." This doesn't mean one has to be competitively superior, only that one has to learn leisure skills and appreciation to become competent. Our health, after all, is related to our self-esteem.

Exercise—and Its Disappearance

Our daily life in the United States is shaped by diverse forces, all of which conspire to minimize movement of the human body. These

> Yes, it's the dirty little secret of the fitness industry. The average active membership in a health club is less than six months. O.K., so you don't belong to one but that treadmill in the garage has dust on it. Look, exercise is like dieting. Diets don't work because people can barely stand to be on them. You have to like what you are eating and you have to like the exercise. What are we talking about here? Pleasure. Fun. Recreation. How does it get to be fun? You've got to develop a little skill. Learn to cook what is good for you. Learn an outdoor activity or a sport or how to swim well. Prepare yourself to have some fun! The health will take care of itself.

forces are diverse and will not be easily overcome. Among the more important factors that minimize the ability to increase exercise necessary to fulfilling work, housework and personal care include galactic cities, single-use zoning, increases in population and population density, automobiles, the decline of walking, TVs and computers, and "labor-saving" devices.

Galactic Cities

What is sometimes referred to as "sprawl" will continue and increase in the Northeast Region. Nucleated cities emerged in the nineteenth century, particularly in the Northeast. They had a well-defined commercial area, known as "downtown." Industry was lined up along the railroad tracks and rivers, and residential areas were arrayed around the edges and segregated along lines of income, ethnicity, and race. At the edge of the city, the countryside began and the boundaries were sharp. Where there were suburbs, they also had sharp boundaries. "There was little debate about where the city was or where the country was."[19]

These cities were replaced by emerging "galactic" cities as the automobile became the primary means of transport. Rather than think of this as urban sprawl, Lewis contends this is a new kind of city.[20] Since rural land was cheap, buildings are spread out horizontally. The Interstate Highway Act of 1956, which financed limited access highways with a mandated gasoline tax, increased the galactic city's viability. This was a new kind of city. "What Americans were doing, far beyond the old urban fringe, was building nothing less than an altogether new form of city—doing all the things that cities had traditionally done, but arranging them in a new geometric form."[21] New cities are inevitably galactic. Northeast Region cities, such as Boston, Philadelphia, and New York City, are in the process of becoming galactic cities.

Characteristics of the galactic city include:

- It has an internal transportation system made up of interstate and limited access highways.

- There is a considerable degree of internal commercial clustering, usually at the intersections of arterial highways. "In contemporary America, the main crossroads occur where interstate and primary highways intersect."[22]

- An industrial clustering that is no longer based on manufacturing but more on high tech, services or "clean" industry housed in industrial parks.

- Residential areas are highly consumptive of space; single houses have lawns and garages.

Traditional forms of rural life have disappeared in most of the Northeast. Farming is less important than residential areas. This is not urban sprawl—it is a new kind of city.

> The new nonurban landscape, in the United States at least, is being shaped largely by people to whom the rural landscape is nothing more or nothing less than an alternative residential location. Whether they be commuters, retirees, or desktop publishers earning a living in their den, to them, the rural landscape is not a productive system or a way of life, but a locational amenity.[23]

Such people are genuinely urban in social outlook, personal relations and the way they make their living. Only in political outlook do they differ with traditional city residents. They resist urban authority and urban government, consolidation, and land use controls.

The dominance of the galactic city will have many implications. Such cities assure the dominance of the automobile as the primary means of travel. Four out of five miles traveled within the United States (including walking) are traveled in automobiles.[24]

Single-Use Zoning

The biggest factor that prevents people from walking and necessitates automobiles for almost all travel is single-use zoning. The prevalence of such zoning prevents life from occurring much as it does in some English villages, even though when Americans describe an ideal place to live they almost always describe an English village. Single-use zoning prevents housing from being intermixed with stores, office buildings, hospitals, etc. Such zoning makes bicycles and walking largely useless as everyday travel. Walking and bicycles are almost useless where big box stores, wide roads for cars, and housing developments are at some distance from one's place of work.

To the extent that there is movement away from single-use zoning, automobile use may be greatly affected, reducing traffic volumes substantially.

Increases in Population and Population Density

Increases in population and population density are of critical importance in many ways. Higher population densities are associated with increased incidence of a variety of diseases, greater participation in welfare, higher rates of suicide, and numerous environmental impacts—from air pollution to toxic chemical releases—which are also correlated to increased industry and transportation infrastructures.[25] Exercising becomes counterproductive if one inhales more pollutants by doing so.

Automobiles

Automobiles will continue to prevail as the dominant transportation form for many reasons. It allows the greatest customization of travel schedules, it is the most heavily subsidized form of travel by the government, it provides privacy, it is more comfortable than mass transit, and it is the only means for negotiating the centerless galactic cities which have emerged as the dominant form of urbanism in the United States. While light rail (e.g., trolleys) will make some gains, the investment costs to develop magnetic levitation or other high-speed train systems is immense and the start up time is more than a decade away at best.

A number of on-board technologies will make driving more automated and further reduce its exercise value. Already, automatic transmissions, cruise control, power steering and low-pressure clutches make driving less physical. On-board computers will guide drivers to less

If we could have a little grocery store in this development, not a big box supermarket but a little grocery store, we could walk there and get milk, bread, cereal, stuff like that. We would get exercise, use less oil, maybe even see neighbors at the grocery store—but it isn't allowed. If we had a pub you could walk to, and a church, and a library and a gym...

My life would not be possible without a car—but it's a pretty good life. I don't think I'd want to live where there were thousands of people around me. I'm used to privacy and I get tired interacting with people all day. You can escape from the world in your car. I like that.

traveled routes and warn of traffic jams. Sensors imbedded in cars will monitor the activity and destinations of other cars on the road. "This technology will conserve fuel and save lives, but the pleasure of driving as you know it will be gone."[26] It will also further devalue driving as a form of exercise, even as more time is spent in cars.

The Decline of Walking

It is estimated that the amount of walking has declined 42 percent in the last two decades.[27] As mentioned earlier, Americans travel four out of every five miles in automobiles. As this has happened, the percentage of overweight Americans has increased by 40 percent.[28] Part of the reason for the decline of walking may be that walking is more dangerous in growing suburban and metropolitan communities.[29] Most states don't or can't use much of their federal transportation funds to make walking safer and more convenient. While states have been spending an average of $72 per person on highways, they spend only 55¢ per person on pedestrian projects.

> Why are you so surprised there isn't much walking, a lack of public transportation or all these giant trucks on the interstate instead of on train tracks? I'll tell you why—The oil companies run the country. A long time ago they bought up all the bus, trolley and train companies and let them run down. The idea was to make everybody own a car and burn nothing but gas. I'm not making this up. Read a little history for God's sake.

TVs and Computers

While there is some evidence that hours spent viewing television by children is declining slightly (some of that decline is being taken up by more computer use), TV viewing remains the number one use of free time in the United States accounting from between 15 and 18 hours of viewing time per week as primary activity and another five hours of secondary activity (which usually means the primary activity was sedentary). Computers and TV both require almost no expenditure of energy. As television and computers become part of everyday life, exercise declines.

Labor-saving Devices

While it has been observed that many labor-saving devices in the household don't save labor but simply raise expectations about how clean the house should be, the multiplication of labor-saving devices—from ubitiquous golf carts to self-propelled lawnmowers to people movers in airports—reduce human movement.

> My neighborhood in summer has all these old guys and gals on rider mowers, cutting the grass and sometimes listening to music through earphones. When they are done with the yard, they drive to a health club for a workout.
>
> Here's my question. Why don't they cut the grass with a push mower? They would get exercise, save money and help the environment by using less gas in both the mower and the car, plus save time by freeing up their afternoon instead of going to the gym. Fine. It's a crazy idea.

The Consequences of Lack of Exercise

Among the consequences of these exercise-reducing changes is the rise of sedentary death syndrome (SeDS; sedentary is defined as less than 30 minutes of moderate physical activity, equivalent to brisk walking, each day) is a syndrome formed by 26 unhealthy conditions.[30] One in ten deaths in the United States is premature due to SeDS. The following defines the scope of the problem:

- The cost of sedentary-related conditions is $1.5 trillion over the next ten years.
- Children are now getting adult-onset (type-2) diabetes.
- Sixty percent of overweight children have at least one cardiovascular risk factor.
- Many children who are in the top 30 percent projected in body weight are already prediabetic.
- Children watching one hour of television a day have less obesity than those watching four hours a day.
- Three out of four adults are sedentary and candidates for SeDS.
- Adult-onset diabetes increased five-fold from 1958 to 1996.
- Moderate exercise could prevent 5.8 million new cases of type-2 diabetes.
- Adult obesity increased 57 percent from 1991 to 1999.

- It only takes 600 additional feet of walking each day by adults for the next ten years to prevent adding ten pounds of fat. The distance to prevent adding ten pounds of fat in the next ten years for 7 through 15 year olds is 1,200 and 730 feet, respectively, because kids have less weight to carry.
- Moderate physical activity reduces colon cancer.
- "Bad" blood lipids are removed from the blood after moderate physical activity.
- The increase in type-2 diabetes at age 65 is largely due to the decrease in physical activity with aging.
- The highest frequency of chronic diseases occurs in the lower income group. An appropriate approach would be to practice primary preventive medicine, including 30 minutes of moderate physical activity each day.
- Moderate physical activity lessens the incidence of the decline in cognitive function with aging.
- A program of physical activity that would delay the entry of older adults into a nursing home by one year would save $50 billion.

All of this means that increasing the exercise level of the American public, particularly older adults, is of critical importance to both restoring and maintaining the public's level of health. It is also critical to coping with the financial catastrophe that awaits government in the healthcare arena. Use of leisure is a critical variable in combating sedentary living and its problems.

The Importance of Leisure in Increasing Exercise

Exercise of the human body may be divided by cultural function in the twenty-first century into three types:

1. *Exercise necessary to fulfilling work, housework and personal care:* human movement that is integral to the tasks of everyday life including behaviors such as walking to and from automobiles, climbing stairs, or mopping a floor

2. *Exercise undertaken as a specific means to improving health or from aversive conditioning:* human movement undertaken primarily

to avoid some negative health consequence or condition or to help ameliorate some negative health condition. This may include prescription exercise, aerobic dance, weight lifting, or home exercise equipment

3. *Exercise undertaken as an inherent part of pleasurable experience or as a pleasure experience:* human movement undertaken as part of an activity that is inherently pleasurable and meaningful, such as play, leisure, flow, gardening, bird watching, hiking, tennis, square dancing, playing the drums, or rowing a boat

In the next few decades, the greatest potential to increase human movement in daily life is by increasing participation in exercise that is an inherent part of pleasurable experience or undertaken as pleasurable experience. In other words, leisure, play, recreation, sport, contact with nature, and so forth. Meanwhile, in the long run, a redesign of communities that allows for and encourages more walking may greatly enhance the exercise value of activities undertaken as a necessary part of paid work, shopping, childcare, and other necessary daily activity. However, during the next ten to fifteen years the ability to redesign and rebuild communities to such standards may be limited.

In terms of prescription exercise, exercise machines, health clubs, and other forms of exercise one does only as a means to the end of better fitness, the evidence is that, on average, people don't stick with such exercise for long periods of time. It is often not fun and sometimes painful. Many of these exercise forms can't be made more complex or follow the skill-challenge model found in flow experience.

Leisure activity that provides pleasure and exercise as a *byproduct* may have the greatest potential to increase exercise because it may become a part of one's style of life and continue for years or even throughout the lifecycle. If you like bicycling, for example, you may go through a "career" as a bicyclist. The same may be said for bird watching, playing basketball, trail hiking, swimming, or a number of other forms of leisure activity. Therefore, as stated elsewhere in this book, providing education for leisure, exposing young people to a variety of active forms of leisure, providing inviting places for such activity to take place, and remembering that socializing is an important part of many forms of exercise, will all become more important in combating our sedentary society.

Other Health Problems of Modern Life

When I compare what my grandparents did and what I do in daily life, they moved their bodies a lot more. My granddad had a garden and used hoes and shovels to plant and weed. My grandmom dried her hair with a towel, scrubbed walls with a hard bristle brush, washed clothes in a sink with a scrubbing board and carried the wet laundry out to the backyard where she hung clothes up to dry on a clothesline with wooden pins. Granddad trimmed the hedge with hand clippers. There were very few "labor-saving devices."

Labor saving seemed like a good idea and when hairdryers, riding mowers and vacuum cleaners became available, my grandparents bought them like everyone else, so they got a lot less exercise. Now they go to the Y three times a week because they don't get enough exercise. I guess that's progress.

While people may live longer, and in many ways, better, in modern society, the profound changes modern life brought about have also produced new health problems. We spend much of our lives sitting, for example, as school children, as workers, and during our leisure. "Sitting for hours on benches or chairs in classrooms is unnatural, and nothing of the sort was ever demanded of Stone Age children.[31] Similarly, the migration of people from warm climates to cold climates required some adjustments in style of living that produced many health problems. When most of life is lived indoors, people more easily transmit communicable diseases. Lack of sunlight may result in insufficient vitamin D. The interior of many dwellings is polluted with smoke, dust, and a variety of toxic chemicals in rugs, insulation, various aerosol sprays let loose in the household, and other hazards. As people who migrated to cold weather climates developed lighter skins, it became more dangerous for them to migrate back to warmer areas, where their lighter skin more easily contracts numerous forms of skin cancer and burns more easily from prolonged exposure to sunlight.

Substance abuse is a greater problem in modern societies because of technological innovations and greater availability. The invention of gin in England resulted in people getting much drunker. Recent innovations which allowed crack to be developed from cocaine, heroin from opium, and the mass production of cigarettes have all resulted in more addiction than would have been found in preindustrial societies. Not only increased supply but also increased potency of numerous drugs have made addiction basically a modern disease. To put this in perspective, U.S. growers produce nearly $35 billion worth of marijuana annually, making this illegal drug the country's largest cash crop— bigger than corn and wheat combined. It is currently worth about $36 billion a year to growers.[32]

Modern eating habits also cause many new diseases. Dental cavities were rare in preagricultural societies. Our diets are not only too high in fat but also the ready availability of cheap food has meant that more people have problems such as high blood pressure. Around 50 million people in the United States have high blood pressure. This situation may not have come about primarily because of too much salt in the diet but due to the fact that blood pressure had to become higher to supply the needs of our increasingly larger bodies. The blood-pressure regulating mechanism, pushed to adjust the system outside the range for which it was designed, often overshoots and causes high blood pressure.[33]

Perhaps even more important is living life in small nuclear families and spending much of everyday life among strangers. Electronic communication also likely affects our psychological sense of well-being but in ways that are not yet understood.

What Is Prevention?

Prevention is such a simple idea, it's a wonder that it was largely forgotten during the twentieth century when the medical model of health and illness dominated. Prevention is simply the commonsense idea that, rather than try to deal with illnesses, accidents, injuries and health problems *after* they occur, you try to organize daily life so they *don't* happen. Rather than having a doctor attempt to treat emphysema, avoid smoking and working in coal mines. Rather than be treated for chlamydia, practice safe sex. Rather than take medicine for constipation, eat a high-fiber diet. Rather than having a fire department that spends all its time training to put out fires, have a fire department expert in code enforcement and public education so the chance of fires is minimized. Prevention puts the responsibility on the individual to behave in ways that minimize illness and injury.

In spite of widespread recognition that prevention is the only sane policy with regard to health, the vast majority of money spent on health in North America, which may be as high as 15 percent of all money spent, is not spent for prevention. While the U.S. Government's Centers for Disease Control has been renamed the Centers for Disease Control *and Prevention*, the vast majority of money they expend is not for prevention.

Table 12.2 Categories of Spending as a Percentage of GNP[34]

Year	Education	Defense	Healthcare
1960	6%	6%	6%
2003	6%	4%	14.2%

You can't see prevention. Local television news programs don't report on people who don't have auto accidents. Most antidrug commercials are made by people who have been addicts rather than by people who have not. Television paramedic shows are about the immediate steps that paramedics take to treat people who are injured or ill; no programs tell the story of people who avoided illness and injury through their own personal habits.

Our social policy for teenagers pays more attention to boys than to girls because boys are more likely to become juvenile delinquents, and our culture prefers to treat visible problems rather than invest in prevention.

Poverty, Health, and Leisure

If health is related to contact with nature, it is also related to poverty. When the former Surgeon General of the United States, C. Everett Coop, recalled his challenges in office, he commented: "When I look back on

> Why isn't prevention more a part of government policy or corporate thinking?
>
> Well, for openers, there's no money in it. Finding a cure for cancer produces lots of jobs, but banning the chemical companies from selling products that are known— known— carcinogens— where's the money there? If there were no obese people, millions of jobs would be lost. The whole diet industry would go down the drain. Then there's the medical profession. If prevention were their goal, they would become a kind of counselor—but the money's in medical testing and operations. Prevention just isn't good for the economy in the short run—and our economy is all about the short run—not what might happen ten years from now.

my years in office, the things I banged my head against were all poverty."[35] Poverty is related to health in a number of ways. Poor people often have less information about ways of preventing illness and injury. They may eat insufficient food or have poor dietary practices. They are more subject to crime. They participate, on average, less in most forms of active recreation and leisure. Their self-esteem is often lower. Additionally, they may have less of a sense of community. In a way, lack of a sense of community represents a kind of spiritual poverty that may afflict people of any income level. Such poverty of the spirit has real consequences for one's health.

Poverty, of course, means many things. While one may be materially or financially "poor," absolute poverty refers to the lack of resources to live a life at a reasonable level—or at all. Comparative poverty, conversely, means that one is economically poor in relation to other people in one's community or society. In such a case, people may compare their possessions to others and judge themselves to be a failure. In particular, it may be the comparative poverty that many Americans experience that contributes to health-related issues, such as crime and low self-esteem. That is, it is not so much the issue of level of material goods owned as the separation of people into have and have-not statuses: winners and losers. This gap is greater in the United States than any other modern nation.

Social policy in the United States makes it much less "healthy" to be poor than in almost any modern nation. Federal support for programs that proved beneficial to health declined during the 1980s.

Today, one in eight American children is hungry. About one-fourth of pregnant women have no prenatal care. Between eight and eleven million children in America are completely uninsured, and large numbers go without needed medical and dental care.[36]

> When I started working at this food bank, I didn't really understand how many people don't get enough to eat. I mean, this is a nation of overweight people, so how could there be hunger?
>
> Well, there is a whole lot of hunger. There are kids who come in here with their mothers—always their mothers—never their fathers. They are clearly hungry. They get excited about canned carrots!
>
> They aren't picky like a lot of other kids. Anything that goes in the bag is a treat—pork and beans—they like it. Canned vegetables—they like it. Peanut butter—they like it.
>
> They're hungry. Why?

Our public and private spending for secondary schools are close to the bottom among industrial nations. Federal support for affordable housing has been cut by two-thirds. Forty percent of the poor now have incomes of less than one-half the amount designated as poverty level by the federal government. These changes in policies have negative health consequences that will likely produce problems that will cost even more money in the future.

Being economically poor, in and of itself, does not automatically have to be related to poorer health. As we have seen, however, it is frequently, but not always, linked with lower levels of education, self-esteem, sense of community and other factors that are related both to use of leisure and health in fundamental ways.

In many cases, the negative relationship between health and poverty, which appears to be financial, is actually a product of intellectual poverty—ignorance. The link between health, longevity and level of formal education is a critical one. Some studies have found that level of formal education was the single best predictor of how long someone would live.[37]

The Weak Relationship between Health and the Medical Profession

There is a tendency to believe that health is a service "delivered" by those in the medical profession (and industry). In reality, the rise of the medical profession has had little to do with improvements in our health. Noted scientists Robert Ornstein and Paul Erlich stated

> to logically approve the huge amounts of money that our government and industry spends for "healthcare," you would have to believe that such service is important to people's health. It is not. To justify such a massive social investment alone, one would also have to believe that the entire medical enterprise, including all the accumulated medical research evidence and training of the past century, has provided a meaningful extension of life. It has not.[38]

We live only four or five years longer than those in, for instance, Britain a century ago, and most of this advance in longevity has been due to advances in sanitation, such as water purification, better sewage systems, and improved hygiene. Research by epidemiologists John and Sonia McKinley demonstrates that medical intervention played an extremely small role in the containment of many communicable diseases:

> Medical intervention in infectious diseases such as tuberculosis, diphtheria, whooping cough, influenza, and the like are responsible for only 3.5 percent of the total decline in mortality since 1900. The major elements in enhancing resistance to disease were improved nutrition and environmental changes that made food purer and safer, especially for infants.[39]

Other studies of the huge expansion of the availability of medical services have found no effect on health or a relatively small effect "in the 5 to 10 percent range, results of much less consequence than such day-to-day factors as marital status, employment, happiness in relationships, and the availability of caregivers."[40] Our state of health is determined largely by factors other than medical treatment. Over 80 percent of the factors that determine our state of health have to do with our environment, our relations with friends and enemies, the quality of our education, our status in the community, and how we think about ourselves. It has only been during the last 30 years that medical practice could be said, on balance, to do more good than harm.

Our state of health is largely determined by how we live our everyday lives, our behaviors, emotions and, sometimes, our luck. Doctors are not a very important part of wellness, although they can sometimes help. What are most important are our own personal habits and our collective societal actions. (It also helps to have the right parents and ancestors.) If all forms of cancer were cured immediately, our life expectancy would go up an average of only two years but "if good nutrition, exercise and good health habits (especially not smoking) were followed, average life expectancy would increase by seven years."[41]

Health and Leisure

What people choose to do voluntarily and for its own sake in their daily lives would seem to have a great impact on their state of health. While there is no universally accepted theory of human motivation, what people do for pleasure, what they find meaningful and what they do when their choice is maximized greatly influence daily life and shape personal habits. While many activities may be undertaken for the sake of "health," as B.F. Skinner[42] and others have argued, such activity declines or disappears when the immediate threat to health appears to be gone. Thus, activity undertaken to escape some negative consequence, such as prescription exercise or joining a health club, rarely continue for long unless the activity in question becomes meaningful or pleasurable for its own sake.

Although theorists and practitioners in health and developmental psychology do not yet recognize the full potential of leisure in the promotion of health, there is evidence that leisure engagement is significantly related to health status. Research suggests that leisure has a positive effect on physical health. For example, the harmful effects of stress on mental and physical health have been well-documented in the literature.

From this perspective, leisure may act as a buffer against the negative effects of stressful life events. For example, Iso-Ahola and Park[43] examined the effects of leisure-generated social support and self-determination disposition on the perceived health of tae kwon do students. Results confirmed that leisure-generated social support was a factor in buffering people against the adverse health effects of stress.

Leisure activity may also contribute to enhancing people's beliefs that they have the capacities to initiate actions, persist with endeavors, and achieve successful outcomes.[44] By learning a new leisure activity, a person may develop commitment, control and acceptance of challenge. Thus, for instance, a gay teenager may find that taking a part in a school play provides an opportunity to gain more control over one part of his life by committing himself to memorizing lines and learning more about acting. This may, in turn, help him accept other more challenging roles and add to his own identity in ways which make him more determined in life and positive in terms of his self-image. A retiree may find that teaching children to swim or becoming an expert on the Civil War renews her belief that she can carry out actions successfully.

Thus, in combination, social support and self-determination are important in helping cope with stress and stay well. Leisure activities are critical variables in providing social support and building and maintaining self-determination.

Leisure also appears to be related to health due to its role in serving as a buffer between stressful life events and illness. Many studies have shown that stressful life circumstances induce both physical and emotional illnesses.[45] In terms of stress buffers, one study found that, of twenty-two factors, only sense of competence, nature and extent of exercise, sense of purpose, and leisure activity helped mediate stress.[46] People who had high levels of leisure participation or who were satisfied with their leisure were less vulnerable to the adverse effects of stress.

Leisure participation helps one cope with life stresses in two ways. First, it helps one's perception that social support is available. Second, participation in leisure activity can help foster self-determination, a disposition which has been shown to contribute to people's coping capacities and health.[47]

> When our baby died, my world fell apart. Jill was devastated, and I was as bad off as she was. I played racquetball with my buds every single day afterward for weeks. It felt great to pummel that ball into the walls—I guess I took it all out on the ball. It relieved the stress. I would still think about it, but once the ball started sailing around the court, I could almost forget about it for a little while. Racquetball kept me sane. It made it easier for me to help Jill too.

Although measures of leisure participation seem important to the leisure-health link, recent research suggests that natural environments are important in promoting health because they provide the opportunity for restorative experiences. For example, Kaplan and Kaplan[48] asserted that natural environments facilitate involuntary attention (which takes no effort at all) and allows for the recovery of directed attention. Directed attention is said to be required to complete work. Kaplan and Kaplan proposed four main benefits of a restorative experience:

1. Recovery of directed attention;

2. The cognitive quiet of soft fascination;

3. Reflection of life, opportunities, and possibilities; and

4. Clearing of the head or removal of residual clutter from the mind.[49]

Joseph Pieper emphasized the value of contemplation in nature by stating, "If we let our minds rest contemplatively on a rose in bud or a child at play, we are rested and quickened though by a dreamless sleep."[50]

While Kaplan and Kaplan and Pieper's assertions are more philosophically or theoretically based, there is some empirical evidence to support their positions. For example, Ulrich[51] compared the recovery of surgery patients whose hospital room windows overlooked nature and those who had the view of a brick wall. Results indicated that those who had a view of nature recovered significantly faster than those whose rooms overlooked a brick wall. Furthermore, several studies support the mood-lifting qualities of natural environments.[52, 53, 54] Overall, their studies of park use and park activities concluded that park use improves positive moods, decreases negative moods, and alleviates stress. Regular park use may have long-term benefits for health and well-being as the benefits of the activities and the environment may have a cumulative effect on individuals.

Despite the many studies which link leisure and health, this relationship becomes much more complex during the later stages of life.[55] The prevalence of chronic illness and disease increases dramatically during the later years. Teague and colleagues contended that approximately 80 percent of elders have one chronic condition, and 50 percent report two or more chronic conditions.[56]

Therefore, a reciprocal relationship between leisure and health becomes more prominent. That is, health problems may influence leisure participation, and leisure participation may influence health. Old age is also associated with stressful life events (e.g., loss of spouse, visual and auditory impairments, caring for a sick loved one), social isolation, and social inequalities (e.g., socioeconomic status, gender) which tend to influence health status.[57] Indeed, these multidimensional influences make the study of leisure and health among elders a complex endeavor. However, two important facts should make the study of leisure and health among older people a priority. First, the proportion of older Americans is rising quickly and will continue over the next 20 years as the members of the Baby Boomer generation enter their "golden years." Second, older people are the largest users of healthcare services in America.[58] Moreover, the prevalence of chronic disease, particularly arthritis, may influence the use of healthcare services later in life. German stated:

> Any focus on control of symptoms and avoidance of severe sequelae along with the prevention of disease and delay of death demands an understanding of chronic disease—first, because chronic disease is closely associated with mortality and morbidity, and second, because of the intimate connection to disability and hence quality of life. Finally, these outcomes of chronic disease have direct bearing on the cost of care, a continuing concern in the current healthcare enterprise and the upcoming reform.[59]

Therefore, it is important to identify factors such as leisure which may prevent or at least delay the onset of chronic disease, improve health and thereby decrease utilization of healthcare services.

Thus, leisure behavior, while not done "in order to," is an arena that has the potential to directly shape your health.

> It's funny but doing what you like to do is often healthier than doing something because you think it will make you healthy. I like to walk and bird watch. You have been walking on a treadmill. After about a year, you stopped completely but I'm still walking for pleasure and bird watching— and have been for forty years.

Study Questions

1. In terms of your own health, what practices and habits do you employ in your daily life which are "prevention" of illness efforts?

2. In what ways do your leisure behaviors negatively affect your health?

3. In what ways do your leisure behaviors positively affect your health?

4. If you made one change in your leisure behavior to positively affect your health, what would it be? Why? How would you change?

Endnotes

1   Capra, F. (1988). *Uncommon wisdom: Conversations with remarkable people.* New York, NY: Simon and Schuster.

2   Henderson, H. (1981). *The politics of the solar age.* New York, NY: Doubleday.

3   Nesse, R. and Williams, G. (1996). *Why we get sick: The new science of Darwinian medicine.* New York, NY: Vintage Books.

4   ibid., p. 9

5   ibid., p. 9

6   Knize, P. (1998, May). Why do so many travelers head for greener pastures—The answer may be a matter of biological necessity. *Conde Nast Traveler, 132.*

7   Nesse and Williams (1996)

8   National Office of Vital Statistics. (1947). *Deaths and death rates for leading causes of death" Death registration states, 1900–1940.*Retrieved from http://www.cdc.gov/nchs/data/statab/lead1900_98.pdf

9   Centers for Disease Control. (2006). Table B: Deaths and death rates for 2004 and age-adjusted death rates and percentage changes in age-adjusted rates from 2003 to 2004 for the 15 leading causes of death in 2004: United States, final 2003 and preliminary 2004. *National Vital Statistics Reports, 54*(19), 4.

10   Stallones, R. (1986). *Public health monograph 76.* Washington, DC: Government Printing Office.

11   Olshansky, J., Carnes, B., Rogers, R. and Smith, L. (1997). Infectious diseases—New and ancient threats to world health. *Population Bulletin, 52*(2), 12.

12   Greger, M. (2006). *Bird flu: A virus of our own hatching* (p.3). New York, NY: Lantern Books.

13   Alberta Centre for Well Being. (1989). *Newsletter* (p. 3). Edmonton, AB: University of Alberta.

14   Dunn (1961). Cited by L. Payne, G. Godbey, B. Orsega-Smith, B., and M. Roy, *The relation between leisure, behavior, and arthritis severity among older adults.* Paper presented October 1999 at the Leisure Research Symposium, National Congress for Recreation and Parks, Nashville, TN.

15   Travis, J. and Ryan, R. (1988). *Wellness workbook.* Berkeley, CA: Ten Speed Press.

16   Ardell, D. (1977). *High-level wellness: An alternative to doctors, drugs and disease.* New York, NY: Bantam Books.

17   Holmes, O. (1856). Editor's drawer. *Harper's Monthly, 13,* 462.

18   Skinner, B. F. (1978). *Reflections on behaviorism and society.* Englewood Cliffs, NJ: Prentice Hall.

19   Lewis, P. (1995). The urban invasion of rural America: The emergence of the galactic city. In E. Castle (Ed.), *The changing American countryside: Rural people and places* (p. 40). Lawrence, KS: University of Kansas Press.

20   ibid., pp. 39–62

21   ibid., p. 46

22   ibid., p. 53

23   ibid., p. 59

24   Robinson, J. and Godbey, G. (1997). *Time for life: The surprising ways Americans use their time*. University Park, PA: Penn State Press.

25   Larsen, D. (1993, January). Density is destiny. *American Demographics, 15*, 38.

26   D'Agnese, J. (2000, October). What you'll need to know in 2020 that you don't know. *Discover*, 58.

27   PR Newswire. (2000, June 15). *Surface Transportation Policy Project: New study links obesity to decline in walking*. Retrieved November 26, 2007, from http://www.highbeam.com

28   Ogden, C., Carroll, M., Curtin, L., McDowell, M., Tabak, C., and Flegal, K. (2006). Prevalence of overwieght and obesity in the United States. *Journal of the American Medical Association, 295*, 1549–1555.

29   Pueher, J. and Dijkstra, L. (2003). Promoting safe cycling and walking to improve public health. *American Journal of Public Health, 93*(91), 1509–1519.

30   Researchers Against Inactivity-Related Disorders. (2007). *SeDS fact sheet*. Retrieved June 15, 2007, from http://hac.missouri.edu/RID/index.htm

31   Nesse and Williams, 1996, p. 153

32   Sullum, J. (2007). America's biggest cash crop. *Reason, April*, 37.

33   Weder, A. and Schork, N. (1994). Adaptation, allometry and hypertension. *Hypertension, 24*(2), 145.

34   Lamm, R. (2003). *The brave new world of healthcare* (p. x). Golden, CO: Fulcrum Publishing.

35   Coontz, S. (1992). *The way we never were: American families and the nostalgia trap*. New York, NY: HarperCollins.

36   ibid.

37   Ornstein, R. and Sobel, P. (1989). *Healthy pleasures*. New York, NY: Addison-Wesley.

38   Ornstein, R. and Erlich, P. (1987). *New world–New mind: Moving toward conscious evolution*. New York, NY: Doubleday.

39   McKinley, J. and McKinley, S. (1989). Quoted in R. Ornstein and P. Erlich (1987), *New world–new mind: Moving toward conscious evolution*. New York, NY: Doubleday.

40   Ornstein and Erlich (1987)

41   ibid.

42   Skinner, B. F. (1978). *Reflections on behaviorism and society*. Englewood Cliffs, NJ: Prentice Hall.

43   Iso-Ahola, S. and Park, C. (1995). Leisure-related social support and self-determination as buffers of stress-illness relationships. *Journal of Leisure Research, 28*, 169–187.

44   Iso-Ahola, S. and Mannell, R. (1985). Social and psychological constraints on leisure. In M. Wade (Ed.), *Constraints on leisure* (pp. 111–151). Springfield, IL: Charles C. Thomas Publishing.

45 Coleman, D. and Iso-Ahola, S. (1993). Leisure and health: The role of social support and self-determination. *Journal of Leisure Research, 15*(2), 111–128.

46 Wheeler, R. and Frank, M. (1988). Identification of stress buffers. *Behavioral Medicine, 14,* 78–89.

47 Coleman and Iso-Ahola (1993)

48 Kaplan, R. and Kaplan, S. (1989). *The experience of Nature: A psychological perspective.* New York, NY: Cambridge University Press.

49 ibid.

50 Pieper, J. (1952). *Leisure: The basis of culture* (p. 42). New York, NY: Mentor-Omega Books.

51 Ulrich, R. (1984). View through a window may influence recovery from surgery. *Science, 224,* 420–421.

52 Godbey, G. and Blazey, M. (1983). Older people in urban parks: An exploratory investigation. *Journal of Leisure Research, 15*(3), 229–244.

53 Hull, R. and Michael, S. (1995). Nature-based recreation, mood changes and stress restoration. *Journal of Leisure Research, 15*(3), 229–244.

54 More, T. and Payne, B. (1978). Affective responses to natural areas near cities. *Journal of Leisure Research, 10*(1), 7–12.

55 Markides, K. and Miranda, M. (Eds.). (1997). *Minorities, aging and health.* Thousand Oaks, CA: Sage Publications.

56 Teague, M. L., McGhee, V.L., Rosenthal, D.M., and Kearns, D. (1997). *Health promotion: Achieving high-level wellness in the later years* (3rd ed.). Dubuque: IA. Brown and Benchmark.

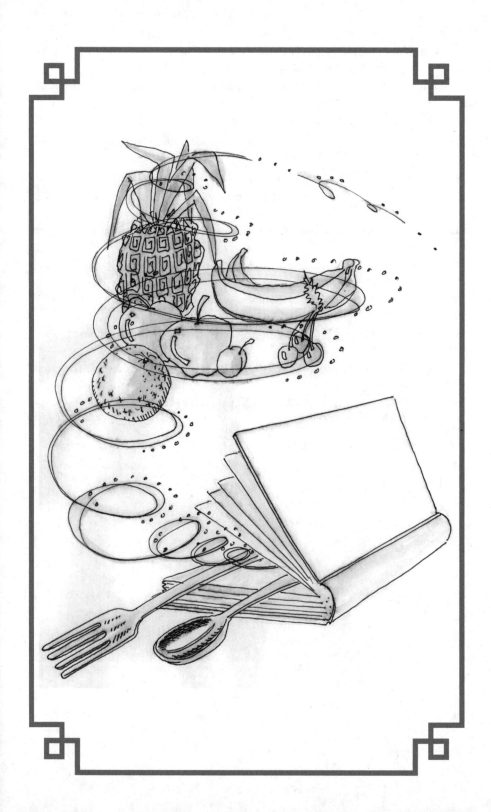

Healthy Leisure—
Celebrating Life

"It is impossible to attempt to engage in leisure for health's sake. Such a reversal of the meaningful order of things is more than just unseemly; it simply can't be done."[1] If this statement is true, how can leisure be related to health? Let's go back, for a minute, and reexamine the definition of leisure presented in Chapter 1:

> *Leisure is living in relative freedom from the external compulsive forces of one's culture and physical environment so as to be able to act from internally compelling love in ways which are personally pleasing, intuitively worthwhile, and which provide a basis for faith.*

This definition is directly related to the issues that determine health. It recognizes that relative freedom from the compulsive forces of our physical environment as well as our culture is a prerequisite of leisure. These freedoms are also critical to good health as we explored earlier. Many of these freedoms are of our own making—how we choose to get rid of garbage, what we choose to eat, how we choose to behave sexually, how we choose to protect ourselves against the elements, how we attempt to keep ourselves and our environment clean. Relative freedom from the compulsive forces of nature depends partly upon nature but, to a great extent, upon us. The same may be said about relative freedom from the external compulsive forces of our culture. We each play some role in shaping that culture in determining if individuals can develop their potential or be free from persecution based upon conditions over which they have little control.

To act from internally compelling love must surely be related to health. Our ability to love must surely be related to leisure. Philosopher Josef Pieper thought that some people could not experience leisure because they could not joyfully celebrate the world and their own life within that world. This inability would seem to be fundamentally related to both leisure and health. Not only is the ability to love related to both health and leisure but also so is the object of our love. If we love money more than anything else, for instance, we may willingly harm the physical environment for short-term gain. If we love some sport or form of outdoor recreation, we may get more and better exercise than we otherwise would. (We may also injure ourselves.) Our ability to love and what we love are related to the will to act. The human will, we are currently finding out, is of critical importance in terms of our response to disease, our ability to recover or live with life-threatening illnesses or injuries, and our physical and mental capacities. To act is to exercise the human will, and leisure, in the above definition, requires acting.

Strangely enough, when we act in ways that are or have become "intuitively worthwhile," it may have greater health benefits than activities which are undertaken as a means to an end. Let's look at some examples. Take dieting. Almost no one who goes on a diet sustains a weight loss for any appreciable amount of time. One expert estimates between 70 and 95 percent of all dieters have not lost weight one year after starting their diet.[2] Most people who begin "prescribed" exercise programs don't stay with them for very long. People whose only motivation for running is to lose weight are likely to stop. People who get more pleasure out of smoking than not smoking are likely to continue. Sound health practices, in other words, often occur only when the individual reaches the point of voluntarily and pleasurably undertaking the healthy activity rather than undertaking it as a painful but necessary part of life. Ironically, many important determinants of our health are based upon what we will do voluntarily and pleasurably apart from any health benefit. For example, you are much more likely to eat lots of fresh vegetables if you have come to prefer their taste and have learned satisfying ways of preparing them than if you have merely been told to do so by your doctor. There may be a period of learning to like them, not only giving your sense of taste a chance to adjust but also acquiring the interest and skills in learning how to prepare them, perhaps by reading vegetarian cookbooks and experimenting with various spices.

In summary, it might be said that we, like other animals, are motivated to a great extent by pleasure, but we are capable of learning to derive pleasure from new experiences—to come to regard them as leisure. This being the case, the extent to which healthy behaviors can become part of our leisure lives, part of what we would voluntarily do for its own sake, may be critical to the extent to which we lead healthy lives.

Some Roadblocks to Celebration

If healthy leisure is partly about the ability to celebrate life and one's place in the world, it is important to understand what may prevent such celebration. Some barriers to celebration are idleness, low self-esteem, low sense of community and self-efficacy, and depression.

Idleness—The Opposite of Healthy Leisure

Healthy leisure is the opposite of idleness, but idleness must be correctly understood. Idleness, in medieval Christian doctrine (*acedia*), referred to people who had renounced the claim inherent in their human dignity. It meant a despairing refusal to be what the person really, fundamentally was—an inability to understand and accept the goodness within. Such people, in effect, did not give the consent of their own will to their own being. They were not at one with themselves. According to philosopher Josef Pieper, sadness overwhelmed such people when confronted with the divine goodness immanent in them.[3]

This "idleness" has been misinterpreted as "lazy" in more recent Christian theology, but the opposite of idleness is not the work ethic but rather a person's happy and cheerful affirmation of his or her own being, of the world and in God—which is to say one's ability to love life. Such idleness and the incapacity for leisure come from the same root.

For people who see little to celebrate in their own lives "work and don't despair" is the common response. You may have received

> I get down between semesters. I just don't have much I want to do. It's funny—I work all semester saying "only three more weeks," "only two more weeks," "only one more week" and then the break comes and there's nothing I really want to do. When I go home, I don't fit in now. A few of my friends are still in town, but after high school everyone went their own way. I watch TV. I help my Mom with housework a bit. I go to the mall. It might sound weird, but I am actually glad when the semester starts again.

such advise when you were growing up—if things are not going well or you are feeling down in the dumps, keep busy and lose yourself in your work. As a temporary solution, this may have made good sense, but as a way of life it may represent a kind of hiding from oneself.

Pieper characterized people who wanted only to work and to lose themselves in work as being willing to suffer without reason. The worker becomes completely absorbed in the social organism, planned for useful ends. The worker lacks the will to undertake his or her own actions with joy but is extremely willing to undertake other people's. Such people are historically the most dangerous because they are most easily trained for war, and the most likely to be recruited into cults or to follow leaders of any type without asking questions. Military training seeks to do this almost universally. Take away the individual's sense of worth and uniqueness. Teach them to act as if they are no different from any other soldier—an interchangeable unit. Teach them to do what they are told without question and that they want to do so. Thus, their own wills become completely subservient to that of the army.

The consequences of this kind of idleness may be physical, mental or emotional idleness—just sitting around, perhaps giving low-level attention to television. "What do you want to do today?" If the answer is "I don't care" leisure isn't possible. This doesn't mean the healthy person doesn't ever watch television or use leisure for escape or diversion. Rather, it means only that they are less likely to use leisure as a way of moving away from something and more likely to use it to move toward something—something they love.

> Have you heard of the firehouse horse? Of course not, you're too young. Horses used to pull fire wagons before there were fire engines. It was said that, when the firehouse horse was set free, he would always head straight back to the firehouse. It was the only thing he knew how to do. When I was freed from my office and retired, I did the same thing—for the same reason. Now I'm back at the office.

Leisure, we should remember, is a mental and spiritual attitude—not simply the result of external factors such as holidays. It involves the ability to get beyond the world of work and apprehend the totality of things: to listen to the universe, to celebrate, and to celebrate the whole of existence. It is built upon the freeing arts (liberal arts) and requires the capacity to love and find meaning in personal, freely chosen behavior. The modern idea of self-esteem is rooted in these ideas.

Low Self-Esteem

Much has been written about the negative consequences of a person having little respect for oneself or judging oneself negatively. What is less often written about is that high self-esteem needs to have some basis. That is, individuals need to have reasons to view themselves positively. There may be as many negative consequences for our society if a person who is highly immoral or willfully incompetent has high levels of self-esteem. (Such situations are unhealthy at a societal level.)

For many individuals who have low self-esteem, there is a tendency to disregard many important issues of personal health—you don't take care of what isn't thought to be worth very much. Leisure and its use may be a critical issue in improving self-esteem.

Leisure can be a critical variable in an individual discovering his or her own strengths, talents and opportunities.

Low Sense of Community and Self-Efficacy

Not only do our feelings about ourselves shape the healthiness of our leisure, so too does our sense of community. Sense of community is critical in our everyday well-being. As psychologist Robert Ornstein and physician David Sobel[4] concluded, need for community is a key part of our evolutionary heritage. The brain's primary function is not to think but rather to guard the body from illness. As Ornstein and Sobel claimed

> Many years ago I worked at a school for delinquent teenagers. One of the residents was a tall, gangly guy who was gay and very effeminate—swishy—in the way he presented himself. He was teased and ridiculed by many other teenagers. He really got abused. We decided to stage a play at the school—a melodrama—and this guy tried out for the role of the villain and got the part. Boy, he could act! Wouldn't you know, after the play "Snidley Whiplash" became grudgingly accepted by the other teenagers. That event wound up being a springboard for a lifetime of involvement in amateur theater for him.

It now appears that the brain cannot do its job of protecting the body without contact with other people. It draws vital nourishment from our friends, lovers, relatives, lodge brothers and sisters, even perhaps our coworkers and the members of the weekly bowling team."[5]

Perhaps it is no wonder that a recent University of Michigan study found that doing regular volunteer work, more than any other activity, dramatically increased life expectancy.[6] The feeling of warmth from doing good may well come from endorphins, the brain's natural opiates which produce not only runner's "high" but also, apparently, volunteer's high.

Community is related to the belief that the world makes sense. Antonovsky and Sagy argued that the capacity to mobilize resistance resources, and the key to holistic wellness, is based on a sense of social coherence which Antonovsky defined as:

> ...a global orientation that expresses the extent to which one has a pervasive, enduring though dynamic, feeling of confidence that (1) the stimuli deriving from one's internal and external environments in the course of living are structured, predictable and explicable; (2) the resources are available for one to meet the demands posed by these stimuli; and (3) these demands are challenges worthy of investment and engagement.[7]

This conceptualization aligns nicely with a conceptualization of leisure that does not view work and leisure as opposites. Both are seen

I volunteered to serve on the park board ten years ago. I was the only woman. The men on the board were all from the old school— "a woman's place is in the home." At first I didn't say much at the meetings. Then when they decided to not have a waterslide installed at the local swimming pool because they were afraid of lawsuits, I spoke up. There are waterslides at many public pools. I started finding out about them, made some phones calls, asked my daughter to look up information on her computer. I also talked to neighbors and they all thought it was a great idea.

At the next meeting, I told the Board we were going to install that waterslide and gave them the evidence. They were reluctant, but I was persistent. Finally, they agreed. Probably because it was 10:30 at night and they wanted to go home. But now, ten years later, when I watch the children go down that slide, giggling, laughing, screaming and having a ball, it occurs to me—I made that happen—me.

"...as responses to a biological need for optimization of arousal,"[8, 9, 10] complexity,[11] challenge,[12] or stress.[13] That is, satisfying recreation or leisure, like satisfying work, involves the creation and acceptance of challenges which "make sense," and which one has acquired skills and otherwise has the resources with which to deal. We need certain levels of arousal, challenge, complexity, stress, or stimulation to make us respond in ways that promote healthy growth, and we also need the resources to have a reasonable chance of dealing with such challenges. In short, healthy leisure involves acting rather than being acted upon. For children, healthy play means the ability to have some "effect" on the environment. Vicarious leisure, allowing oneself to be acted upon by television or narcotics, does not present such challenges and, as principal uses of leisure, would not be healthy.

Not only is individual self-efficacy important in how leisure is used; so, too, is community efficacy. In communities that appear to be power-less and unable to control outcomes that are important to successful community life, there is a greater tendency toward passivity.

Where self or community efficacy are low, leisure behaviors are more likely to be passive, and such passivity is related to addictive behavior. Television viewing, for example, among children, is positively related to obesity in children since it interferes with burning calories through active play. Like excessive eating, drinking or drug taking, it is a passive, consumer-oriented form of entertainment. It is perhaps not sur-prising that a record 10 million children in the United States were obese in 1998 since television, junk food and junk drinks became dominant.

Depression

Depression is the most common psychological problem in the United States, affecting almost 18 million people. About one in four women, one in ten men and one in twenty adolescents worldwide experience depression in some form. It is particularly common among the elderly, often as a reaction to growing older or the death of a spouse or friends.

Our immune system is sensitive to even mild upsets and swings in daily mood. In cases of losing a spouse, the depression of the immune system often begins immediately and may last for as much as a year or more. The symptoms of depression may include persistent sadness or pessimism, loss of interest in many of life's pleasures, including sex, sleeping disorders, fatigue, weight loss or gain, thoughts of suicide, difficulty concentrating and others.[14]

Depression seems to have different causes. A depressive reaction, or "normal depression," can occur as a reaction to a specific event but also can be a side effect of medication, a hormonal change, such as before menstrual periods or after childbirth, or a physical illness, such as the flu.

Depression makes other existing health problems worse. People who suffer from depression are more likely to die from cancer and, among those with coronary heart disease, people with depression are also more likely to die.

While the exact causes of depression are not known, it is currently believed that depression may be caused by malfunction of the brain's neural transmitters, particularly chemicals (such as serotonin) which modulate mood. There also seems to be some genetic predispositions to depression.

MINUS ONE

People are multiplying into nothing.

I go there
by division.

I awoke this morning
nearly gone.

Sun hesitating
upon my cold bridge.

While serious depression is most commonly treated with chemical antidepressants, "...there is good evidence that depression may often be alleviated or prevented with good health habits. Proper diet, exercise, vacations, no overwork and saving time to do things you enjoy all help keep the blues at bay."[15] Moreover, "Hundreds of scientific studies on thousands of people now report that individuals who expect the best, who are hopeful and optimistic, and who regularly enjoy sensual pleasures are, in general, healthier and live longer."[16] Additionally, it appears that the immune system may be strengthened by people who disclose long-held traumatic experiences.

Depression may be linked to a number of addictive habits—smoking in particular. One study found that 60 percent of heavy smokers had a history of depression.[17] About 80 percent of alcoholics and 90 percent of schizophrenics smoke. In terms of depression, it may be that smoking provides the same effects that the brain's mood-controlling neurotransmitters do.

Healthy Living, Healthy Leisure

What is healthy living? What is healthy leisure? Can we simply say a certain activity, such as racquetball, is healthy and another activity, such as television viewing, is not? As you realize by now, the issue is more complex than that. There is also the question of "healthy for whom?" Running five miles may be healthy for one person but very harmful for another. Ornstein and Sobel have developed a theory of health that puts leisure at the forefront. This theory assumes the human desire for enjoyment evolved to enhance our survival. "Doing what feels right and feeling good are beneficial for health and the survival of the species."[18] Pleasure rewards us twice; first in immediate enjoyment and then in improving our health.

The work ethic is not the only cultural barrier to pleasure:

> Combining an archaic religiosity with a sensory-deprived world is to place two prisons together. The result is a life lost not only to this world but also to the next. Redeeming a natural and healthy sensuality requires us to buck strong historical forces. But our health, happiness, and future depend upon understanding and even reversing this deep-rooted cultural denial of pleasure and leisure. Sensuality and spirituality need not conflict.[19]

The following is an attempt to identify some characteristics that might make a leisure activity healthy. You are not asked to uncritically accept these principles, only to consider them in terms of your own life and understanding.

Acting

Healthy leisure involves acting rather than being acted upon. All else being equal, it is healthier to play soccer rather than watch it, to paint a picture rather than watch someone else paint, to make conversation with a friend rather than hear other people talk on television. Turning on the television, of course, is an act but the issue here is more one of whether, in leisure, one diverts one's awareness or consciousness or whether one focuses it on a behavior he or she is drawn toward. Healthy leisure is a joyful act of the human will, and the exercise of the will is as important as the exercise of the body.

One of the more important sayings in relation to health—"Use it or lose it"—appears to be largely true. That which is not stimulated, strengthened, or reinforced through use begins to disappear. If you don't use your arm, your brain or your emotions, they start to wither. In healthy leisure one uses what he or she has been given, not from necessity but by choice.

Creating

Leisure activity which involves creativity is healthier than activity which does not, if creativity is understood in a certain way. Thus, creativity must be considered as "…the production of novel responses which have an appropriate impact in a given context."[20]

> For a long time I watched the women on TV shooting pool—The Black Widow, the Duchess of Doom, all those professional players. They were terrific players—often ran a nine ball rack, used a jump cue stick to make impossible shots. It was fun watching them. Then I decided to take it up myself. I started at a friend's house. Garry taught me a few things about how to hold the cue, not moving your head, getting down to the table, using English on the cue ball. Now I play in a league—I'm not the Black Widow, but I ran five balls in a row last week. It's more fun doing it yourself.

Creativity, therefore, doesn't simply mean doing something novel; it means the effect of that novel approach must advance or improve the activity. Thus, an artist who drops a balloon full of paint on a canvas from a second floor window is not being creative, only novel. Creativity involves advancing the activity in question within the rules or contexts of the situation. In most cases, creativity in leisure comes after a person has learned quite a bit about an activity—a guitar player needs to learn not only chords, time signatures and different methods of strumming and plucking the strings but also harmony.

In learning a leisure activity to the point where one becomes creative, it has been argued that if a person is too closely supervised he or she will produce appropriate responses but not novel ones. If every child learning to serve a volleyball is not allowed to experiment, they may learn an appropriate way to serve but they will not discover novel ones. If, on the other hand, they are given complete freedom to serve however they want, they will likely develop novel serves but ones which aren't appropriate within the rules of the game. Therefore, the balance of freedom and discipline a person has in learning a leisure skill is critical in how likely it is that she or he will eventually become creative.

Meaning

The meaning of life, Csikszentmihalyi suggests, is meaning.[21] In sociological terms, *meaning* is defined as

> an interpretation of the significance of a situation, act, idea or object with reference to how one should respond. Social interaction and social organization are made possible by the existence of culturally shared meanings. However, the subjective significance of the behavior of other persons to an actor (person) is determined by his individual past experience as well as by his internalized culturally defined meanings. Hence, the meaning of a social situation varies to a certain extent from one person to another even in the same culture. Each participant may have subjective meanings that are unique, but at the same time have shared meanings that make interaction and communication possible.[22]

> If you're going to write good poetry, you have to learn the craft first. Robert Frost said that it was mostly perspiration, not inspiration, which produced good poetry. I agree. You do have to have the inspiration. But you need to have written and re-written in meter, with rhyme schemes, open verse, haiku. You need to have read a lot of poetry, gotten criticism, know the difference between an iamb and a spondee. Poetry is actually a lot of work. Most great poets rewrote and rewrote. I guess where I'm going with this is that creativity usually comes out of discipline and learning techniques. You do get the odd genius—Bach was a genius—music just flowed out of him. But most "geniuses" in the poetry world have worked hard to get it right.

Healthy leisure can't occur in the absence of meaning. If you don't interpret an act or situation as having any significance or meaning, it can't produce healthy leisure. Sometimes, such an interpretation is made primarily because of a shared meaning, perhaps riding bicycles on a trail with three long-time riding companions. Other times, the interpretation may be much more at an individual level; you find making pesto pasta for friends an enjoyable experience, while another person who works in a busy restaurant finds it simply something that has to be done to earn money.

Leisure activities have subjective meanings that often must be learned. Boxing may be simply stupid brutality to one person or the "sweet science" to another. Without these meanings, most leisure activities become ridiculous.

> Dad loves to fish. He has taken me out several times—a few times in a boat or just fishing off a bridge. He absolutely loves it. To me, it's just waiting around with a rod in your hand, then watching a fish die. I've become a vegetarian, and Dad can't figure out why.

Giving

Healthy leisure involves giving oneself to an activity rather than trying to take from it. Such giving is an act of trust or faith. As people develop healthy leisure behaviors, they come to "believe" in them. Have you ever talked with someone who loved camping? They "know" the activity is worthwhile—know it is worth doing. Their decision to go camping is therefore not a calculated list of costs and benefits: *What do I give up? What do I get back?* Rather, it is based on belief—*This is a good thing to do. It is worthwhile.*

> When I started taking flute lessons, my Mom said that I should try some other instrument because every girl in school seemed to be playing flute and it would make it hard to get into band. I stuck with it. My school has about twenty good flute players—all of them but Chuck are girls. I love to play. It's fun. I don't care if I make band or not.

Optimism

Healthy people are generally optimistic. They think things will go well. What people believe and expect about their health "may be more important than objective assessments made by your doctor."[23] People who expect bad health are more likely to get it: "…[S]timulating positive moods and expectations not only makes us feel better, but also helps us live longer, healthier lives."[24]

Our attitudes toward life are also related to diseases of the heart: "Research on heart patients reveals more heart attacks and more blockage of the coronary arteries in those who were hostile, irritable, impatient, and self-centered. They tended to hold the anger in and wall themselves off from other people."[25] Being optimistic may be something which can, to some extent, be learned. To be learned, of course, it must be practiced.

Sensuality

> I play volleyball. When we played our big rival—Sacred Heart—I just knew we were going to win. I could see it. It was a really close match. We lost this time, but we play them again. I just know we're going to win that match next month. I can see it.

Healthy leisure involves the senses. Touch, smell, taste, sound, and vision all connect us with the pleasures of the world. Taste is critical in our appreciation of food. It appears that healthy people take delight in the small pleasures of everyday life which use their senses: this means delighting in what they smell, feel, taste, hear, or see. Sleeping, eating, and even the elimination of waste can be pleasurable. In a politically correct society, a no-touching epidemic, described a few decades ago in the *British Medical Journal*,[26] is alive and well in our society. Touching between employees, students and faculty, two males or two females, and almost any touching of children has become suspect:

> The symptoms include a feeling of loneliness and abstraction from one's fellows. Morbid doubts of other people's loyalty, and feelings of insecurity. A fear of unpopularity; an inhibition of feelings. Unusual reaction to others when one is inadvertently touched. Guilt feelings on touching another person. Frigidity. Loss of tenderness and ability to comfort other people in distress. A hesitancy and doubt when confronting people in pain... A strange, inhibited and cold attitude toward strangers and foreigners. Solitary toilet habits; a tendency to keep babies in their prams and young people glued to their desks. Antagonisms to physical forms of punishment... An inability to communicate with people standing nearby in public places and churches... An antagonism to massage as a form of therapy. Shyness and introversion. A tendency to divorce. An incomprehension of people's needs. A preference for television rather than conversation.[27]

Research with babies, even premature babies, has demonstrated the importance of touching and holding babies. Babies who were frequently touched and held have been shown to be much more likely to survive. (The same holds true for rats.) In spite of such findings, "Many of us are not getting our minimum daily requirement of sensual pleasure."[28]

Another aspect of sensuality is the need for heat. Studies indicate the use of saunas, hot tubs, or just hot baths seem to have health benefits. A study of people who used sauna baths found that sitting in a sauna for thirty minutes doubled beta-endorphin levels in the blood. Endorphins are internally produced chemicals that relieve pain and may also produce a sense of well-being and euphoria.[29]

Humor

It appears that humor is critical in terms of health. Healthy people seem to "maintain a vital sense of humor about life, enjoying a hearty laugh, often at their own expense…"[30] The ability to laugh, at ourselves, and at life, is positively related to health and longevity. Norman Cousins wrote of how, having contracted a serious illness, he fought it by viewing comedies and laughing out loud.[31] Our reaction to tragedy may be improved by our continuing ability to laugh. People who take themselves with a great seriousness may rarely laugh, failing to see the humor in their own behaviors. Such seriousness, an inability to laugh at oneself, may be unhealthy. There is wisdom in the old saying: "Laugh and the world laughs with you, cry and you cry alone."

What's not to like? They invited us over and we had this wonderful meal—asiago cheese in Yukon gold mashed potatoes, great black bean soup with sherry, Indian curried vegetables, real whipped cream on the blueberry pie. All kinds of stuff. You should have smelled the kitchen. It's not a big kitchen so it holds the aromas. I love the smell of onions being sautéed in olive oil. Then we got in the hot tub and the water just bubbled up around us. It was hot and the snow was coming down on our faces and shoulders. Once you get your shoulders in the hot water, you need to keep them there. I opened my mouth and caught some snowflakes. I touched Barbara's waist under the water and kissed her. The wind was in our faces, but we were warm. What a wonderful night it was.

I'm not even sure why we started laughing but everybody kept it going, making faces, wisecracks, doing funny walks. We all just suddenly broke out of our seriousness like a bunch of lunatics. I thought the boss was going to fire us all when he walked in. Then—all of the sudden—he made a silly face and we laughed some more. That's the first time we realized he was human—or at least close.

Social Relations

One of the best predictors of how long someone lives is the number of friends they have—or think they have. The quickening pace of life may have made us more productive, efficient and organized—but less spontaneous, less joyful, and less connected to others.[32]

This isolation from others can harm health. You may not actually die of loneliness, as some songs suggest, but nevertheless you may be harmed physically by lack of contact with others.

> I hate exercising in a class—absolutely hate it. But my best friend, Charlotte, asked me to go with her. We've been friends for over twenty years. She asks me to go—I go. And I don't complain.

Some Practical Aspects of Healthy Leisure

There are many practical aspects of healthy leisure. Our personal habits in everyday life shape our health in many ways. What we eat, drink, how much we exercise, how much stress we encounter, our friendships, sexual behaviors and other personal choices define our wellness within the limits of our genetic make-up and our luck. Indeed, these habits are often formed during leisure and sometimes serve as leisure experience. Much of our eating is not physiologically necessary and is done primarily for pleasure. Much of our exercise comes from sport. Cooking may become a hobby. Adolescents are usually introduced to drugs, alcohol, tobacco, and sexual activity during unstructured free time.

Of course, there are more questions than answers about what makes one's use of leisure healthy or unhealthy, but some answers are beginning to be uncovered. Here are a few.

Living in Healthy Environments

Healthy leisure is more likely to take place in certain kinds of environments. In many cases, when we talk about what we would like to do with our free time, we are really talking about longings for specific environments—being near the sea or high in the mountains.

It may be that human beings have a primordial longing for a certain type of environment. If our ways of living have evolved faster than our bodies could adjust, there may be landscapes from the past that we long for, which suggests that people may seek certain types of landscapes which our ancestors roamed. Travel may be a kind of extension of an old longing for a place that provides us with shelter, food and water.

Exposure to nature must be thought of in health terms. One study has found that office workers who have a window with a view of trees experience lower levels of job stress and higher levels of job satisfaction than those with no natural view. According to Kaplan, Kaplan and Ryan, "What we've discovered is that one's capacity to focus and direct attention becomes fatigued in the modern world. People become irritable, erratic, and less competent. Natural environments are the best cure."[33]

A healthy environment means that one can go "outside" in relative safety and find opportunities for contact with nature. It appears that there is a very strong relationship between how long children are outdoors and how much exercise they get. In an urbanizing world, more attention must be paid to keeping nature a part of everyday life.

> **WAVES—LAKE SIMCOE**
>
> Dream signals
> in love with
> the far wash of waters.
>
> Breaking on shore
> like pods of sleep.
>
> Nomads.
> Nuns of the deep.
>
> Ghost breakers.
> Sound of time's cleansing.
>
> Caravan.
> Constant reaching.

Eating

Eating, for most people, can be one of life's greatest joys. It is a part of life, like sleeping, which is both necessary and potentially very pleasurable. The pleasurable tastes and smells are so central to eating that some animals, when they have lost their sense of taste, refuse to eat. For most of us, eating is a pleasure that also happens to provide nutrition.

What we eat, how we eat it and even when it is eaten have some impact on our health. In terms of diet, according to the National Cancer Institute, one third of all cancer deaths can be related to the foods we eat; even the condition of our bones can be strengthened if attention is paid to daily calcium consumption. People in modern nations, particularly North Americans, are in the historically unique situation of having a huge supply of inexpensive food. However, much of what North Americans eat is highly refined and full of fat and sugar. North America, which is blessed with a high percentage of arable land, is a major producer of wheat and corn. So much is produced that, in addition to selling it to other countries, it is fed to cattle to fatten them before slaughter.

In the United States, 70 percent of all grain is fed to cattle and other livestock. Animal feed (e.g., corn, oats, barley, sorghum) is grown on one third of U.S. cropland.[34] In the world, one third of the grain supply goes for this purpose, even though a billion people suffer from malnutrition or starvation. It should not be surprising, therefore, that the amount of energy it takes to produce one gram of protein from animal sources is from six to eight times as great as what it takes to produce a gram of protein from vegetable sources. In particular, cattle are a major source of numerous environmental problems, from the desertification of Africa, where cattle have been inappropriately introduced in semiarid and arid climates, to the production of methane, to simply taking up space. Cows take up 24 percent of the landmass of our planet through designated pasture land.[35] The collective weight of cattle exceeds that of the human beings who eat them. There are 100 million cattle in the United States, most of which will be slaughtered.

A diet centered around eating cows, which have eaten large amounts of grain just before their deaths, helps produce a society in which being overweight is a common problem. Contributing to this is the relatively abundant supply of food all around us. Most of us simply eat too much. Perhaps an example is in order. As a child, I occasionally received a bottle of root beer or cola from my parents. It contained seven ounces. When eleven and twelve ounce soft drinks were introduced, there was great concern raised that these larger soft drinks would harm our health. (They are essentially sugar and carbonated water.) Today, that concern has proved to be a legitimate one, and many young people purchase 32-ounce soft drinks (or even 48) now.

Most food in the United States is grown and processed by a few huge agribusinesses. What they grow and how it is processed is determined by what is profitable, rather than by what provides balanced nutrition. This does not mean such organizations are necessarily evil. It is simply how the market system works. What it does mean is that the purchaser of food needs to be informed and must exercise moderation. The Exercise and Study Questions on page 382 introduces the U.S. Department of Agriculture's recommendations about what one should eat. How do these recommendations compare to what you eat?

◆ ◆ ◆

If eating is thought of in terms of pleasure, it may be the foods that are most appealing to us are highly flavorful. In both eating and preparing food, gaining skill and accepting higher challenges may increase our ability to make a wide variety of foods taste good. Any Neanderthal can roast big chunks of cow body over a fire and find it flavorful, but making pasta primavera or rye bread requires more skill. Learning to use herbs and spices, read a cookbook, then alter recipes can be not only enjoyable but also, as your skill increases, can foster independence in selecting what you eat.

> To transform the biological necessity of eating into a flow experience, one must begin by paying attention to what one eats.... Developing a discriminating palate, like any other skill, requires the investment of psychic energy. But the energy invested is returned many times over in a more complex experience. The individuals who really enjoy eating develop with time an interest in a particular cuisine, and get to know its history and peculiarities... Like all other sources of flow related to bodily skills—like sport, sex and visual experiences—the cultivation of taste leads to enjoyment if one takes control of the activity.[36]

For eating to be transformed into meaningful experience, then, the development of knowledge, skills and appreciations which allow us to accept more complex challenges is required. This process may also lead one toward vegetarianism.

Becoming a vegetarian requires that you know more about what you eat. The more strictly you observe vegetarianism, the more you need to know. Thus, you must acquire some knowledge and skill to cut out all meat but continue to eat fish, acquire more skill if you also avoid eating fish but eat eggs and dairy products, and the most skill if you don't eat meat, fish or eggs and dairy products. Vegetarianism will be increasingly promoted for environmental, spiritual, and health reasons. Consumption of food will increasingly take on environmental, political, and lifestyle overtones as people become more aware that meat-based diets waste millions of tons of grain that could be used to feed people and that cattle do huge environmental damage. Additionally, increased medical costs associated with high-fat diets and increased health and longevity associated with many vegetarian diets will encourage people to eat less meat.

A number of environmental dilemmas are linked to what we eat. Eating cattle, pigs, sheep, horses, dogs, fish, and other animals is linked to numerous environmental and health problems. Vegetarianism, which can produce a perfectly healthy diet if one learns about what to eat, can help eliminate not only some environmental problems associated with methane production and global warming, but also it can help reduce both malnutrition and diseases of affluence—heart attacks, diabetes, and cancer.

There is some indication that a switch from eating animals is underway. In the United States, for instance, not only are Americans eating more poultry and less beef, but also the percentage of consumer spending on meat is declining. These incremental changes may be just the beginning. As those who prepare food become more skilled at preparing vegetarian meals and as the palates of younger people, who are much more likely to be vegetarian, start to exert their influence in restaurants and supermarkets, the movement toward vegetarianism will likely increase.

Not only what we eat but how we eat it and when we eat may be related to health. An important contributor to obesity is eating food very quickly. When we eat too quickly, we may swallow food before we really taste it and not be as

At first, I was proud I couldn't cook. It was a gender thing. Yeah, I didn't even know how to grill a steak. Nothing. My Mom never taught me. Then, when Daren and I got together, we discovered neither of us could cook. We bought fast food and junk food and ate out. Well, it turned out to be expensive and not very healthy, and we both started gaining a lot of weight. So we have a deal. I'm learning to actually cook and he is doing the housework. Yeah, he really is. Check out the carpet. He's pretty devoted to it. What am I cooking? Well, after frying hamburgers and stuff, I started reading cookbooks and watching a cooking show on TV. Also, I've learned a lot about nutrition and how much crap we eat. I follow recipes but now I change them a little to suit our own tastes. Now, I would never use garlic powder—you need fresh garlic—and mince it—don't use a garlic press. I don't feel I let down the women of the world because I learned to cook. Daren, however, has yet to tell his buddies he does all the housework. That's fine by me—as long as he remembers to vacuum behind the couch.

satisfied with a given amount of food. Food must be savored and eaten slowly.

Your Weight

Our ancient ancestors were in a constant battle to get enough salt, fat and sugar. Almost all of them would have been better off getting more of these than they could. Today, the reverse is true for most people in modern nations:

> An overwhelming amount of preventable disease in modern society results from the devastating effects of a high-fat diet. Strokes and heart attacks, the greatest cause of early death from some social groups, result from arteries clogged with arteriosclerotic lesions. Cancer rates are increased substantially by high-fat diets. Much diabetes results from the obesity caused by excessive fat consumption. Forty percent of the calories of the average American diet come from fat, while the figure for the average hunter-gatherer is less than 20 percent. Some of our ancestors ate lots of meat, but the fat content of wild game is only about 15 percent. The single thing most people can do to improve their health is to cut the fat content in their diets.[37]

There it is. Not, perhaps, what you want to hear (nor I), but it is what may do you the most good in terms of health—quit eating so much fat.

Your weight, of course, is only partially influenced by your habits within your own genetic predisposition. While millions of Americans are "overweight," to some extent being overweight has to do with your genetic endowment. If you consume more calories than you burn, you will gain weight. However, some people metabolize food differently than others. We don't know exactly why this happens. What we do know is that being fat isn't always a lack of willpower. If we all ate the same food and the same portions, we still would not develop identical bodies:

> There are many reasons for a person's being obese, including diabetes, thyroid problems, poor diet, insufficient exercise, and heredity. People with a predisposition to gain weight often aggravate their condition by smoking, drinking alcohol

and leading a sedentary lifestyle. Indeed, watching TV is one of the strongest predictors of obesity... While most cases of obesity are related to family history, social environment, diet and other lifestyle habits, there are rare instances in which something specific, such as a thyroid condition, is the cause.[38]

Most attempts to lose weight quickly fail, even though weight loss programs are a billion dollar business in the United States. Many of these weight loss centers assume that obesity is the result of some moral flaw—that fat people lack willpower. However,

> research shows the answer is nowhere near that simple. Strong biochemical and genetic forces come into play every time any of us approaches a plate of food. Lack of willpower has little to do with how your body will eventually process what you eat or how it will respond when you are full.[39]

Being fat, then, is not generally a character flaw anymore than being skinny is. For all our society's talk about diversity, we continue to assume that a given body type is best—often body types displayed in the mass media. People with these body types have a different set of problems—they are highly desired but sometimes it isn't anything personal—they merely represent something considered desirable—like owning a fancy car. Many fashion models, both male and female, suffer from this situation—people seem to admire you, but it has little to do with your personality, morals, imagination or sense of humor—just your shape.

Perhaps the people who are best adjusted can relate to the idea that everything is beautiful in its own way. The least well-adjusted want only trophies—or perhaps they are driven by their genes more than most people.

Doing something about being overweight is difficult. The one thing that is agreed upon is that exercise is critical to any weight loss program. One study found that 95 percent of people on a weight loss program regained any weight they lost if exercise wasn't included as part of their program.

Even if you reduce the number of calories consumed, you may not lose weight. As you reduce calories, your body responds based on the evolutionary assumption that you must be starving and raises all kinds of barriers against weight loss, slowing down your metabolism and storing energy more efficiently.

If you are obese, you must think in long-range terms about your diet and exercise. There is some evidence that a long-term, strict regimen of regular exercise and a moderate, low-fat diet can permanently lower your set point, making it easier for you to sustain a lower weight.[40]

Calorie-counting diets and those which involve fasting are not likely to work in the long run. What is important is three or four moderate meals a day with the large meal being lunch, avoiding sedentary activity, and avoiding the use of food as a reward or eating as a symbol of love. Additionally, most successful attempts at losing weight involve learning more about food and, usually, learning more about preparing your own food. Most restaurants give you what tastes good to most people—butter, sour cream, deep-fried food, lots of fat. For your palate to adjust, you may have to take more responsibility for what you eat.

> It's hard not to gain weight. I'm in sales and on the road a lot. When you stay in hotels and hang around airports, everything you eat is full of fat. I mean, Coke and nachos in an airport or the huge portions they give you in hotel restaurants—it all adds up. A lot of the time I'm so tired from travel I don't work out even when the hotel has a fitness center. Also, when I take clients out to eat, they eat big and so do I, just to make them feel at ease. Everything I just said sounds like an excuse— a really lame excuse.

Addictions and Compulsions

Addiction is another factor that constitutes, in some senses, a use of leisure with health implications. These implications are great since the United States, with less than 5 percent of the world's population, currently consumes an estimated 40 percent of the world's illegal drugs. Thus drugs have become one more resource of which Americans consume far more than their share. Marijuana, whose use is illegal, is probably the largest cash crop in California as well as a number of other states. Cocaine use, for instance, is so widespread that 97 percent of all paper money in circulation in the United States contains traces of cocaine. More than 10 percent of Americans regularly use illegal drugs, costing an estimated $33 billion in lost work time and an unbelievable amount of crime. In essence, selling and using illegal drugs leads to murder.

Most murder in the United States is drug-related. A twelve-city study showed that 53 to 79 percent of men arrested for serious crimes were drug users. Three out of four cities have a waiting period of at least seven weeks for those seeking treatment for drug problems. Drug use has become a routine explanation for many events in the news, from professional sports to train wrecks to oil spills to international relations with Latin America. Illegal drug sales have become a major business for organized crime, from inner-city youth gangs to the Mafia to Vietnamese immigrants.

While addiction is a major problem in our society, there is no clear understanding of what addiction is. This lack of understanding hinders our ability to cope with what is happening. According to Csikszent-mihalyi, "what drugs in fact do is reduce our perception of both what can be accomplished and what we as individuals are able to accomplish, until the two are in balance."[41] While drugs may produce an alteration of the content and organization of consciousness, they do not add to our ability to order them effectively.

Sexual activity, too, may simply be used as a way to impose an external order on our thoughts, of killing time "…without having to confront the perils of solitude."[42] It is, therefore, not surprising that television viewing, sexual activity and drinking are relatively inter-changeable behaviors within many households. What such activities do is focus attention naturally and pleasurably, but what they fail to do is develop attentional habits that might lead to a greater complexity of consciousness. Addictive behavior, then, is undertaken to relieve the pain which may creep into the unfocused mind.

Finally, all these issues are related to a person acting rather than being acted upon. People who have high levels of wellness are more likely to "act" during their free time than merely to be acted on. There is increasing evidence that people who are not physically, socially, or intellectually active start losing their faculties and capacities. "For example, dendrites that connect nerve cells in the brain stay extended with use, but begin shrinking without use."[43]

According to a leading researcher on addiction, Stanton Peele, "The definitive characteristic of every sort of addiction is that the addict regularly takes something which relieves some kind of pain."[44] What the addict takes or does to relieve that pain, however, varies widely. According to Peele, we cannot say that a given drug is addictive, since addiction is not a peculiar characteristic of drugs. Research shows compulsive addictive involvement in sexual behavior, gambling, eating, television viewing, running and other forms of behavior which may be thought of as "discretionary." Furthermore, these compulsions, such as compulsive eating, show all the signs of ritual, instant gratification, cultural variation, and destruction of self-respect that drug addiction does.

> See, you don't get it. You know why? Smack doesn't do it for you, so you're never going to get it. I have to have it. Bottom line: I have to have it. Lock me up, I'll serve my time. Let me out, I'll find more smack. You're always telling me that we're all different. Well, guess what—you're right, Jack.

There is, additionally, great individual and cultural variation in the extent to which use of a drug becomes addictive. More than 90 percent of U.S. soldiers in Vietnam for whom heroin use was detected were able to give up the habit when back in the United States. One generation of Chinese society was devastated by opium use while other opium-using countries, such as India, underwent no such disaster. Some individuals report feeling instantly addicted to heroin after the first use yet others, after years of daily use, quit with no withdrawal symptoms. The addictive personality is likely to accept magic solutions and to suffer anxiety brought about by a discrepancy between society's values and personal lack of opportunity and lack of self-reliance. The increasing gap between what our society values and the ability of those in our country's underclass to obtain it may partially explain why drug use is, increasingly, a phenomenon of poor people. There is also, however, great individual variation in the pharmacological action of drugs and in the ways in which various individuals metabolize chemicals, but these alone do not determine whether a person will become addicted.

Addiction will not be removed from our society by getting rid of all the supply of a certain drug, even if this could be accomplished. It is a pathological process of pain relief which involves many kinds of drug and nondrug behavior. Addiction is a "process rather than a condition."[45] It is a continuum rather than an all-or-nothing condition. The biggest addictions in our culture would appear to be alcohol, nicotine, marijuana, caffeine, eating, prescription drugs and, perhaps, sexual behavior. This listing shows the difficulty in our legalistic approach to addiction prevention. Some drugs and behaviors we associate with addiction are legal, while others are not. Of those which are legal, some are legal and controlled by the state, some are legal and not controlled by the state.

Treating addiction as a disease may be a mistake. As Peele pointed out, behaviors that we have come to define as diseases have grown and, at the same time, we have expanded what we have defined as addictive diseases. Some "experts" claim there are 20 million alcoholics in the United States, 20 million compulsive gamblers, 30 million women who may suffer from anorexia or bulimia, and 80 million Americans with eating disorders. One fifth of all Americans may suffer from anxiety and depression "diseases."

These new behavioral "diseases" raise the danger that we have begun to define all behaviors we don't approve of as "diseases" that need outside intervention even though, in regard to such addictions,

> systematic comparisons indicate that treated patients do not fare better than untreated people with the same problems. This has been shown in the cases of alcoholism, drug abuse, smoking, overweight, and learning disabilities, but it is probably even truer of diseases like PMS and love addiction that to date have been examined mainly in self-help groups and courtrooms.[46]

On the other hand, 40 million Americans have quit smoking, 9 out of 10 of whom received no outside medical help. Most people stop their addictions voluntarily by themselves. Addiction, then, should not necessarily be understood as a disease, particularly since

> by revising notions of personal responsibility, our disease conceptions undercut moral and legal standards exactly at the time when we suffer most from a general loss of social morality. While we desperately protest the growth of criminal and antisocial behavior, disease definitions undermine the individual's obligations to control behavior and to answer for misconduct.[47]

In summary, Peele argued that human beings are self-correcting mechanisms, that knowledge and experience are the best ways people have of learning how to behave in a healthy manner, that the best way to curb undesirable behavior is to insist on standards of decency, and that inter-actions between parents and children are critical in this process.

We may change our attitudes toward addiction within the next decade. Many futurists believe a number of drugs will be decriminalized and will be treated as a controlled substances by the state. In spite of the fact that 40 percent of all those who are serving time in federal prisons are doing so for dealing drugs, law enforcement appears to have little effect on drug use, since one person in ten in our society is a regular user. Legalizing drugs may drastically reduce crime because one-half or more of what we consider crime is drug-related. Further, the spread of AIDS could be reduced since intravenous drug users are currently the most at-risk population, and the shared use of hypodermic needles is directly related illegal drug use. Also, there would be a huge benefit for addicts if they could receive predictable quantities of the drug to which they are addicted. Many could reenter the labor force. The occupation of many addicts now is theft, prostitution, or other forms of crime seen as necessary because of the addiction.

A huge education program is under way in this country concerning drugs, but it must be based on an understanding of what addiction is. Since most people addicted to substances or behaviors voluntarily cease such addiction at some time in their lives, often in their 30s, part of drug education must be to stress responsible ways of behaving to addicts so they do not further injure themselves or others. The message may swing from "stop" to "until you stop, give us a break."

None of this is intended to suggest that addiction is not a problem—It is a huge problem. The illegal drug industry is the second largest in the world, next to armaments. Addiction is more prevalent now than in the past, partially because there is both a readily available supply of tobacco, alcohol, and other drugs and because technology has created more potent drugs.

> More recent innovation facilitated the production of heroin from opium and crack from cocaine, concentrates that are more rapidly addictive than the natural substances. The invention of hypodermic syringes is part of the same story. Similarly, the mass production of cigarettes from newly developed tobaccos that caused relatively little throat irritation greatly increased the incidence of nicotine addiction.[48]

Thus, the potency of many substances associated with addiction have increased, and will likely continue to increase as technology finds more powerful chemical combinations.

If addiction occurs when an individual seeks relief from pain, there is a bigger question to be answered in our society than how to prevent addiction: What are the great sources of pain in our society from which those who are addicted have sought relief? Can meaningful leisure activity help relieve such pain?

Television

Television must be considered separately when considering healthy leisure since it constitutes from one-third to one-half of all our free time. People sit on chairs or couches (or lie on the floor) and watch a television screen. Most typically, they are by themselves or with one other person.

> *O.K., suppose a Martian lands and you try to explain our drug enforcement policy. First, the Martian watches the "Cops" TV show; they spend all their time arresting drug users and dealers. Then you take the Martian to a convenience store and he buys cigarettes, then to a liquor store, then to a coffee house for a strong espresso. Then you take the Martian to a forest area where marijuana has illegally been planted and you tell him that marijuana is illegal but it is the largest agricultural cash crop grown in the United States. Then you go to a pharmacy and fill a prescription for OxyContin, the stuff Rush Limbaugh got addicted to. Then you go back to your apartment with the Martian, and he says he is going back to Mars because "You can't fix stupid."*

Mass communications, especially television and movies, effectively make us all one competitive group even as they destroy our more intimate social networks. Competition is no longer within a group of fifty or a hundred relatives or close associates, but among five billion people. You may be the best tennis player at your club, but you are probably not the best in your city and are almost certainly not the best in your country or planet. People turn almost every activity into a competition, whether it is running, fishing, sailing, seducing, painting or even bird-watching. In the ancestral environment, you would have had a good chance at being best at something.

Even if you were not the best, your group would likely value your skills.

Now we all compete with those who are the best in the world. Watching these successful people on television arouses envy. Envy probably was useful to motivate our ancestors to strive for what others could obtain. Now few of us can achieve the goals envy sets for us, and none of us can achieve the fantasy lives we see on television.[49]

Thus television presents models of behavior, success and beauty that cannot be lived up to, even if one gives "110 percent." Even if school kids want to be like Tiger Woods or Venus Williams, they will not. When they seriously undertake such a goal, there will be millions of losers and only one winner. The link between watching television and obesity and other addictions is that watching television depletes the child's resources for direct experience and interaction with the environment in favor of vicarious experiences and involvements.[50]

Television viewing, for people who are by themselves, like drugs, may keep the mind from having to face depressing thoughts. The introduction of television has also changed the meaning of many leisure behaviors. Going to a bar, pub, or tavern was historically often a place to visit friends, hold conversations with strangers, debate politics, flirt, play darts, pool, cards, pinball machines, video games, organize the softball team, or simply sit in silence. The introduction of television in many drinking establishments radically changed behaviors to sitting, isolated, on a stool, staring at a screen, while getting drunk. Television has also invaded some restaurants, "waiting rooms" and other public places, and the effect has generally been a stoppage of conversation and a decline in reading.

Moreover, the content of television seems to be increasingly vulgar. There is a reason for this:

Television is not vulgar because people are vulgar; it is vulgar because people are similar in their prurient interests and sharply differentiated in their civilized concerns. All of world history is moving increasingly toward more segmented markets. But in a broadcast medium, such a move would be a commercial disaster. In a broadcast medium, artists and writers cannot appeal to the highest aspirations and sensibilities of individuals; manipulative masters rule over huge masses of people.[51]

Television is often vulgar because that is the way to attract a large viewing audience to sell things to. It makes economic sense for it to be vulgar.

Perhaps we need to remember that, even though television may be temporarily overwhelming our use of time, there is historic evidence that discrimination can be learned. As historian Zeldin observed

> It needs to be remembered that at the same time as the British invented the consumer society, they also took to drink as never before, and the United States followed suit, but over the last generation there has been a radical change in attitudes to alcohol, with a move to moderate drinking of high-quality wines rather than mass consumption of anything fermented. Watching television may become addictive, but gradually discrimination is learned.[52]

Not all the effects of television are harmful, of course. Some are very good. Research shows that the more children watched informative television programs at age five, such as *Mr. Rogers' Neighborhood* and *Sesame Street*, the better their high school grades were in each of the core areas on English, math and science. On the other hand, watching cartoons and other entertainment programs predicted lower grades for girls, but not boys. Watching television as a preschooler wasn't related to time spent reading.[53] As one researcher concluded

> There is content that is good for children and helps them to

There are two ways I turn on the TV. One way is just to channel surf. Kind of aimlessly looking for something that diverts me. Sometimes I even watch talk shows when I can't stand the host. The better way, though, is when you turn it on because there's something there you really want to see. I love ice skating. I follow the careers of the skaters, know a bit about judging—and just to see them glide and jump on that frozen surface—always one little twitch away from falling. It's poetry for me—kind of frozen poetry. So when I turn on the TV for something that is meaningful—it's a good thing.

develop in positive directions. There is also content that is bad for children and may produce long-term negative outcomes…. It is the message and not the medium that is most important.[54]

Exercise

Exercise doesn't need to be a painful marathon to be healthful. Puttering in the garden or taking a pleasant walk is sufficient.

Relaxation doesn't need to be twenty minutes of silent meditation. Watching fish in a bowl, laughing at a funny movie, watching football on television, or even taking a quick deep breath at your desk can let you ease off. Many simple pleasures and indulgences are helpful to health.[55]

There seems to be little doubt that appropriate exercise is good for your health and that lack of exercise is extremely bad. The American Heart Association reported in 1998 that physical inactivity is responsible for up to 250,000 deaths a year in the United States—that's about one out of every eight people.

For example, an eight-year study by the Institute for Aerobics Research in Dallas collected pre- and post-health measures of 13,000 people and found that physical exercise can significantly reduce the risk of death from virtually all causes, including heart disease and cancer. Even slight increases in activity among the least fit were found to be beneficial. This later finding suggests that less strenuous activities such as light gardening, dancing, climbing stairs, and perhaps even a good belly laugh may be just as worthwhile, especially for those who cringe at the thought of intense, physical exertion.[56]

In many cases, our notion of exercise is something fairly dramatic, when more moderate forms of exercise are often as healthy or healthier. "We calculate the benefits of running a dramatic marathon, yet ignore the high return of gardening and dancing, which may better promote health."[57] Yet routine forms of exercise, from simply walking up flights of stairs or cutting the grass with a push mower, have health benefits.

Currently, there is no agreement among experts on how much exercise is "enough." While the Surgeon General stated people should get at least 30 minutes of moderate daily physical activity, a report by the Institute of Medicine in 2002 says it should be at least an hour.[58] A key issue in the dispute is whether to focus on inactivity or obesity as the best target for reducing risks of conditions ranging from diabetes to heart attacks. Both, of course, are important, but the Institute of Medicine (part of the national Academy of Sciences) says 30 minutes a day of moderate exercise, such as walking, is insufficient to maintain weight in adults. Those who do less than an hour of exercise per day will have to find more intense exercise forms, such as jogging or riding a bicycle.

Some forms of exercise, however, when carried to extremes, may lead to behavior which may be thought of as addictive. Running, in particular, seems to have become compulsive for some. According to Grant,[59] some runners, although they started running to get in shape, or to lose weight, develop a psychological dependence on it. If they cannot get their daily exercise, they display signs of depression, anxiety, confusion, tension and irritability. Having to stay away longer may produce severe psychological problems such as depression, loss of energy, loss of interest in eating and sexual behavior, insomnia, weight loss and other problems. This is not to imply that serious leisure or specialization in leisure behavior is necessarily a problem. Even with a high degree of specialization, it is possible to maintain balance among work, leisure and family.[60] It does show, however, that such behaviors, to the extent that they let the individual "hide in them" may cause problems.

The importance of integrating exercise into one's style of life is not only that people need exercise routinely but also that "the benefits of exercising go away shortly after you stop doing regular exercise."[61] You can't store exercise up for the winter or even for next week.

Leisure behaviors that involve exercise, if done regularly, have the potential not only to contribute to our enjoyment of life but also to lessen the seriousness of some physical problems. More than 50 million Americans have high blood pressure, for instance, but, as the American College of Sports Medicine reports, by becoming more active you can not only decrease high blood pressure but also decrease your risk of a heart attack or stroke.[62] Our attitude to life and our relationship with other people often counts far more than fitness or medical regimens.[63]

Sex

As discussed in Chapter 10, a lot of sexual behavior may be considered forms of leisure expression. Researchers, however, dwell on sexual dysfunctions, the lethal dangers of sexually transmitted diseases, and catalogue thousands of sexual aberrations. However, they spell out little as to how a pleasurable sexual life contributes to well-being. We found thousands of articles on trauma, physical abuse, and pain, but hardly any sources on the benefits of human touch.[64] In spite of this, sexual relations were rated the activity people liked the most among a national sample of people who kept time diaries.[65]

A recent survey finds there is considerable agreement between males and females on the need for males to be more involved in choosing and using a method of contraception. Both also agree that males should play a bigger role in making sure that contraception is always used. The majority of both males and females also agreed that the female should have the bigger influence on when the couple decides to have children.

What may be surprising, however, was that 20 percent of males claimed to have little or no knowledge about different types of contraception and less than half of males said they knew a lot about contraception alternatives.[66]

Exercise 13.1 and Study Questions

Find the U.S. Department of Agriculture site on the Internet for a discussion of healthy eating habits and The Food Guide Pyramid. At the writing of this book, the URL is http://www.mypyramid.gov.

How do these guidelines compare to what you eat? Compare what is said about healthy eating with your own eating habits in an essay by addressing the following three questions:

1. What, if anything, did you find out about healthy eating that you didn't know?

2. What would you need to do to make your eating habits both healthier and more enjoyable?

3. What would you need to learn about food and cooking to make your eating habits both healthier and more enjoyable?

Endnotes

1 Pieper, J. (1952). *Leisure: The basis of culture* (p. 62). New York, NY: Mentor-Omega.

2 Leder, M. (1990). Slimming down is a hefty $32 billion business. *Centre Daily Times,* January 6. State College, PA.

3 Pieper (1952)

4 Ornstein, R. and Sobel, D. (1987). *Healthy pleasures.* Reading, MA: Addison-Wesley.

5 ibid.

6 Rockefeller-Growald, E. and Luks, A. (1988). The immunity of Samaritans—Beyond self. *American Health,* March, 51–55.

7 Antonovsky, H. and Sagy, S. (1986). The development of a sense of coherence and its impact on responses to stress situations. *Journal of Social Psychology, 126*(2), 213–225.

8 Berlyne, D. E. (1960). *Conflict, arousal and curiosity.* New York, NY: MacGraw-Hill.

9 Berlyne, D. E. (1966). Curiosity and exploration. *Science, 153,* 25–33.

10 Berlyne, D. E. (1971). *Psychobiology and aesthetics.* New York, NY: Appleton-Century-Crofts.

11 Walker, E. (1980). *Psychological complexity and preference: A hedgehog theory of behavior.* Monterey, CA: Brooks-Cole.

12 Csikszentmihalyi, M. (1990). *Flow: The psychology of optimal experience.* New York, NY: Harper and Row.

13 Antonovsky, A. (1987). *Unraveling the mystery of health: How people manage stress and stay well.* San Francisco, CA: Jossey-Bass.

14 Summerville, G. (1996, March). New ways to combat depression. *Population Today, 28*(1), 311.

15 ibid.

16 Ornstein and Sobel (1987, p. 26)

17 Gladwell, M. (2002). *The tipping point: How little things can make a big difference.* Boston, MA: Little, Brown and Company.

18 Ornstein and Sobel (1987, p. 3)

19 ibid., p. 13

20 Bishop, D. and Jeanrenaud, C. (1982). Creative growth through play and its implications for recreation practice. In T. Goodale and P. Witt, (Eds.), *Recreation and leisure: Issues in an era of change* (p. 87). State College, PA: Venture Publishing, Inc.

21 Csikszentmihalyi (1990)

22 Theodorson, G. and Theodorson, A. (1969). *Modern dictionary of sociology* (p. 250). New York, NY: Apollo Books.

23 Ornstein and Sobel (1987, p. 30)

24 ibid., p. 31

25 ibid., p. 28

26 Heylings, P. (1973). Personal view—The no touching epidemic: An English disease. *British Medical Journal*, 2(5858), 111.

27 ibid., p. 39

28 Ornstein and Sobel (1987, p. 37)

29 Heylings (1973, pp. 46–47)

30 Ornstein and Sobel (1987, p. 187)

31 Cousins, N. (1991). *Anatomy of an illness as perceived by the patient: Reflections on healing and regeneration.* New York, NY: Norton.

32 Ornstein and Sobel (1987, p. 12)

33 Kaplan, S., Kaplan, R., and Ryan, R. (1998). *With people in mind: Design and management of everyday nature* (p. 132). Washington, DC: Island Press.

34 Waggoner, P., Ausubel, J. and Wernick, I. (1996). Lightening the tread of population on the land: American examples. *Population and Development Review*, 22(3), 538.

35 Rifkin, J. (1992). *Beyond beef —The rise and fall of the cattle culture.* New York, NY: Dutton.

36 Csikszentmihalyi (1990)

37 Nesse, R. and Williams, G. (1994). *Why we get sick: The new science of Darwinian medicine* (pp. 148–49). New York, NY: Vintage Books.

38 Summerville (1996, p. 629)

39 ibid.

40 ibid., p. 630.

41 Csikszentmihalyi (1990)

42 ibid.

43 Iso-Ahola, S., Jackson, E., and Dunn, E. (1994). Starting, ceasing, and replacing leisure activities across the life-span. *Journal of Leisure Research, 26*, 227–249.

44 Peele, S. (1989). *Diseasing of America: Addiction treatment out of control.* Lexington, MA: Lexington Books.

45 ibid.

46 ibid.

47 ibid.

48 Nesse and Williams (1994, p. 152).

49 Ornstein and Sobel (1987, pp. 220–221)

50 Peele (1989)

51 Gilder, G. (1994). *Life after television: The coming transformation of media in American life* (p. 49). New York, NY: Norton.

52 Zeldin, T. (1994). *An intimate history of humanity.* London, UK: Harper.

53 Wright, J. (1998). *Early viewing of educational television programs: The short and long-term effects on schooling.* Los Angeles, CA: Conference on Free Choice Learning, November 8. National Science Foundation.

54   ibid., p. 19

55   Ornstein and Sobel (1987, p. 3)

56   Heart disease, cancer death rates drop with exercise, study finds. (1989). *Orange County Register*, November 7, p. A11.

57   Ornstein and Sobel (1987, p. 23)

58   Dryfuss, I. (2002). *Experts disagree on how much exercise is enough.* Associated Press, September 19.

59   Grant, E. (1988). The exercise fix: What happens when fitness fanatics just can't say no? *Psychology Today, 22*(2), 24–28.

60   Donnelly, M., Vaske, J., and Graefe, A. (1986). Degree and range of recreation specialization: Toward a typology of boating-related activities. *Journal of Leisure Research, 18*(2), 81–95.

61   Schor, J. (1998). *The overspent American: Why we want what we don't need* (p. 8). New York, NY: Basic Books.

62   ibid.

63   Ornstein, R. and Erlich, P. (1989). *New world—New mind: Moving toward conscious evolution* (p. 24). New York, NY: Doubleday.

64   Nesse and Williams (1994, p. 14)

65   Robinson, J. and Godbey, G. (1999). *Time for life—The surprising ways Americans use their time* (Rev. ed.). University Park, PA: Penn State Press.

66   Kaiser Family Foundation. (1998). Cited in "Teens' changing attitudes toward contraception," *Centre Daily Times*, March 5, p. 3.

Leisure Service Organizations

Many of the leisure activities in which you participate are sponsored by a formal organization. Lots of you have gone swimming at the "Y," gone camping with the Girl Scouts, joined stamp-collecting clubs, become members of theater groups or choral societies, played in parks administered by municipal recreation and park departments, or gone on guided tours arranged by commercial travel agencies. In short, formal organizations play an important part in shaping our leisure behavior.

Leisure Services: An Unrecognized Common History

Many related leisure services dealing with hospitality, parks, play, tourism, sport, outdoor recreation, therapeutic recreation, military recreation, youth services, and others have a common heritage, although it is not often realized. They also have many common goals. All such leisure services find their beginnings and reach their highest potential in the desire to improve the everyday lives of human beings, and in the ability to be entrepreneurial and informed when they do so. Those interested in government-sponsored leisure services sometimes forget the *entrepreneurial* heritage, and those interested in commercial forms of recreation sometimes forget the *helping-and-reform* heritage.

Diverse leisure services also have in common the fact that, *all* leisure services were developed in reaction to the emergence of urbanization and an economy based largely on the manufacture of material goods. As work became more ordered under industrialization, and time became the ordering device, the rest of life, for many, became "free time"—an empty container which could no longer be filled with the old forms of play or the holy days which characterized peasant life. New work patterns, the emergence of capitalism and the unplanned urban environment that accompanied the factory system made former ways of life and leisure obsolete.

Modern leisure was not only the product of attempts to reform the way of life that had developed under industrialization, it was also, and to a greater degree, the "invention" of entrepreneurs who found things people wanted to do during their free time—specifically, things they were willing to pay for.

> Beginning in the eighteenth century with magazines, coffee-houses, and music rooms, and continuing throughout the nineteenth century, with professional sports and holiday travel, the modern idea of personal leisure emerged at the same time as the business of leisure. The first could not have happened without the second.[1]

Modern leisure, then, was largely invented by those in "commercial" recreation and such services, at their best, reflected the same ethic of caring about others as did the best of the recreation reform movements. At their worst, those in the commercial leisure sector cared only about removing money from their patrons, and those in the reform movements cared only about imposing their beliefs on those thought to be inferior.

Caring about others can be exemplified in the history of any form of commercial recreation. In tourism, for instance, a pivotal event was the development of *organized* railroad tours. Thomas Cook, an English minister and Secretary of the South Midlands Temperance

> I have been in this business thirty years and, I can tell you, people don't often know what they want to do with their leisure. They didn't know they wanted to ride a Ferris Wheel until Mr. Ferris invented it and showed it off at a World's Fair. They didn't know they wanted to go to a subtropical swamp in Orlando in the middle of summer until Walt Disney quietly bought up all the land in the area and transformed it into Disney World. Sometimes, uses of leisure get reinvented. Starbucks reinvented the coffee house. Barnes and Noble reinvented the library. The leisure industry doesn't always try to find out what people want to do—they show models of new exciting things to do that people hadn't thought about, but get interested in.

Association, planned an excursion for his members from Leister to Loughborough for the modest price of one shilling. This success led to more organized tours, "package tours," and traveler's checks, all of which helped facilitate travel.

> The success of [Cook's] operations was due to the care he took in organizing his programs to minimize problems; he had close contacts with hotels, shipping companies and railroads throughout the world, ensuring that he obtained the best possible service as well as cheap prices for the services he sold. By escorting his clients throughout their journeys abroad he took the worry out of travel for the first-time travelers. He also facilitated the administration of travel by introducing, in 1867, the hotel voucher; and by removing the worry of travel for the Victorian population, he changed their attitudes to travel and opened up the market. The coincidental development of photography acted as a further stimulus for overseas travel, both for prestige and curiosity reasons.[2]

In this example, we see three factors that shape all forms of leisure and hospitality services at their best, over and over again: the desire to help people, entrepreneurial spirit, and changes in technology which facilitated (or necessitated) such intentions.

Some of this combination may be found in the social reform movements, which brought about many recreation, park, sport, adult education, outdoor recreation, museums, botanical gardens, and other leisure services in the early twentieth century. They evolved, as did commercial recreation, due to changes in how people did work. The Industrial Revolution, which was driven by advances in technology, resulted in the migration from countryside to city, transforming the peasantry into the working class and often doing great environmental damage in the process. From serving as partners in agricultural work, most women were constricted to limited work roles or homemaking and childrearing as primary tasks. From work being interspersed with leisure elements, industrialism put work at the center of social arrangements. Free time became what was left over. Children had no place to play.

In all of these early endeavors, success in contributing to the betterment of humankind was not so much dependent upon whether the organization that ultimately provided the service was "for-profit," "private-nonprofit," or "governmental," but rather on the dedication and vision of the individuals involved. Dorothy Enderis, who served as the Director of Milwaukee's Department of Recreation and Adult Education Department from 1920 to 1948, typified such an individual. Of German heritage, Enderis summarized what may distinguish the truly superior leisure service worker from others:

> *Leut* is the German word for people, and *selig* is holy, and to me, the finest attribute with which you could credit a recreation worker is to say he is leutsig, meaning that people are holy to him.[3]

Hospitality, which today has often come to mean hotel, restaurants and resorts, also shares a history of thinking that people were holy. Historically, according to eminent historian Theodore Zeldin, *hospitality* meant "opening up one's home to total strangers, giving a meal to anyone who chose to come, allowing them to stay the night, indeed imploring them to stay, though one knew nothing about them."[4] This "free" hospitality began to decline as more and more people traveled; it was gradually replaced by the hospitality industry. Zeldin saw that, from the roots of this simple hospitality, a new hospitality might spring:

> A new phase of history begins when this ancient and simple hospitality is succeeded by a deeper hospitality, which alters the direction of human ambition. That happens when people become hospitable to strange ideas, to opinions they have never heard before, to traditions that seem totally alien to them, and when encounters with the unknown modify their view of themselves. When foreign travel becomes a necessity, and no longer an exception, when television news is about distant parts more than about one's own city, when one's emotions are roused by the misfortunes of total strangers, what goes on elsewhere becomes a crucial ingredient in the shaping of one's life. It becomes impossible to decide what to do unless one knows about everyone else's experience. This is a deeper hospitality because it is not just politeness, but involves admitting new ideas and emotions temporarily into one's mind.[5]

Thus, in our current definition of hospitality we see a model that may be extended into a changing world. The tradition of caring about strangers is the common heritage of the *best* of those in all of the leisure services, and this heritage will serve us well in the future. So, too, will the entrepreneurial spirit that the best of those in leisure services exemplify.

While there are many ways to define what entrepreneurship means, what the best of those who have worked in leisure services share is a kind of entrepreneurial spirit that operates on the following assumption:

> A good idea may result in a good product or service that will benefit both those who use the product or service and its developer.

By this definition, the divisions between many forms of leisure services disappear. Entrepreneurs in leisure services bring about a change which benefits others and themselves simultaneously. Thus, a good bowling program for teenagers with mental retardation, a good swimming pool operation at a Florida resort, a good botanical garden in the middle of a big city, a good tour of Amsterdam's "Red Light" District, a good volleyball league for senior women, a good country bed and breakfast, a good arts program for elementary school kids in tough areas of a city, a good restaurant with an imaginative menu, a good trail walk with some interpretation of the plant and animal life seen by the hikers—all have a common core: the entrepreneurial spirit. The entrepreneurial spirit, which has been the

---

This may sound funny but—I work in a hotel. I do staff training and I stress the importance of service. Not just service with a smile, but service based on the idea of really helping another person— really caring about their welfare when they are in our hotel. That also means listening to the guest. Listening can be a very difficult skill to master. How much of what I'm saying now are you really absorbing?

Listening and paying attention are critical. You have to try and learn the guest's habits while they are in the hotel—and then make it easier for them to follow their preferred habits. We often record what we observe about a guest so we can make their stay easier. Some of our employees do this because they get paid to—but you know what, some other staff really start to care about the guests—not faking it—they really start to care—to serve. That's what hospitality is! Our guests can tell the difference.

core of those who excelled at leisure services, will become even more important in the coming era.

Roles of Leisure Service Organizations

There are many ways to identify types of leisure service organizations; one is to identify such organizations by their role. Most leisure service organizations fulfill one or more of the following roles: promoter of specific leisure activities and facilities, culturally neutral provider, social change agent, coordinator of leisure opportunities, provider for the recreationally dependent, enhancement of the physical environment, health promoter, provider of leisure education and counseling, adjustment to institutionalization, and promoter and facilitator of tourism.

> When David and I graduate, we want to start a fitness center that is aimed at older adults. But we want to do a lot of things differently. The whole idea is to make the center a place where they have friendships and support as well as a place for "exercise"— or, as we all say now, "physical activity." We are going to do everything we can to get their kids to visit, and, if they can't, we are going to send online photos of Mom or Granddad on the treadmill, inviting them to encourage their parents. The concept of the place is that exercise doesn't happen in a vacuum. It has to have meaning; it has to be pleasurable. We are going to have juice, coffee, tea, light snacks, colors, uplifting music—maybe Vivaldi—and brief support meetings before they begin. We have a lot of ideas and, as soon as we can get some backing, we will try it out. How about "Friends in Motion" as a name?

Promoter of Specific Leisure Activities and Facilities

Many leisure service organizations seek to interest people in participating in specific recreation and leisure activities with which they are not presently involved. In some cases, this is based on the belief that the leisure activity being promoted is "superior" to other choices of activity the individual might make during his or her free time. Many outdoor recreation organizations act on the assumption that the activities they promote are more worthwhile than other activities.

Bowling centers, for instance, sponsor advertisements concerning the joy of bowling. Some state or provincial leisure service agencies promote various sports and athletic activities in the hope that, if people become involved in such sports, they will become more physically fit, both for their own betterment and that of society.

In some mental hospitals, therapeutic recreation workers encourage emotionally disturbed patients to grow plants, whether or not the patient had such an interest previously, in the belief that it is a valuable step in learning to accept responsibility. In all these cases, the agency wants the person to modify his or her behavior to include certain forms of leisure activity. The leisure service organization serves as a stimulus to awaken this interest. Since a given leisure activity is often valued only after some form of exposure to it, the organization justifies its approach by saying that the individual may not appreciate the happiness found in sailing, for instance, because he or she has never been exposed to it. A child playing basketball all summer in a ghetto area may not desire to go camping until exposed to a camping program and may need to be introduced to such a program one step at a time or on a number of occasions before he or she can decide whether or not it is worth doing.

Culturally Neutral Provider

When acting as a neutral agent, the leisure service organization seeks to provide or sponsor whatever leisure activities, facilities, or services in which its clients express interest. In this role, it is assumed that the agency has no right to impose its own values upon its clients and should cater to existing leisure interests rather than attempting to create new ones. The chief task of the agency is to identify accurately and supply those leisure experiences in which people wish to participate. The determination of leisure desires may involve community surveys, citizens' boards or councils, public hearings, or the collection of information concerning participation in a variety of leisure activities. As stated earlier, it is impossible for the agency to avoid having its own values enter into the decision-making process. The agency, however, may seek to minimize the role its own values play in the operation of its program.

Social Change Agent

Some leisure service agencies attempt to change people's behavior or social condition through the use of leisure activity. Such change goes beyond creating interest in a given activity. In such "social engineering," the leisure activity serves as a means to an end; it is a technique or tool designed to change and, hopefully, to improve society. Some commercial leisure service organizations use golf or tennis as a means of interesting people in purchasing condominiums. Boys' Clubs sponsor after-school programs for teenage boys in the hope of averting delinquent behavior. Nature programs in county park systems may be initiated to change the attitudes of young children toward the outdoors and to foster an attitude of "stewardship" toward the land. Employee-based recreation programs are often sponsored to help attract potential employees and to improve the morale of those already employed in order to improve company productivity. For a leisure service organization to act effectively as an agent for change, however, there must be an ideal situation articulated by the agency as a goal. Sometimes these are criticized for being incomplete or even unworthy. Thus, the goal of providing elderly citizens with "something to do" may be criticized for seeming to assume that the elderly would have nothing to do unless some activity were "given" to them. Another criticism is that the purpose of an activity is often left unseated, as is the question of its importance.

Coordinator of Leisure Opportunities

As a coordinator of leisure opportunities within a community, a leisure service organization seeks to maximize the citizen's opportunities to participate in a wide variety of leisure activities. In this role, the organization takes the initiative in bringing together representatives of commercial, private, and public leisure service agencies in order to share information, avoid duplication of each other's efforts, and plan ways to allow joint cooperative use of each agency's programs and facilities. As a coordinator of leisure opportunities, the leisure service agency tries to make the citizen familiar with the total range of leisure opportunities within his or her community. Often, particular attention is given to informing new community residents about such opportunities. The coordinator role assumes that it is desirable for the agency to take a "systems" approach to leisure opportunity rather than to act independently or in conflict with other agencies. In many cases, the citizen is primarily interested in a given leisure activity rather than in its sponsor. A swimmer, for instance, will be interested in swimming in a clean, well-maintained pool at a nominal cost regardless of the organization maintaining the pool. It is conceivable that many different leisure service organizations could provide this service successfully—commercial neighborhood pools, YMCAs, municipal recreation and park departments, public schools, and so on. Therefore, it would appear desirable for all the agencies that could provide this service to consult with each other to avoid duplicating services. This belief, however, is by no means unchallenged. Grodzins, for instance, has argued that an overlapping of functions by leisure service agencies is actually desirable.[6]

Provider for the Recreationally Dependent

Here, it is assumed that the leisure service agency should direct its major effort toward providing services to those who are highly dependent upon the agency for meaningful leisure experience or who have a minimum of alternatives to the use of these services. Some people are fortunate enough to have a wide variety of leisure opportunities to choose from because of their relatively good health, income, mobility, education, and so forth. While these individuals may depend upon leisure service agencies for some of their leisure experiences, they are not dependent to the same extent as those who are in poor physical or mental health or who have less income, less mobility, or less education. Leisure services organizations try to compensate for this inequity of opportunity in regard to play, recreation, open space, and related areas. There are, of course, no absolute guidelines as to those characteristics that constitute a high degree of recreation dependency. Many would argue that it is possible to be poor and still enjoy a rewarding variety of leisure experiences. When dealing with an issue as basic as where children can play, however, it quickly becomes apparent that in urban poverty areas where apartments are small and overcrowded, children's play opportunities are very limited unless some organized effort is made to provide parks, playgrounds, and leisure activity programs. Individuals with physical handicaps may likewise enjoy a variety of leisure activities with the support of interested organizations in their community, but such help is not always readily available. Thus, the rationale for a public leisure service agency to provide services for the recreationally dependent is that it should be a "provider of last resort," responsible for helping meet the leisure needs and desires of those for whom no one else can or will provide. Much the same argument is presented concerning the responsibility of government to provide employment for those who cannot find work during a recession or depression.

Enhancement of the Physical Environment

Many leisure service agencies have, as a primary role, the protection and improvement of the environment. Many types of leisure activities are dependent upon certain environmental features or conditions that most people cannot supply individually in urban or suburban areas. In addition, the quality of the leisure experience may be highly dependent upon environmental conditions. Boating in a polluted lake is a markedly different experience from boating in a clear, clean one. A number of these leisure activities are often referred to as "resource-based" and include boating, camping, backpacking, hunting, and mountaineering. Leisure service agencies maintain a variety of areas and facilities to accommodate such activities.

*The difference between Americans and Europeans in regard to parks is that Europeans go to the park **as** leisure while Americans go **for** leisure. In other words, Europeans, once they arrive in the park, are at leisure. What you do is important but the main thing is that you're in the park— you are closer to nature. In the States, it's more like the park is a place to do something. Canadians? I always want to say they are somewhere in the middle but now they have so much immigration from Asia that the idea of being in nature is a big reason for park use. Do you think I'm stereotyping? I don't know. Not everybody from China or New York City is the same—but there are tendencies based on culture.*

Some leisure service agencies also perform services that contribute to the "quality of life" of a community, such as planting shade trees, acquiring park land, preserving historical sites and unique natural areas, and protecting wildlife.

Health Promoter

A variety of leisure service organizations provide services aimed at improving or maintaining the health of those they serve. Employee leisure services, for example, often organize activities aimed at improving the physical fitness of workers. Leisure services may also organize social events, festivals, guided tours, or other gatherings to stress healthful living. This role appears to be increasingly important. The most common contribution public recreation and park services make to health appear to be stress reduction and exercise.

Provider of Leisure Education and Counseling

In many cases, organizations concerned with leisure provide information to those they serve about a wide variety of leisure opportunities. Skills and appreciation of specific leisure activities, from karate to flower arranging, also may be taught. In both community and clinical settings, those who provide leisure services may be involved in counseling individuals with a disability or problem that interferes with the satisfying use of leisure. Those in the therapeutic recreation profession provide such services to those with physical and developmental disabilities, emotional disturbances, dependence on drugs, prisoners and parolees, patients in hospitals or hospices, and many others.

Adjustment to Institutionalization

When people move from private residences to large, group-living situations, their leisure resources, and sometimes their leisure, need to change. The institutions served by recreation, park, and leisure service professionals vary widely, but may include: colleges and universities, the armed forces, nursing homes, prisons, hospitals, and other group living situations. The mere act of moving to or from such a living arrangement causes change, and often problems, in one's ability to use leisure. Leisure services help to overcome such problems.

Promoter and Facilitator of Tourism

Many leisure services are involved with promoting and managing tourism and other visitation. They may be primarily involved in promoting an area as a tourist destination, in coordinating conferences and conventions, in managing tourist attractions or resorts, in leading recreation activities for visitors, or they may serve as a retail tourist

> You may think that "institutionalization" means that a criminal or a person who is emotionally disturbed gets put in some concrete box, but college kids are institutionalized too. They have left their homes and come to a large—well—institution. They often live in tiny dorm rooms, eat meals in a huge dining hall and, in many ways, have a slightly higher version of prison life—except for the recreation. They have racquetball courts, a student center, theatre, music, intramural sports, sometimes an environmental center, talks by world-renowned experts, and many other recreation activities and events. In some ways, recreation is the chief difference between prison and college.

agent. All these services and others are necessary to the well-being of the world's largest industry.

Recreation and Leisure Need

You have often heard people around you express their opinions about the need or demand for recreation and leisure. "The kids around here need a place to play." "This town needs a swimming pool." "Why aren't there more movies for the whole family?" "I'd like to learn to play the guitar." It is difficult to try to measure the actual "need" or "demand" for recreation and leisure. While we can determine certain symptoms of people who need food, air, water or sleep, leisure needs are more elusive.

The need for recreation can be conceived in a number of ways. By necessity, the field of service and values inherent in such service must be limited. Agency staff, areas, facilities, and fiscal resources are all limited, and the only alternative to limiting their operation by identifying and delimiting values is to attempt to please everyone—today fighting stream pollution, tomorrow organizing junior competitive sports programs, the next day claiming to be the saviors of the inner city, and finally, claiming to be value-free and just giving the people what they want. While all such activity is potentially worthwhile, and there is great benefit from amalgamating professionals into national organizations with such diverse goals, it is a cop-out to argue that leisure or recreation should be merely concerned with "quality of life" because no specific values are enunciated in such a statement. All human activities affect the quality of life. Additionally, the statement assumes what constitutes superior quality can be readily agreed upon.

In short, some specific concept of public need for recreation must be internalized before recreation or leisure service plans can systematically develop goals and utilize research in that process. Let us examine four concepts of recreation needs identified by Mercer,[7] plus a fifth added by this author in an attempt to determine from what definitions of recreation or leisure and value assumptions these concepts have proceeded to evolve, and how research could be utilized to make such conceptualizations operational. Table 14.1 shows these concepts of need, the definitions of recreation they imply, the value assumptions implicit in them, and the type of research that will facilitate their use.

Table 14.1 Recreation Needs[8]

Conceptualization of Recreation Need	Definition of Recreation	Value Assumption	Information Needs
Expressed Need			
Individual's need for leisure is determined by individual's current leisure activity patterns.	The expression of individual values through participation in freely chosen activities.	Government should be a culturally neutral provider. There is a relatively just distribution of recreation resources. Individuals have a relatively easy and equal access to recreation resources. Individuals don't have a similar need for publicly sponsored recreation services. Variation in need is expressed through differences in participation rate.	Determining what people do during leisure: activities participated in, duration, frequency, sequencing, and scheduling.
Comparative Need			
Need for leisure services of government as systematically related to both supply of leisure resources available to an individual and his or her socioeconomic characteristics.	High autonomy in nonwork activity that is the prerogative of an elite; a right to pursue happiness that is systematically inequitably distributed.	Government should not be a culturally neutral provider. People do not have similar needs for public recreation resources. Those with low socioeconomic status have higher need. There may not be relatively just distribution of resources. Individuals may have relatively difficult and unequal access to public recreation services.	Studies of participation and non-participation and the relationship to socioeconomic variables. Studies of relationship of supply of recreation resources to socioeconomic status.
Created Need			
Leisure need is determined by an individual choosing to participate in an activity after being taught to value it.	Any activity in which, after sufficient introduction, an individual will freely and pleasurably participate.	Government should not be a culturally neutral provider. Individuals often do not know what they want to do during leisure and are happier if given guidance. Leisure activities are substitutable because the individual seeks certain environmental conditions, not specific activities. It is legitimate to use recreation to promote the desired goals of the state.	Case studies examining reasons for participation among various subcultures. Pretesting and post-testing of behavior and attitudes as a result of participation in public recreation services.

Table 14.1 Recreation Needs [continued]

Conceptualization of Recreation Need	Definition of Recreation	Value Assumption	Information Needs
Normative Need			
Experts can establish precise, objective standards to determine desirable minimum supply in quantitative terms. Implies physiological need for leisure.	A set of physiologically necessary yet pleasurable activities undertaken during nonwork time that restore and refresh the individual, prepare him or her for work again, and otherwise contribute to his or her well-being.	Government should not be a culturally neutral provider. Individuals have similar needs for public recreation. Certain well-established recreation resources are inherently in the public interest. Recreation resources should be equally distributed by spacing.	Testing of assumptions of standards [e.g., accuracy of service radii]. Testing relationship between perceived satisfaction and social quality indicators [e.g., crime rate, meeting standards].
Felt Need			
Individual's need for leisure activity as a function of individual belief, perception, and attitude.	What an individual would choose to do given a minimum of constraints or high autonomy. It is a set of personally ideal activities in the mind of the individual which, given the opportunity, he or she will undertake.	Government should be a culturally neutral provider. Many individuals desire to participate in activities that they currently do not. There may not be a relatively just distribution of recreation resources. Individuals often have legitimate reasons for not using public recreation resources. Individuals may not have relatively easy or equal access to public recreation resources. Individuals will be happier participating in what they "perceive" they want to do rather than in what they are currently doing.	Attitudinal research concerning people's desire for recreation experiences, environments, intensity, or desire.

As you can see, the values inherent in these conceptualizations are in conflict. One believes either that each citizen should have an equal amount of public recreation resources or that some subgroup should be given priority. One believes either that government should seek to be culturally neutral, reacting to what the public says about and does during leisure, or that government should promote certain activities and experiences and discourage others. You believe either that experts are in a position to prescribe desirable minimums of certain types of recreation resources or you do not. These conflicts of values and the inability of recreation and park professionals to take stances on them is probably indicative of the fact that, philosophically, there is no unified social movement in public recreation, parks, or leisure services.

Thus, in the public sector, there are no agreed-upon assumptions about how to measure leisure needs. How a public agency measures leisure needs will have a direct relation to how the agency serves the public. For example, if an agency uses only an "expressed need" model of recreation need, it may assume that those who "need" or "demand" to go camping are doing so. Future provision of campsites, therefore, may be targeted to those who already use them. If the same agency used "felt need" as a basis for providing campsites, it would try to provide campsites for those who said they "wanted" to go camping, whether or not they had actually been camping. It is perhaps natural that public leisure service agencies, in a pluralistic society such as ours, increasingly recognize that there is more than one way of determining need for recreation or leisure.

In private, nonprofit, and commercial leisure service organizations, determining recreation or leisure need assumes different dimensions. Private, nonprofit organizations may make assumptions about what changes should be made in society and use leisure activity as a means of bringing about such change. Thus, the organization's concern will not be with leisure needs but with other kinds of need. The YMCA, for instance, may be interested in promoting Christian living. Commercial leisure service organizations often seek to create a need through advertising or by teaching people how to participate in or enjoy their services. They also try to measure felt and expressed need accurately to determine more precisely who uses the type of service or products they provide and who would like to.

Leisure service organizations can never determine "need" for leisure in a completely scientific or objective way. As recreation educator Harlan G. Metcalf stated in his class many years ago, recreation (and leisure) are as broad as the interests of mankind and as deep as his imagination.[9]

The Scope of Leisure Service Organizations

As has been shown, leisure service organizations have a wide variety of roles. We may also distinguish between these agencies according to how they are financed and administered. When this is done, such organizations are often divided into public, private, and commercial categories. Such organizations are compared and contrasted in Table 14.2.

Table 14.2 Comparison and Contrast of Public, Private (Non-Governmental Organizations), and Commercial Recreation[10]

	Public	Private (NGOs)	Commercial
Philosophy of recreation	Enrichment of the life of the total community by providing opportunities for the worthy use of leisure. Nonprofit in nature	Enrichment of the life of participating members by offering opportunities for worthy use of leisure, frequently with emphasis on the group and the individual. Nonprofit in nature	Attempt to satisfy public demand in an effort to produce profit. Dollars from, as well as for, recreation
Objectives of recreation	To provide leisure opportunities that contribute to the social, physical, educational, cultural, and general well-being of the community and its people	Similar to public, but limited by membership, race, religion, age, and the like. To provide opportunities for close group association with emphasis on citizenship, behavior, and life philosophy values. To provide activities that appeal to members	To provide activities or programs that will appeal to customers. To meet competition. To net profit. To serve the public
Administrative Organization	Governmental agencies (i.e., federal, state, and local)	Boy Scouts, Settlements, Girl Scouts, Camp Fire, "Y" organizations, and others	Corporations, syndicates, partnerships, private ownership; for example: motion picture, television, and radio companies; resorts; bowling centers; and skating rinks
Finance	Primarily by taxes. Also gifts, grants, trust funds, small charges, and fees to defray cost	By gifts, grants, endowments, donations, drives, and membership fees	By the owner or by promoters. By the users through admission and charges

Commercial Leisure Services

It is difficult to imagine all the ways in which leisure service organizations shape our leisure behavior or to imagine their sheer size. The commercial sector is by far the most pervasive. As a nation, we spend more of our free time with the products and services of the commercial sector than we do without them. Television and other mass media, travel and tourism, theme parks, professional and commercial sport facilities, and many other commercial ventures occupy, in some manner, the majority of our leisure time. The impact of such commercial outlets on our daily lives is enormous. Commercial leisure resources have been developed to a particularly great extent in the United States. More tourists, for example, visit Disney World than the United Kingdom.

Commercial leisure services are often high-risk ventures since it is difficult to determine on what people will spend their time and money.

Table 14.2 Comparison and Contrast of Public, Private (Non-Governmental Organizations), and Commercial Recreation[10] (continued)

	Public	Private (NGOs)	Commercial
Program	Designed to provide a wide variety of activities, year-round, for all groups, regardless of age, sex, race, creed, or social or economic status	Designed to provide programs of a specialized nature for groups and in keeping with the aims and objectives of the agency	Program designed to tap spending power in compliance with state and local laws
Membership	Unlimited—Open to all	Limited by organizational restrictions, such as age, sex, and religion	Limited by law (local, state, and federal), social conception regarding status and strata in some places, economics—those who have the ability to pay
Facilities	Community buildings, parks (national, state, local), athletic fields, playgrounds, playfields, stadiums, camps, beaches, museums, zoos, golf courses, school facilities, and others	Settlement houses, youth centers, clubs, churches, play areas, camps, and others	Theaters, clubs, taverns, nightclubs, lodges, racetracks, bowling lanes, stadiums, and others
Leadership	Professionally prepared to provide extensive recreation programs for large numbers of people. Frequently subject to Civil Service regulations. Volunteers as well as professionals. College training; facilities growing	Professionally prepared to provide programs on a social group-work basis. Employed at discretion of managing agency. Volunteers as well as professionals	Frequently trained by employing agency. Employed to secure greatest financial returns. Employed and retained at the discretion of the employer. No volunteers

Interest in many leisure activities may rise or fall rapidly. Enthusiasm for activities, such as bouncing on trampolines at trampoline centers, miniature golf, cross-country skiing, bungee jumping, or disco dancing, changes rapidly and makes it difficult for organizations to plan for future development. New forms of leisure activity, such as Internet cafés, spring up overnight. Consequently, commercial organizations often try to diversify their activities or products. They also use advertising extensively to try to create a favorable image with the public.

Commercial recreation may include:

- an individually owned enterprise, such as a dude ranch;

- a local corporation, such as a ski resort;

- a large nationwide corporation, such as a chain of fitness clubs;

- a concession operation where a campsite or other facility is operated on public property under a contractual agreement; and

- a manufacturer-operated enterprise, such as a bowling alley operated by a maker of bowling equipment.[11]

Organizations for Groups with Special Needs

Some leisure service organizations have emerged to meet the leisure needs of a specific subsection of the population. Therapeutic recreation, for instance, refers to both indirect and direct recreation or leisure services provided to special populations such as those with mental retardation, emotional problems, physical handicaps, or other special needs that limit their recreation opportunities. Organizations providing such services include not only residential institutions, such as state schools for those with mental retardation, but also community organizations, such as municipal recreation and park departments and "transitional" organizations such as "halfway houses," sheltered workshops, and others. They also include commercially managed services such as centers for treatment of drug addiction.

Residential institutions serving these groups vary widely in the leisure activities and facilities they provide or allow to be undertaken. Some of the goals of institutionalized leisure services include the following:

1. to aid in adjustment to institutional living;

2. to make the person more receptive to other forms of treatment or therapy;

3. to provide a means for catharsis through wholesome leisure activity and thereby lessen antisocial behavior;

4. to provide opportunities for self-expression;

5. to provide activity that is, in itself, therapeutic and contributes to the improvement or adjustment of the individual;

6. to aid in the acquisition of leisure interests and skills that can be used in the outside world; and

7. to facilitate better intergroup relations within the institution.

Community-based organizations providing therapeutic recreation services may concentrate on making recreation areas, facilities, and equipment available or usable by some special population group; teaching leisure skills; and counseling those they serve in terms of leisure behavior and available leisure resources.

Many private, nonprofit organizations provide leisure services primarily for youth. Such organizations sprang up in the early twentieth century out of concern for children of the urban poor. Many have been concerned, in some way, with "character-building." These organizations, according to Farrell may be religion-oriented, such as the Catholic Youth Organization or YMCA, or social service-oriented, such as the Police Athletic League.[12] They typically involve a central national office with a specialized professional staff, regional offices, and local or neighborhood associations comprised of volunteers.

Another type of leisure organization concerned with a specialized clientele is the employee recreation organization. These usually are involved in providing recreation and leisure services to employees of a medium- or large-sized company. Such organizations may provide athletic programs, social and educational activities, recreation activities for company employees who have retired, lunch time or coffee-break programs at the workplace, or organized vacations. Many employee recreation programs have been initiated by management to improve workers' productivity and the image of the company. Employee recreation services are sometimes organized and financed either by workers or management, but in most cases these services represent the combined financial and organizational efforts of both.

There has been a rapid growth in private, nonprofit leisure services organizations. For instance, the number of national organizations dealing with hobbies and other avocations has increased 178 percent, while those concerned with sport have grown 110 percent during the last 20 years. Although membership in some organizations such as Boy Scouts has declined, there has been huge growth in activity interest groups such as Trout Unlimited and the National Campers and Hikers Association.

The financing of nonprofit agencies comes from a variety of sources. On average about one-half of funding comes from donations, another 27 percent from user fees, 15 percent from government sources, and the remainder from a variety of sources.

According to Szwak,[13] these nonprofit organizations complement government services. Regions of the United States with the greatest number of organizations generally have fewer government services. At the local level, nonprofit organizations, often utilizing large numbers of volunteers as well as trained professionals, are involved in issues as diverse as managing arts festivals to establishing local land trusts.

Nonprofits are likely to increase as a means of providing leisure services at the local, state, and national level. They have a number of advantages in undertaking their tasks:

> Nonprofit organizations may enjoy exemption from corporate income tax, receipt of tax-deductible contributions, exemption from local property and sales taxes, and special treatment in some government-regulated services such as reduced postal rates. The nonprofit sector as a whole receives $50 billion in federal deductible contributions.[14]

Government Leisure Service Organizations

Almost from the beginnings of industrialization in Britain, reform movements sprang up. Reformers often had a variety of motives for seeking to improve the lives of the working class poor. Not only did they want to provide wholesome leisure alternatives to the violence, sex, and drugs which cities provided via prize fighting between both humans and animals, prostitution, and public drinking houses but also they wanted those in the working class to become better workers. Peasants didn't generally make very good factory workers. Not only did they not like to work rigidly prescribed hours, they also were liable to quit if they thought their short-term economic needs—very simple needs—were met. Factory workers frequently did not show up for work on Mondays, taking off what was jokingly referred to as "Saint Monday," perhaps due to a bad hangover.

Activities sponsored and promoted by various organizations within the "rational recreation" movement, primarily for working-class males, included choral societies, brass bands, reading, organized sports, and other activities. For females, the "rational domesticity" movement, although organized and controlled by men, consisted of middle- and upper-class women visiting the homes of working-class women in order to help them become more competent homemakers.

The real success of rational recreationists in Britain, according to Clarke and Critcher,[15] was involving local government in the provision of leisure services and facilities. Land began to be purchased for local parks, and public libraries were established.

> There were still severe restrictions on the use of such facilities; games were banned from parks and libraries' stocks were censored. But the principle of the public provision of leisure out of the rates [local taxes] and with little or no direct charge had been established.[16]

At the same time local government was beginning to provide for public recreation, it also was beginning to control and regulate leisure behavior. The establishment of municipal police forces and the licensing of pubs and other commercial establishments used for leisure both tended to both shape and restrict the leisure behavior of the working class to the ideals of the upper classes. Much of the popular

Our city has the nicest parks. They're clean and safe, and they get used a lot. We aren't in an area with a lot of natural beauty, it wouldn't make anybody's list of top 100 places to live, and it's not very trendy—but we do have our parks. One has a lake with hundreds of waterbirds. There is a tulip festival at another one— that's just beautiful. We're on the prairie, and we love the huge trees with picnic tables under them. Lots of cities claim they are the "park city" but our parks are better, and no—I don't work for the park and recreation department!

activity which took place in the streets, from children's games to street vending, was cleared away to make streets places for travel only or for more respectable shopping. Thus, government came to be more highly influential in both providing and prohibiting certain forms of leisure. During the twentieth century, government became involved in the provision of leisure services at the municipal, state, and federal levels.

Leisure Policy

Changes in government policy suggests that leisure in North America will become more highly developed and reformulated in fundamental ways. Some of these ways would seem to include the following:

1. *Leisure policy will be guided more by responses to need for environmental, social, and economic reform than simply a demand-driven service of government.* An ideological agenda will be developed, and it will be reflected in policy stressing the immediacy need for pragmatic reform concerning the destruction of natural resources for short-term profit; a more frank condemnation of narcissism and open-ended economic greed; the relatedness of leisure experience to a variety of social and environmental problems; and the limitation of individual rights when the exercise of such rights flies in the face of communal well-being, the sustainability of our culture, and our economic solvency.

2. *Leisure services will experience big policy battles as a result of the quickly emerging two-tier society of "haves" and "have-nots."* Policy within given agencies will have to have multiple objectives. On the one hand, such policy will seek to serve the have-nots, for whom quality of experience, aesthetics, convenience, safety, and high levels of specialization in a leisure activity, among other details, are important. On the other hand, agencies will strive to participate in a reform agenda that is concerned with individual responsibility to maintain one's own health, the relatedness of work skills and leisure skills, the ecological necessity for preserving the environment in a more natural state, the creation of less consumptive models of living and leisure use, the re-education of people who are not equipped to function in a changed world, and those who have no homes or future. To a great extent, leisure policy will reflect a preven-

tion strategy in our two-tier society, taking a prevention approach to at-risk youth and low-income families.

3. *Leisure services will partner with other services of government.* Many government services will increasingly recognize a leisure component in what they seek to accomplish. Leisure services will be, to some extent, decentralized throughout government, and policy will be established or made more explicit with regard to leisure for myriad government agencies including those concerned with public transportation, natural resource management, public housing, education, economic develop-ment, crime, health, sewage, global warming, special popula-tions, planning, and other functions. The idea that leisure is the concern of only one agency of government will become obsolete.

4. *Leisure policy will increasingly be concerned with "prevention."* As a concept, the importance of "prevention" will grow dramati-cally as we realize that it makes economic, moral, and physio-logical sense to place more effort in preventing many situations we define as problems *before* they occur, rather than attempting to remedy them after they have become visible.

5. *At the macro level, leisure policy in North America will be increas-ingly cognizant of the fact that our culture's use of leisure is serving as a model for much of the rest of the world.* Television, film, mass tourism, computers, and the globalization of business allow less "developed" nations to see what North Americans do during leisure and to be attracted to our highly consumptive lifestyle with its appealing emphasis upon immediate gratifi-cation, individual fulfillment, and consumption of an ever-increasing array of goods and services. As we become aware of the environmental consequences of other nations attempting to follow our lead (e.g., North Americans consume 40 to 60 percent of the world's illegal drugs and consume a diet which the world's agricultural base could only provide for two billion people), our own leisure policies and other policies will increasingly reflect a movement toward a sustainable environ-ment and society, based upon the recognition that our self-interest dictates reshaping our use of leisure and our ways of life.

Organizational Strategies for Leisure Services

When I talk with top-level bureaucrats from European countries, they remain amazed that the United States has almost no tourism policy. Tourism is one of the biggest industries in the United States, but it just doesn't get recognized as such. I wonder why that is? I guess individual states just take it on themselves but, even at that level, many Governors don't recognize tourism as the second or third biggest economic engine in the state. Curious, these Americans...

The recreation, park, and leisure services organizations are in a process of constant change. While there is no prescription for the future, those who work for leisure service organizations increasingly understand that many of the same forces that are driving changes in the way business organizations function are also reshaping the way leisure services must function in all sectors: private-nonprofit, government, and businesses. These drivers, as identified by Preiss, Goldman and Nagel, include:

- the worldwide spread of education and technology, which increases global competition and accelerates the rate of marketplace change

- the continuing fragmentation of mass markets into niche markets

- more demanding customers with higher expectations

- the spread of collaborative production with suppliers and customers who comprise the value-adding chain

- the increasing impact of changing societal values, such as environmental considerations on job creation, or corporate decision making.[17]

The worldwide spread of education and technology, which increases global competition and accelerates the rate of marketplace change: Almost all customers or clients of leisure services have more options as to what service they will or will not use, and the rate at which these options increase is accelerating. A tourist who wants to plan a vacation may do so through a travel agent, a credit card company, a tourism promotion bureau, an airline, a guided tour company, a local university, and so forth. Tourists can make flight arrangements and book hotels via personal computer (e-mail, the Web); through a travel agent; at the local hotel; or through a national toll-free number. The opportunities when selecting an aerobic dance class or an attraction to visit are huge and diversified.

Changes also take place more rapidly in people's leisure interests and in the constraints they encounter in trying to fulfill them. While many forms of leisure activity have been highly associated with a stage of life, life stages themselves are more varied and subject to change than a decade ago.

The continuing fragmentation of mass markets into niche markets: Mass recreation activities, products and services are disappearing along with mass culture, and even when it looks as though a "mass" activity is occurring, such as an arts festival, closer examination reveals most festivals are multiple niche markets being served by the same festival. Likewise, the options for customers who want to learn about refinishing furniture, playing golf, or to enroll their children in a summer camp have grown exponentially. Part of this represents a kind of mass customization, in which mass leisure markets that grew out of the mass culture produced by the Baby Boomers, are coming apart into niche markets. Thus, in terms of children's summer camps, there are now camps to learn the French language, lose weight, or enhance self-esteem. There are camps for suburban girls to learn to play soccer, camps for children in wheelchairs, and camps for gay teenagers.

More demanding customers with higher expectations: Today, clients or customers of almost all leisure services have increasingly higher expectations about how clean a park should be the morning after a special event, how quickly they should be able to register for an evening class on vegetarian cooking, how many birds they will spot on a guided nature walk, or how few delays there will be in being assigned a campsite for their motor home in a state park. Such increasing demands, combined with more alternatives for participation, mean that successful leisure services must become more agile.

The spread of collaborative production with suppliers and customers who comprise the value-adding chain: The old way of thinking about clients or customers in many leisure services, as with most businesses, was to keep them satisfied but out of your hair in terms of organizational operation. Thus, there were surveys done about satisfaction with programs or facilities but little ongoing dialogue with customers or clients. There might be an advisory council, but it operated on the assumption that the organization already knew what its mission was and that such a mission wasn't subject to question—only to the logistics of how it was provided.

Today, to be successful,

> companies are responding to a new competitive environment by proactively linking dynamically and intimately with customers, not only to give those customers the solutions they ask for, but to work beyond that to find opportunities the customer had never imagined existed. In turn, what *interprises* do for their customers, they expect their suppliers to do for them.[18]

Doing this, of course, means that such a company or organization must establish relationships with clients that may take the organization in unknown directions—it becomes wrapped up in process, not product or service. For those in therapeutic recreation, this must surely mean that the lines between physical, occupational and recreation therapy blur, as do the lines between client and family and friends or between clinical and community practice. The therapeutic recreation employee is wrapped up in the process of assisting the client in adjusting to and minimizing the impact of a disability and does so in terms that have value to that client and/or his or her family.

For undergraduate university students majoring in recreation and park management or leisure studies, this means the "options" within the curriculum must be understood as arbitrary divisions which will frequently make little sense in isolation after they graduate. Thus, outdoor recreation will possibly lead them into tourism issues, which lead to environmental issues, which lead to health issues, which lead to poverty issues, which lead to education issues. Those who want to work with people with disabilities in leisure settings will see the basis of "disability" evolve throughout their lifetime.

Many urban recreation and park agencies are in the process, or will be, of forming coalitions with law enforcement and healthcare agencies in order to respond to the issues their clients identify as critical, such as stress reduction, lowering healthcare costs, fear of crime, and concern about the lives of at-risk youth. These coalitions are already forming.

The increasing impact of changing societal values, such as environmental considerations about job creation or corporate decision making:

These changes, which affect not only what people do during their leisure but, more importantly, the style in which they participate and the benefits sought, occur increasingly quickly. Thus, almost every zoo in the world is today considered obsolete by many visitors, who now believe animals should be viewed in their natural habitat, not cages. A more highly educated visitor recognizes the pacing back and forth of many animals in the zoo as neurotic behavior, similar to the pacing of prisoners in a cell.

Other examples include the fact that many elderly users of conservation areas value convenience and desire indoor restrooms and showers. Gay and lesbian organizations field softball teams in the city league, and teenage vegetarians ask if there is lard in the beans before they will order a burrito at the snack bar. Members of a country club or the state environmental protection agency may ask the manager about use of fertilizers and chemical sprays on the golf course. Environmental issues increasingly present a dilemma for park managing organizations, which must sometimes choose between admitting more paying customers to make up for financial squeezes or better protect the habitat of plants and animals that live in the park.

As leisure becomes a more central part of life, organizations providing leisure services are being challenged to meet heightened expectations of the public.

Study Questions

1. Within the last year, what leisure activities have you participated in that used the services of government recreation and park services?

2. If you could collect only one type of information from people in your home community to determine their need for public recreation, what kind of questions would you ask?

3. Why do you suppose the United States has not developed much national policy pertaining to tourism? Should such policy be developed? Why or why not?

4. Should a "private" golf club be able to restrict its membership based on any criteria it wishes to use?

5. In your leisure, which kind of organizations do you interact with most: commercial, private, or public? Why is that?

Exercise 14.1

Examine the leisure opportunities available to you on one specific day. Select a specific set of boundaries, such as a section of a large city, a small town, or a university campus, and choose a day one to two weeks from the time you start the assignment. Now, seek to identify as many available leisure opportunities as you can through newspapers, brochures, radio, television, magazines, signs, word of mouth, and otherwise. You might do this exercise in a group and divide responsibility for investigating leisure alternatives.

Before starting, determine what you would need to know about a potential leisure opportunity in order to make an "informed" choice about whether to participate. At the end of the exercise, survey members of your group to determine how many of the identified leisure opportunities they knew about.

Endnotes

1 Rybczynski, W. (1991). *Waiting for the weekend* (p. 121). New York, NY: Viking.

2 Holloway, C. (1983). *The business of tourism* (2nd ed.). Plymouth, UK: MacDonald and Evans

3 Butler, G. (1965). *Pioneers in public recreation* (p. 145). Minneapolis, MN: Burgess.

4 Zeldin, T. (1994). *An intimate history of humanity* (p. 437). New York, NY: Harper Perennial.

5 ibid.

6 Grodzins, P. (1966). Sharing of functions: The national recreation system. In *The American system: A new view of government in the United States* (pp. 125–152). Chicago, IL: Rand McNally and Company.

7 Mercer, D. (1973). The concept of recreation need. *Journal of Leisure Research, 5,* 35–50.

8 Adapted from Mercer (1973)

9 Metcalf, H. (1963). Class lecture. SUNY at Cortland, Cortland, NY.

10 Sessoms, H., Meyer, H., and Brightbill, C. (1975). *Leisure services: The organized recreation and park system* (pp. 13–15). Englewood Cliffs, NJ: Prentice Hall.

11 Munson, K. (1978). Commercial and member-owned recreation forms. In G. Godbey (Ed.), *Recreation, park, and leisure services: Foundations, organization, administration* (pp. 133–175). Philadelphia, PA: W. B. Saunders.

12 Farrell, P. (1978). Recreation youth-serving agencies. In G. Godbey, *Recreation, park, and leisure services: Foundations, organization, administration* (pp. 187–201). Philadelphia, PA: W. B. Saunders.

13 Szwak, L. (1989). The nonprofit sector as recreation suppliers. *Trends, 26*(2).

14 ibid., p. 36.

15 Clarke, J. and Critcher, C. (1985). *The devil makes work—Leisure in capitalist Britain.* Champaign, IL: University of Illinois Press.

16 ibid., p. 65

17 Preiss, K., Goldman, S., and Nagel, R. (1996). *Cooperate to compete—Building agile business relationships.* New York, NY: Van Nostrand Reinhold.

18 ibid., p. 8

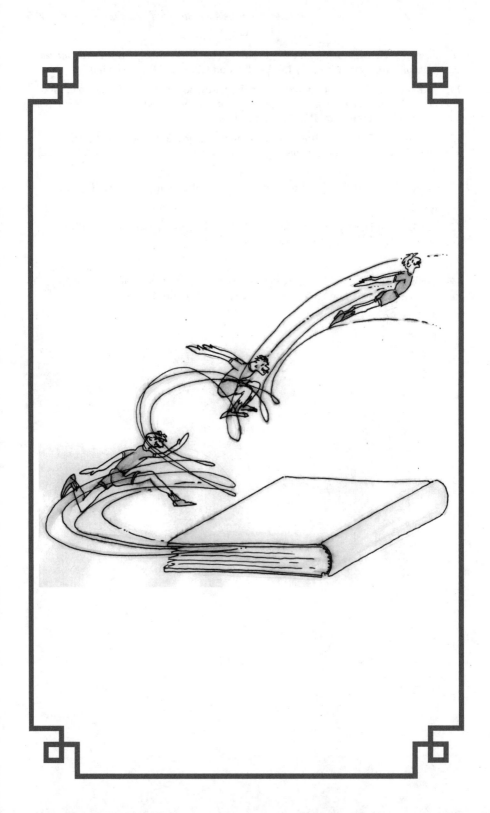

The Future of Leisure

If you are a college student reading this book in North America, you are likely to be young, white, Christian, and middle or upper middle class. (Some of you, of course, aren't any of these). Nonetheless, I want you to think about the people of the world for a minute and what their characteristics are. The vast majority are not white, and there is no country where the White population is replacing itself—All have birth rates below 2.1. Even in the United States, which has a total fertility rate of 2.1, enough to replace the population, Whites have a lower birth rate—1.8. Think about the "ethnic minorities" in your life. Globally speaking, you may be one of them!

Asia has about 60 percent of all the world's people. The United States has less than five percent. Americans are a distinct minority in the world! Your life and your leisure will increasingly be shaped by the other 95 percent of the people in the world. In fact, a book called *A Year Without "Made in China"*[1] has been published about the difficulties of living in the United States for one year without buying anything from China!

Whether or not you are white, you are likely young, yet the world is aging at an amazing rate. The majority of people you will be around for much of your life are likely to be older. Then, there is religion. While Christianity is the religion followed by more people in the world than any other, Islam is growing rapidly. The new converts to Christianity are often fundamentalists, taking a literal interpretation of the Bible.

The vast majority of the people in the world are also not as wealthy as you—or your parents. In effect, you are a minority within a minority within a minority in the world right now and will be even more so in the future. In the past, this might not have mattered so much, but it does now. Your understanding of the future needs to start from this perspective.

In a society as complex as ours, the forces that will have an impact on our leisure are too numerous to identify, and they are changing at a rate that is unprecedented in human history. The "information highway" is transforming not only our use of television, our most time-consuming form of leisure, but also reshaping our basic notions of education and work. It may change our everyday life in many ways—from reading a newspaper (which may exist only on a screen) to "going to" the bank (which comes to you) to making choices about a vacation—since you will have far greater amounts of information about your options.

Our notion of "progress" itself is in a state of evolution. Progress will have less to do with controlling nature for profit and more to do with increasing our quality of life and changing human beings in ways that make it more likely we will survive and lead healthy lives. While humans have devoted centuries to changing the world, the next century will have to be devoted more to changing ourselves.

While no one can identify what changes will shape our world in the next few decades, several trends that will likely shape our leisure behavior in the early twenty-first century and beyond can be identified.

Transforming Human Beings

> People are becoming the subjects rather than the instruments of change. The coming round of progress will alter what people are rather than just what they do or how they live. This raises issues of an altogether different order, and efforts to force them into the old mold offer only confusion.[2]

People may be reshaped in several fundamental ways. Among the most important are genetic selection, mental enhancement and longer life. In terms of living longer, while there are a number of explanations of why we age, there are several methods of increasing the life span of humans which show promise. One of these is calorie restriction. While widespread experimentation with humans remains to be done, in laboratory experiments, animals who are fed less than others show fewer signs of aging and live longer. This is not malnutrition, which shortens life, but merely smaller portions of food with higher nutrition levels.

Another promising avenue of inquiry is *genetic selection*, in which scientists may use their findings about the genetic make-up of strains of animals who live longer, as a way of intervening with humans through drug therapies or gene implantation to extend life. Other genetic approaches, based upon our increased understanding of the genetic make-up of humans, also show great promise in lengthening life. Slowing the aging process may stretch the healthy years of young adulthood, middle age, and early old age. This may actually reduce healthcare costs.

This change has numerous implications for leisure. People will have more years of participation in various forms of leisure expression, perhaps reaching higher levels of specialization in chosen activities. Imagine having eighty years to develop your piano playing skills or your understanding of the Civil War. Other people may go through even more prolonged "menus" of leisure expression, trying out various styles of living, and then moving to yet another way of exercising freedom.

It is also likely that crime will decline, making urban areas safer for many forms of leisure expression. Most crime is committed by males between the ages of fifteen and twenty-five. As such individuals constitute a smaller and smaller percentage of the overall population, crime may decrease.

Mental enhancement will also likely reshape all aspects of life, including our use of leisure. Since it may be that "heredity accounts for 50 to 70 percent of measured differences in intelligence,"[3] the fact that we are going to be provided with a "map" of the building blocks of human beings means intelligence may be enhanced through genetic manipulation. Thanks to the Human Genome Project, which has as its objective to provide a complete understanding of the sequence of nucleotides contained in human chromosomes, humans will be in a position to literally design newborn humans. Parents may be able to select a complete set of genes for their child from a library or other source, perhaps using their own DNA as a framework.

While there are bound to be huge debates over this process, the advantages to parents will likely be so great that it will be hard to resist. Also, as some parents decide to do it, not giving your own child the advantage of enhanced genetic endowment would put them at a lifelong disadvantage.

Designing offspring could shape leisure in a variety of ways. Excellence in music, athletics, the arts and other forms of leisure expression will become commonplace. The use of leisure for educational purposes may increase, while some forms of leisure associated with those of low intelligence, such as professional wrestling, will likely decline in popularity. The content of television will be altered to reflect the desires of a more intelligent viewing audience, and other forms of mass communication will have to readjust. Leisure may even move closer to the ideals of the ancient Athenians.

> When every other child on the gymnastics team was given a new form of steroids, which the experts claim is safe, my kids couldn't compete. The other kids were stronger and faster. So we had a choice. My wife and I talked about it many times but, finally, I gave them the steroids, which you don't even need a prescription for now. They are much better athletes now—very competitive. Where does this all end?

It may be argued that much of the previous could happen, but won't. Currently, much of the population of the modern world are eating diets with larger portions, high-fat, high-salt, and high-sugar. This may start to decrease life expectancies and has already led to an epidemic of diabetes and other illnesses. Global warming and climate change may increase air-borne and water-borne diseases. The growing population of the world and increased material standards of living may pollute, deplete and diminish our natural resources in catastrophic ways. The haves and have-nots of the world may be locked in perpetual struggle. Only the future will tell.

A Postcapitalist Society in Which Knowledge Is the Primary Resource

As the economic basis of the world has moved from hunting-and-gathering to agriculture to mercantilism to industry to a service economy and eventually to an information-based economy, knowledge has become the central resource. To obtain the advances in productivity that the postcapitalist society will need, all organizations will have to embrace both teaching and learning. Knowledge will have to be made more productive, and organizations will have to cope with change by serving more as destabilizing agents instead of their traditional role of stabilizing. What a person needs to know will change every four or five years, making learning a way of life rather than a period of life.

Such a situation will likely mean that our leisure behavior will become more diverse and that the old model of work as forced labor and leisure as a period of recovery from such oppressive activity will make no sense for any but those who remain ignorant. The greatest form of oppression will be to intentionally keep others ignorant. (Perhaps to some extent it has always been this way.) As computers become more accessible and powerful, the exclusivity of knowledge will decline. It will be easier and easier to access knowledge—wisdom will consist more and more of deciding what to access and how to interpret it.

> The way things are going, for most workers you can tell how successful they are by how much their work is like their leisure. The most successful ones have jobs that are basically doing the same things as they would do for free. For the unsuccessful ones, work is the opposite of their leisure. I guess this is an old story.

Globalization of Commerce

Work, trade and the flow of capital are now in the process of becoming globalized. This process shapes the lives of billions of people.

Globalization of commerce has brought with it increasingly differentiated conditions both among countries and within countries. It is also an engine that drives immigration at a startling rate. The top fifth of the world's people now have 86 percent of the gross domestic product and the bottom fifth about one percent.[4] As northern nations have increasingly pressured southern nations to open their economies to foreign trade and investment, about 20 percent of southern residents have increased their wealth; but 80 percent have become poorer.[5] Overall, southern nations have become poorer.

That gives southern nations less and less incentive to manage legal and illegal immigration. The north's emphasis on competitiveness drives southern nations to cut health, education and social budgets, hampering development and further fueling legitimate and unsanctioned emigration. It is a vicious cycle.[6]

This process also makes it certain that "terrorism" and low-intensity wars will become the ways of fighting for the "have-nots" against the "haves." The line between crime and war is disappearing and, as that happens, low-intensity conflicts of attrition will largely replace wars fought from traditional strategies. In 1991, military expert Martin Van Crevald prophetically predicted: "The spread of sporadic small-scale war will cause regular armed forces themselves to change form, shrink in size, and wither away. As they do, much of the day-to-day burden of defending society against the threat of low-intensity conflict will be transferred to the booming security business...."[7] Tragically, he was right. Terrorism as a long-term condition of life will make leisure and especially tourism behavior more deliberate and more subject to sudden change. It may also mean that assurances of safety, predictability and isolation from the increasing conflict between the haves and have-nots will be more appealing.

While globalization will bring sameness to some parts of life—for example, in "McDonaldization,"—in many other ways it will further customize life. While federal governments may seek to "harmonize" currencies, policies, and procedures, leisure behavior becomes more diverse. Even the celebration of holidays becomes customized. As

> In Mexico City, I couldn't get a job at our minimum wage, which is about five dollars a day. The job I did have was one where I had to pay a guy off to keep the job. It wasn't enough to live on.
> I decided to try and cross the border. My wife didn't want me to go but there are three children—no money. So I went.
> Hired a coyote with the only savings of my life. We crossed the border inside a big truck. It was hot as hell and we were dumped at the side of the road near San Diego like trash. I had a contact; Juan let me stay with him and his family for a few weeks. I found out where to go in the morning to get farm work. Now I have a landscaping job. I'm sending money back home. My free time is pretty much just resting or watching a little TV.
> There is a park near the room I rent with eight other guys, and it's pretty safe. I've gone there a few times and watched American kids playing on the playground. My kids would like to play on that playground. One day they will....

political or religious-based holidays become factionalized, Ramadan, Cinco de Mayo or "Chinese" New Year celebrations may occur in San Diego, London, or Jakarta.

The "War" Over Human Consciousness Will Heighten

I was in Bangalore, India, in a housing development. Except for a few minor differences, the houses looked a lot like the ones in Tampa, Florida. There were cars whizzing past—garages in front of the houses, and I felt like I was just down the block from where I live—it was strange—I didn't like it at all. Are we all going to become the same? I guess if we do, there won't be any need for tourism.

How all the previous trends unfold is dependent upon the coming war over human consciousness. It may be argued that the problems of the world are largely due to faulty human perception. Our consciousness, in other words, is false. In effect, as Rifkin, Capra and others have argued, two modes of human consciousness exist. One mode of consciousness perceives reality as separate objects existing in three-dimensional space. Time, in this conception, exists in a straight line. Humans are thought to be logical and can develop techniques to meet their own needs. People who possess such a mode of consciousness, according to Grof: "...typically lead ego-centered, competitive, goal-oriented lives."[8]

They tend to be unable to derive satisfaction from ordinary activities in everyday life and become alienated from their inner world. For people whose existence is dominated by this mode of experience, no level of wealth, power or fame will bring satisfaction. They become infused with a sense of meaninglessness, futility, and even absurdity that no amount of external success can dispel.

A second way of viewing the world may be called, variously, spiritual, holistic, or transpersonal. According to such perceptual bases, reality must be viewed as a series of relationships among all things which are part of some universal consciousness. Humans are part of this universal system, and neither humans nor the larger system of which they are a part are completely knowable through science.

This fundamental division in perception increasingly shapes different visions of the world and which future is desired. Architects may design buildings they view as fortresses or as structures which blend harmoniously with nature. Psychiatrists may view someone with mental illness as an individual who has gone "crazy," or as an organism making an appropriate response in a crazy situation or, indeed, a crazy world. People working in agriculture may view nature as simply a resource to be exploited with chemicals, machines, and techniques in a battle for more food or as a complex series of interrelationships which must be minimally changed to grow food.

Such a division has even brought about increasingly different conceptualizations of time. As Rifkin pointed out, these two fundamentally different concepts of time lead to different political viewpoints and prescriptions concerning the future:

> The new time spectrum runs from empathetic rhythms on one side to power rhythms on the other. Those who align themselves with the empathetic time dynamic are calling for "resacralization" of life at every level of existence from microbe to man. Those aligning themselves with the power time dynamic are calling for a more efficient simulated environment to secure the well-being of society. The rhythm of the first constituency is slow-paced, rhapsodic, spontaneous, vulnerable, and participatory. Emphasis is upon reestablishing a temporal communication with the natural biological and physical rhythms and of coexisting in harmony with the cycles, seasons and periodicities of the larger earth organism. The rhythms of the other side are accelerated, predictable and expedient. Emphasis is upon subsuming the natural biological and physical rhythms and creating an artificially controlled environment that can assure an ever-increasing growth curve for present and future generations.[9]

To a great extent, the future of the world and the future use of leisure will depend upon which of these ways of thinking takes precedence. The qualities and use of leisure in an environment which is increasingly artificially controlled will be fundamentally different from those which we would experience in an environment closer to nature. Leisure behavior would be much less a commodity to be sold in a no-growth economy than in an economy which tries to get eternally bigger.

In spite of the war over human consciousness, several broad trends will likely come about with regard to leisure in the short-term future.

The Clash of Civilizations and A New World Order

> Right now, I can't do anything without thinking about whether or not it will go on my résumé. This is the period of my life when doing things and getting credit for them is really important. I guess it's just a phase but—I really am all wrapped up in it. I like being noticed. This may not change for a long, long time. Just call me a walking résumé.

Globalization takes place in a post-cold war era where "Power is shifting from the long predominant West to non-Western civilizations."[10] Global politics have become multipolar and multicivilizational. Today, the most important countries in the world come from vastly different civilizations and "modernization" of such countries does not mean that they will "Westernize." Although, during the last 400 years, relations among civilizations "consisted of the subordination of other societies to Western civilization,"[11] this pattern has been broken:

> The West won the world not by the superiority of its ideas or values or religion (to which few members of other civilizations are converted), but rather by its superiority in applying organized violence. Westerners often forget this fact; non-Westerners do not.[12]

While it is often assumed that English has become the international unifying language, the percentage of the world's people who speak English is declining, constituting about 7.6 percent of the world's population. Indeed, all Western languages in combination are spoken by about only one out of five people in the world.

In terms of religion, Christianity accounts for slightly less than 30 percent of the world's people. Islam, which accounts for a bit less than 20 percent of the world's population, will continue to increase in numbers since "...Christianity spreads primarily by conversion, Islam by conversion and reproduction."[13] How various religions react to globalization will be diverse and unpredictable. Additionally, the share of the world's population under the political control of various civilizations will shift so that the long dominant "West" will account for only about 10 percent of the world's citizens (see Table 15.1).

Table 15.1 Shares of world population under the political control of civilizations, 1900 and 2025[14]

	Western	African	Sinic	Hindu	Islamic	Japanese	Latin	Orthodox	Other
1900	44.3	0.4	19.3	0.3	4.2	3.5	3.2	8.5	16.3
2025	10.1	14.4	21.0	16.9	19.2	1.5	9.2	4.9	2.8

All these trends mean that the power to shape leisure, popular culture, sport, tourism, hobbies, crafts, mass media, outdoor recreation, and a variety of other behavioral forms related to leisure will be diversified. While global communication networks will show models of leisure from every country, culture, and civilization, it will be increasingly difficult to judge which ideas will succeed.

> I live in Hangzhou, China—one of the most beautiful cities in my country. From the time I was young, my parents taught me that education was everything—Hard work, more hard work and more hard work. There is a joke in China that a child is told by her violin teacher that she is a one in a million violinist. Her mother says: "Yes, so that means there are 1,300 other violinists who are just as good." Competition is out of control, but that's the way it is. Perhaps in the United States, one can afford not to work so hard—perhaps.

In spite of the increased influence of Islam, many historians argue "it's Christianity that will leave the deepest mark on the twenty-first century."[15] The new Christianity, however, will move "...toward the ancient worldview expressed in the New Testament—a vision of Jesus as the embodiment of divine power, who overcomes the evil forces that inflict calamity and sickness upon the human race."[16] The vast majority of Christians today do not reside in Europe or North America. There are an estimated 480 million in Latin America, 360 million in Africa, and 313 million in Asia compared with only 260 million in North America. While it is estimated that the population of the world's Christians will grow to 2.6 billion, which would make it by far the world's largest religion, half of all Christians will be African and Latin American, and another 17 percent will be Asian.

These changes are likely to make Christianity, particularly Roman Catholicism, more conservative, puritanical, authoritarian, and more obedient to authority. A literal interpretation of the Bible will likely become more common.[17] All this will mean that the more liberal brand of Christianity found in much of North America and Europe will increasingly be in conflict with the more conservative Christianity rising in most of the world.

All the changes above imply that people residing in the same country will view leisure activity quite differently in moral terms. Watching MTV, for instance, might be banned by followers of Islam and/or by a more conservative Christian church. Fashion, manners, use of alcohol, sexual matters, gambling, and other aspects of leisure style and activity will be in dispute. The Western influence on leisure activity may be subject to greater challenge. Additionally, women's role in many forms of leisure expression may be challenged anew.

> It isn't right that women have to cover their bodies and faces. Why is it that wherever you get fundamentalists, women have fewer rights? Sorry, I'm not buying it. If the men had to wear that stuff, sweating and barely able to walk, they would go crazy. So there's a problem here. In the United States, people should be free to wear what they want, and I don't think that's what those women want to wear—even if they say they do. They can't fully participate in American life wearing that stuff. In those outfits, you can't even play soccer.

A Decline of Work Hours—The Search for Meaning Through Leisure

Not only has work declined as a portion of the total hours of one's life devoted to work, but also it would appear that such a decline may continue:

> The combination of reduced lifetime working hours and increased life expectancy has caused a huge shift in life experience. While in 1856 half of the disposable life-hours of workers were spent working, the portion has fallen to less than one-fifth today. If the trend continues, soon after the year 2000 half of the years of the average worker will occur before or after work. Even in the working half of an individual's

life, formal work will account for a decreasing fraction of time, one third or less, and should leave more time, for leisure and other activities such as caring for a child (or two) and the home. If the long-term trends continue at their historic rates, the workweek might average 27 hours by the year 2050.[18]

This process of change is of central importance, since formalized work has been the central economic and social fact of industrialized countries. It has been the primary method by which people are socially integrated[19] and has also shaped the use and meaning of free time left over after work.

It seems likely that during the next decade our uses of leisure will be less a matter of diversion or refreshment after work and more a matter of pursuing interests which are central to our lives. Accompanying this trend will be the increasing inability to determine whether or not a person is at work or at leisure merely by knowing the activity in which he or she is participating. Leisure will be different from work because of the individual's attitude toward the activity or the activity's personal meaning to the individual. Sociologists Cheek and Burch have argued already that the difference between work and leisure is not a conceptual one. They stated that:

> All persons clearly know when they are working and when they are off duty. Unlike social life with intimates—kin, friends, peers—or the large social spheres concerned with sustaining myth—such as religion, sports, and politics—work exhibits a fundamentally different pattern of organization. In work, participation is coerced by necessity, only a narrow segment of one's person is required, the selection of co-workers is made by necessity rather than choice, and the timing and sequence of action is usually external to the worker; that is, set by seasons, tools, machines, materials, or work organization—and finally, there is usually a tangible outcome. In short, the significant difference between work and nonwork is not a conceptual one or one that inheres in a specific activity or specific person; rather, the significant difference is in the kinds of social organization that are involved.[20]

Thus, we cannot determine whether Activity A is work or leisure without understanding something about its social organization. While many have speculated that the line between work and leisure is likely to disappear in the near future, it seems probable that leisure will still be distinguishable from work according to how it is organized and with whom it is undertaken. While we will continue to distinguish between work and leisure, the primacy of work may be balanced.

Many futurists believe the next economy will be one that needs very few people to do the "production." Farming, which took one-half the population or more in some economies, now takes less than two percent of all workers. It may be that organic methods of farming will increase the number of people required, but such an increase will still be a much smaller number than what it used to take. The manufacturing of material goods is similarly shrinking in its demands so that there will soon be only 10 percent of the workforce in such endeavors. The same phenomenon may be happening in terms of how many workers will be needed for an information economy, with the advent of hugely increased computation capacity, the progress in developing artificial intelligence, and the increased ability to communicate. Many workers who are being replaced today are not being replaced by other workers, but rather by a combination of robots and computers. While we will doubtlessly continue to "create" work in all of these spheres, the diminishing need for workers in every sector of the economy must surely cause us to ask questions about the necessity of lives built around occupation. To some extent, our first answer to such questions has been to lengthen the segment of life after retirement and to delay entry into the labor force through increased enrollment in colleges and universities. (Granted, going to college for many represents a leisure subculture as much as preparation for work!) However, it is worth noting that these responses will surely be unsatisfactory in the very near future. The distribution of nonworking time must range more broadly over the life span, as must education and work. The portion of life spent at paid work is likely to decrease even further, while the amount of time spent learning will increase. There is, then, the potential for life to be centered around leisure.

The Mass Customization of Life

In the 21st century, technological change is being organized around biological models and biology operates on the principle that difference is better.[21] Today we are beginning what Toffler has called "the Third Wave." In first-wave civilizations, which were basically agricultural, work was not highly interdependent. In second-wave cultures, the synchronization of man's machine led to standardization and centralization. Today, in the emerging third-wave civilization, there is a marked movement toward decentralization and individualization, which is evident in many spheres of life. We are witnessing the mass customization of life.[22]

> The revolution in how work is done is producing a revolution in what work provides: mass customized services based on greatly expanded information about the client or customer. Medicine, for instance, is beginning to be custom made, taking the patient's medical history and physical condition into account.[23]

Some organizations are beginning to prepare for this mass customization. Other organizations and institutions, such as public schools, will follow. Not only will each public school customize pace, duration and sequence of learning but each student will attend and learn in unique time patterns, based on his or her needs and those of his or her parent or parents. As public schools customize their schedules on an individual basis, the leisure and play of children and youth will follow more diverse patterns, often customized at the household level.

While every living thing has its own unique sense of time, the ideal of the industrial society was to treat people *equally* and regiment them to common time patterns. The ideal will now become be to treat people *appropriately*—and that means to have sufficient information about them to recognize their unique needs with regard to time.[24] Daily life will be reorganized with time patterns and schedules that vary for every single person. Treating people equally makes no sense in a decentralized society since we are not interchangeable parts. Treating people appropriately will make more sense, especially as we become even more diverse. The provision of leisure and tourism will be reshaped by this fundamental shift in human relations.

> I've always believed in treating everyone equally. It doesn't matter to me if they're black, brown, yellow or white—I don't even notice. Doesn't matter to me if you're rich or poor, male or female, Republican or Democrat, able-bodied or handicapped—I treat everyone the same—everyone. So don't blame me. I don't even notice anything about anybody.

Greater Use of Leisure for Educational and Religious Purposes

As the nations of the world become more and more interdependent, it will be more and more difficult for anyone to exist independently of others. Your life, in other words, will increasingly be interrelated to the lives of others living in Brazil, China, or France. What happens in Pakistan or Haiti will affect your life in increasingly direct terms. As we become more interdependent, it will be more important that no segment of the world's population remains ignorant. As our power to do harm to each other increases, the power of those with the lowest education levels to do harm to those with higher levels will increase. As much of American literature since Melville and Hawthorne has warned us, as our knowledge increases, our morality must increase correspondingly if we are to survive. In the Western world, and increasingly in the Eastern, we have come to believe that the best chance of improving our morality is more education.

If the previous assumptions are true, leisure may be affected in two ways. First, our use of leisure for educational purposes will become more important. "Continuing education" using both formal and informal methods will become a more important use of our nonwork time. Such education is likely to occur through various media, including television, screen and print, travel and living in other countries, formal instruction, lectures, exhibits, and small group discussions.

Leisure may also be restricted due to our increased power over each other. The major unanswered question of the Western world is whether our collective survival is imperiled if individuals are allowed to be free to pursue their own interests during leisure. It appears that the liberal democratic idea of individual rights being more important than group rights can be maintained only if individuals exhibit more concern for others. When we act, as Jean Paul Sartre said, we must act for all mankind. Our leisure activity will increasingly have to show our ecological understanding. It will, for instance, be less and less feasible to destroy the desert habitat by riding motorcycles and dune buggies over it for the sake of freedom and pleasure. It will be less and less defensible to consume vast quantities of the world's nonrenewable resources during leisure. Education must help show us why.

It is difficult to delineate what the impact of an aging society will be on leisure behavior, since those who are growing old now are likely to be different from those who are already old. The life experiences of those old now are different from those who will be old in coming decades. Since these generational effects mean that old people are not the same now as those in the future, caution must be exercised in trying to estimate how an older population will change recreation and leisure. Today's young adults, for instance, have been socialized into a number of sports which the older generation have not; they also have not lived through the Depression; they are less likely than their predecessors to think that pleasure-seeking is sinful; and they are better educated and in better health.

While we can't assume that tomorrow's older citizens will be the same as today's, perhaps the biggest predictable impact will be the need to "retro-fit" our recreation and leisure resources for an aging population. Public recreation and park agencies cater disproportionately to the adolescent. Many parks have specialized play equipment for the young but not for the old. In many, often unnoticed ways, our recreation and leisure resources are geared to the young. As our population grows older, it is likely that more leisure activities will be undertaken for social rather than achievement reasons, and for expressive rather than instrumental reasons.

Greater Recognition of Leisure's Relation to Health

An older society with higher levels of formal education, and a society increasingly aware of fundamental environmental problems and runaway health costs will be more health conscious in the future. Leisure will be an increasingly important arena in which to positively influence health. Greater emphasis will be placed upon educating for specific leisure skills in the public schools, at the worksite, and within organizations that assist individuals with special needs. The government is more likely to use education rather than criminal prosecution as a means of changing leisure habits relating to drugs.

Organizations involved with recreation, park, and leisure services are also more likely to think of provision of such services in broader terms. Creating a leisurely environment will involve a number of issues, such as noise abatement, in the production of a more tranquil experience. Tranquility will be a higher priority in society. Indeed, the extraordinary health benefits of tranquility are more likely to be recognized. Leisure will be valued as an antidote to stress and, as stress is identified as the culprit in a wide variety of diseases, leisure will increasingly be an ideal.

Corporate Power

As the economy of all countries becomes increasingly internationalized, large corporations have become the most powerful organizational entities, with little allegiance to the country within which they operate. While corporations vary in their environmental sensitivity, they are ultimately driven by the profit motive and must operate in ways which are profitable. In numerous cases, the inability of corporations to restrain themselves has contributed to a world of haves and have-nots. This world is one in which some people make athletic shoes in one country for four dollars a day which are sold in another country for two hundred dollars a pair. A world in which a mining company in the United States can mine gold using techniques which produce one ton of slag for the mining of enough gold for only one wedding band.

Of the largest ten organizational budgets in the world, four are not national governments but corporations. Countries and states compete for corporate relocations, often trashing environmental laws in the process. In numerous modern nations, corporations have come to be the dominant political power. In South Korea, Japan, Taiwan and other Asian perimeter countries, corporations directly shape both the domestic and foreign policies of government.

In many developing nations, corporations determine who will govern and take steps to kill off those they oppose. They also pollute the environment to a remarkable degree. Shell Oil, for instance, has caused 784 separate oil spills in Nigeria, admits to 3,000 polluted sites, has flared off 1.1 billion cubic feet of natural gas, caused acid rain about 10 percent of the days of the year and generally devastated the environment. They have also set up a system described by the World Council of Churches as one in which Shell executives become Nigerian political officials and Nigerian political officials become Shell executives. In countless ways, corporations exploit economically weak nations for short-term profit.[25]

In the United States, "Urged on by a coalition of big industries, one state after another is adopting legislation to protect companies from disclosure or punishment when they discover environmental offenses at their own plants."[26] Corporations are being given exemption from environmental laws if they self-report such offenses. Documents reporting such self-reporting are kept secret by law and cannot be divulged to the public or used in any legal proceedings.

In both developed and developing nations, corporations are part of a "permanent government" that rules regardless of who is elected to political office. As the Editor of *Harper's*, Lewis Lapham, stated:

> The permanent government, a secular oligarchy... comprises the Fortune 500 companies and their attendant lobbyists, the big media and entertainment syndicates, the civil and military services, the larger research universities and law firms.... Obedient to the rule of men, not laws, the permanent government oversees the production of wealth, builds cities, manufactures goods, raises capital, fixes prices, shapes the landscape, and reserves the right to assume debt, poison rivers, cheat the customers, receive the gifts of federal subsidy, and speak to the American people in the language of low motive and base emotion.[27]

Thus, many of the assumptions made about democracy—that people vote in or vote out those who will carry out the policies they favor—simply aren't true.

Certainly, however, some corporations do much good. Many of the advances in science have been due to corporate research and development, and many of the comforts of life, improved medicines, advances in communication and other positive changes have come from corporate involvement. More people visit Disneyland than England each year and they seem free to choose where they go on vacation. If power corrupts, however, then increased corporate power is an increasing problem in the modern world, particularly to the extent that such corporations have no goal or vision other than short-term financial profit by any means.

In terms of leisure, corporations shape the majority of hours of free time for those in modern nations. As mentioned previously, in the United States, television exists only because it is sponsored by corporations seeking to sell their goods and services. (There is a public television network, but it receives less than 10 percent of the viewing audience). Thus the content of television is shaped to reach a maximum audience and generally presents programming which appeals to the lowest common denominator.

The vast majority of tourism in the world is managed and controlled by large corporations — tourists fly to a destination on an airline owned by a large corporation, stay in a hotel owned by a large corporation, take photographs with a camera and have film developed by large corporations, eat in "chain" restaurants owned by large corporations, drink beer brewed by large corporations, and perhaps play golf on a course owned by a large corporation. It may be argued that "marketing" techniques represent the ultimate in democracy, simply finding out what people value, believe, and want and then supplying it to them. Such claims, however, ignore the fact that most Americans have spent thousands of hours watching and reading commercials for the products and services supplied by corporations. Marketing might actually work well as a device for ensuring democracy if advertising did not exist and if people had sufficient education and exposure to various alternative ways of life to make intelligent choices.

Commercial forms of recreation may be satisfying for some people, but they are ultimately supplied to make money for stockholders of a company rather than improve human beings or contribute to their well-being. It might also be said, of course, that government-sponsored recreation is often used as a means of social control, or to keep elected officials in office, or to divert attention from many societal problems with which government has failed to deal.

Minimizing corporate control of much of the modern world would involve limiting corporations by law in ways in which they often formerly were. Such limitations would include: requiring corporations to have a specific purpose, with penalties or removal of corporate privileges if that purpose were not fulfilled or exceeded; requiring a percentage of stockholders to live in the state in which the corporation is licensed; prohibiting corporations from owning stock in other corporations; issuing corporation charters for a fixed period of time; prohibiting all political donations and imposing strict liability on corporate officers and stockholders. Until such steps are taken, however, corporations will continue to be a central component of the permanent government.

Fortunately, some corporations are beginning to believe that their own well-being is dependent upon the well-being of the environment. Large corporations that sell insurance have become concerned about global warming—perhaps because such warming is probably to blame for the increases in violent weather that is raising insurance claims at an alarming rate. There is profit in environmentally sensitive corporate behavior, such as recycling, lightweighting of products, producing 100% recyclable products from recycled material, and other environmentally friendly actions.

In spite of this, the enormous power of corporations to control mass media, constantly advertise and engage in massive public relations efforts to promote their services and products, influence legislation in their favor, and get rid of small competitors remains a problem of growing proportions.

Increased Government Involvement in Leisure but with New Motives and Organizational Forms

In the future, the government at all levels is likely to become more involved in a variety of concerns related to leisure. In part, government will become increasingly involved in leisure for economic reasons. As travel and tourism increase in economic importance, as the economic fate of cities becomes more directly tied to leisure behavior, as the productivity of those with disabilities is increasingly understood to be related to their ability to use leisure in satisfying ways, as successful economic development of communities becomes more and more dependent upon the ability to provide a satisfying leisure environment for workers, government will reinvolve itself for economic reasons rather than reasons of ideology. Both the political right and the political left are likely to see leisure as an important instrument in the economic well-being of the country.

While the government is likely to be more involved in recreation and leisure, the motives which produce such involvement are likely to be different, as are the methods of organization used. Recreation, park and leisure services may pay less attention to "marketing" approaches to services and more to "benefits-based" management through which various recreation areas and facilities are managed to produce benefits specified in advance, such as stress reduction or decrease in the risk of cardiovascular disease. Such services will be judged based on the extent to which these benefits are realized. Government is also likely to operate within new configurations, such as nonprofit corporations, joint ventures with the market sector and "contracting out" some services to other organizations with specialized expertise.

The Feminization of Leisure

Leisure in the near future is likely to be reshaped by women. Younger women are gaining economic parity and a consciousness of how they, and men, might change to benefit society. Women will reshape leisure in the future, not by simply demanding what men have and do, but by developing new visions of what uses can be made of leisure—of what constitutes the ideal. This change is unlikely to be sudden; it may even go largely unnoticed. Slowly, women are being integrated into the world of leisure once reserved for men. More slowly, women will play a coequal role in defining what constitutes the successful use of leisure. As this happens, the commercial sector will begin to market leisure products and services to women more directly. The public sector is increasingly reshaping recreation and park services to the needs and desires of women.

In many nations identified as "developing," women are severely restricted in their ability to travel, to dress as they wish, and to pursue sports. In general, they have little access to leisure. Emerging globalization may play a role in changing this, as may the great amount of migration in the world.

A Rapidly Aging World

The biggest demographic trend going on in almost every country in the world is the aging of the population. As many countries reach populations with 20 to 25 percent of their population ages 65 and over, every aspect of daily life will be changed. While "elderly" people are becoming more diverse, there are central tendencies associated with old age will require increased attention.

Older people, on average, have higher levels of fear of crime, are less tolerant of weather extremes or loud noise, are generally more deliberate in their behavior, commit far fewer crimes, drive and move more slowly, watch more television, exhibit great interest in plant and animal life and in history, are less tolerant of litter, and pay more attention to diet, to name a few. Such changes will reshape leisure in most countries of the world. Use of leisure will also become a huge issue in keeping older adults physically and mentally able to continue living in their own homes.

Thus, although the world may become slower paced overall, there should be less crime, more concern for plants and animals, less participation in sport, more interest in history and more modification of leisure activities to make them more accessible to a vastly older population.

Revolutionary Changes in Environment

Perhaps *the most important revolution* taking place is the transformation of the environment of the planet in ways that have no historical precedent. Such change includes the mass extinction of animal life and plant life at a rate and magnitude never before known in human history. Additionally, we have driven atmospheric carbon dioxide to the highest levels in at least two hundred thousand years, unbalanced the nitrogen cycle, and contributed to a global warming that will ultimately be bad news everywhere.[28]

A combination of exponentially rising consumption and increasing population mean that: "In short, earth has lost its ability to regenerate—unless global consumption is reduced, or global production is increased, or both."[29] Any birth rate above 2.1 means that eventually the weight of humans will exceed the weight of the planet. It is therefore the developing nations who will, in many senses, control the world's future. Since poverty and the second-class status of women are largely responsible for the plague of human population growth, the chances for human survival in most nations, even in the short run, are linked to the elimination of poverty and changes in the rights, education and life chances of women.

Environmentally, we are entering an unprecedented era. In the past twelve years, our federal government has spent $39 billion for disaster relief—up five times over the previous twelve years.[30] Although the causes remain disputed, the fact is that sea level rise in the 20th century was double the rate of the nineteenth century. While the rising water levels will have different effects on the coastlines and shorelines of the world, much of the shoreline of the world will be changed, sweeping many island nations under water in the process. Bangladesh, for example, may suffer a catastrophe.

> There is complete certainty that stratospheric ozone depletion will increase the amount of harmful ultraviolet radiation reaching the surface, while there is high certainty that global warming will increase average temperature and raise sea level. It is less certain, but still likely, that extreme weather and climate events (e.g., intense rain and snowstorms, floods, and droughts) will increase.[31]

Many different gases contribute to climate change, but carbon dioxide is the biggest culprit, producing 60 percent of the human-enhanced greenhouse effect that leads to global warming. While carbon dioxide is naturally present in the atmosphere, levels remained relatively flat until industrialization: after varying within 10 percent for the 10,000 years before 1800, it has increased by 30 percent in the 200 years since.[32]

About all of the carbon dioxide humans put into the atmosphere comes from the supply and use of fossil fuels. Since any massive reduction in the amount of carbon dioxide and other pollutants into the atmosphere will not produce any immediate changes in the ozone layer, we will all live with global warming.

There will likely be major consequences in terms of leisure. Skiing will end many places, including most of the Alps. Many lakes used for recreational purposes will dry up. Forests will lose some varieties of trees and may gain others or simply disappear. One of the biggest questions will be how various species of animal and plant life will redistribute. Hunting, fishing, hiking, birdwatching and many other forms of outdoor recreation will be directly affected.

If there is good news in any of this it may be that much of the non-polluting technology that already exists will be put into place. The vast power of the petroleum industry will be broken. Energy generated from the sun, wind, hydrogen, and huge leaps in conservation will be less polluting or almost nonpolluting. Human stupidity (and greed) is responsible for much of global warming, and the changes that need to be made are often not rocket science. In terms of houses, for instance, one fifth of all energy used may be saved just by situating the house on a lot with southern exposure. The payback for insulation in roofs, walls, doors, all kitchen appliances, solar panels, roof fans, high-efficiency windows and other "innovations" will occur more and more rapidly. In many cases, the technology to combat global warming has existed for some time, but we have not had the will—or the politicians—to change things.

By the way, it is not a stretch to say that one of the big reasons for global warming is the way we elect our political leaders. Traditionally, the United States has been the biggest contributor to global warming (China has just caught up). Because the United States does not have publicly funded elections like most modern nations, those who run for office must raise huge amounts of money—often from corporations in the oil industry or the housing industry—who do not want any changes which are unprofitable in the short run. Elected politicians are reluctant to go against those who have financed their campaigns. Thus, we still allow automobiles to be sold that only get 15 miles per gallon; build many houses with sticks and nails; and install inefficient, "less expensive" appliances and fixtures.

In spite of this, it would be wrong to think that no progress is being made in terms of protecting and enhancing the environment. Indeed, there is a lot of good news. Some environmentalists believe that things are getting much better with regard to the environment, even if they are not getting better as fast as needed. Consider the following:

- Worldwide grain production increased by more than 20 percent during the 1990s, and is one of the reasons that fewer people are starving.[33] While 35 percent of all people in developing nations were starving in 1970, the figure dropped to 18 percent in 1996 and is predicted to drop to 12 percent by 2010.

- The share of people in developing nations with access to clean drinking water has increased from 30 percent in 1970 to 80 percent in 2000.

- Global forest cover has actually increased by a bit less than 1 percent since 1950.[34]

- Sulfur emissions, which are most responsible for acid rain, have been cut by 60 percent in North America and Europe since 1984.

- The rate of world population growth is beginning to slow down.

The huge problem remains, however, that the rate of change in the way humans live that contributes to global warming is not decreasing sufficiently to avoid multiplier catastrophes. Much of the problem is a matter of our understanding and our will. Much, also, is a problem of control; of the media by forces that have purposefully cast doubt about global warming for reasons of profit. The oil industry has been a leader in such deceit.

Environmental change and increasing concern for the environment will customize leisure behavior everywhere. Many beaches will disappear, "tourist seasons" will change and customize, extreme weather events will cancel or interfere with more planned events, attitudes toward exposure to sunlight will become more negative, and environmental degradation will render some leisure environments uninhabitable or more highly regulated. A higher percentage of the land may be protected, and such land may be used for certain forms of leisure that do comparatively little harm.

The consumptive model of leisure prevalent in our society is likely to be reshaped and limited due to ecological problems that threaten our way of life. While Americans currently show only a little willingness to change, we are increasingly aware of the fundamental changes in the environment our way of life has produced since the beginning of the Industrial Revolution. Not only has such change occurred because of the huge growth in the production and consumption of material goods but also due to the cancerous growth of the human population. While it took 1,700 years after the birth of Christ for the world's population to double, it has doubled three times since then in increasingly shorter durations. The 6.6 billion people in the world will double again in a little over 40 years at present rates of growth. Today, the "biomass" (collective weight) of human beings is 360 million tons, which is probably greater than any other animal. Most of the explosive population increase is now attributable to poverty and the low status of women, so lowering the birth rates will have to deal directly with these issues.[35]

While this huge population increase will result in continuous environmental calamities, it is the developed nations, such as Canada and the United States, which do the most environmental harm. The negative ecological consequences of the birth of a North American is about one-hundred times that of, for instance, an Indian, Chinese, or Bolivian person. North Americans, who constitute less than five percent of the world's population, own 135 million of the 350 million automobiles in the world. If the Chinese owned automobiles at the rate we do, the polar ice caps would melt. While North American culture is increasingly serving as a model for much of the world—thanks to increased telecommunications, tourism, the emergent world economy and the widespread use of computers— this model is inappropriate. Every country will have to change, including the United States.

Our own farming practices cannot be sustained even one more century. A third of North American topsoil, which has taken a millennia to produce, is gone. "The basis of human proliferation is not our own seed but the seed of grasses. Corn, wheat, and rice produce plenty of seed; big bluestem and switchgrass precious little. Quadrupeds can live on the stems and leaves of prairie grasses, and bipeds can live on the quadrupeds, but that arrangement leaves bipeds perched on a high, narrow ledge of the pyramid. We are now too plentiful to fit."[36]

Similar dismal pictures may be drawn with regard to global warming, our unbelievably ignorant use of water and chemicals, and a host of environmental problems. Global warming, which is largely attributable to the development of coal, oil, and natural gas as "cheap energy" sources for the masses (particularly in North America), may result in the earth warming three to nine degrees Fahrenheit in sixty years—more than it has in the last 15,000 years—with disastrous results, such as an exponential increase in melanoma and the loss of many coastal cities.

Use of leisure plays an important part in many of these problems. Large jumbo jets taking tourists on holiday from New York City to Hawaii, for example, dump over one ton of carbon particles into the atmosphere. Much of the production capacity of our country is used for leisure-related products. Shopping for material goods is a favorite form of leisure expression. These practices must be altered by more efficient production, taxing consumption, educating for leisure experiences that are less consumptive, and other measures which will move us toward selecting sustainable styles of living.

It was very strange—almost a bad dream. I was at a reception in Wroclaw, Poland with lots of ambassadors, a string quartet playing while good food and wine was offered to the guests. It was a little warm in the ballroom, so I went out on the balcony.

When I sat down, the gentleman beside me turned out to be in the diplomatic corps of Bangladesh. We talked about how pleasant the evening was, and the great hospitality of the Polish people. Then I began to ask about his country.

Bangladesh is a low-lying nation with many islands above the Bay of Bengal. The people are poor, and there are about 140 million of them. I asked about the problem of global warming as it would affect his country.

He stared into the night and, with Chopin playing in the background, told me that a huge portion of his people would likely lose their homes due to higher sea levels. They are unlikely to be able to move to other parts of the country, because it is extremely crowded and poor already. How do you relocate 60 million people?

The United Nations, he said, is not ready to do much about it. We imagined countries with small populations, such as Australia, agreeing to relocate some of the displaced Bangladeshis—but Australia's whole population is only 20 million, and they will likely suffer water shortages from global warming. What will happen?

We walked back into the main ballroom. One of our hosts said, "You don't look like you're enjoying yourself. Is it the food?"

Toward Sustainable Lifestyles

All the changes that will take place in leisure in the short-term future are likely to be shaped by the increasing recognition that the way of life we have been born into cannot be sustained. The consumption patterns of North America cannot be duplicated in the rest of the world, nor can they continue in North America without fundamental damage to our air, water, land, and animal life. We will either change or face declines in our health and quality of life. It is possible that our survival itself is at stake. Reshaping our styles and meanings of leisure will be a fundamental part of this change.

Leisure does not have to mean massive consumption. Much of the research we have examined in this book shows the most satisfying uses of leisure generally don't involve huge amounts of consumption. Also, it does not have to mean ecological damage. During the next decade, it will be more and more difficult to justify a leisure behavior simply because the individual has decided that he or she likes it. Leisure, in the near future, is likely to be shaped by taxation, education campaigns, and policies to encourage leisure behaviors that can be repeated and repeated without serious harm to the individual or the environment. A sustainable society does not mean a society that never changes. Rather, it means a society that protects its ability to adapt and change because minimal harm is being done to the natural world—a world of which we must continue to be a part or perish.

Leisure

A few miles from here a rhinoceros sleeps:
a woman born in a boulder.
Every night her dream is the same:

the armor is pierced.

She glides among the murderous streets
and makes, at last, rhinoceros music,
a Christly cello, centuries ripe.

The morning world is cageless
and naked and near
and whole.

—GCG (1970)

Study Questions

1. What does it mean when we say that the difference between work and leisure is that they involve different kinds of social organization?

2. Do you agree that what we do during leisure increasingly has less connection with our work? Why or why not?

3. In your future, will any of your personal leisure be devoted to continuing education? Please discuss.

4. Do you believe our future society will be better off if the line between work and leisure disappears? Why or why not?

5. Summarize how your ideas about leisure have changed as a result of reading this book.

Exercise 15.1

Discuss some of the more important ways in which you think our society will change in the next ten years and how such changes will alter our recreation and leisure behavior. What new constraints and opportunities will characterize our use of leisure? Will these changes make us more or less satisfied with our leisure lives?

Endnotes

1 Bongiorni, S. (2007). *A year without "Made in China:" One family's true-life adventure with the global economy*. New York, NY: Wiley.

2 Paepke, C. (1993). *The evolution of progress*. New York, NY: Random House.

3 ibid.

4 UN Development Report. (1999). Cited by Mitchell, L. (2002, January 18). American corporations: The new sovereigns. *The Chronicle Review*. Retrieved from http://www.chronicle.com/review

5 Sassen, S. (2002, January 18). Globalization after September 11. *The Chronicle Review*. Retrieved from http://www.chronicle.com/review

6 ibid., p. 2

7 Van Crevald, M. (1991). *The transformation of war* (p. 17). New York, NY: Alfred A. Knopf.

8 In Capra, F. (1988). *Uncommon wisdom: Conversations with remarkable people*. New York, NY: Simon and Schuster.

9 Rifkin, J. (1987). *Time wars: The primary conflict in human history*. New York, NY: Henry Holt.

10 Huntington, S. (1996). *The clash of civilizations and the remaking of world order* (p. 29). New York, NY: Simon and Schuster.

11 ibid., p. 51

12 ibid., p. 51

13 ibid., p. 65

14 Adapted from Huntington (1996)

15 Jenkins, P. (October, 2002). The next Christianity. *The Atlantic Monthly, 290*(3), 54.

16 ibid.

17 ibid., pp. 53–68

18 Ausubel, J. (1998). Reasons to worry about the human environment. *Cosmos 1998: Journal of the Cosmos Club of Washington, DC, 8, 7*.

19 ibid., pp. 1–12.

20 Cheek, N. and Burch, W. (1976). *The social organization of leisure in human society* (p. 41). New York, NY: Harper and Row.

21 Kelly, K. (1994). *Out of control: The new biology of machines, social systems and the economic world*. New York, NY: Addison Wesley.

22 Godbey, G. (2002). Recreation, leisure, and tourism: The next twenty years. Libra Distinguished Lecture Series. University of Maine at Machias, October 24.

23 Anderson, W. (1992). *Reality isn't what it used to be*. San Francisco, CA: HarperCollins.

24 Goldman, S., Nagel, R., and Preiss, K. (1995). *Agile competitors and virtual organizations*. New York, NY: Van Nostrand Reinhold.

25 Montague, P. (1997, May 15). Crimes of Shell. *Rachel's Environmental and Health Weekly [Online serial], 546*, 1–8. Retrieved from http://www.rachel.com

26 *New York Times*. (1996, April 7), p. 29

27 Lapham, L. (1996, August). "Lights, camera, democracy!" On the conventions of a make-believe republic. *Harper's Magazine*, 34.

28 Wilson, E. O. (2002). *The future of life* (p. 23). New York, NY: Alfred A. Knopf.

29 ibid., p. 27

30 McFeatters, A. (2003). U.S. looks to curb rising cost of natural disasters. *Pittsburgh Post-Gazette*, May 7. Retrieved November 26, 2007, from http://www.postgazette.com

31 Fisher et al. (2000). *The mid-Atlantic regional assessment of climate change impacts overview report*. Washington, DC, and University Park, PA: U.S. Environmental Protection Agency and Pennsylvania State University.

32 Low Impact Living. (2007). *Carbon dioxide and greenhouse gas*. Retrieved October 2, 2007, from http://www.lowimpactliving.com/pages/your-impacts/global-warming1?gclid=CKPLlLmRoo0CFRyvgAodhT6gng

33 Lomborg, B. (2001). *The skeptical environmentalist: Measuring the real state of the world*. Cambridge, UK: Cambridge University Press.

34 ibid.

35 Ashford, L. (1995, March). New perspectives on population: Lessons from Cairo. *Population Bulletin, 50*(1), 2–46.

36 Eisenberg, E. (1989, November). Back to Eden. *The Atlantic Monthly, 264*(5), 57–89.

Index

Growing With Care: Using Greenery, Gardens, and Nature With Aging and Special Populations
by Betsy Kreidler

Hands On! Children's Activities for Fairs, Festivals, and Special Events
by Karen L. Ramey

Health Promotion for Mind, Body and Spirit
by Suzanne Fitzsimmons and Linda L. Buettner

In Search of the Starfish: Creating a Caring Environment
by Mary Hart, Karen Primm, and Kathy Cranisky

Inclusion: Including People With Disabilities in Parks and Recreation Opportunities
by Lynn Anderson and Carla Brown Kress

Inclusive Leisure Services: Responding to the Rights of People with Disabilities, 2nd ed.
by John Dattilo

Innovations: A Recreation Therapy Approach to Restorative Programs
by Dawn R. De Vries and Julie M. Lake

Internships in Recreation and Leisure Services: A Practical Guide for Students, 3rd ed.
by Edward E. Seagle, Jr. and Ralph W. Smith

Interpretation of Cultural and Natural Resources, 2nd ed.
by Douglas M. Knudson, Ted T. Cable, and Larry Beck

Intervention Activities for At-Risk Youth
by Norma J. Stumbo

Introduction to Outdoor Recreation: Providing and Managing Resource Based Opportunities
by Roger L. Moore and B.L. Driver

Introduction to Recreation and Leisure Services, 8th ed.
by Karla A. Henderson, M. Deborah Bialeschki, John L. Hemingway, Jan S. Hodges, Beth D. Kivel, and H. Douglas Sessoms

Introduction to Therapeutic Recreation: U.S. and Canadian Perspectives
by Kenneth Mobily and Lisa Ostiguy

Introduction to Writing Goals and Objectives: A Manual for Recreation Therapy Students and Entry-Level Professionals
by Suzanne Melcher

Leadership and Administration of Outdoor Pursuits, 3rd ed.
by Jim Blanchard, Michael Strong, and Phyllis Ford

Leadership in Leisure Services: Making a Difference, 3rd ed.
by Debra Jordan

Leisure for Canadians
edited by Ron McCarville and Kelly MacKay

Leisure and Leisure Services in the 21st Century: Toward Mid Century
by Geoffrey Godbey

The Leisure Diagnostic Battery: Users Manual and Sample Forms
by Peter A. Witt and Gary Ellis

Leisure Education I: A Manual of Activities and Resources, 2nd ed.
by Norma J. Stumbo

Leisure Education II: More Activities and Resources, 2nd ed.
by Norma J. Stumbo

Leisure Education III: More Goal-Oriented Activities
by Norma J. Stumbo

Leisure Education IV: Activities for Individuals with Substance Addictions
by Norma J. Stumbo

Leisure Education Program Planning: A Systematic Approach, 2nd ed.
by John Dattilo

Leisure Education Specific Programs
by John Dattilo

Leisure in Your Life: New Perspectives
by Geoffrey Godbey

Leisure Studies: Prospects for the 21st Century
edited by Edgar L. Jackson and Thomas L. Burton

The Lifestory Re-Play Circle: A Manual of Activities and Techniques
by Rosilyn Wilder

Making a Difference in Academic Life: A Handbook for Park, Recreation, and Tourism Educators and Graduate Students
edited by Dan Dustin and Tom Goodale

Marketing in Leisure and Tourism: Reaching New Heights
by Patricia Click Janes

The Melody Lingers On: A Complete Music Activities Program for Older Adults
by Bill Messenger

Models of Change in Municipal Parks and Recreation: A Book of Innovative Case Studies
edited by Mark E. Havitz

More Than a Game: A New Focus on Senior Activity Services
by Brenda Corbett

The Multiple Values of Wilderness
by H. Ken Cordell, John C. Bergstrom,
and J.M. Bowker

*Nature and the Human Spirit: Toward an
Expanded Land Management Ethic*
edited by B.L. Driver, Daniel Dustin, Tony
Baltic, Gary Elsner, and George Peterson

*The Organizational Basis of Leisure Participation:
A Motivational Exploration*
by Robert A. Stebbins

Outdoor Recreation for 21st Century America
by H. Ken Cordell

*Outdoor Recreation Management: Theory and
Application, 3rd ed.*
by Alan Jubenville and Ben Twight

*Parks for Life: Moving the Goal Posts, Changing
the Rules, and Expanding the Field*
by Will LaPage

*The Pivotal Role of Leisure Education: Finding
Personal Fulfillment in this Century*
edited by Elie Cohen-Gewerc and Robert
A. Stebbins

*Planning and Organizing Group Activities in
Social Recreation*
by John V. Valentine

Planning Parks for People, 2nd ed.
by John Hultsman, Richard L. Cottrell,
and Wendy Z. Hultsman

*The Process of Recreation Programming Theory
and Technique, 3rd ed.*
by Patricia Farrell and Herberta M.
Lundegren

*Programming for Parks, Recreation, and Leisure
Services: A Servant Leadership Approach,
2nd ed.*
by Debra J. Jordan, Donald G. DeGraaf,
and Kathy H. DeGraaf

Protocols for Recreation Therapy Programs
edited by Jill Kelland, along with the
Recreation Therapy Staff at Alberta
Hospital Edmonton

*Puttin' on the Skits: Plays for Adults in Managed
Care*
by Jean Vetter

*Quality Management: Applications for Therapeutic
Recreation*
edited by Bob Riley

*A Recovery Workbook: The Road Back from
Substance Abuse*
by April K. Neal and Michael J. Taleff

*Recreation and Leisure: Issues in an Era of Change,
3rd ed.*
edited by Thomas Goodale and Peter A. Witt

Recreation and Youth Development
by Peter A. Witt and Linda L. Caldwell

*Recreation Economic Decisions: Comparing
Benefits and Costs, 2nd ed.*
by John B. Loomis and Richard G. Walsh

*Recreation for Older Adults: Individual and
Group Activities*
by Judith A. Elliott and Jerold E. Elliott

*Recreation Program Planning Manual for Older
Adults*
by Karen Kindrachuk

*Recreation Programming and Activities for Older
Adults*
by Jerold E. Elliott and Judith A. Sorg-Elliott

*Reference Manual for Writing Rehabilitation
Therapy Treatment Plans*
by Penny Hogberg and Mary Johnson

*Research in Therapeutic Recreation: Concepts
and Methods*
edited by Marjorie J. Malkin and Christine
Z. Howe

*Simple Expressions: Creative and Therapeutic Arts
for the Elderly in Long-Term Care Facilities*
by Vicki Parsons

A Social History of Leisure Since 1600
by Gary Cross

A Social Psychology of Leisure
by Roger C. Mannell and Douglas A. Kleiber

*Special Events and Festivals: How to Organize,
Plan, and Implement*
by Angie Prosser and Ashli Rutledge

*Stretch Your Mind and Body: Tai Chi as an
Adaptive Activity*
by Duane A. Crider and William R. Klinger

*Therapeutic Activity Intervention with the
Elderly: Foundations and Practices*
by Barbara A. Hawkins, Marti E. May,
and Nancy Brattain Rogers

*Therapeutic Recreation and the Nature of
Disabilities*
by Kenneth E. Mobily and Richard D.
MacNeil

*Therapeutic Recreation: Cases and Exercises,
2nd ed.*
by Barbara C. Wilhite and M. Jean Keller

*Therapeutic Recreation in Health Promotion and
Rehabilitation*
by John Shank and Catherine Coyle

Therapeutic Recreation in the Nursing Home
by Linda Buettner and Shelley L. Martin

Other Books by Venture Publishing, Inc.

Therapeutic Recreation Programming: Theory and Practice
by Charles Sylvester, Judith E. Voelkl, and Gary D. Ellis

Therapeutic Recreation Protocol for Treatment of Substance Addictions
by Rozanne W. Faulkner

The Therapeutic Recreation Stress Management Primer
by Cynthia Mascott

The Therapeutic Value of Creative Writing
by Paul M. Spicer

Tourism and Society: A Guide to Problems and Issues
by Robert W. Wyllie

Traditions: Improving Quality of Life in Caregiving
by Janelle Sellick

Trivia by the Dozen: Encouraging Interaction and Reminiscence in Managed Care
by Jean Vetter

Venture Publishing, Inc.
1999 Cato Avenue
State College, PA 16801
814-234-4561; 814-234-1651 (fax)
http://www.venturepublish.com